The Keynesian Revolution and Our Empty Economy

"If you think you know the imprint John Maynard Keynes left on economics and the world, you are in for a surprise. Claar and Forster build a compelling case that Keynes's legacy is moral rather than scientific. Though explicit in his writings, Keynes's moral philosophy and its effects have been overlooked. Keynes turned virtues into vices and vices into virtues. This moral revolution was more fruitful than his scientific innovations. And the fruit is bitter. Economists since Keynes, including Austrian and Chicago critics, have accepted his moral philosophy. Keynesian morals are built into the structures of public and private institutions, policies, and into our desires. We have material prosperity, but it is hollow. This fine book is in the spirit of Wilhelm Röpke, Keynes's most perceptive contemporaneous critic."

—J. Daniel Hammond, *Hultquist Family Professor, Wake Forest University*

"This is a courageous book. It asks economists to not only transcend their standard parameters and to realize that they are students of human conduct but also to grasp that human conduct inescapably has a moral dimension. The authors show that a failure to consider the moral dimension of human conduct leads to the ad nauseum fluctuations in our political life between the socialist left and the fascist right. Economists—indeed all social scientists—need to address the underlying meaning of human life. Consumption is not what life is ultimately about. This book will please neither standard economists nor most contemporary moralists, but to anyone who realizes that morality concerns flesh-and-blood human beings for whom the economic side of life does not exist in splendid isolation apart from the rest of human life, it is an intellectual call to arms. Simply put, once we understand that there is *telos* to human life that is not death, but human flourishing, then we can see that Keynes was manifestly wrong."

—Dr. Douglas B. Rasmussen, *Professor of Philosophy, St. John's University*

"Claar and Forster's thought-provoking book reminds economists of the moral roots of our profession - roots from which common models stem and moral implications are derived whether we acknowledge them or not. In their delightful prose, they use the history of Keynesianism to call the profession to (re)consider its moral foundations and give up the pretense of positive analysis in favor of consciously reflecting on human dignity, the transcendent, and their roles in economics."

—Angela K. Dills, *Gimelstob-Landry Distinguished Professor of Regional Economic Development, Western Carolina University*

"Surrounding us today are messages for simplifying our homes and our lives, for possessing and doing only things that "spark joy"—in short, for re-examining the consumerism that has been rampant in the post-World War II era. Meanwhile, governments pursue economic policies organized around targets for inflation and expectations for growth in national GDP that depend analytically upon the centrality of consumption and anthropologically on what Lord Keynes depicted as the "animal spirits" of mankind. Claar and Forster provide a valuable service by exploring how the 20th-century Keynesian revolution in political economy was wrought despite the availability of alternative paradigms, by explicating the troubling consequences of that victory, and by calling for a new conversation about the moral anthropology, economic theory, and social philosophies that might help us better align public policy with our growing dis-ease at being mere cogs in the machine of producing aggregate demand."

—Lenore T. Ealy, Ph.D., *President, The Philanthropic Enterprise*

"Claar and Forster issue a clarion call to economists to re-examine the normative roots of their profession. They present a cogent analysis of how J.M Keynes's moral vision of a consumption-driven economy is transformed by the Keynesian Revolution into an economics solely geared to serving humans as 'bundles of appetites'. Through a comparative examination of other paradigms in the history of moral reasoning about economic action, they provide a well-reasoned argument for a return to a teleologically-grounded economics."

—Edd Noell, *Professor of Economics, Westmont College, and President, Association of Christian Economists*

"Much to the chagrin of economists, thinking about human betterment requires more than a theory of rational individuals with preferences and resources interacting in markets. We need a framework for thinking about social organization outside markets, and an ethical theory based on more than hedonic calculation. Claar and Forster walk us through past proposals for combining ethics, social organization and markets, and then ask how we might begin to reframe such a relationship today. You will probably not agree with everything here, but you will find much to ponder."

—Ross B. Emmett, *Professor of Political Economy, Arizona State University*

Victor V. Claar · Greg Forster

The Keynesian Revolution and Our Empty Economy

We're All Dead

palgrave
macmillan

Victor V. Claar
Florida Gulf Coast University
Fort Myers, FL, USA

Greg Forster
Trinity International University
Deerfield, IL, USA

ISBN 978-3-030-15807-1 ISBN 978-3-030-15808-8 (eBook)
https://doi.org/10.1007/978-3-030-15808-8

Library of Congress Control Number: 2019934716

This Palgrave Macmillan imprint is published by the registered company Springer Nature Switzerland AG
The registered company address is: Gewerbestrasse 11, 6330 Cham, Switzerland

"Private vices, by the dexterous management of a skillful politician, may be turned into public benefits."
Bernard Mandeville, *The Fable of the Bees*

"I should support all sorts of policies for increasing the propensity to consume."
John Maynard Keynes, *The General Theory of Employment, Interest and Money*

To Wilhelm Röpke, who saw what was happening
and sounded the alarm

Acknowledgements

We are indebted to many who helped us realize the dream of this book over the seven years we have labored to produce it. We begin with Drew Cleveland, who told us to write it. Overhearing our laments at the absence of a major scholarly investigation connecting the Keynesian Revolution in economics to the moral anxieties and dysfunctions of our present economic life, he broke in: "Then the two of you should write one." We are tempted to say: Thanks for seven years of headaches! But we are deeply grateful for Drew's having seen the potential of this work and encouraging us to do it.

The Institute for Economic Inquiry at Creighton University generously convened an interdisciplinary seminar of scholars and students to give us feedback on a draft manuscript of the book. Their reflections were invaluable to us, and drove an extensive revision of the original manuscript. We wish to thank the Director of the Institute, Diana Thomas, as well as Abigail Bodeau, Lenore Ealy, Kevin Gomez, P. J. Hill, Clara Jace, Michael Kotrous, Phil Magness, Alexei Marcoux, Molly Myers, Colin O'Reilly, Douglas Rasmussen, Austin Spillane, and Michael Thomas for their generosity with their time and talents.

The Acton Institute has facilitated the work that went into this book. The institute invited us to co-edit an issue of the *Journal of Markets & Morality* focused on these issues, which was published in Spring 2017. Moreover, we both have led breakout sessions each year at the institute's annual conference, Acton University, for many years, including sessions on the topic of this book and closely related topics. We are grateful for the opportunities Acton has provided, and in particular to Dylan Pahman and Jordan Ballor for their work on the special issue.

We would also like to thank the contributors who submitted articles on this topic and related issues to the special issue of the *Journal of Markets & Morality*, or gave papers at sessions we organized at the 2016 meetings of the Association of Private Enterprise Education and the Evangelical Theological Society: Darrell Bock, Peter Boettke and Patrick Newman, Ross Emmett, Brian Fikkert and Michael Rhodes, Samuel Gregg, Jeffrey Haymond, Klaus Issler, David Kotter, John Lunn, Phillip Magness and Sean Hernandez, Steven McMullen and Todd Steen, Hadley Mitchell, Edd Noell, Daniel Smith and Sean Alvarez, Robert Tatum, and Michael Wittmer.

We rely on the diligent work of many previous scholars who have tilled these fields; among them, Robert B. Ekelund and Robert F. Hébert, Paul Heyne, Mark Skousen, Herbert Stein, Nicholas Wapshott and Phillip Magness stand out. Steven McMullen and Todd Steen's paper in our *Journal of Markets & Morality* issue inspired many portions of the research agenda in our conclusion. Phillip Magness and Per Bylund helped answer questions that arose as we wrote. We would also like to thank the steering committee of the Oikonomia Network, which held a seminar on our research early in the writing process that helped us think about the issues we were dealing with.

Obviously our expressions of gratitude to these persons and organizations in no way suggest they agree with our views, or are responsible for any defects in the final work.

We are most grateful to our families for putting up with the burden that the writing of this book created, and to our universities for giving us the opportunity to do the work, including a sabbatical leave from Henderson State University and a research grant from Trinity International University.

Citations to Classic Works

Classic works such as those of Aristotle or Adam Smith are available in many editions, with no single standard edition. Where appropriate, when citing such works we have supplied the page number of the edition we use, followed (after a semicolon) by standardized references such as book, chapter, and section numbers, so readers using other editions can find the citations without unnecessary inconvenience.

About This Book

This book considers the cultural legacy of the Keynesian Revolution in economics. It assesses the impact of Keynes and Keynesian thinking upon economics and policy, as well as the response of the Chicago and Austrian schools, and the legacy of all three in shaping economic life. The book is a call to restore economics to its roots in moral and cultural knowledge, reminding us that human beings are more than consumers. The Keynesian Revolution taught us that we should be happy if we are prosperous, but instead we feel hollow and morally anxious—our economy feels empty. Drawing on paradigms from earlier historical periods while affirming modern market systems, this book encourages a return to a view of human beings as persons with the right and responsibility to discover, and do, the things in life that are intrinsically good and enduring. Because in the long run, the legacy of our choices will live on long after "we're all dead."

Contents

List of Figures

CHAPTER 1

Introduction: Work Hard and Play by the Rules

America is haunted by a deep and growing anxiety about the structures of its economy. This anxiety crosses all lines of ethnicity, class, religion, party, and ideology; it has been an equally powerful force in the striking rise to power of former fringe figures Donald Trump and Bernie Sanders; in the Tea Party and Occupy Wall Street; and at the kitchen tables of millions of ordinary, apolitical Americans. It is not a mere selfish concern about who gets how much. It is a moral anxiety, a concern about what kind of people we are becoming. Is America still a country where it pays to "work hard and play by the rules," in Bill Clinton's famous phrase? Or have we become the kind of place where cheaters consistently get ahead and slackers get a free ride—where working hard and playing by the rules is for suckers?

Hollow Prosperity and the Empty Economy

America is a prosperous country—by historical standards, breathtakingly so. But we are not satisfied with our prosperity; it feels hollow. The richer we get, the more dissatisfied we seem to become. Where our ancestors were anxious to achieve affluence, we are anxious about our affluence. Our booming economy feels empty.

Ironically, even as economic structures dominated by the aristocratic hierarchies of the past are more and more completely dismantled by the dynamic churn of global markets, our sense that the rich don't deserve their wealth—that the whole system is rigged against the little guy, and it's

V. V. Claar and G. Forster, *The Keynesian Revolution and Our Empty Economy*, https://doi.org/10.1007/978-3-030-15808-8_1

useless to work hard and play by the rules—has steadily increased rather than decreased. People distrust and resent the economic system dominated by bankers and tech entrepreneurs even more than they used to distrust and resent the systems that were dominated by kings and priests.

You can see this feeling of hollow prosperity in the stark contrast between economic policy debates in the early twenty-first century and economic policy debates in the second half of the twentieth century. From Eisenhower through Clinton, public debates about economics were dominated by technical questions. How do we manage the business cycle? How do we keep down inflation? How do taxes and regulations affect growth? How much debt is sustainable? Key moral questions did occasionally take center stage—especially where economic policy intersected directly with matters that were of more than just economic concern, such as racial segregation or health care. And politicians, as always, dressed up technical questions in moral language to whip up popular support for their preferred policies. At the bottom, however, economic debates were managerial—they were about what techniques we should use to manage our affluence. Prosperity was solid enough to be technical.

Those days are over. Economic debates today are all about outrage—which is to say, they are fueled (often unconsciously) by moral anxieties. We fear there is no moral core to our prosperity.

Nationalists are outraged that we don't have big walls and high tariffs to protect our people. How these things are supposed to work in practice almost never gets discussed. In the face of a deeper moral anxiety that our institutions no longer have any moral core, which is supposed to be to take care of their people, mere technical issues are beside the point.

Socialists are outraged that the government doesn't provide free, universal medical care and college education. How these things are supposed to work in practice almost never gets discussed. In the face of a deeper moral anxiety that our institutions no longer have any moral core, which is supposed to be to take care of their people, mere technical issues are beside the point.

From bailouts and bank regulations to basic universal income and Brexit, it's all the same story. People are outraged, and outraged people don't care about technique. If you've been sold a machine that turns out to have a missing button or a misaligned gear, you'll call technical support. But if you think you've been sold a machine that's actually a hollow shell, and doesn't have any of its most important working parts, you're not going to call technical support. You're going to call the cops.

The institutions of economic power—the businesses and financial houses and regulatory agencies and intergovernmental institutions—are still controlled by people who care about how economics works. But they now live in a parallel universe, separate from the public discourse that shapes economic policy. They are struggling to figure out how to do their jobs in a world where nobody trusts them, and nobody cares about technique.

But this change is also visible far beyond public policy debates. It runs much deeper. It goes down to the roots of who we are.

Taking an Uber ride through the streets of Omaha, heading to a seminar at Creighton University, one of the authors of this book noticed a building with an impressive glass dome. Hundreds of small windows fit together in an intricate pattern to form the dome. He remarked to the Uber driver on the building's unusual and impressive architecture.

"Yup," the driver responded. "I put in most of that glass."

The driver, who looked about 75, explained that he had worked most of his life in window installation. Over the course of a long career, he had worked on most of the larger buildings in Omaha. Now that he was beyond the age for that kind of work, driving for Uber allowed him to stay connected to his professional legacy.

"I feel pretty good, driving around the city, seeing all the glass I put in," he said.

But he said it in a bittersweet tone, one that reminded its hearer that it was not only in this driver's personal history that such things felt like they were departing the present for the past. The world where people were allowed to care about that kind of thing—the world where your daily work amounted to something important, something whose worth could not be measured in dollars and cents—seemed to belong to America's past, not just to this driver's past.

Almost nothing is more debilitating in the life of a nation than a pervasive moral anxiety. Wars and disasters may be catastrophic in the short term, but a persistent moral anxiety robs people of dignity and meaning. It destroys people's sense that their decisions matter, that they are moral agents. In some it breeds cynicism, injustice, and exploitation; it breeds anger, resentment, and political extremism in some others; and among still others, a paralyzing state of dependency, learned helplessness and susceptibility to manipulation. Among all but those of the strongest character or firmest faith, it plants a disturbing seed of doubt, nagging away at us, whispering that we can't really be sure our lives have any significance. And slowly, the seeds grow (Berger 1967, 22–24).

The worst part of our anxiety is that we keep trying to fix the problem, but nothing we try seems to help. Politicians in both parties keep affirming their fervent devotion to America's traditional economic virtues: diligence, honesty, entrepreneurship, opportunity for all, and earning your success by doing work that makes the world a better place. They promise, and sometimes they even implement, ambitious plans to preserve our way of life. Yet somehow the scoundrels are always still on top, and the slackers never get off their cans and out of their parents' basements. We have lost our sense that working hard and playing by the rules pays off. And the seeds of meaninglessness continue to grow.

We wrote this book because we believe there is hope America can overcome the anxiety of affluence, the sense that our prosperity is hollow and our economy empty. We are not offering Polyannaism; indeed, we argue that the threat is even worse than most people have yet realized. The causes of hollow prosperity are older and deeper than one election cycle or even one generation. Nonetheless, we believe the problem, though large, is within the reach of human action. Hollow prosperity is not inevitable, even in a growing economy. A dynamic, modern economy is not doomed, by some inevitable law of nature, to become an unbreakable "iron cage" of materialistic selfishness, as Max Weber feared (Baehr and Wells 2002, ix–lxiv).

The moral misdirection that causes our hollow prosperity is the result of a long series of specific choices made by particular people in identifiable times and places. They did not have to make those choices. They could have made better choices. So can we. We live within structures and constraints created by our ancestors' choices, so getting out will be the work of a generation or longer, not of one election cycle. But if enough cultural leaders, especially economic leaders, grasp the deeper causes of the problem and prioritize effective solutions, our moral disorders can be licked. Greater challenges have been conquered before and will be conquered again. Hope will not put us to shame.

What Causes Hollow Prosperity?

Are we really losing the world that Omaha driver looked back on? After all, people have been raising the alarm about moral decay for a long time, yet the world goes on. The limit of nostalgic absurdity may have been reached by Richard Weaver, whose romantic longings for the lost agrarian world of the Old South led him to construct an intellectual history of the West consisting of nothing but unbroken moral decline. Some people like to point out that every generation since the fourteenth century has complained that the generation rising to take its place was morally inferior to itself; to this objection, Weaver boldly replies: Yes, and it was true every time (Weaver 1948, 1–17).

We are not interested in nostalgia, still less in futile attempts to resurrect old social models that have passed away for good reasons. But we think the signs are clear that hollow prosperity is a real problem. Radical movements driven by economic resentments and outlandish policy ambitions used to exist on the fringes of American life, even as radicalism on other issues (civil rights and sexuality, for example) often took center stage and sometimes enjoyed impressive victories. Now, the Tea Party and Occupy Wall Street have been followed by the simultaneous rise of possibly the two most economically extremist candidates ever to have a real shot at the presidency: Donald Trump and Bernie Sanders. There is really no precedent in American history for the current triumph of economic radicalism. The nineteenth and twentieth centuries provide plenty of examples of politicians who were like Trump and Sanders—men who consistently lost elections, or won them only in idiosyncratic constituencies; who were shut out of serious public forums; and who enjoyed what little success they had through niche-market rabble-rousing that attracted little general attention. Now, not only have these two extremists climbed to the tops of their respective parties, but they are the models being emulated by future presidential aspirants.

That kind of thing does not come out of nowhere. This book will argue that the underlying source of the anxiety that our prosperity is hollow is the indifference of our economic systems to moral categories. Our current economic system was not created with the intention that it would promote greed, envy, sloth, gluttony, vanity, and other selfish desires in our economic lives. But that is only because it does not even recognize the existence of these things. It does not see them as relevant to its design and functioning. Worse, as we will show, the conscious indifference of our economic thinking toward moral categories has facilitated an unconscious adoption of economic thought that is much worse than merely indifferent to morality; it actively promotes our worst instincts. Our refusal to think about virtue and higher purposes in economics has made it possible for us to unknowingly adopt economic structures that actively deform us (without our realizing it) into selfish, materialistic economic actors.

The result of this conscious moral indifference and unconscious moral deformation is visible all around us. We find it in business practices that extract money without creating value for the customer; in crony capitalism that uses illicit collusion or government favoritism to enrich big firms and political cronies at the expense of customers, investors, small businesses, and entrepreneurs; in able-bodied people at all levels of the socioeconomic spectrum living in long-term dependency on one-way subsidies from others (the state, churches, friends, and family); and countless other ways. Our conscious indifference to moral categories creates a culture in which we feel like those who have wealth generally don't deserve it—that working hard and playing fair doesn't pay. Our unconscious moral deformation creates a culture in which that perception is increasingly accurate.

This moral indifference and deformation wears many faces. The description above ("greed, envy, sloth, gluttony, vanity, and other selfish desires") may bring to mind thievery and exploitation, squandering wealth on frivolous luxuries and entertainments, or vulgar indulgences of the flesh. These are certainly selfish desires *par excellence*. And no doubt the selfish desires that matter most are those that move us to break the rules of fair play by lying, cheating, and stealing.

But we also find moral indifference and deformation in the civilized idea of "enlightened self-interest" that urges us to restrain our greed, sloth, and lust in the short term for the sake of long-term happiness that is still entirely self-oriented. The outwardly moralistic man—whether aristocratic gentleman or bourgeois shopkeeper—who would never acquire anything except by honest labor, never waste a penny on frivolities, and never touch a woman other than his wife but who nonetheless *lives for the sake of nothing higher than his own personal happiness* is as much a part of the problem as the most insidious crony capitalist.

It is in this sort of person, and not in the more obviously wicked crony capitalist, that the long-term problem lies. His superficial morality of enlightened self-interest is built on nothing solid. This person can offer no compelling justification for his morality. There is no reason to expect his children and their children will remain as honest, frugal, and disciplined as he, for he lacks a strong enough source to stamp this character upon their hearts (Hunter 2000). This is why the moral virtues and higher ends of human activity that would make our economic life genuinely meaningful are not being reliably passed on from generation to generation.

Likewise, while "selfish desires" may bring to mind only the selfishness of individuals, the selfishness of social groups is equally important. The desire of one individual to advance themselves at the expense of everyone else is obviously the paradigmatic type of selfishness. But moral indifference also opens the door to the selfish desires of institutions, demographic groups, religions, movements, nations, and so forth. The economic preferences of groups are fair and right in many cases, such as the demand for equal treatment and expansion of opportunity, or the negotiation of a better deal in a contract. However, as Reinhold Niebuhr wisely observed, our "selfless" devotion to a group or cause is often a vicarious form of selfishness. We feel generous and noble because we are serving something higher than ourselves, but we have only legitimized our own selfish desires by projecting them onto the group. I crush you mercilessly and seize money and power, not because I'm selfish, but only because I'm so selflessly devoted to [insert pure and noble cause here]. And the more aggressively we work for the cause, the more selfless we feel, in a vicious circle that goes on without end (Niebuhr 1932, 1–22, 83–112).

While individual selfishness culminates in the ideology of enlightened self-interest, group selfishness culminates in technocracy and collectivism. People no longer have morally important claims in their own right simply because they are human beings with intrinsic dignity and a calling to be stewards over their own lives. They are not entitled to the freedom to make their own choices, and thus the opportunity to practice love, honesty, diligence, generosity, or any other virtue whatever. People become cogs, to be moved around arbitrarily in whatever way serves the machine. If their current shape does not serve the machine, they can be reshaped at will—or scrapped.

Manifest injustices strike at our sense of moral order like a blow from a sledgehammer. But enlightened self-interest and collectivism can be just as deadly in the long term. The slow and silent selfishness of enlightened self-interest eats away at our sense of moral order like dry rot slowly hollowing out a tree. And the iron vice of collectivism, which grasps the moral order at first intending to fix it, gradually squeezes it tighter and tighter until the life is at last choked out of it.

Economics Shapes Moral and Cultural Life

If we are really losing our grip on the world that Omaha driver looked back to, what exactly was it that allowed that world to maintain moral coherence in its economy? How did we come to lose our grip on it, and how can we start rebuilding it? One of the reasons it's difficult to write about these issues is that we no longer have clear categories for thinking about this ineffable something that makes economies cohere morally. That lack of categories is central to the story of how hollow prosperity arose.

We love economics. We love economics so much because we think it matters—a lot. We owe to the diligent labors of this discipline enormous advances in our understanding of how economic life really works. The economic knowledge that the world around us seems determined to squander in its blind fits of outrage is the fruit of centuries of long and arduous labor. This knowledge is not only essential to any effective approach to urgent social problems, but also to any serious understanding of human life as a whole. We are economic creatures (in addition to much else) and no one can really form a coherent idea of what it means to be human and what life is all about without at least a basic understanding of the knowledge cultivated by the discipline of economics. This is doubly true in the modern world, where we experience our public and common life with our neighbors primarily through economic relations, as opposed to the political and religious forms of unity that made ancient and medieval cultures cohere.

But "economics matters a lot" is a double-edged sword. Dysfunctions in the study of economics will produce defects in our knowledge of economics, which will in turn produce deformities in our economic institutions—and hence in us and our lives. As economics has come into its own as an independent discipline, the enormous new knowledge this discipline has generated gives it enormous power over our lives. Economic institutions are much more socially important now than they ever have been, and their influence over the way we live our daily lives, and thus over how we understand ourselves and our world, is vast.

Our argument is interdisciplinary, or perhaps metadisciplinary. We are not "doing economics" but examining the presuppositions of doing economics. Yet we also are not simply subjecting economics to a unilateral imposition of premises from another discipline, as if we wanted to repeal the independence of the discipline and return economics to its former status as a branch of moral philosophy. We are social scientists who value the enterprise of social science on its own terms. But we recognize that all disciplines rely upon premises that cannot be justified within the discipline; they rely on sources outside themselves. We are constructing a dialogue between economics and moral philosophy, using the lens of each discipline to look at the other and see what we can learn about both. We want economics and moral philosophy to compare notes—on equal terms.

Economics is a moral and cultural system. That is what the dialogue between economics and moral philosophy reveals. If economists want a full understanding of economic behavior—not of something outside economics that is connected or related to it, but economic behavior considered in itself—they have to think about moral and cultural questions.

The economy is a web of human relationships in which people create value and exchange it with one another, and all human action is moral and cultural. Human action is shaped at the deepest levels by morality—by our character; by what we understand to be good, true, and beautiful; and by what rules we believe we are obligated to obey. Equally, human action is shaped at the deepest levels by culture—by formal and informal social structures that help define the meaning of our actions, greatly limiting the ability of individuals to simply make up the meaning of their own lives for themselves.

Think of that Uber driver who used to install windows. His economic work is a source of meaning and purpose in his life, far beyond the paycheck. This meaning and purpose is not something that stands outside of his economic behavior, or even something that exists parallel to his economic behavior in some kind of oil-and-water distinct coexistence. The meaning and purpose of his work is core to his economic behavior as economic behavior.

However, the discipline of economics today has no categories for thinking about his economic behavior in these terms. When asking what he gets out of his job, it rarely looks beyond the paycheck. And through the influence of the institutions that are shaped by the discipline of economics, the economists have taught the institutions that have authoritative voices in our wider culture to think about jobs solely in terms of paychecks as well.

Now think about bigger structures. Have you ever seen a business—Apple, General Motors, Disney, Caterpillar, anybody—talk about itself as if it existed to make money? On the contrary, they all work hard to articulate a mission and vision grounded in some higher purpose that serves human needs and makes the world a better place through their products and services. That is not just PR hokum (although of course there's always a healthy dose of hokum in the world, and business is no exception). For the people who work in a business, that business is not just a platform for making money. The work they do there is a source of meaning and purpose in their lives. Therefore the business itself must have meaning and purpose—a mission worth working for.

The discipline of economics sees a business only as a platform for making money. However, the literature on business management—written by and for the people who actually run businesses—has recognized this as a fallacy for generations.[1] One of the most widely accepted pieces of conventional wisdom in management literature is that employees are much more motivated by a sense of mission than by paychecks, so good business leadership involves articulating a mission that has intrinsic value (i.e. value beyond the revenue it produces) and then running the organization in accordance with that vision.

Yet we don't apply this insight beyond our own lives. Everyone on the shop floor at General Motors cares intensely about the higher purpose of their own work, making products that serve their neighbors and make the world a better place. But they know that the people in the executive suite at Apple are just greedy scoundrels who only care about money. And everyone in the executive suite at Apple feels the same in reverse, about their own work and about the "it's-just-a-paycheck" attitude they assume must predominate on the shop floor at General Motors.

The wider culture gets its categories for thinking about economics from economists, not from the business management literature. Hence our businesses are constantly talking about higher purpose in business, and this discourse has no practical effect on economic policy or our cultural understanding of what economic life is all about. In our own workplaces, where we find meaning and purpose in our own work, we take the mission of the business seriously. But when we hear the CEO of any

[1]Consider, for example, Frederick Herzberg's classic 1968 article, which became the most-requested reprint in the history of *Harvard Business Review* and was reprinted in that journal in full in 2003 (Herzberg 2003). This article, as the title suggests, presented a summary of what was already in 1968 a line of research that had been going on for a generation. After Herzberg, this line of management research was taken up by such prominent figures as Peter Drucker and Michael Porter.

company outside of our own sector talking about meaning and purpose, we dismiss it as PR hokum.

As hollow prosperity grows, we become increasingly aware that something is missing—for example, that we must acknowledge some higher purpose in our work besides the paycheck. Yet generations of moral indifference and deformation in economics has left us without categories for thinking, speaking, and acting about this problem. Unable to do anything, or even to articulate our concerns clearly, we are paralyzed. Hence the feeling that we are losing our grip on the world where such things used to matter. Hence the outrage and the demand that somebody must do something, without thinking about how things work.

From this we draw two conclusions that will shape our argument. Because all human action is moral, every school of economics rests at bottom upon a set of normative presuppositions (what is obligatory?) and teleological presuppositions (what is intrinsically good?). And because all human action is cultural, the normative and teleological presuppositions upon which economics rests are not simply a matter of individual belief and choice from moment to moment. They are that to some extent, but they are also embedded deep in the formal and informal structures of society. Those structures change slowly and are not much susceptible to short-term manipulation.

So economics can neither (1) avoid morality nor (2) individualize morality. If we want to understand economic behavior, we must understand its normative and teleological dimensions. And we cannot reduce those normative and teleological dimensions to arbitrary individual preferences.

We're All Dead: The Keynesian Revolution

In this book, we argue that the moral deformation in our economic system is grounded in a revolutionary transformation in the discipline of economics in the first half of the twentieth century. Chapter 2 outlines the moral and cultural nature of the most important historical paradigms for studying economics—the Nature paradigm of classical Greece and Rome, the God paradigm of medieval and early modern Christians, and the Reason paradigm of the Enlightenment—as well as the reasons they passed away. Chapter 3 shows how economists in the nineteenth century aspired to a morally and culturally neutral social science. In Chapter 4, we describe how Keynes reacted against the moral emptiness of the nineteenth-century approach by offering an economics that was normative but not teleological—a fervent moral crusade, but without any ethical basis or purpose higher than the goodness of satisfying consumer appetites. Chapter 5 traces how the major figures who followed Keynes adopted his moral crusade, but clothed it in the nineteenth-century language of moral neutrality, producing a fully developed Consumption paradigm that claimed to be morally neutral while actually conducting the discipline of economics as a moral crusade to maximize consumption. Chapter 6 reviews how this Consumption paradigm gained extensive influence over the structures of our economic life and broader culture. Chapter 7 looks at the major responses from Keynes' critics in the Austrian and Chicago schools, highlighting how they—ironically—participated in and actually strengthened the process of transforming economics into a moral crusade for the satisfaction of consumer appetites. Chapters 8 through 11 examine the Consumption paradigm through the lens of moral philosophy, asking four key anthropological questions (how do human beings relate to their environment, to the past and future, to one another and to the transcendent?) that reveal the implicit moral and cultural assumptions of their paradigm. The Conclusion in Chapter 12 considers where this history leaves us, and what we might do now to begin constructing a better paradigm for economic study.

The reader will have seen that we are, in the words of one reviewer who commented on the manuscript of this book, "playing the paradigm game." That is, we are describing an overarching set of assumptions that define the discipline of economics in the present historical period, and illustrating the content of this set of assumptions by comparing them with the assumptions that defined the discipline in other historical periods. This method is useful for discovering assumptions that are typically unconscious, and revealing the full meaning of these assumptions by showing how they differ from the assumptions that have prevailed in the past. The Consumption paradigm is so deeply and widely established in our lives that we have to step very far back from our present position before we can see it for what it is.

However, this method is also susceptible to the danger of oversimplification. We are well aware of how much detail and nuance we have left out. For example, in Chapter 2 we describe the "optimism" of the Enlightenment view of human nature, as compared with classical Greco-Roman and Christian views. This is true for the purposes of the present discussion, because the relevant question is how much we can improve social conditions over time. However, if we were asking how much moral virtue it is possible for individuals to achieve if they have the right endowments and circumstances, the Enlightenment view of human nature might actually be the least "optimistic" of the three, rather than the most optimistic. Painting with a broad brush is necessary to our method, and readers should not rely on this book for general intellectual history as opposed to the particular questions we are focused on. But such methods are useful and necessary for our questions; and if you head down to your local paint store, you will discover that they do sell broad brushes.

The first step in the great change we are tracing was moral indifference. Leading economic thinkers of the nineteenth century attempted to remove the moral and cultural categories that lay at the heart of all previous paradigms for understanding economics. Then, in the twentieth century, the Keynesian Revolution returned economics to its historic roots in moral and cultural engagement. But now it had a new, topsy-turvy "morality" that embraced—and even ethically demanded—selfish, materialistic behavior on grounds that such behavior contributed to economic growth and job creation. The moral indifference of the nineteenth-century economists opened the door to the morally deforming structures of twentieth-century economics.

Ironically, as we will see, John Maynard Keynes himself was admirably forthright that he was a moral and cultural thinker. He wanted to reject the moral indifference of the nineteenth-century economists in favor of a new moral crusade for a consumption-oriented society. He insisted that everyone had an ethical duty to spend and consume more and more, for the sake of fueling the economy. For this grand moral vision, he was prepared to destroy traditional pieties and revolutionize ancient social structures.

However, as we will see, the Keynesians who followed Keynes—and who gave final shape to what we now call the Keynesian Revolution—did not share this view. They wanted to eat their cake and have it; they wanted to be morally neutral like the nineteenth-century economists *and* to go on a moral crusade to promote selfish, materialistic behavior for the sake of jobs and growth. The perverse result is a discipline that (1) claims to be morally neutral, "positive and not normative," (2) constantly makes strong moral demands, in spite of this supposed moral neutrality, about how we ought to live and how the institutions that serve as basic structures in our daily lives ought to be managed, and (3) makes these moral demands to promote a way of life that is selfish and materialistic.

"In the long run we are all dead" (Keynes 2013, 65). Nothing captures the dramatic clash between older moral views and the new one that now guides economics as perfectly as this famous rejoinder from John Maynard Keynes to the appeals of old-fashioned economists that we think in longer terms. Older views prioritized what we leave to our grandchildren; Keynes prioritized immediate gratification so completely that the good of future generations vanished from any present relevance. As we will see, even in the short essay he wrote on "Economic Possibilities for Our Grandchildren," for Keynes the good of our grandchildren has no bearing whatsoever on what we ought to do today (Keynes 1963).

Keynes moved the discipline from an older, broader set of moral presuppositions to a new and narrower set of moral presuppositions. Older views were robustly teleological—they had a more fully articulated understanding of what counted as a flourishing human life. They saw productive human work as the source of wealth; they prioritized giving people stewardship over their own lives for their own flourishing as well as the long-term stewardship of civilization for future generations. Keynes replaced this with shallow anthropology and a utilitarian moral ethic. He saw people's desire to consume as the source of wealth, rather than their desire to create; he trusted that people could be so rational, and that reason itself could be so far-seeing, that control of the economy could be safely handed over to elite-educated, plenipotentiary technocrats; and he prioritized short-term gratification over long-term stewardship of civilization.

In Keynes' works, economics is robustly normative, but has almost no teleology. Keynes insists that we have moral obligations (the normative dimension). But his thought is informed by a shallow and materialistic understanding of what is intrinsically good and worth pursuing (the teleological dimension).

The primary figures who followed Keynes were uncomfortable with his openly and even proudly normative approach. They followed the nineteenth-century economists in aspiring toward moral neutrality. So as they built up the system of Keynesianism, they brought back in all the nineteenth-century rhetoric about how economics must be positive, not normative, and refrain from telling people how they ought to live. Yet they retained, and even amplified, Keynes' normative commitments to the elevation of short-term consumption appetites and central economic planning by omnipotent experts.

Needless to say, these are not the usual focal points for the study of Keynes and Keynesianism. Part of the reason we have difficulty seeing these aspects of the Keynesian Revolution is because we are so much its children. We do not find Keynes' breathtakingly radical and revolutionary statements to be radical or revolutionary, or even noteworthy, because to a large extent we think about economics the way he taught us to think about it. Likewise, when we hear economists say that they make no moral claims, and then instantly turn around and give us a long list of things we ought to do, we either do not notice the dissonance or merely smile about it and move on. We have no sense of the floor opening up underneath our feet to reveal an abyss of moral confusion with no bottom.

Of course, the Keynesian Revolution did not take place in a vacuum. Such changes are always part of a larger history that involves many influences. This story could be told with other emphases. However, it was Keynes who gave expression to the grand vision of economics as a moral crusade on behalf of selfish materialism. And it was his followers who blended that vision with the discipline's sharply contrasting nineteenth-century rhetoric of moral neutrality to produce the paradigm out of which the discipline operates today.

But do academic economists really have this much control over how the broader economy and culture think about economics? At the time of the Keynesian Revolution, they did. Universities were at the height of their social power in the first half of the twentieth century. The process of embedding moral presuppositions into a culture occurs primarily in institutions with recognized cultural authority and prestige; culture changes when these institutions change (Hunter 2010, 32–47). The American university was at that time among the most powerful of such institutions. Rival sources of authority, such as churches, remained quantitatively large but had steadily lost their cultural power. And the forces that have eaten away at the university's cultural power in more recent years—intellectual overspecialization, bureaucratic dilution of mission, ideological rigidity, capitulation to student radicalism and entrepreneurial disruption from alternative knowledge sources—were all still in the future.

The Keynesian Revolution in academic economics filtered outward through the mediation of people who presented themselves, essentially, as Keynes' translators. In reality, those who play what is commonly called a "translator" role between the academy and the world of practice are never really just translators. They select some of the insights they glean from scholars and integrate these with other selections of knowledge and experience drawn from more practical sources. And they do so in response to a variety of incentives and pressures. To some extent, they disseminate knowledge and integrate experiences to improve the world of practice; but to some extent they also reshape the knowledge and experiences they integrate to accommodate existing interests in the practical world that can't be changed in the short term, or that they do not wish to change (Hayek 1949).

The Consumption paradigm has had wide-ranging effects on economic policy and practice. In Chapters 8 through 11 we will trace some of its more obvious and important tangible effects. It shapes the arguments we make in debates over tariffs, taxes, immigration, minimum wages, universal basic income proposals, and other hot economic topics. Beyond this, its implications range from the almost-exclusive focus on GDP per person as our overriding measure of economic flourishing to the almost-exclusive focus on fiscal and monetary stimulus as responses to downturns; from declines in new business formation to increases in nonwork and economic dependency; from the explosion of personal and public debt to the collapse of business ethics; from the ever-increasing level of control political leaders have over our lives to the ever-increasing level of vicious polarization in our culture.

Beyond Chicago: Crafting an Effective Response

The Keynesian revolution, like all revolutions, was followed by reactions. Chief among them were the critiques of Keynesianism from two great rival schools: the Chicago school and the Austrian school. These schools fought hard to challenge the dominance of Keynesianism. They racked up some impressive successes, particularly in the last quarter of the twentieth century. But the appearance that they had finally displaced Keynesianism proved fleeting. By the early twenty-first century, under both Republican and Democratic administrations, Keynes was back in the driver's seat, stronger than ever.

We argue that the schools reacting against Keynesianism had limited success because they adopted many of the same inadequate moral presuppositions as Keynesianism itself. They were only a partial reaction. They reacted against Keynesianism's policy conclusions, but not (or not fully) against its underlying anthropological assumptions, utilitarian morality, and social vision.

This was only to be expected. The new social environment created by the Keynesian Revolution established his presuppositions as culturally authoritative. No approach to economics would be seen as legitimate or have much ability to influence culture in mid-to-late twentieth-century America if it challenged those presuppositions at their roots. Such was Keynes' influence that no really radical challenge to his underlying premises would seem plausible, however robustly his policy conclusions were opposed.

As a result, within the profession of economics, Keynesianism's odd combination of the rhetoric of moral neutrality with a moral crusade on behalf of materialistic selfishness is so taken for granted that it can be difficult even to start a discussion of it. The language and boundaries of discourse don't permit a challenge against Keynesianism's moral and social assumptions to be seriously heard, much less robustly debated.

Sociologist Peter Berger, whose research institute has explored cultural, moral and religious questions related to every social science discipline, declared in his memoir that economists were "the one group of social scientists with whom it was generally impossible to work" (Berger 2011, 213). Among other evidence, he pointed to a conference exploring cultural assumptions behind economics that "was a complete fiasco." Berger recounted this exchange:

> Exasperated, the speaker asked, "Don't you accept that some people act for reasons of conscience?"
>
> "Oh, yes," said one of the economists. "Conscience – we call it 'internal price controls'". (Berger 2011, 214)

In this book's conclusion, we offer our reasons for thinking that the conditions for a more effective response to hollow prosperity are emerging. We suggest some basic principles upon which such a response could be built. And we offer some ideas about the first practical steps that could be taken.

In the long run (if our Keynesian friends will forgive the expression) the universe always punishes moral indifference and deformation. We see the signs of that around us, in America's growing anxiety about its affluence—and its growing skepticism that the solution can be found in the economic theories of any of the three major economic schools we consider here. As every entrepreneur knows, every problem is a potential opportunity, and the bigger the problem, the bigger the opportunity. America still has deep cultural wells of wisdom, out of which we can still draw the water we need. We see an entrepreneurial opportunity for a new conversation that speaks to America's anxieties by finding our way toward moral coherence in our economic lives.

We do not know what the final product of that new conversation would look like. As a placeholder, we will propose to call it economics that operates out of a Moral Consensus paradigm. We see such a paradigm as playing a role analogous to, but of course different in some ways from, the role played by what we are calling the Nature paradigm of classical Greco-Roman economic thought, the God paradigm of medieval and early modern Christian economic thought, and the Reason paradigm of the Enlightenment. Each of those paradigms passed away for a good reason, and cannot and should not be restored. Our reasons for stressing Moral Consensus as the focal point of a new paradigm will become clearer in Chapter 11. The task before us is not to impose a moral view on society by force, but to figure out what moral commitments could be authentically shared and publicly institutionalized in an advanced modern economy. This is not a problem to which we already possess a solution; it is a problem for which a solution needs to be built—and that will be the work of at least a generation.

While we do not know what the outcome would look like, we do know that economists—and everyone else who really cares about economics, and is willing to learn something about how it actually works—will be at the center of that new conversation. After all, economics matters a lot. That's why we love it so much. We're thankful to live in such an exciting time!

References

Baehr, Peter, and Gordon C. Wells. 2002. Introduction. In *The Protestant Ethic and the "Spirit" of Capitalism*, ed. Max Weber. New York: Penguin Classics.

Berger, Peter L. 1967. *The Sacred Canopy*. New York, NY: Anchor Books.

Berger, Peter L. 2011. *Adventures of an Accidental Sociologist.* New York: Prometheus Books.

Hayek, Friedrich A. 1949. The Intellectuals and Socialism. *University of Chicago Law Review* 16 (3): 417–433.

Herzberg, Frederick. 2003. One More Time: How Do You Motivate Employees? *Harvard Business Review* 81: 87–96.

Hunter, James Davison. 2000. *The Death of Character.* New York: Basic Books.

Hunter, James Davison. 2010. *To Change the World.* Oxford, UK and New York, NY: Oxford University Press.

Keynes, John Maynard. 1963 [1930]. Economic Possibilities for Our Grandchildren; Scanned by Yale University Economics Department from John Maynard Keynes, *Essays in Persuasion*, Norton, 358–373. http://www.econ.yale.edu/smith/econ116a/keynes1.pdf. Accessed 23 Jan 2019.

Keynes, John Maynard. 2013. *A Tract on Monetary Reform.* Cambridge: Cambridge University Press.

Niebuhr, Reinhold. 1932. *Moral Man and Immoral Society.* Louisville: Westminster John Knox Press.

Weaver, Richard M. 1948. *Ideas Have Consequences.* Chicago: University of Chicago Press.

PART I

The Stakes

CHAPTER 2

From Socrates to Smith: The Moral and Cultural Foundations of Economics

To understand the Keynesian revolution, we must first understand the sort of paradigms for understanding economics that the revolution overturned. For 2300 years, western civilizations understood economics as a moral and cultural system. The economy was seen as rooted in basic imperatives that were a permanent part of human nature, including not only our physical needs but also our needs for meaning, purpose, and ethical direction. This is a point on which the ancients, medievals, and moderns were substantially agreed. In each age, the seamless integration of empirical, moral, and cultural observations was challenged by radical skeptics, and in each age the predominant thinkers defended it using more or less the same arguments; Adam Smith's rejoinder to the cynical Bernard Mandeville in 1759 bears a striking resemblance to Socrates' response to the sophist Thrasymachus in about 380 BC. It was this nearly-two-and-a-half-millennium integration of the empirical, the moral and the cultural in our understanding of economics that lost its grip among leading economists in the late nineteenth and early twentieth centuries (as we will see in Chapter 3), and was finally replaced by the new vision of the Keynesian Revolution.

GDP Per Yak: The Study of Economics Is Always Moral

Economics is as old as humanity. We are social creatures, built to live within a vast web of relationships with others. Our human capacities—to know, to love, to create, to serve—cannot achieve their potential except

V. V. Claar and G. Forster, *The Keynesian Revolution and Our Empty Economy*, https://doi.org/10.1007/978-3-030-15808-8_2

through cooperative action. As Aristotle observed, a beast or a god can be self-contained, but a man cannot. The solitary human being is like a solitary chess piece; it may have its own excellences, such as beauty or strength, but it cannot use them for their original purpose except in cooperation with other pieces. Just as families come into existence through the cooperative action of men and women, households and villages come into existence through economic cooperation (Aristotle 1992, 59–61; I.2). Likewise, at the dawn of the modern era, John Locke argued that the "state of nature" for human beings is not isolated and asocial, as some had claimed. Even without political power to enforce social systems, the natural human state would be characterized by extensive familial and economic structures. It is simply human nature to form these bonds; they exist not because the state enforces them, but because people spontaneously create them through ordinary cooperative action (Locke 1993, 153; II.7.77). Exchanging things we value (goods, services, money, work, etc.) with one another is one of the most fundamental ways we fulfill our natural potential through cooperation.

Our desire to understand economics is almost as old as our desire to understand anything. The philosophers who founded the great intellectual traditions—Socrates, Confucius and so forth—all sought to understand this vast web of relationships through which we exchange what we value. The major world religions have also offered teachings about this sphere of life. Every age of every civilization has had its own philosophy of economics. It would be beyond our purpose to review them all here, but across all these variations there have been a few surprisingly consistent themes, and those are worth noting. In this book we are reviewing the history of economics in the west, particularly in the English-speaking world, but similar observations could be made about the history of other traditions.

At least four basic observations about human nature have been central to western thought about economics all the way back to its earliest philosophers. The first is work; we survive and prosper by applying our productive capacities to the raw material of nature—even in something as simple as the effort we exert to pluck an apple off a tree. The second is property; we claim ownership over all the nonhuman things that human work can control and reshape. The third is exchange; although each of us depends upon work, we do not do all the work upon which we depend ourselves—we obtain much if not most of what we need by trading the fruits of our work for the fruits of other people's work. The fourth is the division or specialization of labor; we do not all do the same kinds of work, but each of us tends to specialize in one kind of work (or a few kinds) and then supply our other needs through trade with people who specialize in other kinds of work.

However, these empirical observations are not the only common thread. Consistently, these and other empirical observations about economics were seamlessly integrated with moral imperatives. It was not only observed that people do survive and prosper through work, but that they ought to do so—sloth was condemned as wrong, because it subtracts from the survival and thriving of the species. Not only do people own property, but they ought to do so—again, for the sake of survival and prosperity—and they ought to be good stewards of what they own. People not only do exchange but should exchange, because exchange is mutually beneficial, and it should be carried out without cheating or fraud. The division or specialization of labor is likewise imperative, because it contributes to survival and prosperity. These moral observations were not considered radically different from the empirical observations they accompanied.

Moral and empirical observations must be integrated because all human action is always both normative (it presupposes rules that prescribe and forbid certain behaviors) and teleological (it has a purpose). Human action cannot be adequately described if it is not morally described. The very act of describing human action is itself not exempt from the ubiquity of normative and teleological presuppositions. Those who describe human action cannot claim to be outside the moral universe they are describing; they are themselves acting as moral agents.

The assertion that all human action is always moral will strike many as jarring, especially in a book about economics. Yet it is easy to see how the discipline of economics reveals, and participates in, the universally moral character of human action.

Economists constantly measure the nation's GDP per person. Yet for some reason they never measure its GDP per yak. They simply assume that people ought to matter to us in a way that yaks ought not to matter to us. This is a moral assumption—a normative claim that demands, on moral grounds, that we recognize a duty to behave in a certain way, namely to structure economic inquiry with particular concern for human well-being and not with particular concern for yaks' well-being. Moral premises are always presupposed even in the very choice of what questions an economist will examine, and what measurements are to be used.

What would economics look like if we didn't make the assumption that we have a moral duty to treat people as more important than yaks?

We might measure the U.S. GDP per yak and compare it with China's, and discover that the Chinese threat to American economic dominance has been vastly overstated. While China's aggregate domestic product has increased dramatically, yaks are common in its Himalayan regions, whereas America is limited to a handful of yaks in zoos. So China's GDP per yak is pathetically tiny compared to America's. Advocates of Tibetan independence might take up this argument with Beijing; China could eliminate a huge drag on its economy by giving yak-laden Tibet back to the Tibetans. What we really should be worried about is not China, but the economic colossus of Monaco. Its one small zoo contains no yaks whatsoever, so—staggering as this is to contemplate—Monaco's GDP per yak is infinite. If you're worried about job security in the gig economy, learn French.

My Life as a Chicken: The Study of Economics Is Always Cultural

In addition to being moral creatures, human beings are cultural creatures. As was observed above, we cannot achieve our potential except through cooperative action. And because all human action is moral, cooperative action is moral—it is normative and teleological. Cooperative action therefore creates socially shared understandings of meaning, purpose, and ethics. Communities develop shared understandings, presuppositions, and stories about how the universe works and what it means to be human. These shared understandings, presuppositions, and stories are what we mean by culture.

The socially shared understandings that constitute a culture are rarely articulated explicitly. For the most part they are implicit, embedded deep in the structures of our relationships and institutions. They can be formulated as explicit propositions, but they do not primarily exist in this form; their primary existence is in institutionalized practices. For example, the idea at the center of the American political tradition—however badly we have failed to practice it—is that all human beings are morally equal and enter the public square with equal dignity. This belief is sometimes formally articulated as a proposition, as in the Declaration of Independence. However, the primary existence of this belief is in the millions of cultural practices that embody it without explicitly stating it, ranging from stigmas against racial discrimination to the practice of forming orderly queues for service in public places (e.g. restaurants, stores, bus stops) strictly on a first-come, first-served basis.

Because we rely so extensively on cooperative action, these cultural presuppositions influence the shape of each person's individual personality and morality. This is not to say that the individual is simply a puppet of social forces. Individuals have free will and make their own choices. This is why cultural structures are complex and dynamic, occasionally changing rapidly and dramatically. But there are limits to free will.

A man is free to announce that he is a chicken. But he is not free to live as a chicken unless the people around him agree to treat him as one. He cannot arbitrarily define the meaning, purpose, and ethics of his own life in simply any way he wants. Too much of our lives is carried out in cooperative action, and therefore represents the shared morality embedded in the structures of culture, for us to have that sort of radical individual autonomy. We are free, but free within cultural constraints.

Economics is therefore cultural as well as moral. The economic structures of a society represent the institutionalization of that society's shared moral understanding of work, property, and exchange. As people work, buy, sell and invest, they are participating in a complex and dynamic system of shared meaning, purpose and ethics that defines the morality of economics in their culture. Their participation in the system may reinforce the system, or reshape it into a somewhat different form. Often it will do both at the same time, reinforcing some aspects of the system and reshaping others.

Consider the huge differences between the ancient, medieval, and modern economic systems. As we have observed, there are important similarities across these systems—most prominently, the moral value of work, property, exchange, and specialization. Yet the differences are also striking. For example, in the ancient world, slavery was accepted as universal, normal, natural, and right. Slavery was one of ancient society's most prominent economic institutions. Even the idea that a world without slavery might be possible did not get much serious consideration; such a world was implausible. Then, after the fall of the Roman Empire, slavery faded away in Western Europe. Historical developments, such as the rise of Christianity, had first rendered a world without slavery plausible, and then rendered a world with slavery implausible. At the same time, quasi-familial bonds between lord and serf became the dominant economic structure, and were as much taken for granted as slavery had been before. But these bonds were eventually weakened by religious, technological, and political developments in the early modern period, and were finally dissolved by the Industrial Revolution. Ordinary workers were given, in principle if not always in practice, the claim of equal moral dignity that we now take for granted as the basis of modern social order (North et al. 2009; Appleby 2010; McCloskey 2010). Ironically, at the same time Europe was elevating the dignity of ordinary workers among its domestic population, it was re-embracing the practice of slavery as its reach expanded into Africa (Frederickson 2002). Economic structures are cultural, and the differences are as important as the similarities.

The history of economic science is simultaneously a history of empirical, moral, and cultural observation. Each figure in this history offers a set of observations about how the economic system does in fact work, how it ought to work, and how both of those facts influence and are influenced by the shared character of a culture. While the seamless integration of these three kinds of observations was occasionally challenged, it was almost universally accepted from the earliest recorded thinkers through the eighteenth century.

The Nature Paradigm: Plato and Aristotle

Economic thought in western culture begins in the philosophy of ancient Greece, which also shaped the culture of ancient Rome. The economic thought of this age operated out of what we will call a Nature paradigm. It began with the assumption that human beings are part of nature and their economic needs and behaviors are part of nature, so conformity to nature and its purposes (they understood nature to have purposes) was their standard for economic thought. This paradigm receded when western thinking about humanity and nature changed in ways that eroded the plausibility of placing nature in that role.

We must begin by recognizing that economics did not exist as a distinct category of thought before the modern era. Classical authors' treatments of what we call "economic" subjects are contained in their books on ethics and politics. There were no books on economics as such until the late medieval period.

Plato

Plato was not the first philosopher in Greece, but he was the first philosopher to address social questions, and (perhaps for that reason) the first philosopher to leave behind a permanent intellectual legacy. Many of his writings are centrally concerned with economics; his *Hipparchus*, for example, examines popular complaints about the evils of "profiteers" and finds that these concerns have some merit, but also tend to be very simplistic and often reflect the ignorance of the complainer as much as the evil of the profiteer (Bloom 1990a).

His most famous and most profound meditations on economics are found in the *Republic*. Like all Plato's works, it unfolds as a dramatic story about Socrates. In the *Republic*, different views of how individuals ought to treat one another and how society ought to be arranged ("justice") come into conflict. The conflict that defines most of the book's drama is the confrontation between Socrates' view that justice is fundamentally a right ordering of the soul, and the view of the sophist Thrasymachus that what we call justice is merely a social convention—a cover-up for a system of exploitation that serves the interests of the powerful at the expense of the weak. As Thrasymachus famously put it, what we call justice is really only "the advantage of the stronger" (Plato 1991, 15; 338c).

In this drama, Socrates represents the seamless integration of empirical, moral, and cultural observation, while Thrasymachus represents the attempt to explain social systems empirically without a moral element. Against Thrasymachus, Socrates argues that human behavior and culture cannot be accurately explained unless we assume that there is moral truth, and that human behavior is related to that truth—the very categories of thought we must rely upon to identify social systems and analyze them empirically presuppose moral commitments. For example, when Thrasymachus argues that in society the strong rule the weak for their own benefit just as shepherds rule sheep for their own benefit and not for the benefit of the sheep, Socrates responds by showing that shepherding itself could not exist on those terms. The concept of "shepherding" becomes meaningless if it simply means "whatever benefits shepherds." While any given shepherd's motives may well be selfish, the activity of shepherding itself can only mean *taking good care of* sheep (Plato 1991, 21–24; 343a–347a). Particular concepts of what is good and bad are presupposed not only in formally moral categories like "justice," but even in empirical categories like "shepherding." At bottom, Socrates' argument is that you cannot strictly separate empirical and moral observation; you are assuming certain concepts of what is good for sheep if you talk about shepherding, regardless of what you say about it.

Moreover, another central feature of Socrates' case is that social arrangements are the embodiment of each society's shared views about justice, establishing the integration of culture alongside the empirical and the moral (Plato 1991, 45, 368c–369a).

Although Socrates' depiction of a utopian city is more famous, his meditations on justice in the *Republic* actually begin with a depiction of a well-run conventional (i.e. non-utopian) city. Socrates offers different prescriptions for justice in the well-run conventional city than he does for his utopia. In the well-run conventional city, justice means that people support themselves by working (Plato 1991, 46; 369d), own private property (46; 369e–370a), exchange with one another and with foreign cities (47–48; 370b–371b), and specialize in one form of labor per person for the sake of efficiency (47; 370b–370c)—including some whose specialty is not production, but buying and selling the goods produced by others in order to facilitate efficient exchange (48; 371c–371d).

As for the utopian city in the *Republic*, Socrates argues that the overwhelming majority of its citizens would live economically in the same way they would live in the well-run conventional city (work, private property, etc.). However, the city would be ruled by a tiny elite class of "guardians" who lived without families or economics, holding their women, children, and property in common. Scholars disagree about the significance of this utopian vision. Some say Plato was advocating it as a serious proposal for real-world implementation, difficult as that might be (Klosko 1981; Morrison 2007). Some say it was a satire showing the absurd results that follow from utopian thinking (Bloom 1991). Some say it was a literary image whose purpose is to illustrate metaphorically the qualities of the good soul (Annas 1999, 72–95). What we can be sure of is that it was not the form of justice he recommended for conventional cities, and even in the utopian city he advocated conventional economics for the vast majority of the population.

Aristotle

Aristotle, Plato's greatest student, generally eschewed utopianism and focused on systematic observation of real cities and economies. He sent his students traveling to 158 cities around the known world, and compiled their observations on political, economic, and other social systems (Schütrumpf 2012). But this empirical emphasis did not move him one inch away from Plato's position on the interdependence of empirical, moral, and cultural observation. To the contrary, all his observations begin from the premise that the universal human aspiration is to live a good life, and this aspiration becomes sustainable only when our view of the good life is moral and exercises virtue (or "activity of soul exhibiting excellence"; Aristotle 1980, 1; I.1 and 14; I.7). For Aristotle, social science exists to answer the question "what is the good life for man?" (Aristotle 1980, 1–2; I.2)

Economics (*oikonomike*) is an expression of ethics for Aristotle; it is the study of the actions through which individuals use the things around them in their pursuit of a good life (Crespo 2008). Besides this central understanding of *oikonomike*, Aristotle makes use of three related, subordinate understandings. First, "the economic" may refer to a person's own talents and abilities available for the pursuit of a good life. Second, it may also describe the habits each of us forms as we practice the virtuous life. Finally, it can describe the systematic study of economics itself—the study of human action in pursuit of moral goals, whether simple or profound (Crespo 2006).

Like Plato, Aristotle recommended work (Aristotle 1992, 57; I.2), property (79; I.8), exchange (81–85; I.9), and specialization (57; I.2). Private property and a market economy in which participants wisely engage in mutually beneficial exchanges ultimately lead to civil peace, effective resource use, and a public morality of mutual respect that grows habitual with time and practice (Aristotle 1992, 81–85; I.9, 106–109; II.3 and 112–119; II.5). Aristotle emphasized that economic activities are integral to the purpose of the family, the household and the village (i.e. the local community; Aristotle 1992, 57–59; I.2). When he turned to larger political structures, he began his observations with a strong warning that economic decisions should be left to private households as much as possible. He acknowledged that some loss of household autonomy is inevitable. But a general transfer of control over economic decisions from households to political systems, and likewise from smaller political units to larger ones, represented a threat to the integrity of all social systems (Aristotle 1992, 101–119; II.1–5). He then offered several specific case studies of cities. One experimented with economic egalitarianism, and the central control of economic activity this requires, and lived to regret it (Aristotle 1992, 126–132; II.7). In another, governance was undermined because people admired wealth more than virtue, and elevated the wealthy rather than the virtuous to public office (Aristotle 1992, 154–159; II.9).

Aristotle also gave fuller expression to some of the economic assumptions of the ancient world that would be challenged in the modern era. Perhaps the most important is a strict separation between economic production and other cultural activities such as politics, religion, philosophy, and art. Following the general mindset of the ancient world, Aristotle included only economic production in his concept of "work" and held that it was suited for the lower classes who possessed lesser human capacities. Elevated cultural activities were "leisure," not "work," and were suited for the higher, more fully human elite classes (Aristotle 1992, 57; I.2, 63–69; I.4–5, 183–185; III.5 and 436–439; VII.15). Closely related to this dualism was the idea that people are destined to certain economic stations by their birth and upbringing; social mobility was assumed to be impossible except in rare cases, and people generally had a responsibility to do the same jobs their fathers did, know their place, and obey their natal superiors (Aristotle 1992, 66–69; I.5). Finally, like all the ancients, Aristotle assumed that the total amount of wealth in the world was relatively fixed—either it did not grow, or it grew so slowly that its growth didn't make much difference. This assumption was the basis of, for example, his very strict prohibition against charging interest on money loans (Aristotle 1992, 85–87; I.10).

Aristotle emphasizes that human beings are morally corrupt; at one point he refers to "that element of badness which exists in each and all of us" (Aristotle 1992, 369; VI.4) As a result, political and economic systems (which Aristotle treats as closely interdependent) are constantly breaking down. Much of his *Politics* is devoted to describing how democracy and oligarchy—the two most common social systems—are each destabilized and eventually destroyed by the competition of selfish desires between the rich (arrogant pride) and the poor (resentful envy; Aristotle 1992, 310–318; V.5–6). Aristotle offers advice on how this decay can be held in check. Among his many recommendations, two stand out as the most important to his thinking. One is sound moral training, so that people in general will behave virtuously, and in particular the ruling class will be just and merciful to the class that is out of power. In an oligarchy, the rich who rule must do justice and show mercy to the poor; in a democracy, the poor who rule must respect the property rights of the rich (Aristotle 1992, 322–332; V.8–9). The other is mixed constitutions; that is, political institutions that give some measure of power to the disfavored class—the poor in an oligarchy, the rich in a democracy—so that no class has unchecked power (Aristotle 1992, 258–263; IV.8–9 and 264–272; IV.11–12).

The Nature Paradigm

We call the economic thought of Plato and Aristotle the Nature paradigm. The role of "nature" in both thinkers is subtle and complex, and defies easy summary. This complexity is there precisely because nature is so important to their thought. (Similarly, Plato's ideas about God are much simpler than Augustine's because God is much more important to Augustine than he is to Plato.) We focus on nature as the common theme in classical thought because a certain understanding of nature is a critical background assumption that gives shape to the economic ideas we have just reviewed.

What sets classical thought apart is the idea that nature has purposes, and human excellence consists in fulfilling those purposes. Aristotle states this explicitly as a foundational principle of his social thought: "Nature, as we say, does nothing without some purpose" (Aristotle 1992, 60; I.2). The role of nature is less explicit and more ambiguous in Plato, given his greater interest in the role of social conventions, but Plato still writes within the general assumptions of a classical view of nature. We see the implications of this view, for example, in the expectation that the basic facts of human social life have always been more or less the same and always will be more or less the same. The basic facts of social life among bears or bats or bees is always the same; why not also humans? That is just how nature works. We also see this in the ease with which classical thinkers assume that human beings should be divided up into classes based on their natural abilities, just as we divide all other living things into classes based on their abilities.

And we see it in the way the paradigm faded. The economic paradigm of Plato and Aristotle gave way to a new paradigm when the rise of Christianity changed the western understanding of nature and humans' relationship to it. Christianity gave the west something higher than nature to use as an ultimate standard. It even placed human beings themselves partly outside nature, standing above it as its official rulers and managers. Obviously "nature" cannot be the ultimate standard for human behavior if humans are given a commission to organize and control nature. Moreover, the doctrine of the fall introduced the conviction that nature in its present state is not just disorganized and in need of tidying up, but actively disordered by adversarial powers.

The God Paradigm: Christian Approaches

Alongside the classical philosophical tradition, the other major intellectual source of western civilization was Christianity and the religious tradition that it inherited (and reinterpreted) from Judaism. The transformation of western thought by the rise of Christianity introduced a new paradigm for economics, which we are calling the God paradigm. It began with the assumption that human beings are created by and under the authority of God, and are placed both within and over nature by God. Their economic needs and behaviors are structured by God's design in creation and are being restored to that design through the redemption of the world in Christ, so conformity to God and his purposes was their standard for economic thought. This paradigm receded when western thinking about humanity and its relation to God changed in ways that eroded the plausibility of placing God in that role.

An analysis of economic themes in the Bible and Christian theology generally would be beyond the scope of this book, although it is worth noting that this topic has been experiencing a renaissance in Christian theological and biblical studies in the early twenty-first century (Blomberg 2000; Schneider 2002; Claar and Klay 2007; Baker 2009; Corbett and Fikkert 2014; Joyce and Forster 2017; Longenecker and Liebengood 2009; Sherman 2011; Wong and Rae 2011; Willard and Black 2014; Waters 2016; Nelson 2017). After the rise of Christianity in the west, the philosophical and theological traditions interacted extensively. From this period through the Enlightenment, the history of western thought—including economic thought—is largely the history of this interaction.

Early Christianity

Early Christian thinkers emphasized their differences with classical ideas about God, but in social ethics there were more similarities. This is visible as early as Justin Martyr and Clement of Alexandria, who argued that Christianity should be legalized because Christians practice the moral virtues recognized by classical society better than their neighbors, and was consolidated in the thought of Augustine. Christians eventually explained the congruence of their social ethics with classical social ethics as a result of the "natural law" written into the hearts of all human beings by God; this term may trace its origin to Augustine's comment that the natural human being, who is at war with God and neighbor because of his sin, is nonetheless drawn to respect a basic level of social harmony by "the laws of his nature, so to speak" (Augustine 1984, 868; XIX.12).

This early emphasis on similarities played out in their approach to economics, establishing a number of continuities between the Nature paradigm and the early form of the God paradigm. The early Christians did not write systematically about economics, but when the topic came up, in general they affirmed their continuity with existing philosophical wisdom—although not with the moral corruption of the political and social *practices* they found going on around them in late Rome (Rhee 2012). The classical fundamentals of work, property, exchange, and specialization were all seen as congruent with biblical teaching. For example, the imperative to support yourself and your household by working had been strongly and repeatedly stressed in the Old Testament wisdom literature, and this imperative was also a consistent theme of the first Christian theologian, Paul, whose writings were accepted as divine revelation on par with Old Testament scripture from the earliest days of Christianity (Exodus 20:9; Psalm 128:2; Proverbs 6:6–11 and 31:10–31; II Thessalonians 3:6–15; and I Timothy 5:8). A line of Christian thought stretching back to the early theologian Irenaeus notes that the Genesis account says God created the world through "work," in contrast to other cosmologies, which held that God or the gods did not work. Irenaeus argued that through the mediation of Jesus and the Holy Spirit, human beings act as co-creators with God through their work, developing the potential of the world that God gave them as raw material. In this, Irenaeus and those following him challenge the dualism of ancient culture that denigrated economic work as compared with the life of the leisure class (Cosden 2006). On the other hand, Origen, Eusebius and those following them embrace classical dualism to a significant degree and reinterpret it to elevate the clergy above economic workers, arguing that economic work is legitimate, but is ethically and spiritually inferior to the special religious works of the clergy (Tait 2014). Moreover, Christian thinkers before the late Middle Ages generally carried forward the ancient world's assumption of a relatively static economy, with consequent prohibitions against charging interest for money loans (which had been forbidden in the Old Testament as well; Waters 2016, 19–39).

A more problematic point of continuity between classical and Christian social thought was the emphasis on moral corruption. Like Aristotle, Christianity teaches that human beings have a systematic tendency toward selfishness (for example Romans 1:18–3:20). However, unlike Aristotle, Christianity teaches that God has intervened in history to overcome this tendency, and that faithful followers of Christ undergo a gradual transformation of their hearts toward virtue (for example Romans 3:21–6:23). To the extent that Christians are influential within their cultures, this transformation of their hearts also creates a cultural environment within which unbelievers are morally influenced—not in a way that saves their souls, but in a way that makes them less corrupt than they otherwise would be (for example Matthew 5:13–16). In the first centuries after Christianity was legalized, this doctrine paved the way for a partnership between church and state, justified on grounds that civilization required the moral influence of the church.[1] In the modern era, Christians have generally embraced religious freedom and sought to influence their cultures either without formal church-state partnership, or with a much more restricted role for such partnership. Christian economic thought is profoundly shaped by complex theological debates over how much virtue Christians can legitimately expect from unbelievers, and what approaches Christians ought to use when seeking to influence their cultures for the better.

The Middle Ages

The God paradigm began to develop in more distinctive directions during the period known as the High Middle Ages, roughly the eleventh through thirteenth centuries. While economics still was not an independent discipline, a few major theologians gave it careful attention. Thomas Aquinas observed that the market system of property and

[1] For example, while Augustine's *The City of God* famously acknowledges that both the "city of God" and "city of man" exist within the Roman civil community, requiring much compromise (see esp. Book XIX), its core argument is that Rome did the right thing to embrace Christianity as its official religion; on the argument that civilization requires the moral influence of the church see esp. Book II.

exchange had the backing of both Aristotle (under natural law) and the Bible (in its prohibitions on theft, fraud and exploiting the powerless). He affirmed what appears to have been the general medieval consensus when he wrote that the "just price" of any good or service was whatever price buyers and sellers agreed to under fair conditions of exchange and subject to general ethical laws, such as the duty of universal goodwill (Wittmer 2017). (Claims that medieval theologians believed in an objectively calculable "just price" do not appear to be supported by historical evidence; de Roover 1958.) Medieval theologians sometimes came into conflict with guilds, denouncing them for using their monopolistic control of skilled trades and easy access to centers of political power to fatten themselves at the expense of those who relied on their services (de Roover 1958). The dignity and importance of work continued to be an important element in Christian theology, experiencing regular revivals as it was championed by figures like Gregory the Great, although the dualism of Origen and Eusebius, with its subordination of the laity to the clergy, also enjoyed periods of dominance (Armstrong 2013).

In the fourteenth century, not long after these currents of high medieval thought, Europe saw the emergence of the first autonomous economic firms—economic institutions, such as banks, that were not directly controlled by dynastic families or the church—as well as more extensive lending at interest (in defiance of church teaching) and other key developments of early capitalism (Stark 2005, 103–128). The inherited ideas of classical and early Christian thinking taught that such developments would be socially harmful, but in fact they seemed to be producing positive results.

Among the most striking of these was economic growth, which benefited the entire community—and which the received wisdom had assumed was not possible. The aggregate economy of Western Europe had begun to grow, slowly but steadily, starting in the twelfth century (Maddison 2007, 382). In some localities, this growth was much more obvious and demanded an explanation.

Eventually, scholars began to question the assumptions that lay behind the longstanding prohibitions on charging interest for money loans. The scholarly movement later known as the School of Salamanca emerged in the fifteenth century to investigate these questions more fully; this represented the first emergence of economics as a distinct field of inquiry. The writings of these scholars laid the theological and philosophical groundwork for moving Christianity toward embracing growth and accepting interest on money loans in that context (distinguishing legitimate loans from biblically prohibited "usury"). Theologians continued to serve as the major scholars of economics well into the seventeenth century; economics was studied as a subfield of moral philosophy and theology (Grabill 2007).

Early Modernity

The Protestant Reformation in the sixteenth century contributed further developments in Christian economic thinking. Luther and the other major reformers directly attacked the Aristotelian and Eusebian dualism that subordinated economic workers to the leisure class; they argued that this dualism was inconsistent with a biblical understanding of both the gospel and the "image of God" in human beings (Wingren 2004). The central importance of this argument to the larger structure of Reformation theology was neglected in twentieth-century scholarship, but is now increasingly appreciated (Veith 2011). As a consequence, Reformation social ethics—particularly under John Calvin (Hall and Burton 2009)—broke down rigid medieval class structures and emphasized the opportunity and responsibility of all individuals to contribute economically. The reformers' emphasis on the dignity and importance of economic work helped lay the groundwork for the emergence of economic growth in the Industrial Revolution. Like Irenaeus, they emphasized the creative element of human work and the Genesis imperative to cultivate (i.e. encourage growth in) the world God had created. This was the primary cultural source for the expanded recognition of human dignity that ushered in the Industrial Revolution (McCloskey 2010).

The economic paradigm centered on the Christian God gave way to a new paradigm when internal religious division and the wars of religion, and later the permanent pluralism of global communications and travel, changed the western understanding of how God related to social systems. Christianity did not decline, but public and social life came to be organized without the assumption of a shared faith. This was required at first by the persistence of theological differences among Christians after the Reformation, which necessitated finding ways of living together without a shared religious assumption as the only alternative to endless religious war (Loconte 2016). As communication and transportation technologies brought the world into closer and closer contact, the need for shared social systems ceased to be a temporary artifact of the

Reformation crisis and became instead a permanent reality (Berger 2014, 51–67). The emergence of social structures that could be shared among people without a common religion made it, in turn, far easier to live and to understand the world in purely secular terms. This provided the social conditions for the emergence, for the first time in history, of a public and sustainable secularism (as opposed to the purely private and, as it were, idiosyncratic atheism of older skeptics like Lucretius; Taylor 2007). In a world where social systems could no longer be based on the assumption of a shared religion, it made sense to seek nonreligious foundations for a paradigm of economics.

The Reason Paradigm: The Physiocrats and Adam Smith

The period known as the Enlightenment saw the rise of a new paradigm of economics we will call the Reason paradigm. It began with the assumption that human beings are rational, and their economic needs and behaviors can be understood and arranged rationally, so conformity to reason and its purposes (they understood "reason" to include moral reason, including teleology or purposes) was their standard for economic thought. This paradigm receded when western thinking about humanity and reason changed in ways that eroded the plausibility of placing reason in that role.

Enlightened Economics

During the Enlightenment, philosophers (including Christian philosophers) detached the idea of natural law from Christian theology. Christian thought up to that point had stressed that while the social world is structured by natural law, it tends to fall apart over time because of human sin—except where the redemptive influence of Christianity and the church infuses Christ's victory over sin into the structures of civilization. However, the basic structure of natural law philosophy that had been built up in the Middle Ages eventually made it seem plausible that the social world could be lawful and stable on its own, without supernatural spiritual influence. Most Enlightenment thinkers still thought the world required God as an explanation of its origin, such that the laws of nature were divine laws requiring our obedience, and some affirmed various forms of Christian belief. However, they generally adopted the view that social systems had sufficient natural integrity to go on of their own accord (Gunton 1998, 117–145).

At the same time, the Enlightenment also retained many key features of earlier classical and Christian thought. While a cultural influence from the church was no longer thought essential to social stability, the basic ethical boundaries for what was permissible in the social system did not much change. The Enlightenment philosophers continued to admonish people to work hard in productive professions, play fair and not steal or cheat, contribute to the well-being of others, and prioritize long-term stability and prosperity over short-term gratification. To the extent that ethics did change, such as in the expansion of opportunity and equal participation in society to the lower classes or in the legitimization of charging interest on money loans, the Enlightenment was mostly carrying forward trends that had begun much earlier—in many cases, as far back as the High Middle Ages (Taylor 2007).

Moral theory was also becoming more naturalistic. In the sixteenth and seventeenth centuries, figures like Niccolo Machiavelli and Thomas Hobbes had attempted to explain human morality solely in terms of a natural calculus (e.g. acts like murder and stealing are wrong because they interfere with the satisfaction of our natural desires). However, these approaches did not gain much mainstream acceptance. Most early moderns retained the historic Christian view that morality could not be explained without a transcendent basis standing above human nature. However, naturalistic approaches to ethics became more widely influential starting in the mid-eighteenth century; David Hume and Jean-Jacques Rousseau were key figures in this movement. In particular, Rousseau's approach was distinguished by the assertion that our emotional sympathy for one another and our desire to see others happy rather than suffering is natural (although it must be protected and cultivated by good education). This more optimistic view of natural human desires made it more plausible that morality could be explained solely in terms of such desires (Bloom 1987, 157–180; 1990b).

In France, the school of thought known as Physiocracy in the second half of the eighteenth century represented the first systematic application of this Enlightenment approach to economics. Physiocrats like François Quesnay believed the laws of nature took precedence over human laws, called "positive law." Rulers might try to get a certain economic result by passing a positive law, but if that result is not what the natural law dictates will happen, the real behavior of human beings will conspire to undermine such policies. For example, if rulers attempt to alleviate a shortage of grain and also avoid a panic by purchasing more grain abroad while passing laws against raising the price of grain, people will respond by buying and hoarding grain in anticipation of further shortages—undermining the intent of the policy. Allowing prices to rise, far from creating a panic, incentivizes more grain production and alleviates the shortage more effectively. Moreover, while positive law is flawed, natural law is perfect and divinely providential; the Physiocrats argued that society would be healthier and happier—and more consonant with the mind of the Supreme Being—if it relied more upon natural law (that is, the spontaneous actions of economic actors in the market) and less on positive law (Rothschild 2013).

Adam Smith

This history set the stage for Scottish philosopher Adam Smith to make his case for the *laissez-faire* ("let them act") view that he articulates in his 1776 book *An Inquiry into the Nature and Causes of the Wealth of Nations.* In his earlier *Theory of Moral Sentiments* (1759) Smith had explained human morality as a result of natural sympathetic sentiments, a theory similar to the one Rousseau had recently begun advocating in France. In *Wealth of Nations*, Smith applied this ethical theory to a market economy.

Smith makes a moral case for both the beneficial effects of economic growth and the preconditions growth requires. He assumes that human beings are essentially self-interested, but that one of their natural self-interests is a desire not to see others suffer (because the suffering of others makes us feel pain in sympathy). Thus a social system that protects rights to work, property, exchange, and specialization, but otherwise leaves people free to do as they please, will be relatively stable and beneficial. It will also produce a growing economy, as people discover and develop new and better ways of working and exchanging. Claar summarizes this point:

> Smith's overarching view is that human interactions, though motivated by self-love, can nevertheless lead to thoroughly pleasing outcomes, whether the outcomes are personal or social. As long as the dignity of humankind is preserved in the freedom to make choices, individuals will...ultimately be motivated to actions that not only benefit themselves but also benefit the other individuals they know and encounter; with time, society's overall

> economic wealth will grow, as will its capacity for great moral good. (Claar 2010, 897)

For Smith and the Physiocrats, the positive and normative were inextricably interwoven (Hutchison 1964, 123–132). The natural law tradition meant that for Smith and the Physiocrats, the word “natural” could capture both positive and normative. As Henry Sidgwick put it:

> By the term “natural” as commonly used, the notion of “what generally is” or “what would be apart from human interference” is suggested in vague combination with that of “what ought to be” or “what is intended by a benevolent Providence”. (Sidgwick 1883, 19)

Smith’s relationship to the classical and Christian traditions is ambiguous. In many ways, he was reinterpreting their commitments into the new idiom of Enlightenment science. The influence of these earlier traditions can be seen in his emphasis on basic human dignity, the creative contribution that people of all social classes make to the economy, the imperative to keep decision-making in the power of individuals and households rather than political systems, and the desirability of opportunity for all. On the other hand, unlike both classical and Christian thinkers, he represents this social system as relatively self-contained, arguing that it will satisfy natural human desires and that this is sufficient to ensure its long-term stability.

The naturalism of the Enlightenment approach can be seen most clearly in Smith’s assumption that physical exertion is the primary element in all economic work. Smith treats work almost entirely in material terms, as a physical activity; the economic value of all commodities is, in turn, equal to the amount of physical exertion necessary to acquire them.[2] This is in stark contrast to Christian thinkers, for whom the transcendent factors of identity, motivation, and purpose are always more important than the physical factor in any activity. Even Aristotle, who drew such a sharp distinction between workers and the leisure class, recognized the importance of the non-physical element in economic work (Aristotle 1992, 73–75; I.7). Karl Marx would later take the purely materialistic understanding of work from Smith, detach it from its roots

[2] “The real price of every thing, what every thing really costs to the man who wants to acquire it, is the toil and trouble of acquiring it” (Smith 1994, 33; I.5).

in classical and Christian ethics, and carry it to its logical conclusion: totalitarian socialism.

There were some respects in which Smith did qualify the naturalism of the Physiocrats. Borrowing a page from classical and Christian approaches, the economic theory of *Wealth of Nations* emphasizes the need for moral training as a precondition of a properly functioning economy. While the first four books present the market economy mostly as a well-oiled machine that runs by itself, the fifth and final book makes it clear that the "parts" needed for this machine to run are virtuous workers and merchants who have been educated to obey basic moral rules. In particular, he worries that the division of labor, carried to an extreme, will reduce some people to working at extremely narrow tasks, possibly narrowing their minds as well. To this end, Smith urges society to offer robust support for schools and churches to broaden people's mental and moral horizons (Smith 1994, 819–875; V.1.iii.2–3). He also includes among the proper functions of government "supporting the dignity of the sovereign," maintaining the shared cultural rituals that strengthen our sense of awe before the guardians of public justice and social order (Smith 1994, 876; V.1.4).

At the same time, he also imports his model of economic markets into the field of moral education. Schools and churches, he argues, should not receive automatic subsidies but should be supported based on how many students or congregants they can voluntarily attract in an environment of free choice and competition. The same market forces that drive businesses to serve customers better will also improve schools and churches (Smith 1994, 819–824; V.1.iii.2 and 846–853; V.1.iii.3). To some extent this makes perfect sense—schools and churches are human institutions like any others, prone to dysfunction and corruption if they are not held accountable to those whom they exist to serve. Freedom of religion has in fact increased the vitality of religion in society and the willingness of different religions to tolerate one another, just as Smith predicted it would (Berger 2014). The early results from school choice experiments are likewise very promising (Forster 2016). At the same time, Smith's conceptualization of schools and (especially) churches as basically the same kind of institutions as businesses confirms the distance between his thought and that of his classical and Christian predecessors. Smith qualifies his naturalism, but he is a naturalist at heart.

Enlightened Answers Raise New Questions

Smith was the last of the great economic philosophers to take for granted the seamless integration of empirical, moral and cultural observation. As we will see in Chapter 3, almost immediately after Smith this integration began to grow problematic for leading economic thinkers, especially in England. Smith's naturalism provided the starting point for this new development. If social systems like economics are constantly falling apart because of human wickedness, as the classical and Christian traditions think, it's important to keep the moral element in mind when analyzing the economy. But if the economic system goes on of its own accord like clockwork, why bother thinking about the "ought" of the economy as much as Smith does? Why not just describe what "is"—won't that give you everything you need? This naturalism had been partially qualified in Smith's own work, as his concern for moral education through schools and churches attests. But these limitations on naturalism had not been widely shared by his predecessors among the Physiocrats, and they were not much maintained among his successors.

It was this nineteenth-century move toward moral neutrality—the subject of Chapter 3—that brought an end to the Reason paradigm. This paradigm was by far the shortest-lived of the three major paradigms. Its enormous theoretical and practical accomplishments came within a short span, but so did the forces that undermined it from within.

The Enlightenment thinkers were able to treat wealth creation, virtue and progress as the morally obligatory purposes of economics only so long as these goals were not deeply examined. Reason remained the standard, but it turned out that reason by itself did not provide grounds for maintaining the integration of empirical and moral inquiry essential to the Reason paradigm. The Enlightenment's confidence was badly shaken when Rousseau's Romanticism called into question the coherence of its aims, holding that wealth creation and social progress were actually inimical to moral virtue. As it became clearer that the Enlightenment had taken for granted the assumptions of Christian metaphysics without realizing it, natural law gave way to utilitarianism. This is the view that actions or rules are morally justified solely by the promoting of human happiness; the morally right thing to do, or the morally right rule to follow, is whatever will maximize general human happiness (understood as pleasure or preference-satisfaction). Utilitarianism was more unambiguously defensible on rationalist grounds, but at the cost of abandoning all moral goals higher than subjective human happiness. Social science began to ask whether it wouldn't be better just to avoid moral questions.

A Cross-Paradigm Hybrid: The American Experiment and Francis Wayland

On the other hand, while English thinkers after Smith began trying to detach economics from morality, the integration of empirical, moral and cultural observation lasted much longer in America. Throughout the eighteenth and nineteenth centuries, American economic thought retained a robust grounding in moral concerns. If anything, this integration got stronger rather than weaker in nineteenth-century America, as explicitly Christian thinking and practice became more influential in the nation's public culture in that century, as compared to the period of the American founding (Noll 1992, 163–285).

The American Experiment

The constitutional democracy and entrepreneurial economy at the heart of the American experiment represent a unique hybrid of paradigms. From its beginnings, American culture has been composed of an unstable mixture of classical, Christian, and Enlightenment thinking (Novak 2003). Enlightenment optimism about human nature, and a resulting confidence that social systems can satisfy natural desires and thus be stable of their own accord without supernatural influence, are clearly present as important elements in early American thought.[3] At the same time, more pessimistic classical elements are at least equally important, giving

[3]From Federalist #9, by Alexander Hamilton: "The science of politics, however, like most other sciences, has received great improvement. The efficacy of various principles is now well understood, which were either not known at all, or imperfectly known, to the ancients. The regular distribution of power into distinct departments, the introduction of legislative balances and checks, the institution of courts composed of judges holding their offices during good behavior, the representation of the people in the legislature by deputies of their own election; these are wholly new discoveries, or have made their principal progress towards perfection in modern times. They are means, and powerful means, by which the excellencies of republican government may be retained, and its imperfections lessened or avoided" (Hamilton et al. 2003, 36).

rise to anxieties among some founders that the social system would inevitably decay, and a sense of urgency about moral education.[4] And while the most famous of the founding figures were very uneven in their theological orthodoxy, they generally articulated a sincere commitment to Christianity (as they understood it) and were importantly influenced by Christian thought traditions; hence we find in many of them the view that Christianity has the power to raise cultures to a moral level higher than what would be possible by natural effort alone.[5] Among the population at large during the founding period, classical influence was less important, while very strong Christian and Enlightenment influences coexisted without much sense of tension between them (Clark 1994; Noll 1992, 83–162).

The paradoxical nature of American culture can be seen in Alexis de Tocqueville's observations on the central role of "self-interest properly understood" in America, including economics. On the one hand, Tocqueville observes that Americans expect the economy, and society in general, to run smoothly and remain successful as long as everyone has an enlightened understanding of what is in his own self-interest, and then acts on this understanding. Here we see the influence of Enlightenment optimism and naturalism (de Tocqueville 2003, 609–612; II.2.viii). At the same time, however, Tocqueville insists that the American concept of what it means to be "enlightened" about your self-interest, far from being secularistic or rationalistic, is extensively Christian. According to Tocqueville, Americans believe that Christian ethical teaching and a very strong cultural influence of local churches is essential to people's achieving enlightenment about their self-interest (de Tocqueville 2003, 613–615; II.2.ix). On this view, in a society where Christianity is

[4]From George Washington's Farewell Address: "Of all the dispositions and habits which lead to political prosperity, religion and morality are indispensable supports…The mere politician, equally with the pious man, ought to respect and to cherish them. A volume could not trace all their connections with private and public felicity…Who that is a sincere friend to it can look with indifference upon attempts to shake the foundation of the fabric? Promote then, as an object of primary importance, institutions for the general diffusion of knowledge" (Washington 2017).

[5]For example, in John Adams' attack on medieval canon and feudal law, he does not call them the greatest systems of tyranny ever, but only the greatest systems of tyranny "since the promulgation of Christianity" (Adams 1985, 5); moreover, he says they were rolled back when "God in his benign providence raised up the champions who began and conducted the Reformation" (6–7).

widely influential, Christian and Enlightenment ideas become complementary. While the naturalism that began growing in English thought was excluded in America by the emphasis on Christianity's unique role, Enlightenment optimism was welcomed—optimistic expectations were justified by the cultural influence of the faith.

Francis Wayland

American clergy in the nineteenth century put great value upon economics as a moral endeavor, and also upon the potential usefulness of economic understanding to lift up humanity everywhere. The late Paul Heyne provides a captivating account of this period in *"Are Economists Basically Immoral?" and Other Essays on Economics, Ethics, and Religion*, a posthumously published collection of his works (Heyne 2008, 213–266).

The nineteenth-century American integration of morality and economics, of Christianity and Enlightenment thought, is vividly illustrated in the 1837 textbook *Elements of Political Economy* by the Reverend Francis Wayland (1796–1865). It became "by far the most popular political economy textbook prior to the Civil War" (Heyne 2008, 240). Wayland's book was so important a contribution to the body of economic thought that Marx quoted Wayland—twice—in *Capital* (Marx 1906, 182n and 231n).

Wayland had not intended to go into the pastorate, moral philosophy or academic life. After his graduation from Union College, he began to study medicine. Upon experiencing a religious conversion, however, he followed a call into pastoral ministry. Wayland read voraciously and eventually transformed himself into an intellectual, serving as president of Brown University for nearly 30 years (Vance 2006).

Wayland's *Elements*, largely a collection of the notes from his lectures in political economy given to the senior class at Brown, brought together the *laissez-faire* economics of Smith and a distinctly Christian articulation of the natural law tradition. It may well be the most systematic and ambitious effort of the post-Smith period to reconcile Smith's Enlightenment science of economics with explicitly Christian theology and ethics. Wayland carries forward into the modern era the long Christian tradition of seeing the created order, including the economic order, as part of God's rich providence.

Consider this passage from the first page of the *Elements*:

> By science, as the word is here used, we mean a systematic arrangement of the laws which God has established, so far as they have been discovered, of any department of human knowledge. It is obvious, upon the slightest reflection, that the creator has subjected the accumulation of the blessings of this life to some determinate laws. Every one, for instance, knows that no man can grow rich, without industry and frugality. Political economy, therefore, is a systematic arrangement of the laws by which, under our present constitution, the relations of man, whether individual or social, to the objects of his desire, are governed. (Wayland 1870, 15)

In this passage and others like it, we can see that Wayland writes in the natural law tradition, and views God as the creator of the laws that govern all of us—not surprising for a Baptist pastor. As Vance observes: "Wayland's teachings show that one can hold to the absolute authority of Scripture *and* be a strong advocate of liberty and the free market...Christianity and laissez-faire economics are not incompatible" (Vance 2006, 404). Wayland understands that economics is not merely about money. For Wayland, our economic relations govern our pursuit of whatever we consider valuable, whether as individuals or as a society. Thus Wayland repeatedly celebrates qualities such as "industry, frugality, thrift, innovation, entrepreneurship, property, competition, the division of labor, labor-saving devices, and capital" (Vance 2006, 404–405).

This passage also shows us how Wayland has assimilated the naturalism of Smith and the Physiocrats in a way that is not really consistent with Christian theology and ethical teaching. Wayland presents it as a "determinate law," comparable to the laws of physics, that "no man can grow rich without industry and frugality." The Bible and historic Christian theology do affirm that it is *usually* the case that wealth comes from diligence and good stewardship; this is, for example, a running theme in the biblical book of Proverbs. However, the Bible and historic Christian theology actually deny that this is a universal law. Because the world is fallen and broken due to sin, material success is not perfectly aligned with virtue; evil, and chaos create misalignments between prosperity and moral worth. This is the primary theme of the biblical book of Job, and is summarized in Jesus' statement that the people killed in a recent accident in Siloam were no worse sinners than the bystanders who survived, with the strong implication of a firm rebuke to anyone who would think otherwise (Luke 13:4).

Earlier Christian writers would have taught the lesson that virtue creates prosperity as a moral precept—a broad generalization about the way the world usually works. The teaching of such general moral precepts is critical to the moral formation of culture in communities. A society that does not teach people to expect that "virtue creates prosperity" at least most of the time cannot sustain virtue and ethical behavior in its economy. However, Wayland speaks in the voice of an Enlightenment scientist studying universal laws comparable to those of physics. To raise these teachings from general precepts to universal laws invites the expectation that the economy rewards virtue and punishes vice on its own, automatically.

Wayland is most memorable when explaining the moral theory imbued within economic theory and its implications for human choice, action, and flourishing. Consider this passage describing the mutual benefits of trade:

> How fallacious is the notion formerly entertained, that, by exchange, only one party is benefitted; and consequently, that what one party gains, the other party loses. Were this the case, no country could grow rich by exchange, unless by impoverishing every other country; and the gain of one nation, would be nothing else than a transfer of the wealth of other countries to itself. On the contrary, precisely the reverse is the case. The most favorable commerce to any one country, is, that by which the riches of both countries are the most rapidly increased. A merchant, whose gains were all derived from the impoverishment of his customers, would very soon have none but paupers for neighbors. A nation, whose traffic caused the impoverishment of another nation, would very soon be obliged to discontinue commerce…And thus, we see, in political economy as in morals, every benefit…is mutual; and we cannot, in the one case, any more than in the other, really do good to ourselves, without doing good to others; nor do good to others, without also doing good to ourselves. (Wayland 1870, 171)

Wayland shows us our economic relationships through the eyes of a modern economist who is also a Christian moral philosopher, for whom the connections between economics and moral theory are obvious and strong. Above all, for Wayland markets afforded great promise for the improvement of the human condition, material and spiritual.

The Experiment Continues

Wayland was not the only clergyman in the United States who remained faithful to economics as moral philosophy; far from it. If Wayland's

Elements was the most popular textbook before the Civil War, Joseph Dorfman describes the Reverend Arthur Latham Perry's 1866 *Elements of Political Economy* as "the most popular treatise in the country" for nearly a quarter century after its publication (Dorfman 1966, 983). Heyne views Perry, professor of history and political economy at Williams College, as the clergy's staunchest defender of *laissez-faire* during the period (Heyne 2008, 257).

The American fusion of Christian and naturalistic thinking—from the idea of enlightened self-interest observed by Tocqueville to Wayland and Perry's natural-law economics—has been a powerful force in human history. It has allowed American culture to harness the power of the Enlightenment's scientific, economic, and political advances without experiencing the extreme secularization and cynicism that have undermined the vitality of cultures in western Europe. The American synthesis provided a metaphysical narrative that motivated, humanized, and morally restrained the endeavors of science, economics, and politics.

At the same time, this synthesis depended upon papering over important contradictions that would later rise to the surface and bitterly divide American culture. In the twentieth century, developments in art, science, religion, and international affairs would force Americans to confront the differences between naturalistic and Christian assumptions about the universe. And even as Wayland was confidently building a Christian economic theory based on the expectation of stable, predictable economic laws ordained by God, economists in England were using the same expectation of stable, predictable economic laws to turn the field of economics itself sharply against the very moral and religious presuppositions Wayland cherished.

Detractors from the Paradigms of Higher Purpose: Mandeville and Malthus

Paradigms integrating empirical, moral, and social observation in economics have been dominant in western civilization, but they have not been without their detractors. We have already seen Socrates' encounter with the skeptical Thrasymachus, a representative example of dialogues that occurred under all three paradigms. In addition to moral skeptics, who are always with us, there were other kinds of critics. For example, figures like Blaise Pascal questioned the empirical validity of the enterprise, arguing that human cultures are so various it is impossible to make generalizations about human behavior that are meaningful enough to inform the design of social systems (Pascal 1901, 61–73). Indeed, if these paradigms had never been challenged, they would not have been laid out with anything like the extensive theoretical articulation they did in fact receive, and consequently we would hardly know what they were or how they worked.

Two particular detractors are especially worth noting for our purposes, for they represented precursors or early harbingers of what would emerge as the Consumption paradigm. One was a skeptic seeking to debunk moral crusaders, and the other was a pastor on a moral crusade to benefit humanity. That the Keynesian Revolution, when it came, would hark back so powerfully to the legacy of two such morally dissonant figures tells us much about that revolution's desire to eat its cake and also have it when it comes to the moral foundations of economics.

Bernard Mandeville

The cynical Dutch author Bernard Mandeville took aim at the moral pretensions of Christian and early Enlightenment approaches alike in his 1714 *Fable of the Bees.* The book depicted conventional morality as a sham, and selfish behavior as the path to success for individuals and society alike. Mandeville popularized the saying "private vice is public virtue," by which he meant that selfish behavior actually had beneficial effects for society. Selfish workers have an incentive to be diligent, frugal, and self-controlled, Mandeville argued. Selfish merchants have an incentive to be efficient and even honest, to keep customers coming back. Meanwhile, the meddlesome schemes of well-meaning do-gooders—whether religious or secular—not only fail to accomplish their goals, they actively interfere with the efficient provision of everyone's needs. The do-gooders never get anything right, and for a simple reason: their plans depend upon people being virtuous.

Adam Smith's response shows how deeply moral the Reason paradigm was at its height. Smith energetically rejected Mandeville's view that it is selfishness that drives all economic decisions. He repudiated the idea that encouraging selfishness is economically beneficial. Classifying Mandeville in his section on "Licentious Systems" of ethics, Smith issues a concise judgment on *Fable of the Bees*: "This author's opinions are in almost every respect erroneous" and the book's "tendency is wholly pernicious" (Smith 2006, 307; VII.4).

Smith's response to Mandeville echoes Socrates' response to Thrasymachus. He argues that moral categories are needed to understand human behavior. Smith observes that Mandeville's argument relies upon a single, central trick, which he repeats in several different ways to apply it to a variety of contexts (Smith 2006, 308–312; VII.4). The trick is to insist that all behavior aimed at doing something morally praiseworthy is really only motivated by a love of being morally praised by others. So all that appears selfless is really an attempt to *look* selfless, i.e. is actually selfish. But Smith points out that such actions would not be considered morally praiseworthy in the first place if human beings really were as uniformly selfish as Mandeville insists they are. Aristotle had made a similar argument in his *Ethics* (Aristotle 1980, 6–7; I.5).

Thomas Malthus

It is difficult to think of a figure in the history of economics more immediately contrasting with Mandeville than Thomas Robert Malthus. Indeed, Malthus was exactly the sort of do-gooder Mandeville detested. A small-town pastor who shepherded village churches in Surrey and Lincolnshire, and later a professor at a college in Hertfordshire, Malthus was intensely concerned about the fate of the poor. He wrote extensively on economic philosophy and policy, drawing upon the writings of Adam Smith and David Hume, and critiquing the English Poor Laws. Although he opposed the economic radicalism associated with the French Revolution and early communistic theories, which he viewed as naïve utopianism, he was a tireless advocate of public policy reforms aimed at improving the economic well-being of the less fortunate.

Malthus has become famous, somewhat unfairly, for a theory that is generally associated with his 1798 *An Essay on the Principle of Population*. In fact, the story is more complicated. Recent scholarship has drawn attention to the fact that Malthus' book focuses on other issues, and does not in fact clearly state the theory now popularly attributed to it (Hammond 2015). It was subsequent interpreters who articulated the theory now called "Malthusianism" and gave it that name, attributing it to Malthus. We do not enter here into the interesting question of whether and to what extent Malthus was a Malthusian. As will become clear, Malthus is important for our purposes regardless of how one answers that question.

The "Malthusian" theory is that economic growth is sabotaged by a general human propensity to favor greater reproduction over greater comfort for the existing population. Economic growth brings with it greater wealth, and thus a greater ability to satisfy our consumption appetites. In the short term, this produces a better life. However, people's consumption appetites are weighted disproportionately toward rearing children rather than consuming one's resources oneself—toward expanding life rather than enjoying life. More people means more mouths to feed, and before long the available resources per person go down rather than up, as the growth in population outpaces the growth in production. Thus, in what has come to be called the "Malthusian Trap," economic development ends in poverty and famine.

While Malthusianism in its full form—the view that economic growth leads inevitably to catastrophe—has been thoroughly debunked, important elements of Malthusianism continue to have enormous social influence. We now know that when economic policy is properly stewarded, productivity growth outpaces population growth by a wide margin. But the "we" in that sentence ("we now know") includes only those who are willing to learn what the discipline of economics has discovered. Concerns about so-called "overpopulation" remain with us. We need not even look as far abroad as China's tyrannical population control policies to find them. The supposed danger of overpopulation is invoked to justify a variety of public policies in all developed countries—and to justify foreign policies under which the powerful, developed nations pressure less-powerful, less-developed nations to suppress the growth they need. If we were willing to learn the lesson of the errors of Malthusianism, we would stop talking about "overpopulation" and start talking about underdevelopment—we would quit bullying developing countries into expanding abortion services and instead help them provide the reliable roads, banks, and courts that their people need to grow sustainably.

However, Malthus' influence is still with us at a much deeper level, in a way that doesn't depend on whether he was a Malthusian. In fact, in one respect Malthus has triumphed. Malthus and his followers introduced a major shift in the underlying anthropology of economics—that is, its understanding of what a human being is.

In the Malthus/Malthusian view, for purposes of economics, a human being is essentially a consumer of resources. The central question for the practice of economics is how to ensure resources are provided for people so they can consume them; the study of economics is to be directed to discovering how this can be done. This was not the focus in any of the three dominant paradigms from before the nineteenth century. For the Nature paradigm, a human being is essentially an embodiment of the highest ends of nature: reason and virtue. For the God paradigm, a human being is the image of God, made to glorify, obey and enjoy God in Christ. For the Reason paradigm, a human being is essentially a thinking and willing being with the capacity to understand, manage, and reform the world. This was not only what they were in general, this was also specifically what they were *for purposes of economics*. The story of how we were conquered by the view that for purposes of economics we are essentially consumers of resources, even as "Malthusianism" was debunked, will unfold in the subsequent chapters of this book.

Mandeville and Malthus, surprising as it may seem, have something important in common. They both envisioned an economics that was largely detached from teleology—from any purpose higher than satisfying people's consumer appetites. An economy in which people have more resources they can use to make their lives more comfortable and enjoyable is a good economy, regardless of other factors; an economy in which people have fewer resources is worse. Higher standards for evaluating whether an economy is good or bad have either dropped out of view to make room for more urgent material concerns (in Malthus) or been deliberately repudiated (in Mandeville).

As we will see, the Keynesian Revolution would have an important place for both these figures.

References

Adams, John. 1985. A Dissertation on the Canon and Feudal Law. In *The Political Writings of John Adams*. Oxford, London and New York, NY: Macmillan.

Annas, Julia. 1999. *Platonic Ethics, Old and New*. Oxford, London and New York, NY: Cornell University Press.

Appleby, Joyce. 2010. *The Relentless Revolution*. Oxford, London and New York, NY: W. W. Norton.

Aristotle. 1980. *Ethics*. Oxford, London and New York, NY: Oxford University Press.

Aristotle. 1992. *Politics*. Oxford, London and New York, NY: Penguin Books.

Armstrong, Chris R. 2013. Refocused Vocation. *Leadership Journal* 34: 44–48.

Augustine. 1984. *City of God*. New York: Penguin Books.

Baker, David L. 2009. *Tight Fists or Open Hands?* New York: Eerdmans.

Berger, Peter L. 2014. *The Many Altars of Modernity*. Berlin and Boston: De Gruyter.

Bloom, Allan. 1987. *The Closing of the American Mind*. New York: Simon & Schuster.

Bloom, Allan. 1990a. The Political Philosopher in Democratic Society: The Socratic View. In *Giants and Dwarfs*, ed. Allan Bloom. New York: Simon & Schuster.

Bloom, Allan. 1990b. Rousseau: The Turning Point. In *Giants and Dwarfs*, Allan Bloom. New York: Simon & Schuster.

Bloom, Allan. 1991. Interpretive Essay. In *Republic*, Plato. New York: Basic Books.

Blomberg, Craig. 2000. *Neither Poverty Nor Riches*. Downers Grove: InterVarsity Press.

Claar, Victor V. 2010. Ethics and Economics. In *21st Century Economics: A Reference Handbook*, ed. Rhona Free. Thousand Oaks, CA: Sage.

Claar, Victor V., and Robin J. Klay. 2007. *Economics in Christian Perspective*. Downers Grove: InterVarsity Press.

Clark, J.C.D. 1994. *The Language of Liberty 1660–1832*. Cambridge and New York, NY: Cambridge University Press.

Corbett, Steve, and Brian Fikkert. 2014. *When Helping Hurts*. Chicago: Moody Publishers.

Cosden, Darrell. 2006. *A Theology of Work*. Eugene: Wipf & Stock.

Crespo, Ricardo F. 2006. The Ontology of 'the Economic': An Aristotelian Analysis. *Cambridge Journal of Economics* 30 (5): 767–781.

Crespo, Ricardo F. 2008. 'The Economic' According to Aristotle. *Foundations of Science* 13 (3–4): 281–294.

Dorfman, Joseph. 1966. *The Economic Mind in American Civilization, 1606–1865*. New York: Augustus M. Kelley.

Forster, Greg. 2016. A Win-Win Solution: The Empirical Evidence on School Choice. Friedman Foundation for Educational Choice, May 2016.

Frederickson, George M. 2002. *Racism: A Short History*. Princeton: Princeton University Press.

Grabill, Stephen J. 2007. Editor's Introduction. In *Sourcebook in Late-Scholastic Monetary Theory*, ed. Stephen J. Grabill. Grand Rapids: Acton Institute.

Gunton, Colin. 1998. *The Triune Creator*. Grand Rapids: Eerdmans.

Hall, David W., and Matthew D. Burton. 2009. *Calvin and Commerce*. Phillipsburg: P&R Publishing.

Hamilton, Alexander, James Madison, and John Jay. 2003. *The Federalist*. Cambridge and New York, NY: Cambridge University Press.

Hammond, J.Daniel. 2015. Malthus, Utopians and Economists. *Research in the History of Economic Thought and Methodology* 33: 179–207.
Heyne, Paul. 2008. *"Are Economists Basically Immoral?" and Other Essays on Economics, Ethics and Religion*. Indianapolis: Liberty Fund.
Hutchison, T.W. 1964. *Positive Economics and Policy Objectives*. New York: George Allen & Unwin.
Joyce, Adam, and Greg Forster (eds.). 2017. *Economic Wisdom for Churches*. Deerfield: Oikonomia Network.
Klosko, George. 1981. Implementing the Ideal State. *Journal of Politics* 43 (2): 365–389.
Locke, John. 1993. *Two Treatises of Government*. London: Everyman Library.
Loconte, Joseph. 2016. *God, Locke and Liberty*. Lanham: Lexington Books.
Longenecker, Bruce W., and Kelly D. Liebengood, eds. 2009. *Engaging Economics*. Grand Rapids: Eerdmans.
Maddison, Angus. 2007. *Contours of the World Economy*. New York, NY and Oxford: Oxford University Press.
Marx, Karl. 1906. *Capital*. Chicago: Charles H. Kerr.
McCloskey, Deirdre N. 2010. *Bourgeois Dignity*. Chicago: University of Chicago Press.
Morrison, Donald R. 2007. The Utopian Character of Plato's Ideal City. In *Cambridge Companion to Plato's Republic*, ed. G.R.F. Ferrari. Cambridge & New York, NY: Cambridge University Press.
Nelson, Tom. 2017. *The Economics of Neighbor Love*. Downers Grove: InterVarsity Press.
Noll, Mark A. 1992. *A History of Christianity in the United States and Canada*. Grand Rapids: Eerdmans.
North, Douglass C., John Joseph Wallis, and Barry R. Weingast. 2009. *Violence and Social Orders*. Cambridge and New York, NY: Cambridge University Press.
Novak, Michael. 2003. *On Two Wings*. San Francisco: Encounter Books.
Pascal, Blaise. 1901. *Thoughts*. London: George Bell & Sons.
Plato. 1991. *Republic*. New York: Basic Books.
Rhee, Helen. 2012. *Loving the Poor, Saving the Rich*. Grand Rapids: Baker.
de Roover, Raymond. 1958. The Concept of the Just Price. *Journal of Economic History* 18 (4): 418–434.
Rothschild, Emma. 2013. *Economic Sentiments*. Cambridge: Harvard University Press.
Schneider, John R. 2002. *The Good of Affluence*. Grand Rapids: Eerdmans.
Schütrumpf, Eckart. 2012. Aristotle. In *Encyclopedia of Ancient History*. Hoboken: Wiley.
Sherman, Amy L. 2011. *Kingdom Calling*. Downers Grove: InterVarsity Press.
Sidgwick, Henry. 1883. *Principles of Political Economy*. London: Macmillan.

Smith, Adam. 1994. *The Wealth of Nations*. New York: Random House.
Smith, Adam. 2006. *Theory of Moral Sentiments*. Mineola: Dover Publications.
Stark, Rodney. 2005. *The Victory of Reason*. New York: Random House.
Tait, Edwin Woodruff. 2014. Duty and Delight. *Christian History* 110: 14–19.
Taylor, Charles. 2007. *A Secular Age*. Cambridge: Harvard University Press.
de Tocqueville, Alexis. 2003. *Democracy in America*. London: Penguin.
Vance, Lawrence. 2006. Francis Wayland: Preacher-Economist. *Independent Review* 10: 401–410.
Veith, Gene Edward. 2011. *God at Work*. Wheaton: Crossway.
Washington, George. 2017. Washington's Farewell Address. Yale Law School Avalon Project. http://avalon.law.yale.edu/18th_century/washing.asp. Accessed 2 Feb 2017.
Waters, Brent. 2016. *Just Capitalism*. Louisville: Westminster John Knox.
Wayland, Francis. 1870. *Elements of Political Economy*. Boston: Gould and Lincoln.
Willard, Dallas, and Gary Black, Jr. 2014. *The Divine Conspiracy Continued*. San Francisco: HarperOne.
Wingren, Gustaf. 2004. *Luther on Vocation*. Eugene: Wipf & Stock.
Wittmer, Michael. 2017. Is a Just Price Enough? *Journal of Markets & Morality* 20 (2): 263–278.
Wong, Kenman L., and Scott B. Rae. 2011. *Business for the Common Good*. Downers Grove: InterVarsity Press.

CHAPTER 3

Just the Facts, Mammon: Aspirations to Moral and Cultural Neutrality

The 2300-year tradition (or series of traditions) approaching economics as an empirical, moral, and cultural phenomenon did not vanish in a day. While it was John Maynard Keynes who decisively instituted the new paradigm that replaced the older ones, he was only able to do so because those older paradigms had undergone almost two centuries of gradual weakening. Even as Francis Wayland was preaching his ingenious synthesis of Christian ethics and Enlightenment economic science in America, across the Atlantic leading economic thinkers were already asking (in effect): If Adam Smith is right that the economic system is relatively stable on its own because it accords with human nature, and human nature is in turn intrinsically good enough to maintain the virtues that sustain the economic system (honesty, diligence, etc.) without extraordinary effort, why does the study of economics need to bother with morality? Why not just analyze facts, leaving normative and teleological questions to the philosophers and theologians who find them interesting? When Keynes developed the new paradigm out of which economics operates today, he was only giving the discipline of economics what its scholars had long been asking for. When the revolutionary leader arrived on the scene, the army of soldiers who would carry out the war was already there—and, as we will see, the man who did the most to make it ready for Keynes' arrival was also named Keynes.

V. V. Claar and G. Forster, *The Keynesian Revolution and Our Empty Economy*, https://doi.org/10.1007/978-3-030-15808-8_3

David Ricardo: First Aspirations to Moral Neutrality

Though there is some scholarly dissent regarding the precise intellectual path leading to the eventual separation of economics from moral philosophy, nearly all scholars point to David Ricardo, who published a series of groundbreaking books in the 1810s, as the economist who first aspired to cut ties between the two. Along with Smith, Ricardo was a major figure in the classical school of economics, a tradition that considered markets to be largely self-correcting, and in which assumptions inherited from classical and Christian natural law philosophy figured prominently.

Ricardo is best known for his articulation of the concept of comparative advantage, a contribution so significant that it is often described as the most important and least obvious idea in all of economics. The principle of comparative advantage demonstrates that it is mutually advantageous for each person to specialize in the production of the good or the service that he can produce at a lower opportunity cost than others, and then offer that good or service in exchange for other goods or services. In such a way an individual can live much more richly than she could if she relied on herself alone to produce everything she needs.

We often overlook the deep truth of Ricardo's comparative advantage discovery because we are surrounded by it. Comparative advantage explains why even starving artists buy art pencils from others rather than making their own. The easiest way for a poor artist to get the pencils he needs is to spend time creating art—or even waiting tables—and use the proceeds from those activities to buy pencils from those who specialize in making pencils and can offer them at very low prices to grateful artists.

What is true among individual producers and consumers also holds among nations. When nations specialize in the production of the things in which they possess a comparative advantage over their neighbors, then both countries will be able to enjoy consumption possibilities that lie beyond their own abilities to produce. This is the reason why both Smith and Ricardo were strong advocates for the repeal of the Corn Laws, trade restrictions designed to protect agriculture in Britain.

Though neither Smith nor Ricardo lived to see the repeal of the Corn Laws, their eventual repeal made it possible for England to grow rich through industrial production of goods like cloth. By specializing in making cloth and using the proceeds to buy goods like corn or wine from other nations, England could live more richly than it would without trade. Comparative advantage also explains why today we refer to the state of New Jersey as "the Garden State": farmers in New Jersey grew rich by growing the food needed by New Yorkers who were busy working at other tasks. Comparative advantage is win-win, whether for individuals or nations, and Ricardo used simple numerical examples to demonstrate both its truth and its power.

It was Ricardo's very numerical examples that initiated the transition of economics from moral theory into a largely quantitative, positive discipline. While Ricardo's keen analytical mind made it possible for him to communicate clearly the power of comparative advantage to its skeptics, it also began the evolution of economics into a mathematical science. As Robert Ekelund and Robert Hébert note, "Ricardo exemplifies the abstract, deductive reasoner" (Ekelund and Hébert 1990, 151). Ricardo began the tradition that typifies economics today because he used his quantitative "ability to forge a general analytic system that yielded sweeping conclusions based on relatively few basic principles" (Ekelund and Hébert 1990, 145). Ricardo doubtless used his gift to promote the flourishing of generations to come. Yet Ricardo's explicit calculations "did much to transform 'the simple system of natural liberty' into a set of simplificatory postulates or a neutral model," as T.W. Hutchison puts it (Hutchison 1964, 25).

Though his work remained within the broad stream of natural law tradition in economics, Ricardo began to discern that the role of the economist might be confined to merely describing the relevant economic laws and relationships on a given topic. He could keep any normative thoughts to himself. As Ricardo himself put it, "it is not the province of the Political economist to advise; he is to tell you how to become rich, but he is not to advise you to prefer riches to indolence or indolence to riches" (Ricardo 2004, 338n).

The Twilight of Classical Economics

Cultural conditions provided fertile soil for the seeds planted among economists by Ricardo. Christianity in the English-speaking world underwent an important change in the nineteenth century. Economists' reaction to the religious change moved them in Ricardo's direction.

Later in this chapter, we will encounter Richard Ely and the Social Gospel movement in the later part of the nineteenth century. However, this was only the culmination of a growing trend across the century.

Popular devotion to the Christian faith in both Britain and the United States was increasing significantly, under the influence of successful revival movements. Equally important, the climate of theological ideas moved decisively away from the more cerebral and rationalistic theologies that dominated the eighteenth century. For some, this meant a shift in standards of doctrinal orthodoxy that elevated fidelity to the text of the Bible while deemphasizing intellectual continuity with existing theological knowledge traditions. For others, including the Wesleyan movement in Britain as well as the largest and most prestigious denominations in the United States, there was a new fervor for social activism on behalf of moral causes. It was this second group that would eventually produce the Social Gospel movement.

The public-policy crusades of this second group brought them directly into the path of economists, especially as their concern for the poor led them to advocate economic policies they thought would alleviate poverty. During much of the nineteenth century, public debates over policy—including economic policy—often centered on religious claims. This did not always take the form of "the Bible says X, therefore we must implement policy Y, end of discussion." But it sometimes did take that form, and in that century of passionate revival movements, there was usually less room for rational deliberation than there ought to have been. Opposition to policy *Y* (say, high tariffs) could be equated with disobedience to biblical teaching *X* (say, care for the poor). Not enough space was being made for considering whether policy *Y* might in fact undermine the goal of teaching *X*—that high tariffs intended to protect the poor might actually harm them (Heyne 2008, 256–264). The emotionalism of most nineteenth-century Christian political theology would have shocked the more academic minds, steeped in natural law traditions that recognized prudence as one of the four cardinal virtues, that dominated theology in the seventeenth and eighteenth centuries.

This background should be borne in mind as we review the growing uneasiness of economists with moral demands. Granted, scholarly economic books written by economists for economists do not usually offer much direct comment on theological trends, or on the daily give-and-take of political discourse. But the increasing intensity of religious demands for public policies that were regarded by the economists as unwise, if not reckless, is an important historical context. Economists drawing sharp divisions between empirical and moral claims were saying, in effect: "We do not object to your demand that we care for the poor.

That is not our department. The divinity school is across the courtyard, second building on your left. But if you want a specific public policy, you cannot simply quote the Bible and pound the table. Show your work." In this light, their aspiration to moral neutrality, while misguided, is not unsympathetic. Among other things, it allowed them, unwittingly, to serve as an ark in which the cardinal virtue of prudence was saved from the utter shipwreck it might otherwise have made.

Nassau Senior

Hutchison points to 1836 as a landmark year in the drift of economics away from the normative and teleological concerns of moral philosophy because of the publication of two highly influential works: Nassau Senior's *Outline of Political Economy* and John Stuart Mill's *On the Definition of Political Economy* (Hutchison 1964, 23). Seeking to emulate the success of the natural sciences, Senior and Mill built upon the implicit fact/value distinction in David Hume's works to expand the gap between empirical and moral observations in economics. Though the explicit drawing of a "positive/normative" distinction came later, many economists had already begun to refer to a distinction between "science" and "art" in economics. In 1883, Sidgwick identified Senior and Mill and the fathers of this contrast: "The present general recognition of the distinction between the two terms, in its application to economic matters, is due, I think, to the combined influence of Senior and J.S. Mill, and cannot be traced further back" (Sidgwick 1883, 15n).

Senior strove to transform economics into a respectable discipline that could deservedly take its place next to the rapidly developing natural sciences. Both a lawyer and economist, Senior "was totally engrossed in that unexciting though necessary stage of development of any academic discipline: identifying basic principles and organizing them, along axiomatic lines, into a genuinely scientific framework," Ekelund and Hébert write (Ekelund and Hébert 1990, 158).

In his *Outline*, Senior draws a somewhat chilling distinction between wealth and happiness. He argues that economics is only about wealth, while political legislation ought to concern itself with values such as the broader welfare of society. Senior was comfortable making claims about wealth because they were easily quantifiable, because such claims are a better fit for a young discipline desperately seeking scientific status. The truly scientific economist should never render opinions or advice. Thus

Senior distinguishes between the "science of legislation" and that of political economy:

> [The science of legislation] requires a knowledge of the general principles supplied by political economy, but differs from it essentially in its subject, its premises and its conclusions. The subject of legislation is not wealth, but human welfare...On the other hand, the subject treated by the political economist...is not happiness but wealth...His conclusions, whatever be their generality and their truth, do not authorize him in adding a single syllable of advice...The business of a political economist is neither to recommend nor to dissuade, but to state general principles. (Senior 1836, 129–130)

This passage makes two things clear. First, Senior was already sowing the seeds of an eventual focus upon pecuniary gains and other strictly quantifiable outcomes in economics. Second, Senior believed the political economist needed to emulate his counterparts in the natural sciences. If not, economics would never succeed or be taken seriously as a scientific discipline.

Senior's opening address to the Statistical Science section of the thirtieth meeting of the British Association for the Advancement of Science, held in 1860, is especially telling. According to Senior, the professional economist must at all times put forward an utterly scientific persona. To admit "art" (i.e. precepts) to any conversation would sully the scientific credibility of the economist and his fledgling science. Senior warns what will happen to the advice-giving, moralizing economist:

> Whenever he gives a *precept*, whenever he advises his readers to do anything, or to abstain from doing anything, he wanders from science into art, generally into the art of morality, or the art of government...We cease to be scientific as soon as we advise or dissuade, or even approve or censure. (Senior 1861, 183–184)

John Stuart Mill

Mill is an important part of our story in three ways. First, he was the key popularizer of the ethical theory of utilitarianism. The shift from natural law ethics to utilitarian ethics within the intellectual world that grew out of the Enlightenment marked a critical turning point for the Reason paradigm. As we suggested in the previous chapter, utilitarianism was an attempt to rescue the moral element of the Reason paradigm as the natural law tradition, with its Christian metaphysical premises, became less attractive among thinkers following the Enlightenment legacy. (Christianity, as we have seen, maintained a vigorous presence in society at large, but grew steadily less influential among those dedicated to the Reason paradigm.) A vitally important element in this shift was utilitarianism's attempt to maintain a strong normative element (telling us with moral fervor what we ought and ought not do) while minimizing teleological elements (telling us what is intrinsically good). The natural law tradition held up many things as intrinsically good, from rationality and moral virtue to material well-being and social progress. Utilitarianism holds up nothing as intrinsically good beyond individuals' subjective experience of pleasure—or, in the more precise language of later utilitarianism, their subjective experience of preference-satisfaction. This subjective experience is still held to be intrinsically good, but it is the only intrinsic good. Rationality, virtue, prosperity, and progress are only good insofar as we value them and experience subjective preference-satisfaction when we enjoy them. The attempt to hold on to a robust normative morality with little or no teleological content helped pave the way for the Consumption paradigm.

Closely related to Mill's utilitarianism is his second role, that of popularizing the famous (not to say notorious) *homo economicus* model of human action in economics. Mill drew on his utilitarian ethical assumptions to flesh out an anthropology to provide a basis for modeling economic behavior. The *homo economicus* model assumes that each of us is a utility maximizer, constantly weighing the anticipated marginal cost of a given action against its expected marginal benefit(s), and choosing whatever yields the largest amount of preference-satisfaction. As we will see in more detail in the next chapter, Mill's original articulation of the model rested upon a very reductive set of assumptions about what matters most for people's economic decision-making; Mill's original *homo economicus* is very focused on maximizing short-term pleasure while minimizing effort. Here, in addition to contributing starting points for the Consumption paradigm, Mill's model also provided a foil for Keynes. Keynes provided a more complex vision of *homo economicus* that helped explain aspects of real-world economic behavior Mill's model couldn't account for. As we will see, two of Keynes' most famous contributions to economics—his idea of "sticky wages" and what has come to be called "the paradox of thrift"—can be read as major revisions of Mill's *homo economicus*, making important shifts in the underlying anthropology. Keynes does this in the service of Mill's original underlying goal: to build an economic anthropology without teleological assumptions.

But Mill, in spite of his dedication to a moral theory (utilitarianism), also contributed to the unfolding division between empirical and moral observations in economics. He was well-suited, both in ability and philosophy, to extend the analytical approach of Ricardo in his *Principles*—a book Mill had already mastered by the age of fourteen (Ekelund and Hébert 1990, 171). Widely regarded as the last of the great classical economists, Mill was internally conflicted between the arithmetic elegance of production relationships in economics and the often troubling realities of unequal income and wealth distribution they produced. Mill observes that even though economics cannot be used to make pinpoint predictions regarding economic outcomes, economics can nevertheless be useful inasmuch as it can be used to identify underlying tendencies that give insight into a (hopefully narrow) range of possible outcomes (Alvey 2000).

Mill lived through an era during which there was both public and intellectual criticism of the legacy of the classical school, including many socialist critiques. On such distributional issues Mill was sympathetic to the critics. Yet he remained firmly planted in the classical tradition of *laissez-faire*, insisting that intervention only be invoked as a last resort, and that the "art" be kept entirely separate from the "science": "Science is a collection of *truths*; art, a body of *rules*, or directions for conduct. The language of science is, This is, or This is not; This does, or does not happen. The language of art is, Do this; Avoid that" (Mill 1844, 124).

A slightly longer quote from his *System of Logic* shows even more clearly that Mill builds a wall between empirical observation and moral evaluation. Echoing Senior's tone, Mill positions the scientist, regardless of discipline, as the discoverer of truth and never the dispenser of advice or wisdom:

> Propositions of science assert a matter of fact…A proposition of which the predicate is expressed by the words *ought* or *should be*, is generically different from one which is expressed by *is* or *will be*…A scientific observer or reasoned, merely as such, is not an adviser for practice…Whether the ends themselves are such as ought to be pursued, and if so, in what cases and to how great a length, it is no part of his business as a cultivator of science to decide, and science alone will never qualify him for the decision. (Mill 1856, 527–528)

Any student who has taken even a single course in modern economics will recognize the distinction Mill makes here; it sounds eerily similar to passages that appear near the beginning of virtually every introductory economics textbook on the market today.

For example, note how similar Mill's italicized language (italics in original) is to this passage from the first chapter of *Essential Foundations of Macroeconomics*, a typical introductory textbook today:

> Disagreements that can't be settled by facts are *normative statements* – statements about what *ought to be*. These statements depend on values and cannot be tested....Economists as social scientists try to steer clear of normative statements....Disagreements that *can* be settled by facts are *positive statements* – statements about what is....A positive statement....could be right or wrong, and it can be tested. (Bade and Parkin 2013, 13)

With the exception of the specific words "normative" and "positive" in the 2013 passage, as well as a subtle difference in how they appeal to the role of "science," the two quotations sound nearly identical. Economists are to embrace their role as quantifiers of the economic order, but "steer clear" of value judgments. The positive/normative distinction had been made in Mill, even if it had not yet been named as such or formally codified in the profession at large.

Transition from Classical Economics

If Mill is regarded as the last of the "great" classical economists, Irishman J.E. Cairnes may have been the last of the classical economists. Two themes are clear in Cairnes. First, like his immediate predecessors, Cairnes longed for the day when economics could take its place alongside the natural sciences. As he wrote in his 1873 *Essays in Political Economy*: "Political economy is a science in the same sense in which astronomy, dynamics, chemistry, physiology, are sciences" (Cairnes 1873, 253). Second, marking a decisive shift from his classical predecessors, Cairnes was frustrated by the tendency to conflate economic science with the espousal of *laissez-faire* economics. Against contemporaries like French thinker Frédéric Bastiat, Cairnes argued the young science of economics could not afford even the appearance of sanctioning any particular point of view—even one that leading economists generally agreed on. According to Cairnes, economics "has nothing to do with *laissez-faire* any more than with communism…It stands apart from all particular systems, and is moreover absolutely neutral as between all… It pronounces no judgment on the worthiness or desirableness of the ends aimed at in such systems" (Cairnes 1873, 255–256). Cairnes may be regarded as the last classical economist, but his writing here stands directly opposed to Smith and the classical economic school. Smith saw deep intrinsic moral value in growing the wealth of nations, and argued that a system of *laissez-faire* was good because it made this possible.

William Stanley Jevons was a brilliant analyst who significantly extended the use of mathematics and statistics in economics. Jevons was so fascinated by statistical correlations that at one point he observed that economic activity was highly correlated with sunspot activity, and concluded that sunspots must be causing fluctuations in commercial activity! For Jevons, then, the only impediment to making positive economics a precise predictive science was that we lacked the necessary data. As he wrote in his 1871 *The Theory of Political Economy*: "I know not when we shall have a perfect system of statistics, but the want of it is the only insuperable obstacle in the way of making economics an exact science" (Jevons 1911, 12).

Finally, Henry Sidgwick shared Cairnes's frustration with those who conflated economic science with *laissez-faire*. In 1883, Sidgwick gave this voice to the emerging divide between positive and moral observation:

> We shall gain in clearness, by distinguishing the problems of economic science from the political or ethical problems that are commonly combined with them, and stating the former in a purely positive way; asking not "What *ought* government, or workmen, or masters, or philanthropists, to do?" but "What will be the effects of their own wealth and that of others, if they do so and so?" (Sidgwick 1883, 24)

Note the prominence of the word "positive," an important step toward the formal articulation of the "positive/normative" distinction that would emerge just seven years later in the work of an economist named Keynes.

German Historicism and the American Social Gospel

While British economists of the classical school were steadily moving toward a wider divide between empirical and moral observation, and American economists of the classical school were still feeling Francis

Wayland's old-time religion, other movements took the relationship between economics and morality in different directions. An alternative to the classical school of economics, called historicism, would emerge and become dominant in Germany. Historicism won followers in Britain as well, among those who were dissatisfied with the direction the classical school was taking. In America, the economics of German historicism was a major influence on the rise of the Social Gospel movement.

The historicists believed economics had made a mistake in aspiring to develop as a purely abstract, deductive science. They had grave concerns about the increasingly theoretical models of economics and their detachment from the real historical development of institutions. As Friedrich List, a major founder of the German historical movement, put it in his 1856 *National System of Political Economy*: "Let theory build upon nature and experience, and it may yet accomplish great good" (List 1856, 275). The historicists argued that the study of economics should be subsumed within a broader study of history, including social realities and the forces behind their change and development.

Economists in the historicist school made their primary focus the study of the existing laws, institutions, and culture of society in an effort to reform institutional arrangements for the benefit of society. For historicists, it wasn't necessary to sit around theorizing about and formulating generalized ideas like *homo economicus* or the laws of supply and demand. These abstractions weren't anchored in concrete evidence. They were harshly critical of any sort of economics that began from first principles about the nature of the world and the nature of man, and then derived subsequent understandings from those first principles (Buchholz 1989, 176). For the historicists, you couldn't understand anything about human economic relationships without first turning to the primary source material: history.

While classical economists, at least in Britain, were working hard to dissociate themselves from advocacy, economists of the historicist school moved in the opposite direction. German historicism was closely associated with activism for nationalist and socialist economic policy. Consider these passages, from List's *National System of Political Economy*:

> It is the interest of every great nation to make the national confederation of its productive powers the main object of its exertions, and to consider their international confederation as second in importance to it. (List 1856, 131)

> We have proved historically that the unity of the nation forms the fundamental condition of lasting national prosperity; and we have shown that only where the interest of individuals has been subordinated to those of the nation, and where successive generations have striven for one and the same object, the nations have been brought to harmonious development of their productive powers.…We have further tried to prove in the last chapter how the law of union of powers exhibits its beneficial operation in the individual manufactory, and how it acts with equal power on the industry of whole nations. In the present chapter we have now to demonstrate how the popular [i.e. classical] school has concealed its misunderstanding of the national interests and of the effects of national union of powers, by confounding the principles of private economy with those of national economy. (List 1909, 132)

Critics called these economist-activists *Kathedersozialisten*, or "chair socialists"—what English-speakers might call "armchair socialists."

The great foil of the German historicists was the emerging "Austrian school" of economics, which developed over time through Carl Menger, Ludwig von Mises, and Friedrich Hayek. The Austrians were not moving as aggressively toward a larger role for mathematics and statistics than the English classical economists. But they did begin from highly general theories about human behavior that struck the historicists as abstract and ahistorical—too detached from the concrete realities of particular nations and their histories to be either accurate or practically valuable.

Interestingly, the historicists rarely drew any distinctions between the debate over abstract, theoretical economic methods and the debate over *laissez-faire* public policies. In fact, as we have already seen, in the late nineteenth century that connection was already becoming tenuous. By the 1880s, the highly theoretical, orthodox approach to economics was being influenced by new currents of thought and not just by *laissez-faire* (Moore 2003, 5–6, 17, 23–24). But List's *National System of Political Economy*, for example, talks about the methodological fight (abstract v. historical) and the political fight (*laissez-faire* v. socialism) as if they were all one thing. As we will see below, one of John Neville Keynes' frustrations with the historicists was their tendency to caricature their opponents.

German historicist economics was highly influential in the emergence of the Social Gospel movement in the United States. The Social Gospel was the congruence of two trends: the movement of the largest and most prestigious American denominations toward a heavy emphasis on social activism, noted above, and the emergence of a highly moralistic school of socialist economics, provided by German historicists.

The founding of the American Economic Association (AEA) in 1885 was a key point in the emergence of an approach to academic economics closely aligned with the Social Gospel movement. The founder of the AEA, Richard Ely, stands at the crossroads of German historicism, the Social Gospel, and a morally activist approach to the discipline of economics. Ely had been a doctoral student of leading German historicist Karl Knies at the University of Heidelberg. In addition to the AEA, in 1891 Ely founded the Christian Social Union, a major Social Gospel religious organization.

To see the deep resonance between American Social Gospel economics and German historicism, compare the quote above from historicist List with the opening paragraph of Ely's manifesto for the creation of the AEA:

> We regard the state as an educational and ethical agency whose positive aid is an indispensable condition of social progress. While we recognize the necessity of individual initiative in industrial life, we hold that the doctrine of *laissez-faire* is unsafe in politics and unsound in morals; and that it suggests an inadequate explanation of the relations between the state and the citizens. (quoted in Heyne 2008, 257)

The passages are not identical. List goes further in calling for state control of the economy. But both strongly assert a leading role for the state in directing and managing everyone's economic life, and both identify the sound practice of academic economics with public-policy advocacy of an expansion of the state's economic role.

John Neville Keynes and the *Methodenstreit*

A Cambridge economist by training, John Neville Keynes wrote relatively little and spent most of his academic life as a university administrator. Yet his main contribution to the profession, his 1891 *Scope and Method of Political Economy*, arrived at a pivotal moment for the economics profession in England. It came to serve as the definitive statement of what would be known as the "Cambridge method" in economics.

John Neville Keynes' *Scope and Method* also afforded a significant legacy to his son, John Maynard Keynes. The success and impact of the latter's *General Theory* owes much to the former's *Scope and Method*. Though the disconnection of economics from its deep roots in traditional moral theory had been evolving for some time, as we have seen, it was John Neville Keynes who gave us the formal distinction between the normative ("what ought to be") and the positive ("what is") in economics. This distinction was used to firmly separate economics from the normative and teleological traditions that were integral to the classical, Christian and Enlightenment paradigms. Without his clear and influential articulation of the normative/positive distinction, his son's *General Theory* might never have been written.

The language John Neville Keynes has bequeathed to economics recognizes only one moral category, "normative," and does not recognize the teleological. This is only natural, because if the normative is excluded, by logical necessity the teleological will be excluded. Teleological judgments always imply normative judgments. Any statement that philosophy (or piety, or prosperity, or pleasure) is intrinsically good entails the statement that we ought to act, all other things being equal, in ways that increase the enjoyment of it. Therefore once the profession had excluded the normative, there was no need to say it was excluding the teleological. This was implied. On the other hand, as the example of utilitarianism shows, the reverse is not the case. You can have normative judgment without teleological judgment, or at least without more than the most minimal and subjective teleological judgment. Thus the Consumption paradigm would later bring normative judgment back into the discipline, without bringing back the teleological judgments of the earlier paradigms.

An Unlikely Peacemaker

John Neville Keynes wrote at a time of considerable upheaval in British economics. Up to this point, the field had experienced plenty of internal debates, but it had not often been subjected to truly radical criticism of its ideology or methods. This peace was interrupted by two assaults during the late nineteenth century: Marxism and historicism.

Marxism is the more important of the two for purposes of general political and intellectual history, but it is less important for the history of paradigms in the discipline of economics that concerns us here. Marx inspired revolutionary movements that remade world history and that continue to play an important role both in geopolitics and in intellectual life. That, to be fair, is something neither Ricardo nor Mill can boast of having done (although Adam Smith can). But Marxism is simply not very important to the development of paradigms in academic economics. The moral universe of Marxism quickly detached itself from the moral universe of the discipline; the most interesting debates within Marxism soon migrated to the topic of politics, concerning how Marxism was to gain and retain power, rather than how economies function. Marx's original economic theories have been long discredited even among those who still call themselves "Marxists." As a paradigm for how to live life and for revolutionary political action, Marxism was (and is) enduring and important; as a paradigm for the study of economics, it is more comparable to what we have called the "detractor" voices of Mandeville and Malthus than to paradigms of primary importance like those of Smith and Keynes.

By contrast, the conflict with the historicists, and the resolution of that conflict in John Neville Keynes' *Scope and Method*, played a key role in the emergence of the paradigm within which we now study economics. Keynes skillfully restored the peace among British economists who were divided over historicism. In doing so, he defined the intellectual framework within which the new paradigm of economics would emerge.

As historicism gained momentum in both Germany and Britain during the second half of the nineteenth century, a major conflict over the methods of the discipline erupted in both nations. In Germany, the conflict over economic methods was known as the *methodenstreit* ("battle of methods"; von Mises 1984). This conflict was connected with the British debate over historicism, producing a British *methodenstreit* (Ekelund and Hébert 1990, 250). Jevons participated in this debate on the anti-historicist side (Ekelund and Hébert 1990, 453).

John Neville Keynes wrote his *Scope and Method* during the hottest days of the British *methodenstreit*, and he artfully used the book to seek an enduring peace. He was eager to stop this family squabble among the British economists for two reasons. First, he thought that—just like any other family squabble—the *methodenstreit* was embarrassing. In his view the infighting among economists was getting in the way of the significant progress the profession had made in gaining respectability among the other sciences. Second, he thought the battle was diverting precious resources from the study of economics. If economists would simply drop their rhetorical weapons they could redirect their energies from unproductive uses—ideological war—to productive scholarly activities that would continue to advance the discipline (Moore 2003, 6). To that end, as Gregory Moore puts it, he "employed some deft rhetoric to hasten the end of the long and acrimonious debate," making the British *methodenstreit* appear to be nothing more than a simple misunderstanding (Moore 2003, 5).

Keynes did not sympathize with the historicists. On the contrary, the young John Neville Keynes had an analytical mind and initially began his Cambridge career studying mathematics in Pembroke College. He soon transferred to the moral science program, which included economics. Although economics was still included among the moral sciences, Keynes' mathematical mind seems to have been attracted to the increasingly analytical orthodox view of economics—using deduction to arrive at conclusions based upon a fairly restrictive set of assumptions. He enjoyed the sheer elegance of the method, and at Cambridge his teachers included both Sidgwick and Alfred Marshall (Moore 2003, 9).

Keynes was also frustrated by the arguments of the historicists. In his view, they were not critiquing the orthodox approach; they were critiquing a caricature of it (Moore 2003, 12–13). And he was unimpressed by the academic progress—or lack thereof—made by the historicists. He thought their thinking was "sloppy" (Moore 2003, 8). During a series of meetings of the Moral Science Club devoted to an ongoing translation of the works of Adolph Held, a notable German historicist, Keynes wrote in his diary: "If this is a fair specimen of German political economy, I don't think we have much to learn from them. I gained no new ideas and my old ideas were not made clearer" (Keynes various, entry for May 2, 1879, 7831(2)).

After teaching at Cambridge—mostly logic, primarily because Marshall dominated the economics lecturing at that point—Keynes was named to the lectureship in political economy at Balliol College, Oxford, in 1885. He was finally able to devote his energies fully to economics and its methodology. Marshall had previously held this same post, and lobbied on Keynes' behalf to help him gain it (Moore 2003, 10–11 and 13–14).

Marshall's impact upon Keynes' career was not limited to helping him secure this lectureship. Marshall, widely thought to be the orthodox economist most sympathetic to the arguments of the historicists, also had a tremendous influence upon the approach and tone of Keynes' *Scope and Method*. Reading many drafts of Keynes' book, Marshall repeatedly urged Keynes to take a conciliatory tone toward the historicists, helping the book become instrumental in resolving the British *methodenstreit* (Moore 2003, 8, 14–15).

Marshall's help was not easy for Keynes to accept. Always the orthodox economist, mathematician, and logician, Keynes was not personally sympathetic to the historicists' criticisms of the beauty and elegance of abstract economic models. As a result, Keynes found Marshall's efforts to direct him toward a diplomatic tone frustrating and, at times, demoralizing. In his diary entry for June 2, 1888, Keynes wrote: "It will be a poor book. But I suppose I must go on with it now" (Keynes various, entry for June 2, 1888, 7837). Keynes seems to have viewed Marshall's criticism as pompous and inappropriately self-absorbed, and his efforts add nuance the book's tone as mere meddling (Moore 2003, 8).

Institutionalizing the Positive/Normative Distinction

Though Keynes may not have always welcomed Marshall's comments on *Scope and Method*, the resulting book brilliantly resolved the British *methodenstreit* by acquiescing to many of the views of the historicists, and then pointing out how those views may be accommodated within the existing orthodoxy. Economics did not need to be rewritten; it merely needed to find a place within it for historicists' views. Keynes' strategy was to state the claims of the historicists, assent to their validity, and then point out how they might be reconciled with existing orthodoxy.

To make room for historicists within economic orthodoxy, Keynes gave full voice to the positive/normative distinction that had been steadily evolving from Ricardo all the way through Sidgwick, one of Keynes' contemporaries at Cambridge. Keynes' argument is that all of economics needs to be organized around a central core of theoretical abstraction, involving models that elegantly reflect the general tendencies of human interactions and their resulting outcomes. Having first used these analytical tools to establish the fundamental principles of their field, economists could add any relevant real-world institutional details later, as elaborations upon the basic models. Rather than permit historical-institutional realities to drive the overall direction of economics, as the historicists would have preferred, Keynes' solution subsumed historical and institutional economics into the discipline by relegating it to its own subfield (Moore 2003, 6, 20–22, 28–31).

Toward that end Keynes argued that the central core of economics lies in its positive aspects only—the discernment of economic laws: "We ought at least to recognize as fundamental a positive *science of political economy* which is concerned purely with what is" (Keynes 1965, 36). He adds: "The attempt to fuse together enquiries as to what is, and enquiries as to what ought to be, is likely to stand in the way of our giving clear and unbiased answers to any set of questions" (Keynes 1965, 48). And: "It is not…the function of science to pass ethical judgments; and political economy, regarded as positive science, may, therefore, be said to be independent of ethics" (Keynes 1965, 60–61).

Beyond the positive central core of economics, Keynes also admitted room to two other areas of inquiry: normative science and art. Keynes defined normative science as "a body of systematized knowledge discussing criteria of what ought to be, and concerned therefore with the ideal as distinguished from the actual" (Keynes 1965, 34). The other area, art, includes the application of both positive and normative economics to matters of policy (Keynes 1965, 34–35). However, even while admitting the potential value of both normative science and art, Keynes clearly argues for a strict separation between them and the positive core of economics, observing that any attempts to consider moral questions will get messy: "Even if philosophers are agreed as to the facts, they may still arrive at contrary solutions…because they differ as to the true ideal of human society" (Keynes 1965, 52).

Keynes thought it crucial that economics get positive theory right first, independent of normative considerations. He considered pure analytical deduction to be the best approach for arriving at accurate conclusions. And though the historicists wanted to focus on the historical evolution of institutions, Keynes championed static modeling and abstract understanding as the primary goal. Once the basics were accurately modeled and understood, historical dynamics could be added later (Moore 2003, 27–28, 31–33).

Setting the Stage for a Revolution: The Legacy of John Neville Keynes

Upon its publication, *Scope and Method* was "widely accepted as the definitive methodological tract in the field of political economy in the late Victorian period" (Moore 2003, 5). The book also made possible the success of Marshall's *Principles of Economics*—a book that would go on to become the most widely used economics textbook in the world.

As Moore puts it, Keynes "supplied the methodological underpinnings of Alfred Marshall's majestic synthesis of late-Victorian theoretical opinion" (Moore 2003, 5). Sidgwick also contributed to *Scope and Method*'s healing of the British *methodenstreit*; though he was certainly one of the orthodox economists, he had remained above the fray during the conflict, lending a supportive context to Keynes' efforts to bring about peace with the historicists (Moore 2003, 6).

But with the success of *Scope and Method*, economics was decisively detached from its historic roots in normative, and hence also teleological, observation. Keynes and Marshall had drawn up the divorce papers for a split between moral philosophy and economics. As an obituary for Keynes remarks: "Keynes was actively involved in the proceedings which led to the separation of economics from moral science at Cambridge" (Broad 1950, 404). Alvey points out the reason the *Scope and Method* and its successors had this effect: "A moral science seems harder to achieve once the emphasis is on mathematics, if only because the technique becomes the focus" (Alvey 2000, 1241).

The significance of this transition is most obvious in Marshall's and Keynes' success, along with their Cambridge colleagues, in creating an economics program separate from the moral sciences program within which the study of economics had previously been housed. The first economics program exam at Cambridge was given in 1905, with Keynes among the examiners (Broad 1950, 405).

This legacy of John Neville Keynes lives on in the discipline's continuing insistence that because economics is a science, it is separate from moral theory. Two Nobel prize winners in economics make this clear. Milton Friedman, in his *Essays in Positive Economics*, writes: "Positive economics is in principle independent of any particular ethical position or normative judgments" (Friedman 1950, 3–4). George Stigler makes a similar pronouncement: "It does not seem necessary to retread familiar ground to show that economics as a positive science is ethically...neutral" (Stigler 1959, 522).

As we have seen, this dogma is presented to students early in introductory textbooks, to make sure no one gets far in the study of economics without internalizing this key piece of orthodox doctrine. Many view the removal (or apparent removal) of moral concerns from economic study as essential for economics to evolve into a mature discipline. As Kenneth Boulding has put it, "economics...only became a science by escaping from the casuistry and moralizing of medieval thought" (Boulding 1970, 117).

There have been economists who have mourned this divorce (or apparent divorce) of economics from moral philosophy. They have taken up the argument made by Socrates against Thrasymachus and by Smith against Bernard Mandeville—that no empirical observation is truly free from moral presuppositions.

Two voices from opposite ends of the political spectrum—a socialist and a champion of free markets—saw clearly what was happening. Socialist Gunnar Myrdal opened his 1958 *Value in Social Theory* with this assertion: "A 'disinterested social science' has never existed, and for logical reasons cannot exist…our very concepts are value loaded" (Myrdal 1958, 1). Anti-socialist Wilhelm Röpke spoke out in 1941 against "the positivist puritanism with regard to value judgments and the reproachful insistence on so-called scientific 'Objectivity'," which he said was "not far from being a real impediment in our academic activities" (Röpke 2015, 498). Röpke was one of the cofounders of the Mont Pelerin Society, an elite association of classical liberal and libertarian intellectuals, in 1947, and became its second president (after Hayek) in 1960. But he resigned from the society at the end of the following year, in an acrimonious dispute over the editorial independence of the society's journal (Butler undated). The dispute's acrimony arose from deeper tensions over the society's turn away from wider moral philosophy into narrower economic ideology (Hammond and Hammond 2013).

Myrdal and Röpke were right. As we saw in Chapter 2, if economists really did remove their normative assumptions, they could end up analyzing GDP per yak. The ubiquitous metric "GDP per person" is one of those concepts Myrdal was referring to when he said "our very concepts are value loaded." Its moral assumptions are not obvious to us only because they are so ubiquitous we have ceased to notice them. But voices like Myrdal's and Röpke's are rare, and not typically part of the mainstream of modern economics.

In practice, the positive/normative distinction means economists tend to take the preferences of consumers as given, telling themselves *de gustibus non est disputandum* ("tastes cannot be disputed"). Yet consumers are also human beings, and this model reduces them to mere calculating machines. Hutchison summarizes the convenient reduction of the human being in modern economic analysis:

> The analysis of [the] consumer's preference and choice...encouraged in a superficial way the view that social values, the ends of policy, and value-judgments generally, were relative and subjective, as contrasted with the "objective," "positive" propositions of economic science. In the new analysis... "utility," in some versions at any rate, was explicitly emptied of any ethical significance and simply meant "desiredness." The economist simply took consumers' tastes and desires – for beer or Bibles – as given, and it was regarded as irrelevant or even "illegitimate" for him to pronounce on their rightness or wrongness. Complete neutrality between consumers' valuations and preferences was the attitude the economist could and should adopt; and the same held good – it was implied – with regard to social desiderata and the objectives of economic policies. (Hutchison 1964, 40)

Making a Revolution Possible: The Palace Gates Open

One more major development was needed to prepare the way for John Maynard Keynes to lead a revolution that would overturn the old economic order. The success of the *Scope and Method* made it clear that the discipline of economics wanted to jettison moral and cultural analysis. But the wider world was not yet ready to accept such a change.

Professional economists are not the only people who influence our thinking about the economy. Many other gatekeeping leaders and institutions have socially recognized authority to say what is morally acceptable in our culture, including in the economy. At the time of the *methodenstreit*, almost all those gatekeepers outside the discipline of economics were still solid defenders of moral and cultural views of economic systems. If the Keynesian Revolution had been carried out by the elder Keynes in the 1890s rather than by the younger Keynes in the 1930s, it probably would have failed—put down by a palace guard of pastors, politicians, business leaders, artists, intellectuals, and others who saw themselves as guardians of traditional moral order with a responsibility to defend it.

But this palace guard was badly shaken—both in their power to uphold the old order and their sense of responsibility to do so—by a nearly perfect storm of interlocking events in the late nineteenth and early twentieth centuries. A combination of military, diplomatic, religious, artistic, and scientific events brought the western world to a moment of crisis in the 1920s, in which the gates of the cultural palace were unexpectedly flung wide open. The timing, for John Maynard Keynes' revolutionary purposes, was just about flawless.

The West's Crisis of Confidence

By general agreement, one of the most important turning points was World War I. The unprecedented atrocities of the war discredited the Enlightenment assumption—by now buried deep in the roots of western institutions—that the progress of modern civilization would march forward like clockwork and bring us a better and better world every year. Even the end of the war brought no sense of restoration to moral order. On the contrary, the great powers, in negotiating the peace, engaged in cynical manipulations and shamelessly seized money and power under the cover of high rhetoric about justice and democracy. For many, particularly among cultural elites in positions of power and influence, the advance of civilization was now something to fear rather than welcome. Moral authorities associated with the traditional social system, such as the dynastic families of Europe and the mainline Protestant denominations in America, lost a significant portion of their credibility as the system they backed seemed more and more unworthy of their spiritual imprimatur (Johnson 1991, 13–27).

This great shake-up of public faith in civilization and its moral authorities suddenly lent credibility and energy to two existing radical movements (one in Europe, one in America) whose explicit goal was to oppose existing cultural elites. In both cases, these domestic rebellions rendered their cultures unable to defend themselves with full confidence. And the battles that they began in the wake of World War I are still with us, still rendering western cultures unable to assert themselves morally.

In Europe, reaction to the horrors of war and the cynicism of peace brought the modernist movement in the arts and literature from the margins to center stage. Why exalt beauty when ugliness can be just as fascinating? Why shun deviant sexual desires when we can explore them? In short, why believe human nature conforms to traditional ideas of what is good and noble? Did the war teach us that? Do our supposedly refined and virtuous aristocrats model it? Isn't it just so much propaganda to keep us all working hard at our jobs and following the rules, so the fat cats can stay rich and powerful? Let's open ourselves to the possibility that a full expression of the human soul in all its amazing potentialities is to be found in the things that the aristocrats and the bourgeois call evil rather than what they call good. European cultures would never be able to act in solidarity again; the acid of modernist cynicism renders any attempt to champion virtue or tradition presumptively suspect (Johnson 1991, 6–10).

Meanwhile, in America, theologically conservative Protestants both inside and outside the mainline Protestant denominations had been in growing conflict with the leadership of those denominations, who had long held the keys to power and legitimacy in American religion. In the second half of the nineteenth century, as the mainline moved more and more decisively away from the historic commitments of Christianity on a range of topics—the inspiration of the Bible, the divinity of Christ, the historicity of miracles, and many others—resistance movements had grown. Outside the high citadels of religious power, the growing ranks of local churches affiliated with various holiness, charismatic and dispensationalist movements were coalescing into a larger movement called "fundamentalism"; meanwhile, inside the citadels, conservative scholars like B.B. Warfield and J. Gresham Machen gathered an intense following by denouncing theological liberalism (Marsden 2006, 43–140).

The boiling over of this conflict into a full-scale division of American Protestantism began almost simultaneously with American entrance into World War I. American participation in the horrors of the war dramatically politicized and radicalized the fundamentalists, who were drawn almost entirely from pietistic traditions that valued pacifism and distrusted political power. In the ensuing mainline/fundamentalist conflict, the mainline conservatives felt compelled to cast in their lot with the fundamentalists against their own denominations (Marsden 2006, 141–198).

It is difficult to describe in a small space the enormous social consequences of this division of American Protestantism. Although America was founded on an idea of religious freedom that prevented the state from formally aligning itself with Protestantism, until the early twentieth century there had never been much doubt that Protestantism was the predominant moral compass of American culture generally. The law did not force people to go to a Protestant church, but in a thousand little ways, Protestantism was presumptively privileged in the norms of the culture (Noll 1992). After the division, however, no one could say with any certainty what "Protestantism" meant. It became very difficult to say what was normative and what was forbidden in American culture when the traditional standard of legitimacy suddenly meant all things to all people. Although American culture would take longer to "seize up" than European culture, and the seizure took the form of a persistent conflict between overconfident sides (now called the "culture war") rather than a general loss of cultural confidence, the result was the same—a culture unable to act (Hunter 2010).

As these parallel rebellions gained steam in the 1920s, two more major blows fell upon the old order. Starting in 1919, a series of astronomical observations provided solid empirical support for the Theory of Relativity. The idea that we live in a neat, rational, systematic physical universe—historically affirmed not only by Newtonian physics and Enlightenment philosophy but by Christian theology stretching all the way back to the early Middle Ages and even by the brightest of the Greco-Roman lights before then—seemed to have been discredited. To the shock and horror of the theory's key champion, Albert Einstein, confirmation of physical relativity was widely misunderstood to imply that everything—logic, morality, beauty—was merely arbitrary and ultimately chaotic and meaningless (Johnson 1991, 1–5).

At almost the same time, the psychoanalysis of Sigmund Freud gained mainstream institutional acceptance. All in one year—1920—Freud gained fame participating in a government inquiry into cruelties inflicted in mental hospitals, the first psychiatric "polyclinic" was opened in Berlin, and one of Freud's students launched an academic journal (Johnson 1991, 5–8).

Freud attacked the old moral order directly at its deepest roots. He sought to deconstruct our feelings of guilt for our actions, explaining that they were not what they seemed to be—the natural accompaniment of real moral failure on our part—but rather a by-product of adjusting our natural behavior to the needs of civilized society (Freud 2010). This deconstruction of moral guilt brought him into direct conflict with Christianity, which he dismissed as a delusion.

This struck a double blow against the old order, one Freud had intended and one he had not. The availability of a legitimate explanation for guilt other than the Christian one suddenly made it much easier for social elites to legitimately disaffiliate themselves from Christianity. At the same time, just as the Theory of Relativity had been popularly interpreted in ways that horrified Einstein, in the prevailing climate of distrust toward civilization Freud's ideas were taken, much to his dismay, as *discrediting* guilt. The individual is not a morally responsible agent in the ultimate sense, as the Greco-Romans, Christians, Enlightenment philosophers and Freud himself had all thought; all our profound sense of personal moral agency and responsibility was just a by-product of adjusting to life in society. Now that we know its true source, why continue to take it seriously? Where Freud had sought to understand the process of adjusting our behavior to the needs of society in order to help facilitate that process more smoothly, the main impact of his ideas was to make people feel like such adjustment was largely unnecessary and even illegitimate. What right did civilization have to tell us our natural appetites required adjustment? Marx had already shown how the credibility of civilization's moral claims was compromised by its economic interests; Freud seemed to be putting the final nail in the coffin for the legitimacy of those claims. Christianity taught that our natural appetites are disordered by sin, but if Christianity is false, why not take our natural appetites as the standard of legitimacy and demand that civilization bend to them, rather than they to it? (Johnson 1991, 8–11).

As a result of all these crises, everything now seemed uncertain. Morality, religion, politics, economics, art, and even the laws of physics were all arbitrary. The old order was no longer plausible on intellectual grounds, theological grounds, aesthetic grounds or moral grounds. Moreover, the terrible war and the cynical peace that followed it seemed to show that there was not even much *prudential* value in supporting the old order. In the nineteenth century, people might have felt an obligation to prop up civilization even if they had doubts about its inherent value, because it at least imposed some limits on violence and injustice. But after that civilization produced the Great War?

Business and the State

The most important change that helped pave the way for the Keynesian Revolution was a transformation of the relationship between business and the state. The war had enormously increased the size of the state in all affected countries. Rather than shrink their authority after the war, governments began entering into collusive partnerships with large businesses to exercise unprecedented, extensive control over everyday life. Even in the UK and America, which had less precedent for such collusion, businesses flocked to these arrangements in pursuit of easy revenue (Johnson 1991, 14–18).

In America, this change also had a religious source. Mainline Protestantism began prioritizing large-scale social reform, an undertaking known as the Social Gospel movement. It did this both for its own theological reasons and also to differentiate itself from the fundamentalists, who were characterized by suspicion of government. As part of the Social Gospel movement, the mainline denominations—which at that time still exercised titanic social power in American culture—embarked upon a major campaign to align themselves with the growth of the state, and to demand the politicization of ordinary life as a basic principle of Christian ethics. This campaign never really ended. After the decline of the mainline churches, it was maintained largely intact in a secular form, but retaining its moral and even spiritual fervor—by the progressive political left (Bottum 2014).

Likewise, in Europe the artistic modernists demanded government expansion and nationalization of cultural institutions (so they could be handed over to the modernists for reform; Johnson 1991, 9). And, in a fantastic irony, the growth of the state was fueled in part by the new distrust of civilization—the state could be a powerful weapon in the hands of idealistic reformers eager to undo the damaging effects of modern life (Johnson 1991, 16–17).

In earlier periods, such massive state control of and/or collusion with businesses would have been rejected as a gross violation of the basic commitments of western civilization. This would have been especially true in America, where limitations on the state had been so central to the nation's traditions of political identity and legitimacy. But the breakdown of moral authority left no one with the power to challenge the growth of the state and the politicization of the economy along with the rest of everyday life.

A Window into the Old and New Orders

This perfect storm of challenges undermining the old social order is dramatically summed up in a book that almost derailed the 1919 Paris peace conference after World War I. Historian Paul Johnson calls this publication "one of the most destructive books of the century, which contributed indirectly and in several ways to the future war [that the author] himself was so anxious to avert" (Johnson 1991, 30). Others render an opposite judgment, holding that the book's analysis was vindicated by the inability of the world's major powers to avoid another war. Either way, the book's legacy is a window into both the collapse of the old moral order and the nature of the new one that has replaced it.

Titled *The Economic Consequences of the Peace*, this book spoke into a decisive historic crisis. The great powers of Europe were proving unable to broker any postwar settlement. One factor was low levels of trust, due to their history of cynical manipulations; another was their own moral confusion—their inability to appeal credibly to moral principles to resolve disputes (Johnson 1991, 23–28). One especially brilliant delegate to the conference sought a path out of the impasse through what he saw as a technical solution that would sidestep difficult moral questions: economic management. The key to peace was not settling the moral and cultural questions of military security and national identity, which led to endless disputes about where borders should be drawn and which populations had a right to live where. The key to peace was for political leaders to focus on creating prosperity for their people; once everyone was getting richer, old disputes and grudges would matter less to them (Johnson 1991, 28–30).

When the peace conference leaders rejected these ideas, this delegate stormed back home. He was outraged by the dishonest political intrigues of the conference leaders, and even more by his sense that they were irresponsibly squandering a golden opportunity to make a new world order—one built on technically managed economic growth rather than the old, historic moral sources of solidarity in nationality and religion. He published *The Economic Consequences of the Peace*, a scathing indictment that exposed the dishonesty of the great powers' leaders for all their people to see, and intemperately denounced their failure of vision. The political fallout from this angry expose made the Paris negotiations even more difficult. Johnson contends that the book materially contributed to the lack of a stable postwar settlement—and thus to the eventual onset of World War II (Johnson 1991, 30–48). From another perspective, the catastrophic political failures of the great powers in the 1920s and 1930s can also be taken to vindicate the book's skepticism toward those powers. Either way, there was a clear breach between the old order of dynasties and denominations, with their traditions and legacies, and the new order of technocrats promising peace through managed prosperity.

The delegate was John Maynard Keynes.

References

Alvey, James E. 2000. An Introduction to Economics as a Moral Science. *International Journal of Social Economics* 27: 1231–1251.

Bade, Robin, and Michael Parkin. 2013. *Essential Foundations of Macroeconomics*. New York, NY: Pearson.

Bottum, Joseph. 2014. *An Anxious Age*. New York, NY: Image.

Boulding, Kenneth E. 1970. *Economics as a Science*. New York: McGraw-Hill.

Broad, C.D. 1950. Obituary: Dr. J.N. Keynes (1852–1949). *Economic Journal* 60: 403–410.

Buchholz, Todd G. 1989. *New Ideas from Dead Economists.* New York: Plume.

Butler, Eamonn. 2019. A Short History of the Mont Pelerin Society. undated, 11–14. http://rybn.org/thegreatoffshore/THE%20GREAT%20OFFSHORE/1.ENCYCLOPEDIA/MONT%20PELERIN%20SOCIETY,%201947/DOCS/A%20SHORT%20HISTORY%20OF%20THE%20MONT%20PELERIN%20SOCIETY%20By%20Eamonn%20Butler.pdf. Accessed 30 Jan 2019.

Cairnes, J.E. 1873. *Essays in Political Economy.* London: Macmillan.

Ekelund, Robert B., and Robert F. Hébert. 1990. *A History of Economic Theory and Method.* New York: McGraw-Hill.

Freud, Sigmund. 2010. *Civilization and Its Discontents.* New York: W.W Norton.

Friedman, Milton. 1950. *Essays in Positive Economics.* Chicago: University of Chicago Press.

Hammond, J. Daniel, and Claire H. Hammond. 2013. Religion and the Foundation of Liberalism. *Modern Age* 55 (1): 35–51.

Heyne, Paul. 2008. *"Are Economists Basically Immoral?" and Other Essays on Economics, Ethics and Religion.* Indianapolis: Liberty Fund.

Hunter, James Davison. 2010. *To Change the World.* New York: Oxford University Press.

Hutchison, T.W. 1964. *"Positive" Economics and Policy Objectives.* London: George Allen & Unwin.

Jevons, W. Stanley. 1911. *The Theory of Political Economy.* London: Macmillan.

Johnson, Paul. 1991. *Modern Times.* New York: HarperCollins.

Keynes, John Neville, Various. *The John Neville Keynes Diaries.* Cambridge University Library.

Keynes, John Neville. 1965. *The Scope and Method of Political Economy.* New York: Augustus M. Kelley.

List, Friedrich. 1856 [1841]. *The National System of Political Economy.* Philadelphia: J.B. Lippincott.

List, Friedrich. 1909 [1841]. *The National System of Political Economy.* London: Longmans, Green, and Co.

Marsden, George M. 2006. *Fundamentalism and American Culture.* Oxford and New York, NY: Oxford University Press.

Mill, John Stuart. 1844. *Essays on Some Unsettled Questions of Political Economy.* London: John W. Parker.

Mill, John Stuart. 1856. *A System of Logic.* London: John W. Parker and Son.

von Mises, Ludwig. 1984. *The Historical Setting of the Austrian School of Economics.* Auburn: Ludwig von Mises Institute.

Moore, Gregory. 2003. John Neville Keynes's Solution to the English Methodenstreit. *Journal of the History of Economic Thought* 25 (2003): 5–38.
Myrdal, Gunnar. 1958. *Value in Social Theory*. New York: Harper & Brothers.
Noll, Mark A. 1992. *A History of Christianity in the United States and Canada*. Grand Rapids: Eerdmans.
Ricardo, David. 2004. *The Works and Correspondence of David Ricardo*. Indianapolis: Liberty Fund.
Röpke, Wilhelm. 2015 [1941]. A Value Judgment on Value Judgments. *Journal of Markets & Morality* 18 (2): 497–514.
Senior, Nassau W. 1836. *An Outline of the Science of Political Economy*. London: W. Clowes and Sons.
Senior, Nassau W. 1861. Opening Address. In *Report of the Thirtieth Meeting of the British Association for the Advancement of Science*. London: John Murray.
Sidgwick, Henry. 1883. *Principles of Political Economy*. London: Macmillan.
Stigler, George. 1959. The Politics of Political Economists. *Quarterly Journal of Economics* 73: 522–532.

PART II

The Keynesian Revolution

CHAPTER 4

Keynes' Revolutionary Vision: Consumer Satisfaction as Moral Crusade

Our story thus far might lead us to expect economics in the twentieth century to take a radically different direction from the one it actually took. The ambition of the leading nineteenth-century economic thinkers was to move away from normative and teleological principles—from speaking about what *should* be done or what is intrinsically *good*—in favor of observational investigation. We might therefore expect economics to have spent the twentieth century questioning the assumptions that lay behind its models, constantly collecting a wide variety of data to test those assumptions, and refining the models to conform more closely to the data. We might expect to hear it praised for its willingness to examine its assumptions, and at the same time blamed for its refusal to get involved in the urgently important practical decisions of economic policy and strategy. The daring upstarts on the margins of the discipline would be those who got beyond mere theory to develop an economics that actually had something to say to governments and businesses about how they should manage their economies.

This is precisely the reverse of what we find. Economics in the twentieth century developed in such a way that it now serves as the omnipresent voice of authority in economic decision-making, summoned daily by every business and government agency to give judgment on what we ought to do, and unfailingly eager to give such judgments. It is more and more widely blamed precisely for its failure to revisit its assumptions—for adhering rigidly to theoretical models that haven't been reconsidered (much less experimentally tested and revised) in

V. V. Claar and G. Forster, *The Keynesian Revolution and Our Empty Economy*, https://doi.org/10.1007/978-3-030-15808-8_4

decades, if not generations, and that don't correspond to the facts of real life or provide even roughly accurate predictions. The daring upstarts on the margins of the discipline are those who turn away from practical questions and instead go into laboratories and do something that was until recently unthinkable: run controlled experiments on test subjects to examine whether the discipline's core assumptions fit the data. It was for his role in promoting such inquiries that Richard Thaler received the 2017 Nobel Prize in Economic Sciences.

The difference is the Keynesian Revolution—from its origin in Keynes himself to the construction (largely after his death) of a systematic economic paradigm based on his ideas—and the adoption of that paradigm by the discipline and its influence on society at large. In this chapter we will look at Keynes himself. Subsequent chapters will trace the emergence of the Consumption paradigm in the work of his successors and the rise of that paradigm to dominance in the discipline and in our economies.

The Scope of the Revolution

The vast scale of the Keynesian Revolution, the total reinvention of the discipline of economics it effected, is difficult to convey. Keynes himself foresaw how revolutionary his ideas would be. In a New Year's Day letter to George Bernard Shaw in 1935, Keynes wrote:

> I believe myself to be writing a book on economic theory which will largely revolutionize – not, I suppose, at once, but in the course of the next ten years – the way the world thinks about economic problems....I can't expect you or anyone else to believe this at the present stage, but for myself I don't merely hope what I say. In my own mind I am quite sure. (Davidson 2002, 4)

He was right. This vast estimate of his own importance was not at all greater than the reality turned out to be.

Perhaps the quickest way to get a sense of how big a change it was is to recall that before Keynesianism, there was no such thing as a formal filed of inquiry called "macroeconomics." Today, we distinguish macroeconomics (the study of aggregate economic phenomena across nations or other large populations) from microeconomics (the study of how particular individuals, firms, etc. make economic decisions). Before the Keynesian Revolution, there was no macroeconomics; there was only economics, and it was all what we now call microeconomics.

Keynes was the father of macroeconomics. There were economists and politicians carrying out fiscal and monetary analysis prior to the *General Theory of Employment, Interest and Money*, but their activities were largely founded in economic theorizing and some very limited data analysis. Few economists had modeled the determination of things like national income or national unemployment rates until Keynes came along, and when they did, it was rarely for prescriptive purposes. Instead, constructions like Irving Fisher's equation of exchange, or his 1926 articulation of "A Statistical Relation Between Unemployment and Price Changes" (which would later come to be known as the Phillips curve), tended to be more descriptive than prescriptive (Fisher 1911, 1926; Phillips 1958). They described relationships among macroeconomic variables without necessarily employing those descriptions in any specific national policy recommendations.

The invention of macroeconomics was revolutionary. The Keynesian Revolution not only invented half the discipline from scratch, but the more socially influential half. Macroeconomics has far more influence outside the discipline than microeconomics. Macroeconomists tend to have much more influence over public policy than microeconomists. This not only puts macroeconomists in the position of speaking for the discipline to political leaders, it also puts macroeconomists in a commanding position over microeconomists in speaking to the culture at large. Political discourse is one of the most influential cultural powers in any civilization, so those who speak into politics speak into the shape of our civilization—the way we structure and understand our daily lives—with a powerful voice. Moreover, public policy shapes the economic decision-making structure within which individuals and firms make economic choices, so mircroeconomists end up working with the world macroeconomists create.

And Keynesianism had a moral goal—a set of normative principles—for what it would do with that political and social influence. This is perhaps the most important reason the Keynesian Revolution is the key turning point in how the discipline of economics relates to society at large. The Keynesian Revolution, with its invention of macroeconomics and its corresponding revision of the rest of the discipline to accommodate that invention, didn't just place economics in a position to speak to public policy. As we will see, it positioned economics as a moral crusade for a reform of society.

Homo Economicus: A Brief Biography

The Keynesian Revolution had this transformative impact throughout the discipline because it revolutionized the anthropological model that stood, and still stands, at its center: *homo economicus*. Just as Einstein changed all of physics when he changed our understanding of just a few of the central concepts upon which the whole discipline was based, the Consumption paradigm built by Keynes and his followers changed economics by changing our understanding of *homo economicus*. The path of the discipline in the twentieth century did not follow the pattern we might have expected from the empiricism of the nineteenth century because of this central change.

When economists model economic behavior, they rely on the simplified theoretical construct of *homo economicus*—an autonomous, rational chooser who always strives to maximize the satisfaction of his preferences, and who has a limited set of preferences to maximize. The first version of this model emerged in the late nineteenth century, at the same time the discipline was formalizing the positive/normative split. As we have seen, John Neville Keynes' predecessors longed to take their place alongside the natural sciences like chemistry and physics, predicting with precision the choices human beings would make under a given set of circumstances. And they genuinely believe they could do it. With normative questions set aside, economists like Jevons, armed with powerful new tools—supply–demand diagrams, data sets, and new statistical methods like the *t*-test—believed precise predictions of human behavior were not only possible, but lay within reach.

The puzzle is what happened next. The next logical step would be for this newly empirical discipline to regularly revisit the assumptions behind *homo economicus*, refining them as needed in light of real-world data and evidence. Yet the discipline was so fervently devoted to following the facts that it repudiated millennia-old normative commitments on grounds that they might bias observation, so the job to be got on with was observation. The embarkation of economics on this new era of purely positive inquiry was understandably delayed as economists debated the appropriate methods for such an inquiry in the *methodenstreit*. But then, with the conflict over methods behind them, the economists neglected to subject the *homo economicus* model to a highly critical positive inquiry, whether freed from normative questions or not. Economics after the *methodenstreit* does not test the *homo economicus* model, but reify it, building upon it a new moral vision of economics for a new moral vision of humanity.

As we will see, Keynes lay at the heart of this change in who *homo economicus* is and how the discipline uses him. He changed both the content and purpose of the model, and the two changes were related. In content, while *homo economicus* was always "rational," Keynes radically changed the meaning of the model's rationality. Keynes shifted it to an instrumental rationality (where reason only calculates which means will achieve our ends, and has nothing to say about ends) from the Reason paradigm's substantive rationality (where reason tells us not only how to achieve our ends, but which ends we ought to achieve). Keynes detached *homo economicus*' rational decision-making from the last vestiges of the Reason paradigm, with its fixed goals of enlightening education for individuals and reform and progress for societies, and planting the model firmly within a new, post-Enlightenment rationality in which any actor who calculates a connection between means and ends is "rational" regardless of their ends. As a result, where the older *homo economicus* pursued productive ends, the new one pursues only its own enjoyment in pleasure and leisure—where reason no longer dictates ends, we gravitate to the ends of our irrational nature.

This change to the content of the model went along with a change in its purpose; instead of an empirical model to be investigated, Keynes' *homo economicus* was a social model to be imposed. Economics, for Keynes, was a moral crusade to remake society in the image of the new *homo economicus.* The connection between the two changes, to the content and to the purpose of the model, is this: they were grounded in a moral vision, a normative account of the meaning of human life, and one very different from the vestigial-Enlightenment Reason paradigm that had shaped the nineteenth-century *homo economicus.*

To understand the significance of the Keynesian Revolution, then, we must begin with a brief pre-history of *homo economicus.* We must see who *homo economicus* was when Keynes arrived to appreciate who he became under Keynes' tutelage.

Mill's Model

It was inevitable that the nineteenth-century empirical turn in economics would begin with a very simple model of economic behavior. Scientific inquiry cannot proceed without a model, and when a discipline begins a new mode of inquiry, as economics was doing at the time, it must use an untested model because there are not yet any tested models in the new inquiry. Whatever model the inquiry begins with will inevitably look simple and inadequate in retrospect, once empirical inquiry has falsified some (perhaps many) of its assumptions and compelled us to revise it.

The challenge of modeling the economic behavior of human beings lies in their most distinctive quality: their ability to think and make decisions in ways that are unique to each person. Under very similar circumstances, two very similar people might make completely different choices—even in something as trivial as which beverage to drink on a hot summer day. Even the same person might make different choices on two very similar occasions. Human beings not only think and make decisions, but do so according to unique internal blueprints of tastes, preferences and priorities—blueprints that are sometimes highly consistent, and sometimes prove ephemeral.

Economics had to come up with a way of thinking about human thoughts and choices—a model of the human person. Yet any such model must be a caricature compared to the literally incomprehensible complexity of what real people typically think and do. This was especially so as the discipline embarked upon a new era of empirical inquiry. Scientific progress does not mean we never have an oversimplified model, it means we are constantly striving to test all our models against reality and improve them.

We find building blocks of the *homo economicus* model in the works of Adam Smith and the Physiocrats, and even in some elements of the earlier classical and Christian schools of thought. But it is much more clearly articulated by Mill during the sunset of the classical era in economics:

> What is now commonly understood by the term "Political Economy" is not the science of speculative politics, but a branch of that science. It does not treat of the whole of man's nature as modified by the social state, nor of the whole conduct of man in society. It is concerned with him solely as a being who desires to possess wealth, and who is capable of judging of the comparative efficacy of means for obtaining that end. It predicts only such of the phenomena of the social state as take place in consequence of the pursuit of wealth. It makes entire abstraction of every other human passion or motive; except those which may be regarded as perpetually antagonizing principles to the desire of wealth, namely, aversion to labor, and desire of the present enjoyment of costly indulgences. (Mill 2000, 97)

Mill reduced human beings, at least as far as formal economics was concerned, into individual decision-making units that were calculating, wealth-maximizing, costly-indulgence-enjoying and labor-averse—and, for purposes of economics, nothing else. Economists following this model make similar assumptions about business; the fundamental assumption underlying the theory of the firm is that firms maximize profit.

Mill does not suggest the economic person labors merely in the hope of acquiring essentials such as food for his belly or a pillow for his head, much less Aristotle's "equipment" for virtue or the means of glorifying God. The focus is upon wealth accumulation for its own sake, as modified by our propensity to spend that wealth on "costly indulgences" for pleasure and our propensity to relax from the task of wealth creation. Both these modifying factors involve enjoying wealth, either by purchasing things we like or by living off it without working.

Also, note the relationship between gaining wealth and enjoying wealth (the other two factors, spending and relaxing). Gaining wealth is decidedly primary. It is wealth accumulation that defines the discipline of economics as against other areas of inquiry—Mill is concerned with wealth creation simply because that is what economics is for him. Costly indulgences and relaxation enter the picture as distractions or obstacles to wealth accumulation, not for their own sake.

Mill's *homo economicus* is greedy. On the other hand, he at least regards squandering money on frivolities and sloth as vices.

This would not have been an edifying model for economics in any event, had the discipline continued to rely on it. The problem is not simply that it is reductive. Any scientific model must reduce the complexity of reality to a manageable level—that is what models are for. The problem is that it is reductive in the wrong way.

Mill's version of *homo economicus* grows out of the movement away from teleology taking place both in the discipline of economics and in Enlightenment-derived thought generally in the nineteenth century. Paradoxically, it connects both to Mill's utilitarian moral theory and to his desire to separate moral questions from economics. Utilitarianism, as we have seen, strives to be normative without being teleological; it wants to be able to tell us what we ought to do with robust moral authority, while making as few claims as possible about what is intrinsically good. *Homo economicus* connects with the desire to minimize teleology. It does not quite eliminate teleological claims—it assumes, for example, that wealth is good and toil is bad, and that rational calculation to achieve these ends is good—but it is probably as close to the minimal amount of teleological assumptions a discipline could possibly make and still conduct discourse. At the same time, because of the emerging positive/

normative split, Mill's *homo economicus* was not intended to connect to the normative side of his utilitarianism. Mill did not want to remake the world in the image of *homo economicus*.

How Scientific Models Work

It's easy to understand why economists like Mill and, later, Alfred Marshall made simplifying assumptions: the real world is messy. Economics is not everything, and some limiting principle must be found to help us discover basic and reliable ways in which human beings interact (Emmett 2014).

A simple model, even one as sharply reductive as Mill's version of *homo economicus*, can be the starting point for fruitful inquiry even though, because it is reductive, it will not always fit the facts. In fact, it can be a fruitful starting point *precisely because it fails to fit the facts.* Uncovering conflicts between what our model predicts and what we find in the real world, and then explaining those conflicts, is the meat and potatoes of science. It is by investigating such conflicts that we learn things we didn't know before.

For example, suppose we adopt the very simplest and most naïve form of the *homo economicus* model as a basis for investigating ethnic discrimination in business hiring. Based on our naïve model, we might expect that businesses will never discriminate by ethnicity in hiring, except to the extent that they are forced to do so by external pressures such as discriminatory laws and social norms. A rational, profit-maximizing business would always prefer to select the most productive person available for the wage the firm is willing to pay, which in turn is driven by the price the firm can charge its customers. However, upon empirical investigation, we find that firms sometimes do discriminate even when they don't have to. These data would then prompt us to modify our model, revising *homo economicus* to fit the facts. Economists working with *homo economicus* have in fact pursued several strategies for adjusting the model to account for ethnic discrimination in hiring (Arrow 1998). One strategy is to think of the model in terms of survivor analysis—*homo economicus* shows us, not what businesses always do, but what behavior helps them survive economically. So it points to what kind of behavior we should expect to emerge over the long run, as discriminatory businesses are eliminated through Darwinian economic competition. (How long a run is required is of course another question, dependent upon the extent to which it is economic pressures that determine survival, as opposed to non-economic factors like the aforementioned discriminatory laws and norms.) Another strategy is to broaden our definition of what the businesses' goals are—to recognize that businesses have more goals than our initial, naïve version of *homo economicus* admits. A business is a social and cultural entity that has its own community beliefs and norms. Do some businesses value not just profits but also ethnic loyalty, and thus seek to pursue both, making tradeoffs between the two according to some implicit scheme of comparative valuation?

These and other strategies for modifying simple models into more complex models are how science progresses. Modifications to an existing model give new insight into behaviors that would otherwise seem irrational.

The bad news is that there are limits to how far a model can be developed. Adding even small complexities to mathematical models renders the analysis intractable. That is, the math gets very messy very quickly. There is a limit to how complex our models can get, and we reach that limit far before we have even come within hailing distance of modeling any given individual's behavior.

This is not so big a problem if our expectations from economics are modest. In fact, the more sophisticated versions of the *homo economicus* model actually in use among microeconomists today do give us something of value. It's a useful starting point for generating plausible hypotheses for what we might expect a typical economic actor to do in many kinds of typical economic situations. For all the limits of the model, much real-world economic behavior roughly conforms to it in important ways. When you buy bananas in the grocery store, you evaluate their quality and price, and make a cost-benefit analysis in pretty much the way the *homo economicus* model predicts. If you have a choice between buying five individual bananas at a dollar each or a bunch of five for $4, you will always go for the latter option, if the bananas are comparable in quality. When economist and stand-up comedian Yoram Bauman explains the rational-choice assumption in economics, he rewrites it as: "People are stupid, but they're not *that* stupid."

However, the limits of the model are essential to its value. *Homo economicus*, even in Mill's very simple version, works perfectly in grocery-store-type situations. For economic decisions where bigger, more qualitative questions are important, the model becomes harder to apply. Mill's *homo economicus* couldn't even begin to calculate—for example—whether to enlist in the armed forces. "What is worth dying for?" is a question that shapes many of our critical economic decisions, but it is a question about which Mill's *homo economicus* tells us little. Even the question of which college to enroll in involves questions of identity and cultural formation alongside more materialistic concerns about prospective future income. Of course, as we have observed already, it is possible to develop the model in more sophisticated ways that allow us to examine a broader range of questions, such as (in the example discussed above) ethnic discrimination. However, that development must proceed carefully, with an awareness of the model's limits. Many were shocked when economist Gary Becker used a very simple *homo economicus* model to explain marriage decisions in terms of people maximizing their own interests in a competitive marketplace for mates; Becker was right to think that the discipline of economics should have something to say about those kinds of intimate decisions, but he was wrong to explain them using a model designed to explain how we buy bananas (Becker 1974).

Fast Forward: How We Use the Model Now

The model's limits have an important implication: The less we demand economics do for us, the less dangerous the limits of the *homo economicus* model are, and the more likely we are to know those limits and not go beyond them. Economics at its best attempts to do with models precisely what Albert Einstein suggests in an aphorism popularly attributed to him: "Everything should be made as simple as possible, but not simpler." It is a good thing to simplify the analysis when, in doing so, the key questions at hand may be considered more clearly.

However, our expectations from economics today, and hence from *homo economicus*, are no longer modest. Our society now turns to economics to inform our general picture of how the world works, and to make many specific decisions for us. Economists use their models to guide enormous systems of political power, business organization, and financial structure.

For example, roughly eight times per year, the Federal Reserve holds its two-day Federal Open Market Committee meeting, at which it decides whether to tinker with interest rates throughout the economy. Though the Fed cannot change interest rates directly, it does have the power to manipulate the rate of interest that banks charge each other for a short-term ("overnight") loan, and all other interest rates move along with this rate. This power over what it costs to get access to capital gives the Fed a breathtaking power to control economic activity of all types, at all levels of the economy. Why does the Fed do this? After all, an interest rate is simply a price, just like the price of an orange or a haircut. And the Fed wasn't originally created to steer the economy. In 1913, Congress created the Fed to be the banking system's "lender of last resort"; in a bank panic, the Fed could ensure the liquidity needs of banks that might otherwise fail. But things have changed since 1913. Now, the Fed has a "dual mandate"—to manage the U.S. economy in pursuit of full employment and price stability. Economic thinkers from classical Greece through the Enlightenment warned their readers, consistently and strenuously, against the idea that a central authority could exercise that level of power even over the economy of a small agrarian city, much less an economy of the staggering size and complexity of the modern United States.

Or consider fiscal policy. Prior to the twentieth century, entities like the U.S. Congress usually attempted to keep the federal budget somewhere near balance. As of this writing, however, the U.S. federal debt is larger than ever, and the debt-to-GDP ratio is the highest it has been since World War II. Congress is ready to jumpstart the economy with huge, un-paid-for spending whenever the Fed can't seem to get things going by lowering interest rates. The American Recovery and Reinvest Act of 2009 made available $787 billon to stimulate economic activity in the wake of the global financial crisis.

Why do we give a tiny group of politically insulated economists virtually unlimited power to manage our lives using interest-rate manipulation? Why is Congress so willing to overspend in a crisis, and then make no effort to retire the debt during the subsequent recovery?

Here we come to the role of moral vision. Economic life constantly presents us with new exigencies and dilemmas. People need some kind of moral vision to help them understand how they ought to make economic choices. And policymakers, like everyone else, must make choices according to some scheme of assumptions about what is right and wrong.

The nineteenth-century economists wanted to supply people with technical knowledge about economics, but remove themselves from the moral questions that economic life always raises. Meanwhile, the collapse of confidence in society's older moral traditions and institutions, recounted at the end of Chapter 3, left the policymakers without other plausible sources of moral commitments to inform policy.

This moral vacuum was a golden opportunity for a brilliant intellectual who had a clear moral vision to offer for economics. Keynes offered people, especially policymakers, the moral guidance they were looking for in economic life. The nineteenth-century economists thought they were clearing away religion to make way for science. As it turned out, their displacement of older normative visions from economic thinking simply cleared the way for a new and equally enthusiastic normative vision.

No one can say what would have happened if, after the *methodenstreit*, the economists of the twentieth century had set themselves to dispassionate reassessments of the *homo economicus* model. What we can say is what they actually did do. They discovered, in Keynes, a new and exciting normative vision for economics, one that reified *homo economicus* (a new version of the model, revised to suit the new moral vision) as the normative ideal for human life. And they demanded that the economy be drastically reformed in light of that ideal, in order to drag the ignorant and the recalcitrant into the glorious future of moral fulfillment as autonomous wealth-maximizers, costly-indulgence-enjoyers and labor-avoiders.

What Was Not New in Keynes: The Policies

What was new and revolutionary in Keynes was not any of his particular critiques of existing economic theory. Many of these were laid out by others before him.

J. Ronnie Davis, in his 1971 *The New Economics and the Old Economists*, emphasizes the extent to which American economists, including supporters of *laissez-faire*, were already embracing elements of what would come to be called "Keynesian" fiscal policy prescriptions during the first half of the Great Depression (Davis 1971). Frank Knight, a hard-core free marketer and founder of the Chicago school, wrote a striking letter to Congress supporting the Wagner bill for fiscal stimulus spending: "Economists are completely agreed that the Government should spend as much and tax as little as possible at a time such as this – using the expenditure in the way to do the most good in itself and also to point toward relieving the depression" (quoted in Davis 1971, 16). This letter came one week after a dozen University of Chicago economists, responding to an inquiry from a member of Congress, co-signed a letter that advocated countercyclical fiscal policy as a means to counteract the business cycle, and using debt financing to do so if necessary (Davis 1971, 25).

It has been suggested that a number of young economists known as the Stockholm School, including familiar names like Erik Lindahl, Bertil Ohlin and Gunnar Myrdal, advanced ideas that would have been called "Keynesian" if they had appeared after, rather than before, the publication of the *General Theory* (Steiger 1976). However, this interpretation has been credibly challenged (Patinkin 1978a, b, 1982). More plausible is what Martin Kragh calls "the Wigfross connection": Ernst Wigforss, who served as Minister of Finance in the government formed by the Social Democratic Party in 1932 and heavily influenced Swedish economic policy between the wars, anticipated key ideas found in the *General Theory*; he supported policy encouragement of more consumption and less saving during economic downturns, and advocated government public works projects as stimulus (Kragh 2014).

Robert Nash and William Gramm trace the concept of the paradox of thrift—a concept we will discuss below—even further back. They point to John Robertson's 1892 book *The Fallacy of Saving*, which warns against "industrial paralysis" caused by high savings rates. Robertson even used the word "paradox," warning that the potential destructiveness of high savings rates was "no idle paradox" (Nash and Gramm 1969, 397).

What Was New in Keynes: The Moral and Social Vision

What was new in Keynes was the moral vision in which he tied those critiques together, and upon the basis of which he issued a clarion call for a moral crusade to remake society. Keynes was no bloodless technocrat or musty academic. He dedicated his life to a moral vision, and his work to advancing it. He lived a full and active life in which economic theorizing coexisted with other intellectual and artistic pursuits. Among the arts, he was particularly drawn to theater, due in large part to the influence of his father. He surrounded himself with other intellectuals, artists, and musicians, and seemed to thrive in that environment. He was a member of the legendary Cambridge Apostles. The Apostles is a multi-disciplinary intellectual society that, once a week, invites one of its members to deliver prepared remarks, with open discussion following. While the Apostles consists primarily of students, others holding positions at the university are often counted among the society's members.

The Bloomsbury Group

Keynes' more intimate gathering of the intellectual and artistic elite was the Bloomsbury group. Named for an area of London, Bloomsbury consisted of leading British intellectual figures. These included Leonard and Virginia Woolf, E.M. Forster, Clive and Vanessa (Woolf) Bell, Duncan Grant and one of Keynes' closest friends, Lytton Strachey. While the group gathered many hangers-on and marginal associates over the years, and eventually even writers who were not personally associated with the group were described as "Bloomsbury group" writers if their ideas were influenced by (or just similar to) those of the group, Keynes was one of the group's dozen or so core members (Rosner 2014, 2).

The influence of the Bloomsbury group on the intellectual and artistic life of the western world was enormous. "It might well be said that no other English-speaking gathering of friends in the past two hundred years has achieved such prominence or exerted such sway," writes Victoria Rosner (Rosner 2014, 2). They influenced diverse fields, from art and literature to logic, philosophy of science and political philosophy.

Bloomsbury was held together by a distinctly modern and materialistic moral vision, one that drew together most of the threads involved in "throwing open the palace gates" in the history recounted at the end of Chapter 3. Heavily influenced by G.E. Moore's 1903 *Principia Ethica* and A.N. Whitehead's and Bertrand Russell's 1910–1913 *Principia Mathematica*, the group took pleasure in seeking pleasure, and questioned all sorts of existing mores, attitudes, and conventions. They questioned everything, including what constituted beauty, truth, and goodness. In this their attitude was highly agnostic. Though they weren't sure what the highest forms of pleasure might be, their sense was that they could be found only among their greatest loves—in intimate relationships and in things like the arts, theater, and music—rather than in more pedestrian forms of enjoyment (Rosner 2014; Mullin 2014).

Keynes himself emphasized that the Bloomsbury group had a moral vision directly opposed to all previous morality—so much so that he even described it as a form of immoralism. He wrote of the bohemian ethos of the group: "We repudiated entirely customary morals, conventions and traditional wisdom. We were, that is to say, in the strict sense of the term, immoralists" (Skidelsky 2009, 148).

Members of the Bloomsbury group were deeply disdainful of what we now call "consumerism." They renounced the pursuit of happiness through the accumulation of wealth and material things. Such pleasures are fleeting and artificial, drawing us away from our authentic selves. The pathway to happiness lay in the appreciation and discussion of such things as art, literature, and philosophy, carried out within intimate relationships of friendship and romantic (or at least sexual) partnership.

The Bloomsbury group stood militantly opposed to the vision of the good that had dominated the Enlightenment—the vision that had formed the basis of the Reason paradigm in economics. In their view, the Enlightenment's intense social focus on the productive virtues of diligence, frugality, and self-control drained people of their humanity. In the economy created by the Enlightenment, the worker was reduced to a drone in an economic beehive. Bloomsbury thought the Enlightenment's vision of a "rational" society had reduced human beings to nothing but dehumanized workers—factors of economic production (Mini 1991, 49–67).

The Bloomsbury group wanted to clear away the last vestiges of the Enlightenment's substantive rationalism (its view that reason could tell us our ends as well as our means) and make way for a new human consciousness, one that would not begin with rationality. Of course, one could not live without calculating. But the task of calculating was instrumental; you could not calculate your way into valuing beauty above ugliness, or a painful truth above a comforting lie. Reason was to be ruthlessly subordinated to its proper purpose: enjoying the experience of life. Calculating was merely about means; enjoying one's life was the end (Mini 1991, 68–83).

Adam Smith, as we have seen, had been worried about the tendency of the division of labor to reduce people's daily lives to the performance of narrower and narrower tasks. The risk was that the human being would disappear into the mere worker/drone. Smith insisted upon the role of educational institutions like schools and churches in maintaining people's full humanity.

The Bloomsbury group rejected such ameliorative approaches. To them, you could not live a fully human life if your day job was on a factory floor. The ruthlessly utilitarian demands of business exerted a pervasive warping effect on the whole life and worldview of those devoted to their service; the proper response is not to ameliorate but to stand against the Benthamism of business (Mini 1991, 104–124).

Bloomsbury Elitism: A Higher Life for Higher People

This does not mean the Bloomsbury group wanted to shut down the factories and liberate the drones. Far from it! While they strove to detach themselves from consumerism, the elite Bloomsbury intellectuals did enjoy the longer lifespans, cures for diseases, ready availability of money, and many other material benefits provided to them by the modern economy with its millions of drone workers (Gerzina 2014).

This was no self-contradiction, for it was an essential element of the Bloomsbury group's view of the good life that only a few could live it. The Bloomsbury elites did not think the factory drones were capable of kind of intellectual, artistic, and literary life they enjoyed. They thought the drone-like narrowness of factory life suited the common man, for the common man was a drone in his soul. When it came to both intellectual inquiry and social mores, Bloomsbury saw themselves as a group of, if not "know-it-alls," at least "know-it-more-than-anybody-elses." As Robert Ekelund and Robert Hébert put it, they "considered all issues (philosophy, social convention, art, literature and music) with the utter frankness and conceit born of a firm belief in their own intellectual superiority" (Ekelund and Hébert 2007, 514).

What they objected to was not the drone-like life of ordinary people. It was the idea that the productive virtues appropriate to the factory drones were morally good and socially beneficial. On the contrary, for the Bloomsbury group these virtues led to the cultural emptiness of bourgeois society with its endless consumerism. What the Reason paradigm saw as social progress toward justice and comfort, the Bloomsbury elites saw as shallow and materialistic life.

What was needed was for superior lights like themselves to assume cultural leadership. They could benefit from the productive power of the modern economy and use it to live the kind of lives that are alone worth living: lives devoted to the proper human ends, namely the artistic and literary enjoyment of which only elites like themselves were capable. Leonard Woolf wrote of the group: "We were in the van of the builders of a new society" (Mullin 2014, 19).

The Bloomsbury critique of the Enlightenment vision is closely connected with the change Keynes introduced in both the content and the purpose of the *homo economicus* paradigm. In content, "rationality" in the Reason paradigm had included calculation to achieve ends, but it also included recognition of the right ends—ever-increasing levels of useful knowledge, acquisition of moral virtues involved in using that useful knowledge effectively, and reform of society to spread the benefits of that knowledge and virtue. Mill's *homo economicus* was introduced in an intellectual climate where these assumptions were still deeply embedded, if only unconsciously. At the very moment Mill was disclaiming moral commitments in economic science, he introduced a model of economic rationality that was plausible and acceptable because it was assumed that this was the model on which the Enlightenment social vision would thrive. In the Bloomsbury group, this rationality of ends as well as means was viewed as disconnecting people from the ability to enjoy life. The Bloomsbury elites wanted to pursue the good life, but they did not see reason as the ultimate source of our knowledge of what is good. Reason helps us analyze our experiences of the good, but it is those experiences—themselves pre-rational or super-rational—that constitute our knowledge of the good (Mini 1991, 68–83).

The only "rationality" possible within this view is a rationality of means. Experience of good things tells us what is good; reason helps us understand how to have more such experiences. You are rational if you calculate your means to accomplish your ends, whatever your ends are. This leaves the bourgeois drones free to continue living their "rational" drone lives, but liberates the bohemian elite from the constraints of bourgeois life goals.

In purpose, Mill's *homo economicus* was not intended to be imposed on anyone, but was intended only an observation (however crude or reductive) of how people made their daily grocery-store-type economic decisions. The Bloomsbury group felt that they could take control of the drones' culture and reform it for the drones' own good.

Scholarly Misreadings of Keynes and Bloomsbury

The Bloomsbury group's sense of its own elite status, its sense of entitlement to live a superior life not suited for the factory drones, helps to solve an otherwise baffling puzzle in Keynes scholarship. Among Keynes scholars who attend to the moral dimensions of the *General Theory* and the elevated aspirations of the Bloomsbury group, it is common to read the *General Theory* as laying out an economic system that will bring the Bloomsbury life to the masses. The baffling puzzle is how it is possible for Keynes to be the most influential economic thinker of the twentieth century—by orders of magnitude—and yet the economic life produced during the period of his overwhelming influence represents very much the reverse of a Bloomsbury lifestyle.

Legendary Keynes biographer Robert Skidelsky represents the typical approach of assuming that the goal of the *General Theory* must be to provide a Bloomsbury life for everyone. How, then, did we get a world in which the purpose of economic systems is to maximize the satisfaction of consumer appetites? In a book assessing Keynes' legacy, Skidelsky says pluralism was our fatal weakness: "Maximizing the quantity of goodness in the universe cannot provide an agreed criterion for economic action, because rational people disagree about what is good. Economics therefore is bound to take wants as data and treat the maximization problem in terms of want satisfaction" (Skidelsky 2009, 137). Skidelsky elaborates further on this theory, with additional possible causes, in a book he co-authored entitled *How Much Is Enough?* (Skidelsky and Skidelsky 2012, 15–42).

However, maximizing the satisfaction of consumer appetites was not a wrong turn that somehow came after Keynes. As we will see below, it is at the heart of the *General Theory.* Of course, it's true that the maximize-consumer-appetites approach is also highly incentivized by the challenge of social pluralism—in a society that does not agree about what is good, the easy shortcut is to say that we can build an economy without raising such divisive questions, by simply giving everyone whatever they happen to want. But this consumption-maximizing approach was Keynes' original goal in the *General Theory.* Keynes never aspired to build an economy that would bring the Bloomsbury life to everyone. No such aspiration is expressed anywhere in the *General Theory.*

Ironically, Skidelsky's major biography of Keynes shows more sensitivity to the real moral content of Keynes' thought. A reviewer comments:

> If we just sit tight and wait for the world to come around to us, [Keynes is saying,] we may not be here when it arrives. Pleasure delayed is often pleasure denied. Skidelsky, particularly in the first two volumes (for some reason, the thread is dropped in the third), is deft in bringing out this moral implication of Keynes's work; but he is troubled by it, too. He seems to feel that something is dangerous about a society in which there is no philosophical bridge between private happiness and social welfare, a society in which individual life is the only thing that has meaning, and everything else – institutions, customs, traditions, values – is understood to exist only to serve our present happiness. (Menand 2002)

In *Keynes, Bloomsbury and the* General Theory, a scholarly book focused entirely on the relationship between the Bloomsbury group and Keynes' economics, Piero Mini encounters the same conundrum and offers a different explanation. He shows how the anti-materialistic values of the Bloomsbury group—their dedication to art and literature, and their rejection of crass bourgeois society with its advertising and its relentless pursuit of consumer satisfaction—are visible in Keynes' other writings. From the existence of these connections, he draws the inference that the economics of the *General Theory* must be intended to be anti-materialistic, and stand against an economic life focused on satisfying consumption appetites (Mini 1991, 158–191). Where Skidelsky thinks that Keynes was really as influential as we think, but was subverted by other factors, Mini concludes that Keynes must have actually failed to exert lasting influence on the way we think and live. Far from his having been an influential figure of the first rank, the triumph of a materialistic, consumption-oriented economy in the twentieth century proves that Keynes never really had an important role in designing the economic world in which we live (Mini 1991, 192–211).

Skidelsky and Mini have missed the social dualism in the Bloomsbury worldview—their sense that the world is divided into an enlightened artistic elite, like themselves, and factory drones incapable of rising to their higher level. Keynes' economic theory assumes the Bloombsury view of the common man as a materialistic and manipulable drone. That was not the life Keynes and his Bloomsbury peers wanted for themselves, but it was the life they thought the ordinary person was doomed by his inner shallowness to live. The economy built by Keynesianism was, and still is, an economy that assumes almost everyone will live as a drone—and by structuring our daily economic life on that assumption, it forms us into those drones.

Manifesto: The *General Theory* as Revolutionary Document

It is notoriously difficult to develop a comprehensive understanding of Keynes' works, and it is not our intention to take on such an ambitious undertaking here. He was prolific writer, and a thinker who was working out the consequences of his own ideas in real time. His economic philosophies were constantly evolving throughout his life, and he did not live long enough to publish a synoptic or retrospective work at the end of his explorations. People have spent lifetimes climbing the mountain of Keynes' writings and not come away with a clear synthesis. So great is the challenge that it is common among economists to speak of "exegeting" Keynes' works, as if they were ancient texts. Among other Keynes scholarship, we are particularly indebted to Ekelund and Hébert (2007) and Claar and Klay (2007).

Our goal here is far more limited. It is to highlight how key ideas in Keynes' central writings, especially his most famous and influential work, the *General Theory of Employment, Interest and Money*, pointed to a new moral vision for economics. In identifying key economic ideas in Keynes, we are not offering any major departure from consensus interpretations of what was important in his ideas. We are operating within the standard understanding of the Keynesian model as "translated" from the *General Theory* by Sir John Hicks and later Alvin Hansen (a history we will return to in the next chapter; Hicks 1937; Hansen 1953). Our goal is not to argue that existing Keynes scholarship has misidentified what ideas are important in Keynes, but to prompt a fresh consideration of the moral significance of those ideas.

The *General Theory* arrived at just the right moment to be successful. The world was seven years into the Great Depression, with no foreseeable end. During the worst year of the Great Depression in the United States, the unemployment rate was 25%, and only about 70% of the nation's productive capacity was being utilized. Traditional economics had neither foreseen the crisis nor made any contribution to resolving it that the popular mind could appreciate. Against this backdrop Keynes published the *General Theory.*

Employing a mix of rhetoric and basic mathematical modeling, Keynes explained his theory of the business cycle and interest rates, contrasting it with the views of classical economists like his Cambridge contemporary A.C. Pigou. Keynes positioned the *General Theory* as a rejoinder to Pigou's (1933) *Theory of Unemployment*, though he implicates everyone that had worked within that tradition as far back as David Ricardo. In a note on page three, Keynes writes: "I have become accustomed…to include in 'the classical school' the *followers* of Ricardo, those, that is to say, who adopted and perfected the theory of Ricardian economics, including (for example) J.S. Mill, Marshall, Edgeworth, and Prof. Pigou" (italics in original). Keynes specifically points his criticism at Ricardo and his successors to differentiate himself from Marx, who had used the term "classical economists" to refer to "Ricardo and James Mill and their *predecessors*" (italics in original; Keynes 2013, 3). Thus, Keynes isn't criticizing the entire classical legacy; he intends to criticize the general-equilibrium claims about the economy that had been articulated by Ricardo and his successors down to Pigou.

One way to view the *General Theory* is to consider it a rejection of what is called Say's Law: the theoretical claim that markets will not remain in disequilibrium. Jean-Baptiste Say, at least in the interpretation of his works that was standard at the time, contended that any temporary glut or shortage in one market must have its own unseen offsetting shortage or glut in another market, or in a combination of other markets.[1] For example, if there is currently too much lumber being produced (i.e. too much for one sort of use in one market), it must also be true that other markets are currently getting too little of it. For classical economists like Say, the price system would quickly eradicate any such disequilibrium, redirecting the resource from the use where it's less valuable to the use where there is currently a shortage. For Say, shortages or surpluses were ephemeral deviations from a condition of a general equilibrium for all markets. Say didn't necessarily believe that such adjustments were instantaneous—unlike the way we sometimes model them. The point was that markets were always either in equilibrium or adjusting toward equilibrium. The colloquial expression of Say's Law is that "supply creates its own demand," meaning that, in the aggregate, anything that exists will be allocated to its most-highly valued use:

> It is worthwhile to remark that a product is no sooner created than it, from that instant, affords a market for other products to the full extent of its own value. When the producer has put the finishing hand to his product, he is most anxious to sell it immediately, lest its value should diminish in his hands. Nor is he less anxious to dispose of the money he may get for it; for the value of money is also perishable. But the only way of getting rid of money is in the purchase of some product or other. Thus the mere circumstance of creation of one product immediately opens a vent for other products. (Say 1834, 138–139)

Say's Law applied to everything in the "real" economy, meaning things other than money: hours of labor, pairs of shoes, soybeans. Though we

[1]We leave aside controversies over the accuracy of the standard interpretation of Say. On this topic see Sowell (2016).

carry out our market transactions using money, and express values in money prices, money is a "veil" though which we engage in exchange of value for value. For the classical economists, money was simply a lubricant that made any adjustments from short-term disequilibria to eventual market-clearing positions much faster and easier than one would see in an exclusively "real" economy (in which we all participated only in barter transactions, without money). As a consequence, the economic focus was on the equilibrium position; it was the position toward which economic movement was inevitable and universal.

When applied to financial markets, one implication of Say's Law was that aggregate household savings should be identical to the overall level of borrowing, and that interest rates—whether long or short term—are constantly adjusting to bring these quantities into equilibrium. Households save when interest rates are sufficiently high to make saving attractive. Firms borrow only when the interest rate is sufficiently low to make borrowing profitable. Thus, interest rates move quickly to equilibrate the quantity of saving and the volume of lending. Households could never save "too much"; it was impossible. Households would save the amount that was right for them given the rate of interest. High interest rates would indicate a high demand for savings and also induce households to save more, while low interest rates would induce households to save less when there was less demand for their savings. After all, the opportunity cost of spending your money (or hiding it in your mattress) is the interest income you could have earned by putting it in the bank as savings.

The essence of the *General Theory* is that the classical economists were mistaken to put the focus of their analysis on equilibrium, since markets are never in equilibrium. Keynes explains that he calls his theory a "general theory" because it isn't limited to explaining what happens when markets are in equilibrium (Keynes 2013, 3). Markets are normally in a state of disequilibrium, so our models should be ones that attempt to explain why economies are not at full employment most of the time, rather than why they might momentarily be so. The probability that a complex economy would ever reach a general-equilibrium state is effectively zero, even if—like a stopped clock telling the right time twice a day—the general-equilibrium models might occasionally be accurate.

Interpreted this way, the *General Theory* is the story of what forces move us away from full employment (i.e. economic equilibrium), not what moves us toward it. The question is not what is orderly, but what is chaotic. This led Keynes to bring economics straight to the same place modernists were bringing art and Freudians were bringing psychology: the darker realms of the human psyche. Keynes would famously speak of this psychic netherworld in terms of "animal spirits."

The New *Homo Economicus* in the *General Theory*

Mill's version of *homo economicus* is a key target in the *General Theory*. Keynes doesn't rely on the actual phrase "*homo economicus*," which was less commonly used then, but Mill's model emerges as a target of Keynes' attack almost immediately. The first chapter of the book lays out what Keynes means by a "general theory"—that is, one that doesn't focus on equilibrium. The second chapter sets up as his foil what Keynes calls, in the title of the chapter, "The Postulates of Classical Economics." And while other classical economists like Say and Ricardo are mentioned, it is the works of Mill from which Keynes actually draws block quotations to illustrate the postulates he has set himself to attack.

The anthropological model behind those postulates takes longer to emerge. The concerns that are front and center in the second chapter are more technical. Over the course of the book, however, the key critiques of classical economics that are now widely recognized as constituting the heart of Keynes' attack—"sticky wages" and "animal spirits," interest rates and the "paradox of thrift"—concern the anthropology of Mill's *homo economicus*.

One reason Keynes' attack on Mill's anthropology is not more widely recognized is that while Keynes was eager to highlight his disagreements with Mill and mainstream economics, the successors who followed Keynes and built the paradigm of Keynesianism from his ideas were not. On the contrary, as we will see in Chapter 5, they described Keynes' approach using the language of moral neutrality that dominated the discipline before Keynes' arrival. This made Keynes more palatable, and allowed the discipline to ignore those aspects of the *General Theory* that were unpalatable—above all its open and proud moral crusade for a revolutionary reform of society, which didn't accord with the discipline's view of itself as detached scientists.

Refining Mill's Model: Business Cycles and Sticky Wages

Understanding Say's Law, especially as it applies to labor markets and household saving, is essential to understanding Keynes' theory of the business cycle. In Keynes' opinion, Say's Law couldn't possibly square with the Great Depression. There was clearly a glut of labor—unemployment—but wages simply were not adjusting as rapidly as the classical economists had suggested. If wages were as flexible as the classicals claimed, there would be no unemployment over the longer term; instead of becoming unemployed, people would either end up working for lower wages in the same jobs, or finding other activities to keep themselves occupied. Yet during the Great Depression, there appeared to be significant and persistent unemployment. Wages did not appear to be delivering general equilibrium, even though Say's Law says that all available labor will be employed (though with no guarantees about the level of wage that would clear the market).

On the classical theory, prices should gravitate downward when there is a surplus of anything, so there should never be persistent unemployment in any economy. Under Say's Law, if demand has fallen for goods and services, thereby reducing their market prices that should—at first lead to layoffs in those particular industries. But Say's Law claims there will always be sufficient demand to employ all available resources, like labor, though that may require a market-driven decrease in wages paid to labor. Whatever causes a recession, the glut of labor should naturally lead to a new market equilibrium in labor markets—an equilibrium in which the market wage is lower than it used to be, but one in which every person who is willing and able to work for that lower wage is doing so. Though the new equilibrium level of employment is lower that it was before the recession began, under the classical, Say's Law view, there is no long-term "unemployment" in the formal sense. Someone who loses a job will be unemployed until they find another one, but if a person is permanently "out of work" it means that person is not willing to work for available wages, and is therefore out of the labor force rather than unemployed. For example, stay-at-home spouses are not unemployed; they have chosen to stay out of the labor market because they prefer caring for their children over accepting available jobs at the prevailing market wage.

Keynes' theory is that persistent unemployment does happen, because wages are "sticky." In this theory, wages paid to labor do not adjust as rapidly to new equilibrium levels as prices for donuts, diamonds or detergents do. Keynes believed wages were especially "sticky downward," meaning they would be even slower to adjust if the adjustment would be downward.

Keynes and his successors have offered a variety of explanations for this phenomenon. The most obvious is that human relations make it difficult for managers to cut wages whenever the market suggests they should do so, and however deep the market suggests they should be cut. Shopkeepers don't hurt the feelings of Halloween candy when they slash its price drastically on November 1, but it's a lot harder in human terms for them to tell employees that their labor has to be marked down.

There are other reasons wages might be slow to adjust following a decrease in the demand for labor. For instance, multi-year collective-bargaining agreements, especially if they are overlapping among multiple unions, could put contractual constraints on the speed of wage adjustments. Another possibility is that currently unemployed workers may be reluctant to attempt to underbid currently employed workers for their jobs because it's unseemly (Solow 1980).

Regardless of the reason, if Keynes is right, Say's Law could still hold over the longer term, but periodic and unpredictable gluts of unemployed workers can be expected over shorter time horizons. With this powerful critique of the classical view of unemployment, Keynes proved himself both a bold economic thinker and one who had the intelligence to back up his boldness.

This observation could have been the starting point of a very different kind of revision of Mill's *homo economicus* model. Wages are sticky because people have dignity. Economics cannot limit itself to understanding people's desire for wealth, consumption, and comfort. People also want recognition, respect, and relationships with others. These desires affect economic behavior in fundamental ways.

However, that is not the direction in which Keynes took his revision of Mill. In the *General Theory*, Keynes points out that wages do not fluctuate in the same way other prices do, but he does not investigate the reasons beyond a few quick observations. He displays no interest in human dignity or in building an economic model that takes account of our need for recognition, respect and relationships. He does not pursue this adjustment of Mill any further than the problem of unemployment requires. In fact, the stickiness of wages is for Keynes a problem to be overcome! Reducing unemployment, not affirming human dignity, is the goal. On this point, Keynes revises Mill only far enough to show that traditional market mechanisms will not provide the kind of solution Mill thought they would for the problem of unemployment.

Reinventing Mill's Model: Instrumental Rationality and "Animal Spirits"

Along with this critique of Mill's model, which was an important achievement insofar as it accurately showed how Mill had failed to account for the stickiness of wages, came elements of a radically new economic worldview. Keynes offered a different understanding of what drove labor markets, grounded in a different general view of human behavior and leading toward a different organization of society as a whole. Behind this was a new and different economic anthropology—a new *homo economicus*.

In Keynes' view, the major driver of the business cycle couldn't be found in any quantifiable measures like household income, taxes, or the prices of productive inputs like steel or oil. Keynes believed that during a recession or depression, the fundamental cause lay in insufficient private demand for goods and services. That is, households and firms simply weren't buying enough stuff to keep everyone and everything employed, despite Say's claims to the contrary. The reason was that households and firms simply didn't feel like buying enough stuff. According to Keynes, insufficient private spending was caused by mood swings in the economy:

> ...there is the instability due to the characteristic of human nature that a large proportion of our positive activities depend on spontaneous optimism rather than on a mathematical expectation, whether moral or hedonistic or economic. Most, probably, of our decisions to do something positive, the full consequences of which will be drawn out over many days to come, can only be taken as a result of animal spirits – of a spontaneous urge to action rather than inaction, and not as the outcome of a weighted average of quantitative benefits multiplied by quantitative probabilities.... Thus if the animal spirits are dimmed and the spontaneous optimism falters, leaving us to depend on nothing but a mathematical expectation, enterprise will fade and die. (Keynes 2013, 161–162)

He goes on to write that in economic decision-making we are "often falling back for our motive on whim or sentiment or chance" (Keynes 2013, 163).

These "animal spirits" are, for Keynes, the shock that starts the business cycle. And in the recessionary case, consumers and firms grow pessimistic because they got up on the wrong side of the bed, because it's cloudy outside, or because they have a tummy ache. A couple who has saved up a 20% down payment to build a new house decides to continue renting for a while; a firm that had arranged a small business loan decides not to sign the papers after all; a family foregoes their annual tradition of new church clothes for Easter. In a recession or depression, a systemic wave of shared pessimism sufficiently widespread causes a quantifiable decline in the overall demand for goods and services. People, lots of people, are buying fewer goods and services, with little idea why they have this inclination.

To be fair, Keynes doesn't attribute all human action or inaction to mere whimsy:

> We should not conclude from this that everything depends on waves of irrational psychology.... We are merely reminding ourselves that human decisions affecting the future, whether personal or political or economic, cannot depend on strict mathematical expectation. (Keynes 2013, 162–163)

But it is important not to allow such caveats to obscure the important move Keynes is making.

Keynes stresses that he is resisting the tendency of the *homo economicus* model to reduce the human being to a calculating automaton, like a robot. But for this robot he substitutes something essentially capricious—something beastlike. The robot of Mill's Enlightenment rationality has been replaced with an animal.

Mill's *homo economicus* did have a robotlike quality. This was partly owing to the extreme reductiveness of the model, eliminating the complexity of higher teleological values to focus on limited goals; Mill's model was merely wealth-maximizing, costly-indulgence-enjoying and labor-averse. Keynes' point about sticky wages is such a potent critique of the traditional economic model precisely because real people are not like Mill's robots. They want things that wealth-maximizing robots can't understand.

But the robotlike quality of Mill's model was also partly owing to the fact that Mill thought its specific goals—wealth, pleasure, and leisure—were dictated by reason. Mill's *homo economicus* acts like a hyper-rational robot partly because it has so few ultimate goals, but also partly because those goals it does have are understood to be (1) rational, and (2) not a matter of choice, but demanded by rationality.

Where Mill's robotlike anthropology was substantively rational, Keynes' animalistic anthropology is only instrumentally rational. Mill's *homo economicus* is rational actor who occasionally makes mistakes, but has fixed aims, and for that reason will reflect over time and learn from past errors. This model grew from the Enlightenment's Reason paradigm, in which all humanity was doing the same thing—pursuing the same set of fixed, rational ends and thus learning over time. The choices of Keynes' *homo economicus* are instrumentally rational in that they calculate means to achieve ends; hence the caveat in the quote above. But while these choices are instrumentally rational, they are substantively irrational. The economic actor for Keynes has goals that are arbitrary and ephemeral.

When the economy has faltered due to the shared whimsical pessimism of many, what is a caring member of the know-it-more-than-anybody-else elite supposed to do? For Keynes, it seemed cruel to wait out a demand-driven recession, even if eventually the skies would clear and people would shake the fog from their brains, and at last follow through on their prior plans (the house, the loan, the bright new suits, and dresses). Instead of waiting for demand to return on its own to its pre-recession level, Keynes insisted that the humane thing to do was for the state to step in right away and shore up the decline in the demand for goods and services. Wherever there had been layoffs due to a decline in sales, government could step in and do the spending instead, and people could return to their pre-recession jobs. And it was perfectly acceptable to use budget deficits for this if necessary, provided government used the increase in tax revenues during the eventual boom to retire the debt that had been incurred during the bust.

Refining Mill's Model: Money-Holding and the Paradox of Thrift

Disequilibrium in the labor market wasn't the only major instance of disequilibrium in Keynes' theories of recession. The other instance lay in the saving decisions of households. When banks and other financial institutions make loans (mainly to businesses financing investments in inventory, capital goods such as machines, or new technologies), the money they are loaning comes from savings (from households). The more people put money into financial institutions through savings, the more money those institutions have available to loan out. The potential disequilibrium is a divergence between the amount of loanable funds made available by savings and the amount of loanable funds demanded by borrowers. Much as classical economic theory suggests that we should see wages constantly adjusting to align the amount of labor supplied with the amount of labor demanded, it suggests that we should see interest rates—the price of loans—constantly adjusting to align the borrowing of firms with the saving of households.

It's helpful to break this assessment down by considering the planning decisions of savers and borrowers individually. Michael Jacobs and Anil Shivdasani break down the decision on the borrower (firm) side:

> Say, for instance, an investment of $20 million in a new project promises to produce positive annual cash flows of $3.25 million for 10 years. If the cost of capital is 10%, the net present value of the project (the value of the future cash flows discounted at that 10%, minus the $20 million investment) is essentially break-even – in effect, a coin-toss decision. If the company has underestimated its capital cost by 100 basis points (1%) and assumes a capital cost of 9%, the project shows a net present value of nearly $1 million – a flashing green light. But if the company assumes that its capital cost is 1% higher than it actually is, the same project shows a loss of nearly $1 million and is likely to be cast aside. (Jacobs and Shivdasani 2012, 120)

A profit-seeking business won't sink more into the cost of a project than the expected increase in revenues the project is expected to generate. Firms will undertake new projects only when the net present value of a project (that is, its expected revenues, minus costs, and discounted into "present dollars" to account for the delay in realizing the revenues) is expected to be larger than zero. This means firms will undertake more projects when interest rates are low, and put more projects on the back burner as interest rates rise. The key here is that an interest rate is just a price, and it works like any other price; in this case, it happens to be the price to use someone else's money for a while.

Having looked at the demand side of the loanable funds market, let's consider the supply side. Here we find households: from passbook savers and 401(k) savers to angel investors and venture capitalists. Big or small, all savers are ultimately households. One consideration we all make every week is how much to save or spend out of our current income, and that is affected by what rate of interest the bank is offering us for putting our money into savings. When interest rates are low, there's not a strong incentive to save; the opportunity cost of not saving is low. We aren't missing out on much if we don't save. But as interest rates rise, the opportunity cost of not saving also rises. If someone is indifferent between saving a dollar and spending it at an interest rate of, say, three percent, an interest rate higher than three percent would move that person to part with that dollar for a while.

Putting together the supply of loanable funds provided by saver-households in a given period with the demand for loanable funds by borrower-firms in that same period should generate an equilibrium price for a loan. This is just another supply and demand price coordination, like in any other market.

This requires the market for interest rates to be free of arbitrary interference, just as the markets for footballs and tea can connect supply to demand because they're free to find the price that clears the market. Freely functioning interest rates help coordinate the saving plans of households with the investment plans of firms. Households loan to firms only when it is perceived to be mutually beneficial by both parties.

Keynes believed that, in the case of a downturn, such a model is too simplistic to account for what he observed in the behavior of savers. He thought households were saving more money than the classical economists would have predicted; as a consequence, they were demanding fewer goods and services.

Thus, alongside anemic animal spirits, another source of a downturn can lie in "too much" saving by households. Of course, moral codes from the ancient world to the modern day have said that saving is generally a virtuous behavior on the part of households. But Keynes thought that in the case of saving, what seems good for the individual may be bad for the overall economy. If the consequence of additional saving is a reduction in the demand for goods and services that in turn leads to layoffs, that additional saving is destructive rather than constructive.

This phenomenon is what Paul Samuelson famously described in a highly influential textbook as the "paradox of thrift." Keynes summarizes it in the *General Theory*:

> The reconciliation of the identity between saving and investment with the apparent 'free-will' of the individual to save what he chooses irrespective of what he or others may be investing, essentially depends on saving being, like spending, a two-sided affair. For although the amount of his own saving is unlikely to have any significant influence on his own income, the reactions of the amount of his consumption on the incomes of others makes it impossible for all individuals simultaneously to save any given sums. Every such attempt to save more by reducing consumption

> will so affect incomes that the attempt necessarily defeats itself. It is, of course, just as impossible for the community as a whole to save *less* than the amount of current investment, since the attempt to do so will necessarily raise incomes to a level at which the sums which individuals choose to save add up to a figure exactly equal to the amount of investment. (Keynes 2013, 84)

Keynes thought households were saving too much because they were spending too little.

The challenge for this theory comes from the fact that when households save money in banks or other financial institutions, those institutions turn around and loan the money out to firms. A dollar saved in a bank by a household is a dollar ultimately spent by a firm that took out a loan from that bank. It is the job of loanable funds markets to set interest rates (prices) connecting supply and demand so money that goes into the bank as savings goes out again as loans. Changes in savings rates should not cause an overall change in the aggregate demand for goods and services.

To work, Keynes' theory needed an explanation for why households would keep at least a portion of their savings as cash in hand (or in the mattress)—savings that don't become loans because they don't go into financial institutions. That means Keynes needed a theory of why people might hold at least a portion of their savings in cash, at home, out of the loanable funds market and earning them no interest, rather than putting their money in the bank and earning interest.

In the *General Theory*, Keynes articulates three distinct motives for households to hold their savings as cash rather than in interest-bearing forms that would ultimately be used by firms for investment expenditure: a transactions motive, a precautionary motive, and a speculative motive. The transactions motive is straightforward: People hold cash in preparation for cash expenditures they plan to make. The precautionary motive is also straightforward: People hold cash in excess of the cash expenditures they expect to make in a given period because life is unpredictable and they want to have extra cash on hand in case they need it. This is why people often, even in contemporary society, withdraw additional cash in advance of a road trip than they might normally hold in their wallets if they weren't leaving town. Keynes believed the transactions and precautionary motives for holding cash were sufficient to overcome the opportunity cost (that is, the loss of the interest the money would earn in the bank) for at least a portion of household saving. Finally, according to the speculative motive, people may choose to hold cash simply because it is a low-risk asset—the risk being whether the value of cash will be eroded by inflation (Keynes 2013, 165–173).

In the close of the section, Keynes states that these three motives for liquidity may be thought of as the equivalent of "hoarding": "The habit of overlooking the relation of the rate of interest to hoarding may be a part of the explanation of why interest has been usually regarded as the reward of not-spending, whereas in fact it is the reward of not-hoarding" (p. 174). This means that it's not really saving that is the problem for Keynes: the problem is hoarding. With hoarding, money that could have been used for either consumption purchases by households or investment spending by firms does neither. As a consequence, aggregate saving can indeed—at least over the short term—be larger than aggregate investment since not all savings a channeled to the loanable funds market.

These motives to hold cash in hand, according to Keynesian theory, can undermine the ability of central banks to alleviate a downturn by putting more money into the economy. Central banks seek to perform "monetary stimulus" by increasing the cash reserves of commercial banks during a downturn. The idea is to reduce interest rates, which will encourage firms to make new investments and get the economy going again. Today, the Fed accomplishes this by purchasing bonds from commercial banks, exchanging one form of asset for commercial banks (securities they hold) with another (bank reserves). However, Keynesian theory holds that if interest rates are already perilously close to zero, savers will prefer money-holding to bond-holding, because with interest rates so low, money will look like a more sensible asset to hold than bonds. As long as money-holding, or "hoarding" as Keynes called it, is perceived to have at least some positive benefit, then there is little reason to believe households would be inclined to lend to firms rather than to continue to hoard cash when interest rates are near zero. Savers maximize their hoarding, and further attempts at monetary stimulus are doomed. Keynes writes:

> There is the possibility…that, after the rate of interest has fallen to a certain level, liquidity-preference may become virtually absolute in the sense that almost everyone prefers cash to holding a debt which yields so low a rate of interest. In this event the monetary authority would have lost effective control over the rate of interest. But whilst this limiting case might

> become practically important in future [*sic*], I know of no example of it hitherto. (Keynes 2013, 207)

Keynesians call this a "liquidity trap," since it arises from households' desire to have extra liquidity by holding their cash in hand.

And so we return once again to fiscal policy—fiscal stimulus rather than monetary stimulus. In an economic downturn, it is our duty to use fiscal policy to restore the economy to full employment. As we saw above, Keynes recommends government spending as the antidote to anemic animal spirits; the same idea is extended to cover savings and interest rates. Just as discouraged consumers stop buying and discouraged firms shelve new projects, discouraged households hoard money rather than spend it or lend it. Government must spend money on goods and services to restore aggregate demand to its pre-recession levels.

These challenges to classical economic assumptions refine Mill's *homo economicus*. All three of the reasons Keynes gives for people holding more cash than the classical economists assumed was rational are, in fact, rational reasons. To that extent, Keynes is not changing the rationality of Mill's *homo economicus*, he is correcting its application. Rational economic actors will in fact hold more cash than the classical economists thought, because the classical economists hadn't recognized these rational reasons for holding money.

Reinventing Mill's Model: A Penny Saved Is a Penny Wasted

The deeper change to Mill's model comes where we're not looking for it, in the relationship between gaining wealth and enjoying it. Mill had identified three qualities of *homo economicus*: he maximizes wealth, enjoys costly indulgences, and avoids labor. Of these, the first (gaining wealth) was primary and the other two (enjoying wealth) were secondary. As he says in the passage quoted above, it is gaining wealth that defines economics as an activity. Wealth maximization was the purpose of economic life. Productivity is primary. The other two factors, the desire to enjoy wealth by consuming costly indulgences and avoiding work, were brought in only because they ran counter to the desire to gain wealth. They were obstacles to productivity—which would clearly have to be included in any study of productivity, but they are not the goal.

Keynes reverses the relationship between gaining and enjoying wealth in his analysis of saving. He places indulgences and leisure first, and reduces the desire to gain wealth to a secondary status. For Mill, the goal is to produce and build over time, and the two kinds of enjoyment appear as distractions or obstacles to that end. For Keynes, we only gain wealth because we want to enjoy it.

Homo economicus does not cease to be greedy in Keynes' version. He has not overcome the lust for money; he still believes, like Mill's version, that the path to happiness lies through the acquisition of money. He has only overcome the primacy of money over pleasure. Keynes' *homo economicus* strives after money just as Mill's does, but Keynes' version strives after money in order to enjoy pleasure and leisure, where Mill's strived after money in order to build up a store of reserves. Neither vision is morally edifying, but Mill's at least partook of the productive virtues and shunned the unproductive vices. Keynes has the worst of both worlds: endless pursuit of money *and* idolatry of the things money buys.

Here we see Keynes' Bloomsbury elitism. As we have seen, Mini is puzzled that the rise of Keynes was followed by the triumph of materialistic greed and idolatry of consumer pleasures, given that the Bloomsbury group firmly rejected greed and consumerism. But Keynes does not offer us an economy in which the many rise to the Bloomsbury level, becoming lovers of art and literature. In Keynes' economy, the greedy and consumptive bourgeois remain exactly what they are. Worse, the structures of the economic system are designed on purpose to keep them that way, because their lust after consumer pleasures is taken to be the source of economic productivity.

This reversal of the classical relationship between gaining and enjoying wealth is central to Keynes' reasoning throughout the section on saving and interest. He says:

> An act of individual saving means – so to speak – a decision not to have dinner today. But it does not necessitate a decision to have dinner or to buy a pair of boots a week hence or a year hence or to consume any specified thing at any specified date. Thus it depresses the business of preparing today's dinner without stimulating the business of making ready for some future act of consumption. It is not a substitution of future consumption-demand for present consumption-demand, it is a net diminution of such demand. (Keynes 2013, 210)

Mill's model had aligned with Ben Franklin's famous dictum that a penny saved is a penny earned, but for Keynes a penny saved is a penny wasted. We are not building anything up over time, passing on an accumulated store of resources to future generations. Whatever we don't spend today goes to waste for as long as we fail to spend it.

Thus, while holding cash as opposed to depositing money in a bank may not be intrinsically irrational for Keynes, the traditional emphasis on encouraging people to save their money instead of spending it is. Classical economics, grounded in the Reason paradigm with its productive virtues, eschewed costly "indulgences" in favor of the moral virtue of thrift. Keynes removed the moral imprimatur associated with "thirft," setting the stage for his successors to use that term in a negative construction—the "paradox of thrift" is that thrift leads us into a "trap."

This change to Mill's *homo economicus* is connected to the first one, the change from substantive to instrumental reason. Substantive reason, relying on teleological assumptions inherited (perhaps unconsciously) from the Reason paradigm, dictates productive ends that produce wealth. When ends are no longer dictated by reason, enjoying wealth becomes the end. With reason removed, we gravitate to our irrational nature.

Economics as Moral Crusade

The *General Theory* is economics as moral and social crusade. Alongside its trenchant and fruitful critiques of key weak points in classical theory, it reinvents the job of the economist from detached scientist to social reformer. The people are suffering. The problem is urgent. And the source of the problem is not vice or economic illiteracy, but movements in the dark recesses of the psyche that are not amenable to rational or moral improvement. Those who know how to save the people from their own anemic spirits have a moral obligation to step in and do so. If this requires expanded political power over the economy, then economists must fight for expanded political power over the economy. Those who favor the old ways appear not as colleagues who belong to a different school of thought within the same academic discipline, but as enemies of righteousness.

Like Mill's utilitarianism, Keynes' social vision was normative without being teleological. Unlike Mill and the other nineteenth-century economists, however, Keynes had no scruples about his normative mission. He wanted to tell us how we ought to live, and he didn't hide that fact.

Consider how starkly the following passages contrast with the nineteenth-century aspiration to detached, positive science without normative content:

> The outstanding faults of the economic society in which we live are its failure to provide for full employment and its arbitrary and inequitable distribution of wealth and incomes. (Keynes 2013, 372)
>
> There remains an allied, but distinct, matter where for centuries, indeed for several millenniums, enlightened opinion held for certain and obvious a doctrine which the classical school has repudiated as childish, but which deserves rehabilitation and honor. I mean the doctrine that the rate of interest is not self-adjusting at the level best suited to the social advantage but constantly tends to rise too high, so that a wise government is concerned to curb it by statute and even by invoking the sanctions of the moral law. (Keynes 2013, 351)

One may agree or disagree with the particular policies Keynes advocates as he is calling for economists to lead a moral reform of society. Either way, a call for economists to lead a moral reform of society is what this is.

It was obvious to Keynes that an economic theory should produce a social philosophy that shapes public policy and society at large. The reshaping of society he envisioned was vast. Immediately following the first of the quotes above, he launches into an argument that his theory removes some of the justification for permitting large disparities in wealth to continue—that is, the justification for not establishing heavily redistributive tax regimes. He explains that his theory does point toward allowing market economies to continue, as opposed to socialism, but with an interventionist state (Keynes 2013, 372–374).

The book ends with a prediction that implementing his economic ideas will bring on a massive conflict with entrenched interests, to be overcome by the power that will accrue to his ideas because of their truth and justice (Keynes 2013, 383–384). Here is how Keynes speaks of economists who disagree with his views:

> One recurs to the analogy between the sway of the classical school of economic theory and that of certain religions. For it is a far greater exercise of the potency of an idea to exorcise the obvious than to introduce into men's common notions the recondite and the remote. (Keynes 2013, 350–351)

That is not how Einstein talked about physicists who doubted his theories about relativity.

In the *General Theory*, economics abandons its nineteenth-century ambition to moral neutrality. It no longer seeks a place alongside chemistry and physics as a detached, disinterested, purely positive observer. It becomes, once again, a practical discipline with a moral vision.

But now the moral vision is radically different. Instead of the virtue, piety, or the progress of humanity, the moral vision of the *General Theory* is an animalistic *homo economicus* whose only economic goal is to satisfy his own consumption appetites. The people must be elevated, for the sake of righteousness, into greater and greater autonomous wealth-maximizers, costly-indulgence-enjoyers and labor-avoiders—not, to be sure, on Mill's robotlike model, but on a beastlike model, driven by irrational animal spirits. We are no longer just observing *homo economicus*; we are on a great moral crusade to get people to the shopping mall to buy, buy, buy for the sake of humanity.

In the aftermath of the September 11, 2001 terrorist attacks, the people of the United States anxiously turned to their president to guide them on what they should do in that hour of trauma and fear. He told them that if they wanted to serve their country in its time of need, they should go shopping. If they wanted to make an even bigger sacrifice for their country, they should go to Disney World (Basevich 2008). He issued this high and noble summons to the American people because he was surrounded by economists urging him that if he wanted to avoid economic catastrophe, he needed to keep the economy bustling with consumption. This is the triumph of the moral and social vision of John Maynard Keynes.

References

Arrow, Kenneth. 1998. What Has Economics to Say About Racial Discrimination? *Journal of Economic Perspectives* 12 (2): 91–100.

Basevich, Andrew. 2008. He Told Us to Go Shopping, Now the Bill Is Due. *Washington Post*, October 5.

Becker, Gary. 1974. A Theory of Marriage. In *Economics of the Family*, ed. Theodore W. Schultz, National Bureau of Economic Research, 299–351. Chicago: University of Chicago Press.

Claar, Victor V., and Robin J. Klay. 2007. *Economics in Christian Perspective*. Downers Grove: InterVarsity Press.

Davidson, Paul. 2002. *Financial Markets, Money and the Real World.* Cheltenham: Edward Elgar.

Davis, J. Ronnie. 1971. *The New Economics and the Old Economists.* Iowa City: Iowa State University Press.

Ekelund, Robert B., and Robert F. Hébert. 2007 [1990]. *A History of Economic Theory and Method.* New York: McGraw-Hill.

Emmett, Ross. 2014. Economics Is Not All of Life. *Econ Journal Watch* 11: 144–152.

Fisher, Irving. 1911. *The Purchasing Power of Money.* London: Macmillan.

Fisher, Irving. 1926. A Statistical Relation Between Unemployment and Price Changes. *International Labour Review* 13: 785–792.

Hansen, Alvin. 1953. *A Guide to Keynes.* New York: McGraw-Hill.

Hicks, J.R. 1937. Mr. Keynes and the 'Classics'; A Suggested Interpretation. *Econometrica* 5 (2): 147–159.

Gerzina, Gretchen Holbrook. 2014. Bloomsbury and Empire. In *Cambridge Companion to the Bloomsbury Group*, 112–127. Cambridge and New York, NY: Cambridge University Press.

Jacobs, Michael, and Anil Shivdasani. 2012. Do You Know Your Cost of Capital? *Harvard Business Review* (July/August): 118–124.

Keynes, John Maynard. 2013 [1936]. *The General Theory of Employment, Interest and Money.* Cambridge: Cambridge University Press.

Kragh, Martin. 2014. The 'Wigforss Connection': The Stockholm School vs. Keynes Debate Revisited. *European Journal of the History of Economic Thought* 21: 635–663.

Menand, Louis. 2002. Buried Treasure. *New Yorker*, January 20.

Mill, John Stuart. 2000 [1874]. *Essays on Some Unsettled Questions of Political Economy*, 2nd ed. London: Longmans, Green, Reader & Dyer.

Mini, Piero V. 1991. *Keynes, Bloomsbury and the General Theory.* London: Macmillan.

Mullin, Katherine. 2014. Victorian Bloomsbury. In *Cambridge Companion to the Bloomsbury Group*, 19–32. Cambridge and New York, NY: Cambridge University Press.

Nash, Robert T., & William P. Gramm. 1969. A Neglected Early Statement of the Paradox of Thrift. *History of Political Economy* 1: 395–400.

Patinkin, Don. 1978a. On the Relation Between Keynesian Economics and the 'Stockholm School'. *Scandinavian Journal of Economics* 80: 135–143.

Patinkin, Don. 1978b. Some Observations on Ohlin's 1933 Article. *History of Political Economy* 10: 413–418.

Patinkin, Don. 1982. *Anticipations of the General Theory? And Other Essays on Keynes.* Chicago: University of Chicago Press.

Phillips, A.W. 1958. The Relation Between Unemployment and the Rate of Change of Money Wage Rates in the United Kingdom, 1861–1957. *Economica New Series* 25 (100): 283–299.

Pigou, A.C. 1933. *The Theory of Unemployment*. London: Macmillan.

Rosner, Victoria. 2014. Introduction. In *The Cambridge Companion to the Bloomsbury Group*, ed. Victoria Rosner. Cambridge and New York, NY: Cambridge University Press.

Say, Jean-Baptiste. 1834 [1803]. *A Treatise on Political Economy*, 6th American ed., trans. C.R. Prinsep. Philadelphia: Grigg & Elliot.

Skidelsky, Robert. 2009. *Keynes*. New York: PublicAffairs.

Skidelsky, Robert, and Edward Skidelsky. 2012. *How Much Is Enough*. New York: Other Press.

Solow, Robert. 1980. On Theories of Unemployment. *The American Economic Review* 70: 1–11.

Sowell, Thomas. 2016. *Say's Law: An Historical Analysis*. Princeton: Princeton University Press.

Steiger, Otto. 1976. Bertihl Ohlin and the Origins of the Keynesian Revolution. *History of Political Economy* 8: 341–366.

CHAPTER 5

Forging the Consumption Paradigm: A Morally Neutral Moral Crusade

The original thinker and the "-ism" constructed from his works are never the same things. There is daylight—sometimes a lot of it—between Plato and Platonism, Calvin and Calvinism, Descartes and Cartesianism, Malthus and Malthusianism, Darwin and Darwinism. The gap between Keynes and Keynesianism is of great importance to understanding the Consumption paradigm.

The rise of Keynesianism changed Keynes' open moral crusade into a concealed one. Keynes was frank and aggressive in his normative claims, and his corresponding ambition to revolutionize society. The followers who produced Keynesianism as a school of thought maintained his moral crusade. However, his frankness about the crusade did not survive the transition. Keynesianism merged Keynes' social revolution with the rhetoric of moral neutrality that the discipline had inherited from the nineteenth century. Where Keynes was normative, Keynesianism is crypto-normative. It makes moral demands while simultaneously claiming to make no normative demands, out of respect for the positive/normative divide.

We have already seen in previous chapters how extensively normative the discipline of economics is today. Economists regularly tell us what we should or should not do, even as they claim not to. This chapter is the story of how that strange dissonance came to be. Other historical factors were of course at work—the German historicists did not simply vanish after the *methodenstreit*, and did their best to pull the discipline in the direction of normativity. However, Keynesianism proved to be an even greater source of normativity for economics in the English-speaking world.

V. V. Claar and G. Forster, *The Keynesian Revolution and Our Empty Economy*, https://doi.org/10.1007/978-3-030-15808-8_5

The two most important shapers of Keynesianism were Sir John Hicks and Paul Samuelson. Hicks became an authoritative interpreter of Keynes to the profession, providing a defining interpretation of Keynes' landmark work. Hicks took the very difficult text of the *General Theory* and created an intelligible system of economic technique that could be plausibly read as based on Keynes' work. Samuelson contributed additional interpretive work, including the famous Keynesian Cross. At least as important, however, was his role as a textbook author. When Samuelson found Keynesianism, it was discussed almost exclusively among specialized experts. Samuelson made Keynesianism a standard part of economics textbooks for undergraduates, establishing its impact on the discipline as a whole. And Samuelson's textbooks also insisted on the positive/normative distinction, combining Keynes' moral crusade with the rhetoric of moral neutrality.

Two sections in this chapter are significantly more technical than the rest of this book. Readers not interested in following all the technical ins and outs can skip those sections (we have marked them) without loss of continuity.

The Keynesian Revolution, Keynesianism, and the Consumption Paradigm

Keynes' impact on economics as a visionary intellectual and moral revolutionary is unparalleled, simultaneously wide in scope and deep in effect. He redefined the subject, purpose, and methods of economics. That is the Keynesian Revolution in its fullness—a discipline radically transformed, not just in its technical methods, but in its understanding of itself.

By contrast, what economists call "Keynesianism" is more narrowly understood as an economic school defined by certain technical assumptions and methods. This "-ism" emerged only partially from Keynes' own writings. Keynes' works were very difficult to read even for experts. Keynesianism owes at least as much, if not more, to the interpreters and intellectual translators who formulated and proposed theories explaining "what Keynes really meant."

This transition from Keynes to Keynesianism was not the development and refinement of a method introduced by Keynes. It was the creation of an economic method, partly arising from Keynes' own work, but created by his successors. This method would embody Keynes' assumptions and put into practice the moral crusade upon which he launched the discipline of economics.

We must draw some careful distinctions between the Keynesian Revolution, Keynesianism, and what we are calling the Consumption paradigm:

- **The Keynesian Revolution** is a commonly used phrase that refers to a historical series of events through which the influence of Keynes greatly transformed the discipline of economics, including the creation of macroeconomics.
- **Keynesianism** is one school of thought within economics. It stands alongside other schools of thought, most notably what are called the Chicago school and the Austrian school.
- **The Consumption paradigm** is our term for the paradigm that now dominates the discipline of economics in all its major schools of thought, in a manner analogous to the dominance of the Nature, God and Reason paradigms in earlier periods.

We should note two further points.

First, while Keynesianism is not identical to the Keynesian Revolution, the success of Keynesianism was essential to the broader success of the Keynesian Revolution. There could not have been a Keynesian Revolution if Keynes' ideas could not be put into practice in the discipline—if there were not Keynesian methods for conducting Keynesian analysis to produce Keynesian results. But economists reading Keynes' original works did not come away with any clear idea of how to put his ideas into practice. The Keynesianism created by his followers solved that critical problem for Keynes by creating a workable technical method.

Second, it is important to note that economists who are not part of the Keynesian school—even those who are fierce critics of Keynesianism—are nonetheless part of the discipline as transformed by the Keynesian Revolution. They mostly study economics within the Consumption paradigm. To be fair, some of them resist key elements of the paradigm, such as Keynes' embrace of economic planning. But this resistance has not yet involved a comprehensive break with the paradigm as a whole. First steps toward such a break have been taken by some, but that trail has not been followed to its end. We will get into that story more properly in Chapter 7.

John Hicks and Making Sense of Keynes

Hicks' classic 1937 article, "Mr. Keynes and the 'Classics': A Suggested Interpretation," is a standout example of how the academic equivalent of marketing can change the world of ideas (Hicks 1937). Prior to the publication of this essay, economists had struggled to interpret the theory outlined in the *General Theory*. And, as we shall see, Hicks' interpretation wasn't the only influential interpretation of Keynes—though most economists agree that Hicks' interpretation was the most influential.

What Did Keynes Really Mean?

Brian Snowdon and Howard R. Vane write that the debate over what Keynes was really driving at in the *General Theory* remains unsettled. Even Keynesians disagree among themselves regarding what Keynes himself meant, and whether or not the tradition of Keynesianism is really "Keynesian" (Snowdon and Vane 2005, 55). Snowdon and Vane supply a few colorful quotations, including ones from prominent Keynesian economists such as Paul Samuelson and John Kenneth Galbraith:

> *Nobel laureate Robert Lucas:* I still can't read Keynes….I find it carelessly written, not especially gracefully written, sometimes dishonestly written. I don't like the bullying tone. I don't like the sort of British aristocratic stuff….The *General Theory* is a political response to the Depression and to the discrediting of conventional economics that resulted from it. (Klamer 1984, 30, 50, 56)
>
> *Keynes popularizer Paul Samuelson*: It is a badly written book, poorly organized; any layman who, beguiled by the author's previous reputation, bought the book was cheated of his 5 shillings. It is not well suited for classroom use. It is arrogant, bad-tempered, polemical, and not overly-generous in its acknowledgments. It abounds in mares' nests and confusions: involuntary unemployment, wage units, the equality of savings and investment, the timing of the multiplier, interactions of marginal efficiency upon the rate of interest, forced savings, own rates of interest, and many others. In it the Keynesian system stands out indistinctly, as if the author were hardly aware of its existence or cognizant of its properties; and certainly he is at his worst when expounding its relations to its predecessors. Flashes of insight and intuition intersperse tedious algebra. An awkward definition suddenly gives way to an unforgettable cadenza. When it finally is mastered, we find its analysis to be obvious and at the same time new. In short, it is a work of genius. (Samuelson 1946, 190)

> *John Kenneth Galbraith*: The *General Theory* was published long before it was finished. Like the Bible and *Das Kapital*, it is deeply ambiguous, and, as in the case of the Bible and Marx, the ambiguity helped greatly to win converts....When understanding is achieved after much effort, readers hold tenaciously to their belief. The pain, they wish to think, was worthwhile. And if there are enough contradictions and ambiguities, as there are also in the Bible and Marx, the reader can always find something he wants to believe. This too wins disciples. (Galbraith 2001, 233–234)

Indeed, in the preface to the *General Theory*, Keynes explains that the book is the culmination of his lifelong "struggle of escape from habitual modes of thought and expression....The difficulty lies, not in the new ideas, but in escaping the old ones, which ramify, for those brought up as most of us have been, into every corner of our minds" (Keynes 2013, xvi–xvii). In this quote we see especially clearly the power and influence of the Bloomsbury way of thinking in Keynes' approach to macroeconomics: Throwing off naive conventional wisdom in favor of the much clearer insights one can gain if one refuses to be blinded by the preconceptions of prior generations and traditions.

The *General Theory* is in some ways like an ancient text whose meaning is at least partially subject to the interpretation of the reader, and it has had a variety of interpretations since its publication. Snowdon and Vane delineate three, and refer to them as hydraulic Keynesianism, fundamentalist Keynesianism, and modified general-equilibrium Keynesianism (Snowdon and Vane 2005, 70–71). The hydraulic interpretation is by far the one that gained the greatest number of adherents in the first 15 years after the book's publication. It begins with the earliest interpretation: the one provided by Hicks.

Making Keynes Plain

Known primarily for his work in microeconomics, a body of work that led to an eventual Nobel Prize, Hicks provided one of the earliest popular interpretations of the *General Theory*. Though his 1937 paper, "Mr. Keynes and the 'Classics'; A Suggested Interpretation," gave the *General Theory* the shove that would launch a new school of economic thought, Hicks first introduced the book to the profession in a review essay he was invited to contribute to the *Economic Journal* (Hicks 1936). This was a daunting undertaking for Hicks: The general editor of the

Economic Journal from 1912 to 1944 was none other than Keynes himself! (Royal Economic Society 2018). But beyond this, Hicks faced enormous time pressure to get the review in. The *General Theory* came out in January of 1936; according to Hicks's own recollection in an interview with Arjo Klamer, Hicks was asked to deliver the review to the journal by April! In the same interview, Hicks confides that being invited to write that review was "one of the greatest honors I have received," even to the extent that he views it as a greater honor than his Nobel Prize. Hicks believed he was selected to write the review because the journal editors thought he "was not a member of their gang but could be relied upon to take the book seriously" (Klamer 1984, 176–177).

But there may have been another factor in the anointing of Hicks to write the review of the *General Theory* for the readers of the *Economic Journal*, the members of the Royal Economic Society. Daniel B. Klein and Ryan Daza suggest that, while Hicks was reluctant to weigh in on any particular judgments regarding economic policy actions, Hicks had nevertheless been thinking—prior to the publication of the *General Theory*—along quite similar lines. They quote Hicks as saying:

> I was aware, before I left [the London School of Economics] in 1935, and before the appearance of Keynes's General Theory, at the beginning of 1936, that the direction in which my mind was moving was not dissimilar to his. (He told me so himself, in some correspondence I had with him). (Klein and Ryan Daza 2013, 370–371)

Thus it appears that Keynes was aware that Hicks's thinking at the time was evolving in ways similar to Keynes' own.

Klein and Daza suggest that Hicks's attraction to Keynesian modes of thinking was neither an immediate conversion nor even a gradual one, and perhaps not even a lasting one. Young Hicks may have very well been a social democrat, then shifted for a time in the direction of Hayekian classical liberalism, only to drift away from that perspective by the mid-1930s. But identifying precisely when these shifts may have taken place is challenging because, as noted above, Hicks wrote little that conveyed clearly his opinion on matters of economic policy. Nevertheless, regardless of where Hicks might have been ideologically when the *General Theory* was published, David Laidler contends that "these two papers [the review essay and "Mr. Keynes and the Classics"] helped to set monetary economics moving in what Hicks later came to regard as the wrong direction" (Laidler 1990, 481).

By the time Hicks presented a draft version of "Mr. Keynes and the Classics" at the September 1936 meetings of the Econometric Society, he had quite an impact. As Hicks explains it in talking to Klamer, at that point not many economists had picked up the book, and the ones who had most likely had given it only a cursory glance (Klamer 1984, 177). So the perceived novelty of Keynes, at least as Hicks interpreted him, owed much to Hicks. The paper was a big hit, and graduate students in economics read it even today.

What was it about "Mr. Keynes and the Classics" that made it so influential in conveying Keynesianism? Hicks provided the most intelligible interpretation of the book available at the time. And he didn't take 384 pages of terse text to expound it, as Keynes had. He reduced it to a mere 16 pages. More than that, Hicks supplied something altogether novel: a diagram. Keynes had included diagrams of his own in the *General Theory*, but none that so conveniently condensed so much of the book into a single diagram as Hicks did with his *IS–LM* diagram. (Hicks' original version used the label *LL* rather than the *LM* we use now.)

Whether or not the *IS–LM* diagram accurately captured what Keynes was getting at in the *General Theory*, it added an elegance of presentation the book itself had lacked. Hicks' diagram was used to teach Keynesian economics throughout the period from the 1940s to the 1970s (Leijonhufvud 1998, 1002). The *IS–LM* diagram is sometimes referred to as the "Hicks-Hansen" diagram, to convey that it is Hicks' model, augmented by refinements later added by Alvin Hansen.

One simply cannot overstate how influential the Hicks-Hansen *IS–LM* model has been in the teaching of macroeconomics since Keynes, as well as the actual modeling macroeconomists engage in when assessing policy. As Axel Leijonhufvud observes, "*IS-LM* became…not only the vehicle for popularizing Keynesian ideas and the mainstay of macroeconomic textbooks but, for several decades, the main organizing conception for macroeconomics in general. Even the very large macroeconometric models of several hundred equations were generally disaggregated *IS-LM* structures" (Leijonhufvud 1998, 1002).

The *IS–LM* Diagram

This is a technical section. Readers not interested in following the technical argument may skip to the next section without loss of continuity.

The *IS–LM* diagram contains two curves, the *IS* curve and the *LM* curve. The *IS* curve depicts each possible combination of the interest rate, *r*, and the level of output and income, *Y*, that represents equilibrium in the goods and services market. The equation that underlies the graphical *IS* relationship equates national income with all of the spending carried out by the eventual purchasers of the goods and services that earned that income by producing those goods and services. If we assume no foreign sector, the *IS* equation is simply

$$Y = C(Y - T) + I(r) + G,$$

which says that national income is equal to national expenditure by households on consumption goods (*C*) plus expenditures by firms on capital goods (*I*) and government purchases of goods and services (*G*). In this formulation, we take government purchases as exogenously determined, i.e. not dependent on other variables in our formula (perhaps set by prior budgetary appropriations). We assume there is an inverse relationship between the interest rate, *r*, and the level of capital investment by firms. And we assume household expenditures on consumption goods are positively influenced by increases in disposable income, represented by the difference between total income *Y* and the net taxes paid by households, *T*.

Because increases in the interest rate, *r*, will lead to a decrease in new projects by firms, it follows that there is an inverse relationship between the interest rate and national income. Thus, if the interest rate is on the vertical axis and the national income is on the horizontal axis, the *IS* curve is drawn with a negative slope, as depicted in Fig. 5.1.

The *LM* curve represents equilibrium in the money market, tracing out the various combinations of the interest rate, *r*, and national income, *Y*, that equate the supply of money to the demand for it. (We assume the supply of money is exogenously determined.) Or, to use Keynes' language, the *LM* curve equates the supply of money to the current liquidity preference of individuals to hold their wealth in a monetary form rather than in an interest-bearing asset such as bonds. We assume that the supply of money is exogenously determined by the central bank. Thus the *LM* equation may be expressed as

$$\frac{M}{P} = L(r, Y),$$

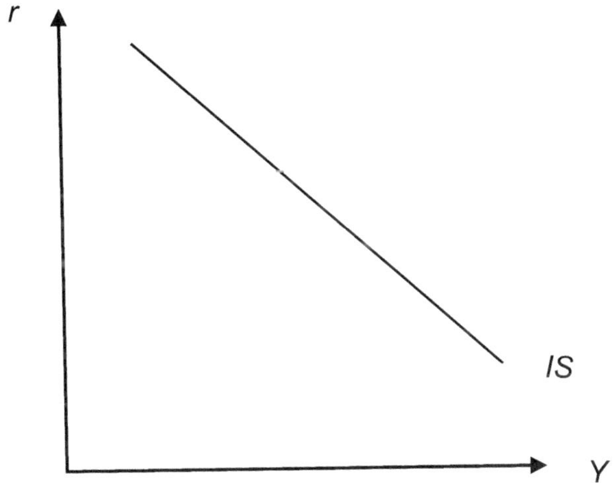

Fig. 5.1 The *IS* Curve (*Note* This figure is a creation of the authors' based upon the *IS* equation (see text))

where the left-hand side represents the real supply of money, which is the number of dollars in the money supply, *M*, in light of how high or low the level of prices (*P*) is. If prices are low that increases the real purchasing power of each dollar in the money supply, and vice versa. On the right-hand side we have a liquidity-preference (i.e. money demand) function, where the quantity of real money demanded is a function of both households' incomes and also the rate of interest. We assume higher rates of interest on non-monetary assets like bonds will reduce the demand for money, since it bears no interest. Regarding the relationship between national income and the demand for money, we assume that as household incomes rise, people will want to hold higher monetary balances on average in order to finance additional expenditures. This is still true in the electronic-payments world of 2018, since economists generally consider the funds in your "checking" account as part of your money holding, inasmuch as your checking account is used mainly to finance payments (though now likely through your debit card rather than your checkbook) and also because checkable deposits rarely pay much interest compared to alternative assets. Since at any moment in time we take the left-hand side of the equation (the real money supply) as given, it figures

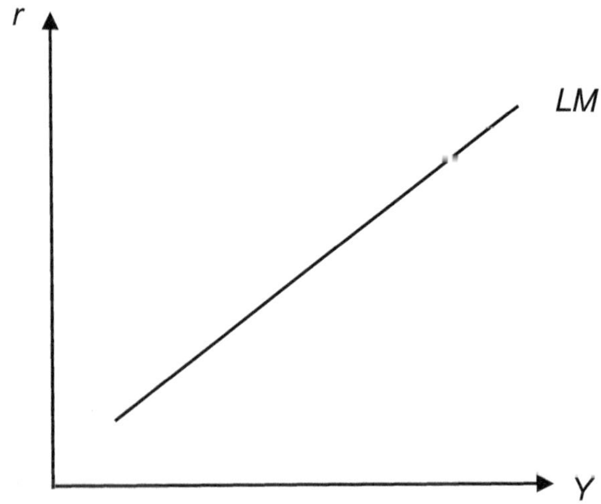

Fig. 5.2 The *LM* Curve (*Note* This figure is a creation of the authors' based upon the *LM* equation (see text))

that to maintain the equality between the (fixed) value on the left-hand side and the amount of money people wish to hold on the right, *Y* and *r* must be positively related. For example, suppose national income *Y* rises. Now recall that we assumed that as incomes rise, people wish to hold greater monetary balances. Given our assumption that the supply of money is exogenously determined by the monetary authority and held fixed, the increased demand for money in the face of a fixed supply of it will put upward pressure on the rate of interest. This leads to an *LM* curve that has a positive slope as depicted in Fig. 5.2.

Like most diagrams in economics, the two curves are most useful when combined in the same diagram, as depicted in Fig. 5.3. At the intersection point, we can identify the unique combination of the rate of interest and the level of output/income that equates the supply of and demand for goods and serves, as well as the supply of and demand for money. This is why one can think of the *IS–LM* model as a "general equilibrium" model: it brings several markets into equilibrium simultaneously. In this case, it represents general equilibrium throughout the economy.

Armed with this basic background, we are now positioned to model a recession and a suggested Keynesian policy response. Consider Fig. 5.4.

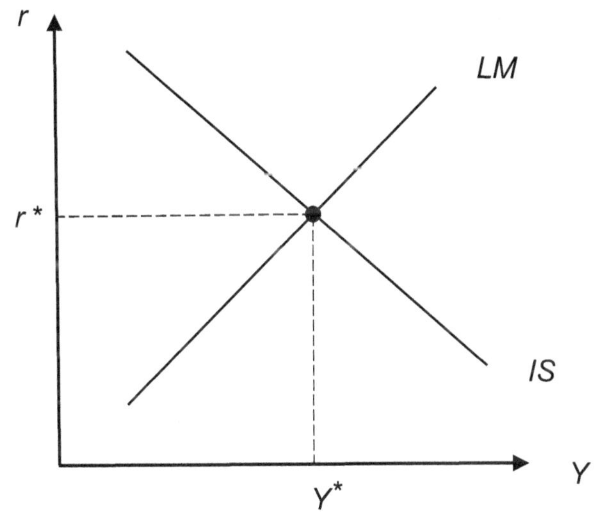

Fig. 5.3 The *IS–LM* diagram (*Note* This figure is a creation of the authors' based upon the *IS* and *LM* equations (see text))

We see a leftward shift of the *IS* curve—perhaps because Keynes' animal spirits have made firms more pessimistic about the future and, as a consequence, less inclined to borrow money at every rate of interest. If so that reduces investment demand (I), results in layoffs in those firms and industries that would have produced those capital goods otherwise, and the laid-off workers now reduce their own spending levels, too. Once the economy has settled following that initial shock, we find we are now in a recession: less total output and income, and lower interest rates due to the decrease in the demand for loanable funds by firms. We depict this shock and the eventual new equilibrium in Fig. 5.4, where the new *IS* curve lies to the left of the original one, and where the new intersection of the original *LM* curve and the new *IS* curve lies at a lower level of output and at a lower rate of interest. This is what a Keynesian recession looks like.

Prior to the wave of pessimism the economy had been at point A. But given the reduction in spending on capital goods by firms, the ensuing layoffs, and the smaller paychecks of laid-off workers, the economy

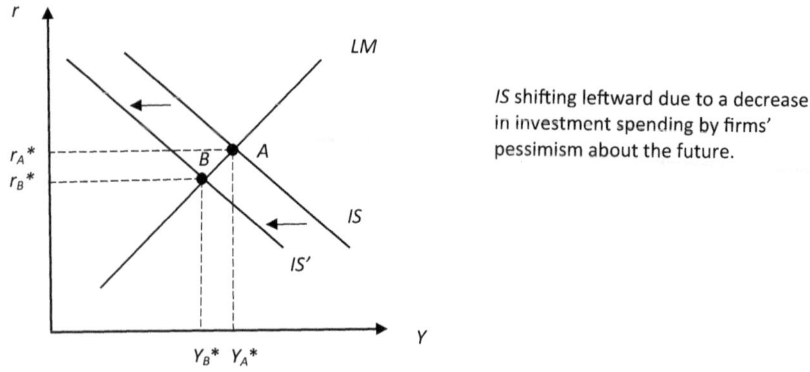

Fig. 5.4 A Keynesian recession (*Note* This figure is a creation of the authors' based upon the *IS* and *LM* equations (see text))

eventually rests at its new general equilibrium, point B—where the level of output is lower than it had been previously.

Given that our model economy is now in an animal-sprits-driven recession, how does it get out? Well, supposedly one could wait until firms develop rosy feeling about the future and begin to invest again. But that might take some time, and as good Keynesians, we know that in the long run, we're all dead. So a hydraulic Keynesian wants to end the recession by pushing the *IS* curve back where it came from. But if firms remain pessimistic, and households have less income due to recession-driven layoffs, where will the additional spending come from to offset the decrease in spending by pessimistic firms? The formula itself tells us. If people think that neither *C* nor *I* will increase soon, there's only one sector left on the right-hand side of the *IS* curve to turn to: *G*, government spending. If politicians exactly offset the initial reduction in investment spending by firms with an increase in government purchases of goods and services, politicians can push that pesky *IS* curve back precisely where it came from and restore the economy to point A, with higher levels of output and income, and more people working again.

Hicks, Chief of the Macro Tribe

After Hicks gave economists an easy way to understand what "Keynesianism" meant, the Keynesian Revolution was enthusiastically embraced by young economists first in England, then America. That it was the young who were more likely to contract the Keynesian fever is a theme among many histories of this process (Stein 1969, 163). Nobel laureate and Keynesian economist James Tobin, who earned his bachelor's, master's, and doctoral degrees from Harvard in 1935–1947, reflects upon the Keynesian youth movement as he observed it as an undergraduate at Harvard: "Keynes's uprising against encrusted error was an appealing crusade for youth. The truth would make us free, and fully employed, too" (Breit and Hirsch 2009, 97). In Tobin's words: "Harvard was becoming the beachhead for the Keynesian invasion of the new world. The senior faculty were mostly hostile….The younger faculty and the graduate student teaching fellows were enthusiastic about Keynes's book" (Breit and Hirsch 2009, 98). Nicholas Wapshott records that the anticipation of the publication of the *General Theory* was so great among the Harvard undergraduates that they placed advance orders for it in 1935 so that the moment it was printed they would be the first in the Americas to read it (Wapshott 2011, 167). Samuelson sums up the spread of Keynesian fever among the young: "The *General Theory* caught most economists under the age of 35 with the unexpected virulence of a disease first attaching and decimating an isolated tribe of South Sea Islanders. Economists beyond 50 turned out to be quite immune to the ailment" (Samuelson 1946, 187).

One older economist who did embrace Keynes as translated by Hicks, with enormous consequences, was Hansen. As we have noted, the *IS–LM* diagram is called the "Hicks-Hansen" diagram. It was Hansen who did the most to bring Keynesian ideas across the pond to the new world. As economic thought historian Mark Blaug has put it, "Alvin Hansen did more than any other economist to bring the Keynesian revolution to America" (Blaug 1985, 79). His 1941 *Fiscal Policy and Business Cycles* as well as his 1953 *A Guide to Keynes* cemented his reputation as the greatest American scholarly interpreter and communicator of Keynes; he is sometimes called "the American Keynes." Samuelson was his graduate student.

The legacy of the *IS–LM* diagram in marketing what was perceived to be Keynes' thinking, and was actually Hicks' gloss on Keynes, is critical. To understand its influence, consider a satirical essay published by Leijonhufvud in 1973, roughly 38 years after the publication of the *General Theory* and 37 years after the publication of "Mr. Keynes and the 'Classics.'"

In the essay, "Life Among the Econ," he describes the members of the economics profession as though they are primitive tribal peoples. Leijonhufvud plays the role of the anthropologist who has made studying the curious "Econ" tribe his life's work. He differentiates "castes" among the Econ, with the primary distinction being one between the "Micro" and the "Macro": "While the Micro assert their superiority over the Macro, so do the Macro theirs over the Micro, and third parties are found to have no very determined, or at least no unanimous, opinion on the matter" (Leijonhufvud 1973, 329).

Further on in the essay, Leijonhufvud explains the totems of the two castes, "Micro" and "Macro":

> To the untrained eye, the totems of major castes will often look well-nigh identical. It is the great social significance attached to these minor differences by the Econ themselves that have made Econography (the study of Econ arts and handicrafts) the central field of modern Econology. As an illustration, consider the totems of the Micro and the Macro. Both could be roughly described as formed by two carved sticks joined together in the middle somewhat in the form of a pair of scissors. (cf. Fig. 5.5)
>
> Certain ceremonies connected with these totems are of great interest to us because of the indications that they give about the origin of modelmaking among the Econ. Unfortunately, we have only fragmentary accounts by various travelers of these ceremonies and the interpretations of what they have seen that these untrained observers essay are often in conflict. Here, a systematic study is very much needed.
>
> The following sketchy account of the "prospecting"-ceremony among the Macro brings out several of the riddles that currently perplex Econologists working in this area:
>
> The elder grasps the LM with his left hand and the IS with his right and, holding the totem out in front of himself with elbows slightly bent, proceeds in a straight line – "gazing neither left nor right" in the words of their ritual – out over the chosen terrain. The grads of the village skip gaily around him at first, falling silent as the trek grows longer and more wearisome. On this occasion, it was long indeed and the terrain difficult … the grads were strung out in a long, morose and bedraggled chain behind their leader who, sweat pearling his brow, face cast in grim determination, stumbled onward over the obstacles in his path… At long last, the totem vibrates, then oscillates more and more; finally, it points, quivering, straight down. The elder waits for the grads to gather round and then pronounces, with great solemnity: "Behold, the Truth and Power of the Macro". (Leijonhufvud 1973, 331–332)

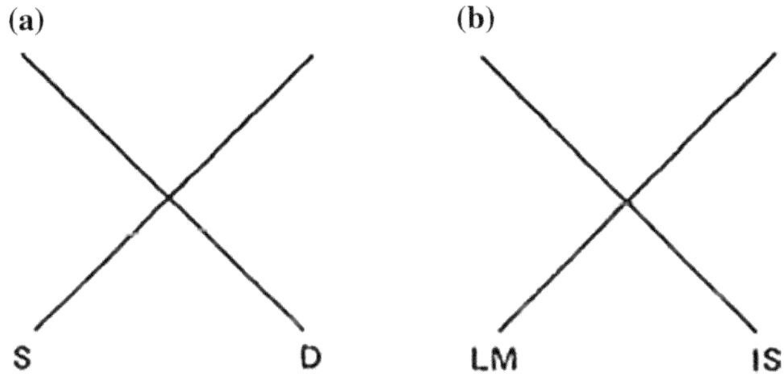

Fig. 5.5 Totems of the Micro and Macro (Copyright 1973 Western Economic Association. Reprinted with permission)

Clearly, at this point in the history of economic thought, Leijonhufvud considered the *IS–LM* diagram among the "Macro" to be just as defining as the supply-demand diagram is to the "Micro." As anyone who has taken Econ 101 knows, the supply-demand diagram lies at the dead center of microeconomics. To say that the *IS–LM* diagram occupies an analogous position in macroeconomics is to convey a sense of how important Hicks was to the emergence of Keynesianism.

Paul Samuelson Popularizes Keynes

If "Mr. Keynes and the 'Classics'" succeeded in winning over professional economists to the Keynesian way of thinking about economies and the individual actors within them, Samuelson's textbook *Economics: An Introductory Analysis*, whose first edition was published in 1948, introduced Keynes to generations of students in colleges and universities. Students from disciplines across the university, who had no intention of taking another econ course after the introductory level, got Keynesianism from Samuelson. Students who went on to make economics their profession assimilated Keynesianism as one of the first steps into the discipline, setting the framework for what would come after. With coauthor William Nordhaus, who joined the byline in 1985, the 2010 edition of *Economics* is the book's 19th edition.

Table 5.1 Publishing history of Samuelson's *Economics*

Edition number	*Year of publication*	*Copies sold*
1st	1948	121,453
2nd	1951	137,236
3rd	1955	191,706
4th	1958	273,036
5th	1961	331,163
6th	1964	441,941
7th	1967	389,673
8th	1970	328,123
9th	1973	303,795
10th	1976	317,188
11th	1980	196,185
12th	1985	N/A
13th	1989	N/A
14th	1992	N/A
15th	1995	N/A

Data source Kenneth G. Elzinga, "The Eleven Principles of Economics," *Southern Economic Journal* 58 (1992): 861–879

Kenneth Elzinga supplies sales numbers for the book from its initial publication through its decline due to the rational-expectations revolution coming out of the University of Chicago in the 1970s. The figures are summarized in Table 5.1.

The book has sold a total of over four million copies over its run (Chiang 2017, 91). When one remembers that new textbooks get resold over and over again in the used textbook market, the impact of Samuelson is staggering.

But Samuelson's book was also the model for generations of new textbooks to come. Until very recently, most books that succeeded Samuelson were using Samuelson as a starting point.

The success and impact of Samuelson is legendary. Referring to the $1.4 million advance his company paid to Harvard's N. Gregory Mankiw to write a new textbook, executive editor Paul Shensa said: "Every economics editor in the business has been looking for the new Samuelson since the 1970s" (Nasar 1995).

Another indicator of his impact is how quickly Samuelson was awarded what is popularly known as the Nobel Prize for economics, and the Nobel Endowment's lavish praise for how wide his influence had been.[1] The economics prize is relatively new, compared to the original Nobel prizes; the Nobel Foundation had given prizes in all of Alfred Nobel's original categories by 1901, but the economics prize was not given until 1969. In that year, the prize was shared by two European economists: Norway's Ragnar Frisch and Jan Tinbergen from the Netherlands. But in 1970, the second year the prize was given, its recipient was a lone American economist: Paul Samuelson. He was awarded the prize on grounds that "his work influences practically all branches of modern economics" (Nobel Media AB 2019).

A Morally Neutral Moral Tract

Samuelson's textbook was ground zero for one of the most important developments of the Consumption paradigm: its combination of the nineteenth-century rhetoric of moral neutrality with Keynes' vision of economics as a moral crusade. Even as discussion and debate about Keynes' ideas had been raging among specialists, the discipline at large had continued to describe itself as positive and not normative. Naturally, one of the most important places where a discipline describes itself is in its introductory textbooks. Samuelson's textbook carried on this practice, explaining the positive/normative distinction to students and asserting that the discipline of economics is concerned only with the positive. At the same time, he advocated the policy conclusions demanded by the Keynesian project. Thus the original nature of those policies—a revolutionary aspiration to remake society in accordance with a new moral vision in which gratifying consumer appetites is the highest aspiration of human endeavor—was concealed.

In an insightful discussion of the philosophy of the positive/normative distinction in economics, Will Heath used Samuelson's textbook as a representative example of the discipline's prevailing view (Heath 1994). Heath quotes the following from the Samuelson textbook (in one of the later, co-authored editions):

[1] Unlike the other "Nobel" prizes awarded each year, the economics prize is not funded through the initial endowment given by Alfred Nobel. The official name of the prize is the Sveriges Riskbank Prize in Economic Sciences in Memory of Alfred Nobel. It was established in 1968 by a gift from the Sveriges Riksbank—Sweden's central bank—to the Nobel Foundation on the occasion of the 300th anniversary of the bank.

> Positive economics describes the facts and behavior in the economy. What are the causes of poverty in the United States? What will be the effect of higher cigarette taxes on smokers? How has the economic performance of socialist countries compared with that of capitalist countries? These questions can be resolved only by reference to facts … they are all in the realm of positive economics.
>
> Normative economics involves ethical precepts and value judgments. Should the government give money to poor people? Should the budget deficit be reduced by higher taxes or lower spending? Should the socialist countries introduce private property and stock markets? These issues can be debated, but they can never be settled by science or by appeal to facts. There are no right or wrong answers to these questions because they involve ethics and value judgments rather than facts. (Heath 1994)

Heath correctly characterizes this as "a fairly standard view" (Heath 1994).

Yet Mark Skousen shows, in a careful review of the textbook's content as it developed through multiple editions, that it was far from neutral when it came to how our economies ought to be organized. Skousen reviews 15 editions, from the first edition in 1948 through the fifteenth edition published in 1995. He traces the ways the text evolved after its initial publication, responding either to current events or new advances in economics.

It's important to note that Samuelson's textbook isn't exclusively a textbook in macroeconomics. Like most introductory textbooks in economics, it considers both microeconomics—the study of decisions and actions taken at the individual, household or company level—and macroeconomics. Organized that way, the book can be used in a two-semester course sequence at any college or university, with "micro" covered in one term and "macro" covered in the other. Because not all students take both courses, most publishing companies also issue "splits": shorter books that contain only the micro or macro portions of the full volume. But because we are focused here mainly on the influence of Keynes on the discipline we will direct our attention mainly to the macro portions of Samuelson's text, assessing what made it both so Keynesian in its approach and also so influential more generally. To this end we will rely heavily on Skousen's meta-analysis of the first 15 editions of the book, including editions that included William Nordhaus as coauthor (editions 12–15, published in 1985–1995).

Samuelson himself, in the introduction to the fourteenth edition, suggests that such an undertaking might prove worthwhile: "A historian of mainstream-economic doctrines, like a paleontologist who studies the bones and fossils in different layers of earth, could date the ebb and flow of ideas by analyzing how Edition 1 was revised to Edition 2 and, eventually, to Edition 14" (Skousen 1997).

Before diving into his analysis, Skousen reminds us that the seeds of economic thinking that are planted during one's study of economics have lasting consequences for broader society:

> Looking back at Samuelson's text is like looking into a mirror that reflects many of our past beliefs. If we are uncomfortable with some of what we see in the mirror, then we must also feel uncomfortable with the version of economics that was taught, and perhaps also uncomfortable with the impact that the teaching of economics may have had on the economy. (p. 138)

Samuelson understood this too, and says as much in the front matter to the seventh edition:

> When the election of 1984 rolls around, all the hours that the artists and editors and I have spent in making the pages as informative and authentic as possible will see to me well spent if somewhere a voter turns to the old book from which he learned economics for a rereasoning of the economic principle involved. (Skousen 1997, 150)

Samuelson has also famously quipped: "I don't care who writes a nation's laws—or crafts its advanced treaties—if I can write its economics textbooks" (Nasar 1995). Sylvia Nasar quotes Worth editor Paul Shensa: "economists are prosyletizers" (Nasar 1995).

The Samuelson textbook does not just describe, but advocates Keynesianism. Admittedly, the line between describing a view and advocating it can be hard to define. Some allowance can be made for the fact that no textbook author perfectly conceals the author's biases.

However, in his review, Skousen comes down firmly for the view that Samuelson is a Keynesian evangelist. He points to a variety of evidence for this interpretation. The first several editions contained a biographical sketch of only one influential economist: John Maynard Keynes, whom Samuelson refers to as a "many-sided genius" (Skousen 1997, 139). The Keynesian Cross was printed on the cover of the first three editions. The macro half of the book actually preceded the micro portion—an approach that was novel at the time, signaling not only a reversal of priorities, but the extent to which incorporating the new macroeconomics as one half of the discipline was demanding that economists rethink the entire discipline (both halves).

Samuelson portrays hydraulic Keynesianism as settled science, even in the 1948 edition. He says Keynesian expenditure theories are "increasingly accepted by economists of all schools of thought," and that most of the consequent policy prescriptions were "neutral" (Skousen 1997, 139).

Even before publishing his first edition, Samuelson already understood the power of Keynes to fundamentally change the trajectory of future textbooks. In 1946, reflecting on the decade since the publication of the *General Theory*, Samuelson notes:

> Instead of burning out like a fad, today ten years after its birth the *General Theory* is still gaining adherents and appears to be in business to stay. Many economists who are most vehement in criticism of the specific Keynesian policies – which must always be carefully distinguished from the scientific analysis associated with his name – will never again be the same after passing through his hands….
>
> It is perhaps not without additional significance in appraising the long-run prospects of the theories that no individual who has once embraced the modern analysis has – as far as I am aware – later returned to the older theories. And in universities where graduate students are exposed to the old and new…analysis, I am told that it is often only too clear which way the wind blows.
>
> Finally, and perhaps most important from the long-run standpoint [*sic*], the Keynesian analysis has begun to filter down into the elementary textbooks; and as everybody knows once an idea gets into these, however bad it may be, it becomes practically immortal. (Samuelson 1946, 188–189)

One can see the truth of Samuelson's reflections in an excerpt from his 2009 *New York Times* obituary. Not only did Samuelson influence Keynesian thinking during the middle of the twentieth century, but his legacy lives on well into the present day:

> The textbook introduced generations of students to the revolutionary ideas of John Maynard Keynes, the British economist who in the 1930s developed the theory that modern market economies could become trapped in depression and would then need a strong push from government spending or tax cuts, in addition to lenient monetary policy, to

restore them. Many economics students would never again rest comfortably with the 19th-century view that private markets would cure unemployment without need of government intervention.

That lesson was reinforced in 2008, when the international economy slipped into the steepest downturn since the Great Depression, when Keynesian economics was born. When the Depression began, governments stood pat or made matters worse by trying to balance fiscal budgets and erecting trade barriers. But 80 years later, having absorbed the Keynesian teaching of Mr. Samuelson and his followers, most industrialized countries took corrective action, raising government spending, cutting taxes, keeping exports and imports flowing and driving short-term interest rates to near zero. (Weinstein 2009)

Samuelson's role as an advocate was almost inevitable. He fell madly and deeply in love with the *General Theory*. We don't need to speculate about that. Samuelson says so himself in 1946, two years prior to the publication of his textbook:

I have always considered it a priceless advantage to have been born as an economist prior to 1936 and to have received a thorough grounding in classical economics. It is quite impossible for modern students to realize the full effect of what has been advisably called 'The Keynesian Revolution' upon those of us brought up in the orthodox tradition. What beginners today often regard as trite and obvious was to us puzzling, novel, and heretical. To have been born as an economist before 1936 was a boon – yes. But not to have been born too long before!

'Bliss was it in that dawn to be alive,

But to be young was very heaven!'The *General Theory* caught most economists under the age of 35 with the unexpected virulence of a disease first attacking and decimating an isolated tribe of south sea islanders. Economists beyond 50 turned out to be quite immune to the ailment. With time, most economists in between began to run the fever, often without knowing or admitting their condition. (Samuelson 1946, 187)

Nasar reports that Samuelson, despite his claim in the third edition that he didn't have any "single Great Message" (p. 3) in mind, was a dedicated Keynesian evangelist working tirelessly on the first edition:

> Without an advance or, for that matter, any publishing deal at all, he labored for three years while teaching at the Massachusetts Institute of Technology to turn the novel ideas of Lord Keynes into breezy prose, crystalline examples and simple diagrams. (Nasar 1995)

It is to the most famous of those diagrams we now turn: the Keynesian Cross.

The Keynesian Cross

This is a technical section. Readers not interested in following the technical argument may skip to the next section without loss of continuity.

Where Hicks simplified Keynes into the *IS–LM* diagram, Samuelson's Keynesian Cross diagram further simplified Hicks' representation of the *IS* relationship. Even today, economics professors can quickly assess "how Keynesian" a new textbook is by simply flipping through the pages of the book and asking two questions: Does it have a Keynesian Cross? If so, can the chapter that contains it be omitted without losing other essential material?

Recall that the *IS* equation represents equilibrium in the market for goods and services according to a national income identity, stating the nation's total expenditure in a given period is equal to the value of the income earned by the producers of those goods and services:

$$Y = C(Y - T) + I(r) + G.$$

In this formula, we assume the interest rate, r, is currently fixed.

We illustrate the Keynesian Cross in Fig. 5.6.

The main message of the Keynesian Cross lies in its slope. Notice that neither the spending plans of firms (I) nor government (G) is influenced by the size of GDP (Y). So the only channel in the *IS* relationship that relates buying plans in the economy to the level of income is the consumption term. The slope of the $C+I+G$ line is driven exclusively by what Keynes referred to as the "marginal propensity to consume": the fraction of each dollar of additional income households will devote to new spending of their own. Should the spending plans of firms increase due to increased optimism, or should government decide to purchase more goods and services, then the $C+I+G$ line will shift upward so it will be parallel to the original line. This means that any autonomous

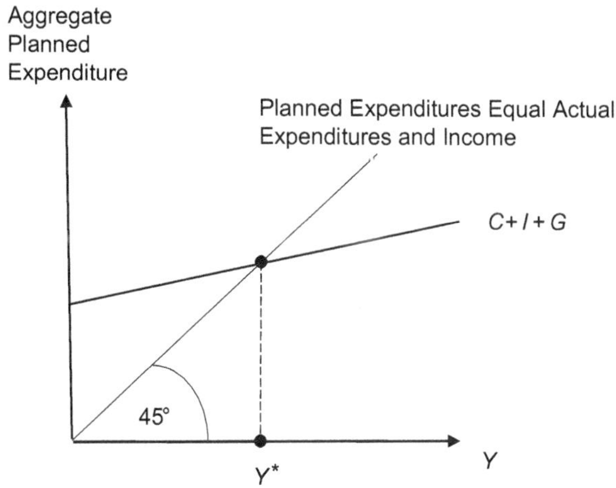

Fig. 5.6 Samuelson's Keynesian Cross (*Note* This figure is a creation of the authors' based upon the *IS* equation (see text))

increase in either investment or government spending will increase the total level of output by more than the initial increase in spending.

Economists refer to this impact as the expenditure multiplier. The intuition is straightforward. If government decides to buy more staplers, the stapler company will need to increase its number of workers. With the additional income now being paid out by the stapler company, those workers engage in further spending activities of their own, which will lead to more employment in other sectors as well as more household income. Via these ripple effects from the initial increase in government expenditure, the total impact on national income will be a multiple of the initial increase in spending.

The magnitude of that multiplier is determined by the marginal propensity to consume. The more inclined households are to consume their additional income rather than save it (that is, the steeper the slope of the $C+I+G$ line), the greater the overall impact of any attempts to stimulate the economy via fiscal expenditures.

Which leads to a second major distinctive of Samuelson: the paradox of thrift.

Samuelson Christens the Paradox of Thrift

As we have seen in Chapter 4, Keynes argues in the *General Theory* that more saving is not necessarily beneficial for the aggregate economy. Saving today can actually have the paradoxical effect of reducing overall saving if today's additional saving comes at the cost of foregone consumption, thereby reducing incomes for others throughout the economy and reducing their levels of saving as well.

Keynes did not exactly get this idea across in the clearest possible terms. As he wrote:

> The reconciliation of the identity between saving and investment with the apparent "free-will" of the individual to save what he chooses irrespective of what he or others may be investing, essentially depends on saving being, like spending, a two-sided affair. For although the amount of his own saving is unlikely to have any significant influence on his own income, the reactions of the amount of his consumption on the incomes of others makes it impossible for all individuals simultaneously to save any given sums. Every such attempt to save more by reducing consumption will so affect incomes that the attempt necessarily defeats itself. It is, of course, just as impossible for the community as a whole to save *less* than the amount of current investment, since the attempt to do so will necessarily raise incomes to a level at which the sums which individuals choose to save add up to a figure exactly equal to the amount of investment. (Keynes 2013, 84; italics in original)

Clear as daylight!

Samuelson coined and popularized the term "paradox of thrift," which frames the basic idea in a clear and intuitive way, with the publication of the first edition of his textbook. He calls it a paradox because it clashes with one of the most widely held and economically important moral norms in society, a norm held by Nature, God and Reason paradigms alike:

> The "paradox of thrift" is a paradox because in kindergarten we are all taught that thrift is always a good thing. Benjamin Franklin's *Poor Richard's Almanac* never tired of preaching the doctrine of saving….What is good for each person separately need not be good for all; under some circumstances, private prudence may be social folly. Specifically, this means that the attempt of each and every person to increase his saving may… result in a reduction in actual saving by all the community. (Samuelson 1948, 270–271)

Samuelson had connected Keynes' idea to something that was familiar and psychologically important to the average person.

"Paradox of thrift" rendered this idea much more powerful in policy conversations than the concept alone would have been without this highly effective brand name. Most of us tend to think of the habit of personal saving as something virtuous: resisting the temptation of immediate gratification, and foregoing present consumption for the sake of even greater consumption possibilities in the future, as well as resources upon which to draw in the event of an unforeseeable "rainy day." Yet in Samuelson's first edition, and somewhat echoing Bernard Mandeville's "Fable of the Bees," Samuelson comes close to making it sound like a private virtue (personal saving) may in fact "become a social vice" (Mandeville 1998, 253).

In multiple editions, including the first, Samuelson directs his criticism of "excess" saving to those with the greatest ability to do so, the wealthy. He portrays that view as a justification for progressive taxation: "To the extent that dollars are taken from frugal wealthy people rather than from poor ready spenders, progressive taxes tend to keep purchasing power and jobs at a high level" (Samuelson 1948, 174).

The Moral Crusade Repackaged as "Business as Usual"

Samuelson produced a Keynesian method that could actually guide policy, directly and in detail. Keynes had aspired to remake the world. Samuelson crafted the tools to do it. In the section above on the Keynesian Cross, we walked through how a policymaker could use the Cross to respond to a recession on Keynesian principles.

The Keynesianism refined and popularized by Samuelson, and the Consumption paradigm that it made possible, carried on Keynes' moral crusade to remake the world in the image of his *homo economicus*. In the passage from Samuelson on the paradox of thrift quoted above, note the clearly normative discussion of "what is good" for individuals and for the economy as a whole. Samuelson remarks: "private prudence may be social folly." That is strange language for a supposedly morally neutral discipline.

Critically, Samuelson carried on Keynes' aspiration to remake society. As Skousen shows, the textbook advocates specific, normative views about how society should be organized. These are often presented as mere observations about how the world is in fact being organized, but the normative intent is unmistakable. Samuelson argues that economic growth changes the nature of the social contract: "Our social conscience and humanitarian standards have completely changed" (Skousen 1997, 144). "With affluence come[s] greater interdependence and the desire to meet social needs, along with less need to meet urgent private necessities" (Skousen 1997, 143). This is not neutral observation but political philosophy masquerading as empirical science.

Skousen traces how Samuelson consistently advocates the expansion of state power to control the economy through all 15 editions of the book. This is not limited to advocating expansion of the redistributive and regulatory programs that are routine in liberal economies across a variety of policy areas. That was always an important priority; Skousen traces the many public policy controversies, from price controls on health care to how high taxes should be to how much we should spend on welfare, medical care, retirement, and other transfer programs, upon which the supposedly neutral observer Samuelson advocated his opinions in the textbook (Skousen 1997, 143–146). But beyond this, Samuelson advocated moving toward much more fundamental changes in the nature of the social order.

Starting with the fifth edition in 1961, at a time when Samuelson was an economic advisor to the president of the United States, he displayed a disturbing tendency to advocate the claims of the totalitarian Soviet planned economy. Accepting official Soviet data, Samuelson informed his readers that Soviet growth rates were "considerably greater than ours" (Skousen 1997, 148). Skousen points out that "the fifth through the eleventh editions showed a graph indicating the gap between the United States and the USSR narrowing and possibly even disappearing" (Skousen 1997, 148). The twelfth edition replaced this graph with a table showing the Soviet economy growing at a shocking rate of 4.9% per year between 1928 and 1983 (Skousen 1997, 148).

The thirteenth edition of the textbook was published in the fateful year of 1989. It contained this declaration: "The Soviet economy is proof that, contrary to what many skeptics had earlier believed, a socialist command economy can function and even thrive" (Skousen 1997, 148). That is a statement that would have given pause even in 1929; we struggle for words adequate to characterize its publication in 1989.

After 1989, in which year the slaves of the Soviet tyranny finally began to succeed in removing the spikes of its iron boots from their necks, Samuelson stopped giving full credence to Soviet claims. Question marks appeared next to Soviet economic data in the textbook, so readers would be alerted to the fact that a government that had deliberately killed about 35 million of its own citizens in order to ensure its command economy would "function and even thrive" may not have provided fully trustworthy statistics about its growth rates. Only in 1995 did Samuelson actually remove the laudatory coverage of the Soviet economic miracle, replacing it with a tardy but welcome declaration that communism was a failed model (Skousen 1997, 148).

This is a failure of special significance in the author of the discipline's most influential textbook. Samuelson was, of course, far from the only economist in the English-speaking world who was taken in by the chicanery of Soviet economic statistics and the alluring promise that "a socialist command economy can function and even thrive." But not all economists who saw command economics as plausible were in a position to advocate that plausibility in the top training manual for the formation of our leading economic minds. If too many economists were flirting dangerously with command economics literally right up until the Berlin Wall fell, it was in part because Samuelson taught them to.

As we have seen, even as Samuelson was meditating on the emergence of a new social consciousness and advocating central economic planning, he also continued the nineteenth-century tradition of admonishing young economists that economics is morally neutral. He didn't see himself as a moral crusader, and neither did macroeconomists following his lead in the 1950s and 1960s. They thought they were doing purely positive science, without normative assumptions. It was just business as usual—at least, the new "usual" that was being established by the Keynesian Revolution.

The Keynesian Cross allowed economists to approach policymakers with numbers and formulas, which seemed merely technical and neutral rather than carrying a moral idea. Diagrams and mathematical formulas don't come across as if they were treatises on how society should be organized. But the analysis they embody always begins with moral assumptions.

The data show *X*, the economist says to the policymaker; therefore, to combat the recession, you should change rate *Y* by amount *Z*. In this sentence, the normative word "should" is a Trojan Horse that smuggles in the whole constellation of Keynesian moral assumptions—the new *homo economicus*, instrumental rationality, appetites as ends in themselves, and an elite class that controls and manipulates the lives of ordinary people. The neutral technical expert is a crypto-moralist—a moral crusader in disguise.

References

Blaug, Mark. 1985. *Economic Theory in Retrospect.* Cambridge and New York, NY: Cambridge University Press.

Breit, William, and Barry T. Hirsch (eds.). 2009. *Lives of the Laureates.* Cambridge: MIT Press.

Chiang, Eric P. 2017. *Microeconomics.* New York: Worth.

Galbraith, John Kenneth. 2001. *The Essential Galbraith*, ed. Andrea D. Willams. Boston: Houghton Mifflin.

Heath, Will Carrington. 1994. Value Judgments and the Principles of Economics Textbook. *Southern Economic Journal* 60 (4): 1060–1064.

Hicks, J.R. 1936. Mr. Keynes' Theory of Employment. *Economic Journal* 46: 238–253.

Hicks, J.R. 1937. Mr. Keynes and the 'Classics'; A Suggested Interpretation. *Econometrica* 5: 147–159.

Keynes, John Maynard. 2013 [1936]. *The General Theory of Employment, Interest and Money.* Cambridge: Cambridge University Press.

Klamer, Arjo. 1984. *The New Classical Macroeconomics.* Brighton: Wheatsheaf.

Klein, Daniel B., and Ryan Daza. 2013. John R. Hicks. *Econ Journal Watch* 10: 366–377.

Laidler, David. 1990. Hicks and the Classics: A Review Essay. *Journal of Monetary Economics* 25: 481–489.

Leijonhufvud, Axel. 1973. Life Among the Econ. *Western Economic Journal* 11: 327–337.

Leijonhufvud, Axel. 1998. IS–LM Analysis. In *The New Palgrave: A Dictionary of Economics*, vol. 2, ed. John Eatwell, Murray Milgate, and Peter Newman, 1002–1004. London: Macmillan.

Mandeville, Bernard. 1998. *The Fable of the Bees or Private Vices, Public Benefits*, 2 vols. Indianapolis: Liberty Fund.

Nasar, Sylvia. 1995. A Hard Act to Follow? Here Goes. *New York Times*, March 14.

Nobel Media AB. 2019. Paul A. Samuelson—Facts. https://www.nobelprize.org/prizes/economic-sciences/1970/samuelson/facts/. Accessed on 20 Jan 2019.

Royal Economic Society. 2018. History of the *Economic Journal.* http://www.res.org.uk/view/HistoryEconomicJournal.html. Accessed on 8 Feb 2019.

Samuelson, Paul A. 1946. Lord Keynes and the General Theory. *Econometrica* 14: 187–200.

Samuelson, Paul A. 1948. *Economics.* New York: Mc-Graw Hill.

Skousen, Mark. 1997. The Perseverance of Paul Samuelson's *Economics. Journal of Economic Perspectives* 11: 137–152.

Snowdon, Brian, and Howard R. Vane. 2005. *Modern Macroeconomics: Its Origins, Development, and Current State*. Cheltenham: Edward Elgar.

Stein, Herbert. 1969. *The Fiscal Revolution in America*. Chicago: University of Chicago Press.

Wapshott, Nicholas. 2011. *Keynes Hayek*, 167. New York: W. W. Norton.

Weinstein, Michael M. 2009. Paul A. Samuelson, Economist, Dies at 94. *New York Times*, December 13.

CHAPTER 6

"We Are All Keynesians Now": How the Revolution Transformed Our Economy and Culture

The Consumption paradigm has spread from the academy to the political and cultural structures of our lives. This was accomplished in part by the policy influence of economists. But it also occurred through public discourse. Economic issues are of urgent concern to millions of ordinary people who need help understanding the bewildering complexity of the modern economy; the ideas of economists provide forms and boundaries to the general public discussion of economics. In particular, one economist gained enormous influence by combining macroeconomic ideas derived from Keynes with the sociological ideas of another source, producing a synthesis that was far more culturally potent than either of the originals had been on its own.

The university as an institution was at the height of its influence in American society and culture when the Keynesian Revolution and the Consumption paradigm conquered the academic discipline of economics. To control the boundaries of discourse within an academic discipline will always have a major effect on the workings of society at large in any modern, developed nation. But in the middle of the twentieth century this power was at its peak. Rival sources of authority, such as churches, remained quantitatively large but had lost their earlier levels of power to influence the structure and public discourse of society. The forces that have eaten away at the university's cultural power since that time—intellectual overspecialization, bureaucratic mission dilution, capitulation to student radicalism, ideological rigidity, and entrepreneurial threats from alternative knowledge sources—were all still in the future. From its home

V. V. Claar and G. Forster, *The Keynesian Revolution and Our Empty Economy*, https://doi.org/10.1007/978-3-030-15808-8_6

base in the academy, the Consumption paradigm achieved a breathtaking level of influence over American society.

In the previous chapter, we described a tale of two diagrams: The *IS-LM* diagram and the Keynesian Cross. Hicks used the *IS-LM* diagram to convey his interpretation of the *General Theory* to a generation of economists who either couldn't make sense of the book on their own, or who hadn't picked it up in the first place. Hicks' "Mr. Keynes and the 'Classics'" followed the publication of the *General Theory so* quickly—from February 1936 to April 1937—and the *General Theory* was such a challenging book to digest, that it's likely many serious economists either hadn't fully assimilated the book or hadn't even read it when Hicks appeared to offer a useful shortcut to understanding. Hicks' "hydraulic" interpretation of Keynes became the baseline interpretation from which all other interpretations would be assessed. Then Paul Samuelson moved the conversation about Keynes from an inside debate among specialists to the heart of the discipline, changing the discipline's entire structure by cementing the place of "macro" alongside—and giving a new shape to—"micro." And Samuelson combined the normative prescriptiveness of Keynes with the nineteenth-century rhetoric of moral neutrality, creating a crypto-normative paradigm.

In this chapter, we trace the unfolding influence of this Consumption paradigm on wider public policy and discourse. The broad and sweeping infusion of the paradigm has influenced not only our economic systems, in fiscal and monetary policy, but the way we see ourselves in relation to the economy. Where our prior understanding of economics had always been driven by its usefulness in the pursuit of an intrinsically (i.e. teleologically) good life, today we are more likely to see it as useful in the satisfaction of our consumption appetites.

The Keynesian Revolution Goes Beyond "Keynesianism"

In assessing the social impact of the Keynesian Revolution and the Consumption paradigm it created, it is important to recall the distinction drawn at the beginning of the previous chapter between Keynesianism and the Keynesian Revolution. Keynesianism is a specific school of thought within mainstream economics that exists alongside other schools, most notably the Chicago and Austrian schools. The Keynesian Revolution was a reinvention of the entire discipline of economics, including the creation of Keynesianism but also defining the conditions within which all modern economics is conducted. Where Keynesianism represents one part of mainstream economics, the Keynesian Revolution transformed the entirety of mainstream economics as we now know it.

Our claim in this chapter is not about the policy and cultural influence of Keynesianism, it is about the policy and cultural influence of the much broader Keynesian Revolution and its Consumption paradigm. Keynesianism, the school, has had ups and downs. It would probably be fair to say that over the course of its history, it has been more up than down. But this is beside the point.

In 1965, *Time* magazine quoted University of Chicago economist Milton Friedman—a key founder of the Chicago school and perhaps the most notorious critic of Keynesianism in the popular press for most of the twentieth century—as saying: "We are all Keynesians now." *Time* also noted that Friedman had served as Barry Goldwater's economic advisor and called Friedman "the nation's leading conservative economist" (*Time* 1965, 74ff.).

In one way, this widely quoted quotation didn't get the story quite right. In a letter to *Time*, Friedman said the magazine quoted him correctly, but out of context: "As best I can recall it, the context was: 'In one sense, we are all Keynesians now; in another, nobody is any longer a Keynesian.' The second half is at least as important as the first" (*Time* 1966, 15ff.).

However, in 1968 Friedman himself would make it clear just how profoundly right *Time* had been. While it had botched the quote, it was right in asserting that Keynes and his followers had so thoroughly revolutionized America's economic discourse and systems that even Keynes' strongest critic, an advisor to the most libertarian major-party presidential candidate in American history, was operating within Keynes' paradigm. Offering further clarity on what he meant when he said that we were all Keynesians in one sense but not in another, Friedman wrote: "We all use the Keynesian language and apparatus; none of us any longer accepts the initial Keynesian conclusions" (Friedman 1968, 15). According to Friedman, Keynes and his followers invented the "language and apparatus"—the conceptual framework and the tools of analysis—now used by all economists, and the only differences that have emerged within economics since Keynes arise from the fact that in his early work using these tools, Keynes had not immediately gotten all the conclusions exactly right.

The most important word in Friedman's sentence is "initial." It indicates the real relationship between Keynes and subsequent economics. All economists are now traveling down the road Keynes and his followers put them on. If they differ from Keynes on some particulars, that is only because they have gone further down his road than he did, and have refined his initial conclusions in light of further discoveries within the same paradigm.

The relationship between the Keynesian and Chicago schools will be examined more specifically in the next chapter. Here, the point is to appreciate how extensive was the influence of Keynes and his followers upon public policy and discourse, reshaping the nation's economy, and with it, our understanding of the meaning of our daily lives.

Keynes in His Time: Celebrated, not Obeyed

It was the Keynesian Revolution, not Keynes himself, that accomplished this level of influence. On the contrary, during his lifetime Keynes had little influence on public discourse and even less on public policy. And this was despite the fact that he was a celebrity.

While Keynes is best remembered today for his *General Theory*, it wasn't the *General Theory* that first gained Keynes a public platform. On the contrary, it was Keynes' already-famous name that earned a hearing for the *General Theory*. The book is notoriously difficult to read, and had Keynes been a relative unknown when it was published, it's not clear how much impact it might have made.

We have already seen that Keynes shot to fame with his 1919 *Economics Consequences of the Peace*, and became a member of the highly influential Bloomsbury group. *Economic Consequences* spoke to issues of enormous public importance as the postwar shape of Europe was being determined, and created a sensation. According to Herbert Stein, the book became a sensation for a variety of reasons. It painted harshly critical portraits of the key players involved in the process, attacking major political figures on both personal and policy grounds. The book gained additional fame when the postwar collapse of the German economy and subsequent rise of National Socialism made it appear prophetic to many. Thus, as Stein puts it: "The book established [Keynes] as a person to listen to" (Stein 1969, 134). Stein also notes that, in *Economic Consequences of the Peace*, one can already detect Keynes' wariness of capitalism and its major players—a stance that made Keynes' thinking attractive to many in the intellectual class: Keynes "always saw the society run by bankers, businessmen, and politicians to be in great danger, but he also always saw the possibility of saving the society by listening to the intellectuals" (Stein 1969, 134–135).

Keynes' prior fame helps explain why Hicks' article offering a highly simplified interpretation of the *General Theory* was embraced so quickly, so widely and so conclusively as a functional substitute for the book itself. Because of Keynes' fame, everyone—at least, everyone in economics who specialized in questions like unemployment and interest rates—would have felt intense pressure to digest the book and have an opinion about it. This was a daunting task, for which Hicks provided a welcome shortcut.

Economic Consequences launched Keynes into a successful career publishing books and giving talks on economics, in addition to forays into journalism. He established himself as a major public intellectual:

> Keynes was honored in his own country, even in the 1920s; he was widely read, he was in great demand as a speaker, he was editor of the leading professional academic journal, chairman of the board of a high-prestige magazine, advisor to the Liberal Party, and a member of important government committees. He was honored, but his advice was not taken. (Stein 1969, 141)

Stein's final note that "his advice was not taken" brings us to the irony of Keynes' celebrity. During his own lifetime, Keynes was a celebrity thinker, but he was not yet an influential voice when it came to the design of real-world public policy. Keynes himself lamented this, writing in a 1931 collection of essays: "Here are collected croakings of twelve years—the croakings of a Cassandra who could never influence the course of events in time" (Keynes 1931, xvii).

Though Keynes would not live to see it, his status as a Cassandra was to be dramatically reversed.

Economics After Keynes: Obeyed, not Celebrated

Today, our understanding of what economic life is, and what the discipline of economics is, is entirely shaped by the Keynesian Revolution. We can see this in examples ranging from the high end of political power to the jokes we make on an everyday basis.

The most obvious impact is in the creation of large new policy and organizational apparatuses, which exercise enormous power, based on the Consumption paradigm. Since 1946, in what was at the time a very direct concession to Keynesian influence, presidential administrations have appointed a Council of Economic Advisors (Stein 1969, 197, 204). Its job, and the job of other institutions, is to help the president manage the national economy. This ensures that the president is regularly engaged in using the power of his office for the purpose of managing the economy. The mandate of the Federal Reserve Bank has been changed to include not only keeping prices stable, but also managing the business cycle. Many other examples could be cited. As these policy institutions carry out their mission, they control systems that have an enormous influence over our lives.

Consider: John F. Kennedy, champion of Keynesianism, cut taxes to stimulate consumption. Ronald Reagan, knight in shining armor of the anti-Keynesians, cut taxes to spur savings and investment. Both used fiscal policy as a way of managing the economy, manipulating our behavior using incentives created by government action, with the end goal of maximizing consumption possibilities. Whichever party you vote for, you're voting to be governed by the Consumption paradigm.

As these institutions reshape our economic systems, they also reshape our understanding of the meaning of our daily lives. The narratives and norms embedded in their discourse, implicitly and explicitly, exercise an authoritative and formative influence over the self-understanding of those whose lives they control. The example cited in Chapter 4 of the president of the United States asking people to serve their country by going shopping after the September 11 terrorist attacks stands out as one of the most shocking examples of how moral narratives of higher purpose and self-sacrifice have been supplanted by the new dominance of economic discourse in the Consumption paradigm. It is, admittedly, an extreme example, but it is an extreme example of a power that is exercised over us in less crude ways every day of our lives.

The Keynesian Revolution's view of what economics is—bloodless technical management that accomplishes no morally good purpose—has penetrated our culture so pervasively that we unconsciously rely on it to make jokes. In a *New Yorker* cartoon by Ed Arno, the host of a party is introducing a guest to another guest: "I'd like to introduce you to Marty Thorndecker. He's an economist, but he's really very nice"

(*New Yorker* 1974). One of the authors of this book, as a graduate student, heard one of his professors make a joke with the students in his undergraduate lecture by telling them that economists like him set their watches with the atomic clock.

More profoundly, core human concerns that are right at the center of our economic lives are no longer considered "economics." One of the authors of this book assigned students in an economics class to write responses to the Economics Focus column in the *Economist* newsmagazine. On one occasion the column covered newly published research suggesting that female musicians are more likely to land symphony jobs if the auditions are conducted using a divider that allows the audition committee to hear the musicianship of the performer but not observe the musician's sex (Goldin and Rouse 2000). The intention was to show that economics is a social science that explores human choices of all kinds, and affords us an opportunity to examine more clearly how we live our lives. But in class and in written responses, it became clear that the students did not perceive this research as having anything to do with economics. At times they said so quite directly: "What does this have to do with economics?" The research wasn't about unemployment rates or inflation rates or business revenues or investments, so it wasn't economics, even though it was about vitally important economic behaviors.

John Kenneth Galbraith and the Popularization of the Paradigm

We will examine only two of the many channels through which the Consumption paradigm became influential beyond the academy. We offer these as examples that illustrate the process. Much more was involved, of course. But if these are only examples, they are examples that have great importance in their own right.

John Kenneth Galbraith's book *The Affluent Society* greatly magnified the cultural influence of the new approach to economics by combining it with a more sociological approach to economic life. He merged the Consumption paradigm of economics with the philosopher Thorstein Veblen's cultural critique of economic development. Galbraith's mixture of Keynes' macroeconomic thought with Veblen's sociology of economics produced an explosive combination that greatly magnified the influence of both.

Veblen had been born in Wisconsin to parents who had emigrated to the United States from Norway. He famously challenged central assumptions of neoclassical economics (Buchholz 1989, 177). After earning a Ph.D. in philosophy at Yale, and apparently drifting without ongoing employment for several years, he made his way to Cornell, where economist J. Laurence Laughlin served as his mentor in economics. Soon thereafter, Laughlin moved to the University of Chicago and was successful in finding a position there for Veblen as well.

Veblen's 1899 *The Theory of the Leisure Class* rejected the dominant approaches to economic analysis that were being developed by the latter-day successors of the old classical school. Like Marx, Veblen is primarily interested in overthrowing the dominance of the rich in favor of the exploited. However, Veblen avoids the class struggle framework of Marx, offering us a different set of heroes and villains. Veblen's villains are businessmen, as in Marx, but the heroes are the creative, innovative engineers working within the businessmen's corporations.

In Veblen's storyline, it's the engineers rather than the proletariat who revolt. They are sick of settling for the paycheck offered to them by employers who are more interested in producing substandard products that need to be frequently replaced, or selling add-ons to inferior products, rather than simply making better products in the first place. The businessmen are blinded by money and cannot see what the engineers might do if their creative energies were turned loose (Buchholz 1989, 183).

Following in the footsteps of the historicist school, Veblen suggested that only an aggressive government could rein in the ruthless, money-hungry businessmen. However, he had little hope that such plans could succeed (Buchholz 1989, 184). And, like most of the historicists, he was much better at condemning the work of the other economists than he was at formulating new models consistent with his own radical theories.

Galbraith: "Resolved to Go to the Temple"

John Kenneth Galbraith simultaneously worked within the Keynesian economic paradigm while offering the iconoclastic social analysis of the historicists and Veblen. And he communicated these ideas very successfully to the broader public outside of academia.

Like many other aspiring economists in the mid-1930s, Galbraith had also contracted Keynesian fever. Galbraith and his wife planned their 1937 wedding and ensuing honeymoon so that their wedding trip would take them to Cambridge, where Galbraith would be able to study with Keynes for a year; Keynes, alas, was absent from campus while recovering from what would become a series of heart attacks (Wapshott 2011, 164). Nonetheless, in his memoir *A Life in Our Times*, Galbraith reflects on this plan to travel to Cambridge to see Keynes: "I had resolved to go to the temple" (Galbraith 1981, 70).

Galbraith spent most of his career on the faculty at Harvard, after beginning his career by earning a doctorate in agricultural economics from the University of California-Berkeley. Throughout his academic career he also commanded a considerable public spotlight, as Keynes had in England in earlier decades. He is probably the only specialist in agricultural economics to become a bestseller and leading public intellectual in the age of mass media.

Galbraith's public life was colorful and influential. After he served in a variety of public posts during World War II, Henry Luce hired Galbraith to serve as editor-in-chief of *Fortune* magazine from 1943 to 48. Galbraith also served as advisor to both Presidents Kennedy and Truman, and held the post of U.S. Ambassador to India in the Kennedy administration from 1961 to 63 (*Encyclopædia Britannica* 2019). Galbraith appeared on the cover of *Time* magazine twice: once during his service as ambassador to India (January 12, 1962)—where he appears with two other ambassadors nominated by Kennedy—and another soon after the publication of his *The New Industrial State* where he appears alone with the caption "John Kenneth Galbraith: The All-Purpose Critic" (February 16, 1968). By way of comparison, Friedman appeared on the cover just once (December 19, 1969), and Keynes himself appeared just once (posthumously, on the December 31, 1965 cover; *Time* 2019).

The Affluent Society and the Dependence Effect

Galbraith is perhaps best remembered for a series of three books with a simple formula for combining the Keynes and Veblen lines of thought. They offered up a robust Veblenian attack on the sociology of wealth, and argued that a big dose of Keynesian public policy could cure what ails us.

The heart of Galbraith's argument is that corporations are now so big that consumers are no longer in the driver's seat in determining what gets produced and at what price. Throughout all three books—*The Affluent Society* (1958), *The New Industrial State* (1967) and *Economics and the Public Purpose* (1973)—Galbraith ridicules the tradition of Adam Smith, in which self-interest leads to the social interest as if by an invisible hand. Against this, he points to the considerable market power and advertising budgets wielded by large corporations. He also paints the market-clearing efficiency of the price system under assumptions of perfect competition as, in the words of Todd Buchholz, "on the same fantastic list as Tinkerbell, Santa Claus, and Snow White" (Buchholz 1989, 188). The myth of consumer sovereignty upon which modern economics so prides itself is akin to the spell placed on Sleeping Beauty—it keeps us asleep, so we don't wake up to the ways in which advertising has put the big bosses in control.

Madison Avenue advertising executives relentlessly plot to sell you a broad variety of goods and services that are largely indistinguishable from other goods and services that already exist. Buchholz uses this example: You are standing in line to buy a box of Cocoa Puffs cereal. You remark to the person next in line that you really needed that box of Cocoa Puffs, and you really like them. And you are glad they were there when you needed them. But that next person in line turns out to be John Kenneth Galbraith, and his take on your relationship with Cocoa Puffs is dismissive. Galbraith might say to you: You fool! You don't love Cocoa Puffs, and you definitely don't need Cocoa Puffs. You have been duped into thinking you need or like or want Cocoa Puffs, but you only think that because a multilevel marketing campaign insidiously suggested to you that you like Cocoa Puffs. In fact, things have gotten so out of hand that you don't even really know what you need or like or want anymore. You are not free to choose anything: Marketing has decided that for you (Buchholz 1989, 188).

Galbraith's diagnosis—hard-nosed CEOs hiring expensive advertising executives to convince us we simply must have the absolutely latest and greatest of everything—is not unfounded. As journalist Danny Cross put it: "The toothpaste aisle is the worst. There are only like two toothpaste companies, and they make about 1,000 different types" (Cross 2013). You don't have to be a wild-eyed Marxist to see the state of modern marketing as a poor reflection on our moral character.

Galbraith's solution, however, wasn't to help the American consumer living in the era of *Mad Men* become more discerning and self-controlled. He did not propose a movement to awaken us from our collective hypnosis, calling us to live simpler and happier lives through the classical virtues of prudence and frugality. That would have required him to see the consumer as a responsible moral agent.

However, Galbraith did not see the consumer as a responsible moral agent. He said we suffered from the "dependence effect." Our desires aren't our own. We only think they are because they have been injected into our subconscious minds through television and other means. We are too easily manipulated to develop habits of discrimination and resistance:

> If production is to increase, the wants must be effectively contrived. In the absence of the contrivance the increase would not occur. This is not true of all goods, but that it is true of a substantial part is sufficient. It means that since the demand for this part would not exist, were it not contrived, its utility or urgency, ex contrivance, is zero. If we regard this production as marginal, we may say that the marginal utility of present aggregate output, ex advertising and salesmanship, is zero. (Galbraith 1958, 129–130)

Galbraith envisioned only one way to overcome the dependence effect. He argued that we were headed for a dystopian future in which we all became helpless automatons in service of big business, unless government intervened on our behalf. We needed to adopt democratic socialism and central economic planning, so key decisions could be carried out by planners who had clearer heads about what needs to be produced and how. Trusting economic decisions to the whim of the so-called market really just left us to be helplessly manipulated by the rich and powerful. As Robert Ekelund and Robert Hébert observe:

> Galbraith's neglect of the individual, and especially of the individual's intellectual independence and his preferences, leads him to argue that individuals cannot discern what is in their own best interests. The usefulness of the price system in allowing individuals to register their choices between economic and social alternatives (for example, to choose less costly gasoline more pollution rather than more costly gasoline and less pollution) is similarly ignored or discounted. Galbraith and others have felt frustration at the distribution of income and the level of social-goods provision that free markets provide. This frustration had led them to champion the extension of government as a palliative. (Ekelund and Hébert 1990, 477–478)

Notice how extensively Galbraith's approach reinforces the anthropology of the Consumption paradigm. We are bundles of appetites, and stuff we can enjoy is what we are after. We do not discern good ends rationally, but are at the whim of our animal spirits—which respond powerfully to stimuli (advertising). The purpose of the economy is to satisfy consumer appetites, and rational elites should manipulate consumers to maximize their satisfaction. Even if we hadn't been taken in by radio jingles, we'd still be after stuff, it would just be other stuff. The problem is not that we are seeking to satisfy consumption desires and nothing more, it is that we do not control our own consumption desires. That's why we need government to control them for us, to decide what stuff we really need. Do we need two different scents of laundry detergent? Central planners will tell us. The goal is not to elevate consumer behavior, but to eliminate producer parasitism.

The degree of influence Galbraith had upon the ways Americans think about economics and talk about economics and internalize economics cannot be estimated precisely. By one measure, Galbraith connected more directly to the American public than Keynes ever had back in England. Nicholas Wapshott states that Galbraith "through writing over a thousand newspaper and magazine articles became the chief popularizer of Keynesian ideas" (Wapshott 2011, 170). Reflecting on this activity, Galbraith himself says:

> This was a revolution without organization. All who participated felt a deep sense of personal responsibility for the ideas; there was a varying but deep urge to persuade. But no one ever responded to plans, orders, instructions, or any force apart from his own convictions. That perhaps was the most interesting single feature of the Keynesian Revolution. (Galbraith 1975, 138)

Galbraith's reach with the American public was astounding. *The Affluent Society* is number 46 on the Modern Library's list of the best nonfiction books.

Samuelson and Friedman: Battle of the Laureates

Galbraith was not the only economist who captured the attention of the American public. Samuelson, the titan of Keynesianism, and Friedman, anti-Keynesian giant of the Chicago school, communicated frequently with the American public through a dueling series of columns in *Newsweek*. From 1966 to 1982, the two wrote op-ed style columns every three weeks (Mata 2015, 2). In these columns, they offered their contrasting opinions about the economic issues of the day.

It's likely that Americans have never been so frequently exposed to the leading economists of their day than in the 1960s. Galbraith, recall, had the cover of *Time* all to himself early in 1968, just after the 1967 publication of his second major work, *The New Industrial State*. Keynes had the *Time* cover all to himself, posthumously, at the end of 1965. Tiago Mata details the ubiquity of economists in public media in the 1960s, especially during the Kennedy and Johnson administrations (Mata 2011).

It was a critical time for economics, as the Chicago school was building up its comprehensive challenge to Keynesianism. As Mata observes, "Samuelson was a strong candidate for the title of the discipline's foremost Keynesian," and Friedman "was engaged in an intellectual project of creating an alternative to Keynesian macroeconomics" (Mata 2015, 12–13).

Friedman and Samuelson were each paid about $20,000 per year—a considerable sum given the value of the dollar at the time—for their services (Mata 2015, 2). But they likely valued their relationship with *Newsweek* far more because it offered an opportunity for these two academic economists to make their cases on policy directly to the American public. An added attraction was that Friedman and Samuelson had nearly full editorial control over their respective columns (Mata 2015, 3).

Mata has conducted a meta-analysis of their columns. It reveals that even the very words the two chose signaled their differences. For example, Samuelson used the word "economics" 207 times and "economist" 221 times. In contrast, Friedman uses them just 49 times and 82 times respectively (Mata 2015, 23).

What's most intriguing is the topics they covered most frequently. As the word counts above suggest, Friedman was less inclined to invoke the authority of economics and economists than Samuelson. But their shared focus throughout the period was upon what people typically regard as macroeconomic topics. Mata aggregated all their columns and classified the topics and keywords mentioned most often by both in about 20 "bins." Far and away the most common, covering more than a fourth of their entire body of work in *Newsweek*, is the following bin: "interest rates, federal reserve, cent year, years ago, money supply, exchange rates, rate cent, recent years, tax rates, inflation" (Mata 2015, 28).

The next three bins in size order contain keywords on similar macro-themed topics. Together, these top four bins occupy roughly two-thirds of Samuelson's and Friedman's total contributions to *Newsweek*.

To some degree, this outcome is understandable due to the period in which they were writing. The stagflation misery of the 1970s would have pushed these topics to the fore in any set of economic columns. But these focal points also reinforce the view that economics is all about manipulating the money supply, strangling inflation and managing exchange rates.

After *Newsweek*, the battle moved to television in the 1980s. Galbraith's BBC production of *Age of Uncertainty* was followed by Milton and Rose Friedman's PBS series *Free to Choose*, accompanied by a best-selling book.

Regardless of where the battle was joined, the battle succeeded in giving the public an impression that economics is mainly about unemployment, inflation, the Fed, and what your disposable income is. In public discourse, macro had crowded out micro, and the Consumption paradigm was reinforced. The issue between the Keynesians and their critics was what was the best way for government to manipulate the economy to maximize the satisfaction of consumer appetites.

Why were the Keynesians' critics reinforcing the basic assumptions of the Consumption paradigm, such that their debates reinforced rather than challenged those assumptions? In the next chapter, we turn to that question.

References

Buchholz, Todd G. 1989. *New Ideas from Dead Economists*. New York: Plume.

Cross, Danny. 2013. There Are Too Many Types of Toothpaste. *CityBeat*, December 4.

Ekelund, Robert B., and Robert F. Hébert. 1990. *A History of Economic Theory and Method*. New York: McGraw-Hill.

Encyclopædia Britannica. 2019. John Kenneth Galbraith. https://www.britannica.com/biography/John-Kenneth-Galbraith. Accessed 21 Jan 2019.

Friedman, Milton. 1968. Why Economists Disagree. In *Dollars and Deficits*. Englewood Cliffs: Prentice-Hall.

Galbraith, John Kenneth. 1958. *The Affluent Society*. New York: New American Library.

Galbraith, John Kenneth. 1975. How Keynes Came to America. In *Essays on John Maynard Keynes*, ed. Milo Keynes, 132–141. Cambridge: Cambridge University Press.

Galbraith, John Kenneth. 1981. *A Life in Our Times*. New York: Ballantine Books.

Goldin, Claudia, and Cecilia Rouse. 2000. Orchestrating Impartiality. *American Economic Review* 90: 715–741.

Keynes, John Maynard. 1931. *Essays in Persuasion*. London: Macmillan.

Mata, Tiago. 2011. Trust in Independence. *Journal of the History of Behavioral Sciences* 47: 359–379.

Mata, Tiago. 2015. Milton Friedman and Paul Samuelson, Columnists of *Newsweek*. *Journal of the History of Economic Thought*, forthcoming; working paper manuscript dated April 15, 2015. http://www.eshet.net/conference/paper_view.php?id=1321&p=39. Accessed 21 Jan 2019.

New Yorker. 1974. Cartoon. November 18.

Stein, Herbert. 1969. *The Fiscal Revolution in America*. Chicago: University of Chicago Press.

Time. 1965. We Are All Keynesians Now. December 31.

Time. 1966. Letters. February 4.

Time Cover Store. 2019. https://www.timecoverstore.com. Accessed 21 Jan 2019.

Wapshott, Nicholas. 2011. *Keynes Hayek*. New York: W. W. Norton.

CHAPTER 7

Two Counter-Revolutions: The Chicago and Austrian Schools and the Consumption Paradigm

Any good revolution inspires a counter-revolution. Keynes inspired two. The older Austrian school and the newly formed Chicago school each rejected some key elements of Keynes' thought. This led to the division of the discipline into three schools—Keynesianism, Austria and Chicago. The disputes among these schools are the most important factor defining the landscape of modern economics.

However, the attention-grabbing conflict between these schools conceals a deeper uniformity. Both counter-revolutions accept most of the key elements of the Consumption paradigm. Most importantly, they accept Keynes' redefinition of the purpose of economic systems: to maximize consumption possibilities. They also accept Keynes' redefinition of Mill's *homo economicus*, which lay at the heart of the new focus on maximizing consumer satisfaction—they accept the instrumental rather than substantive understanding of rationality, and they accept the reversal of the relationship between gaining wealth and enjoying wealth.

So total was the victory of the Keynesian Revolution that doubting the core premises of the Consumption paradigm is no longer plausible within the discipline of economics. Challenging these core premises is not provocative, it is ridiculous—beneath consideration. Recall from the Introduction Peter Berger's "one group of social scientists with whom it was generally impossible to work."

To some extent, Keynes' rivals may have adopted the core elements of his paradigm because they were persuaded by the force of his arguments.

V. V. Claar and G. Forster, *The Keynesian Revolution and Our Empty Economy*, https://doi.org/10.1007/978-3-030-15808-8_7

And to some extent they may have accommodated themselves to the Overton Window—that is, they may have foregone deeper challenges to the paradigm simply because they felt raising such challenges to be futile, given the paradigm's dominance. Either way, they accommodated themselves to the core elements of the paradigm and focused on challenging Keynes on subordinate questions.

As Milton Friedman himself, the giant of Chicago, said (in words we quoted in Chapter 6): "We all use the Keynesian language and apparatus" even though "none of us any longer accepts the initial Keynesian conclusions" (Friedman 1968, 15). The discipline has used Keynes' methods, and his conceptual framework of what economics is, to revise Keynes' "initial" conclusions as it carries forward what remains Keynes' grand project of reinventing economics to serve consumer satisfaction.

This is not to say that there are no important differences between the three schools. It is to say that the differences, important as they are, are mostly differences within the Consumption paradigm and not about the Consumption paradigm. Moreover, we are not saying that there are no individual exceptions—economists here and there who go further in challenging the roots of the Keynesian Revolution. But the typical or representative models of the two counter-revolutionary schools operate more or less within the Consumption paradigm.

What the Counter-Revolutions Do Challenge

To understand what the three schools have in common, it is valuable to begin with some broad observations on what they disagree about. These disagreements, after all, define the boundaries of the schools. And starting with an understanding of the key disagreements serves as a precaution to help prevent us from overestimating the level of agreement between them.

Most conspicuously, both Austria and Chicago resist Keynes' tendency toward aggregation—the narrowing of the subject of economics to the study of impersonal social abstractions. They insist that studying the economy means studying the countless millions of "microeconomic" decisions each person makes every day. The Austrian school goes furthest in this direction, emphasizing that policymakers should avoid tinkering and strive instead to provide clear and fixed rules of honest exchange along with stable money, so individual economic actors (persons, companies, etc.) will know what is and is not permitted and what the value of a dollar will be, and can arrange their lives accordingly. While Chicago economists are more willing to encourage some forms of tinkering, especially with the money supply, for the sake of aggregate goals, they also want to keep the individual economic actor methodologically in view. All economic activity, they emphasize, resolves to the decisions of individual actors, so there is less that can be accomplished by government tinkering, and what that tinkering can accomplish is of less value.

As a consequence of this difference, they come into sharp conflict with Keynesians over the effectiveness of Keynesian policies. Austria and Chicago are free-market oriented, opposing the Keynesian calls for interventionist government. This conflict plays out on a variety of fronts. Austria and Chicago doubt the capacity of economists (and hence of the policymakers relying on economists' advice) to know enough about the preferences and choices of individual economic actors to be effective in intervening in the economy, in most if not all cases. Moreover, they emphasize the costs involved in the interventionist state; fiscal stimulus is paid for with some combination of taxes, borrowing or inflation, each of which has a negative impact on the same aggregate outcomes that the stimulus is supposed to stimulate. Finally, and most emphatically, they emphasize the dangers involved in giving political elites the power over our lives that is needed for economic management; "government failure" must be taken into account alongside "market failure."

Additionally, the Austrians have not shared in the narrowing of economic methods since Keynes. Economists in the Keynesian and Chicago schools use quantitative mathematical approaches almost exclusively. Austrians do use math, but they also make use of the qualitative methods that prevailed before the Keynesian Revolution. Like Keynes himself, they mix equations with other methods.

The Austrian Response: A Slow and Incomplete Resistance

The Austrian school predates Keynes, and played a pivotal role—often underappreciated—in the development of some of the most important concepts in modern economics. Understanding these contributions is important to understanding the inadequacy of its response to Keynes.

Austrian Accomplishments in the Marginal Revolution

The Austrians played a major part in what has become popularly known as the Marginal Revolution. This occurred when economists brought together three powerful concepts: opportunity cost, the subjectivity of economic value, and decision-making at the margin (hence "marginal" revolution).

Israel Kirzner suggests that Austrian economist Friedrich von Wieser may have supplied the earliest formal expositions of the notion of opportunity cost (Kirzner [undated]). The whole edifice of modern economics depends upon this essential concept; its formalization was for economics something like what the invention of the numeral zero was for mathematics. Informally, the idea of opportunity cost is familiar from the saying "there's no such thing as a free lunch." Whatever you do, you have to give up the opportunity to do other things in order to do it; therefore, everything you do has costs. Benjamin Franklin articulated the concept in his 1748 *Advice to a Young Tradesman*, where he wrote:

> Remember that time is money. He that can earn ten shillings a day by his labor, and goes abroad, or sits idle one half of that day, though he spends but sixpence during his diversion or idleness, ought not to reckon that the only expense; he has really spent or rather thrown away five shillings besides. (Franklin 1748)

But it took Austrian economists like Wieser to formalize the concept and incorporate it into economic analysis so that today, every college student learns about opportunity cost within the first week of an introductory economics class.

Three economists all arrived, independently, at the concept of the subjectivity of economic value at about the same time: British economist Stanley Jevons, mentioned in Chapter 3; Frenchman Léon Walras; and Austria's Carl Menger, founder of the Austrian school (Stigler 1950). The subjectivity of economic value is the idea that the economic value of a good cannot be determined fully by the material value of the good or the cost to produce it. Those things matter, but so does the perceived usefulness of that good to the person who is assessing it for use. Each of us has unique preferences and purposes, and these are subjective. A bottle of really fine wine is worth a lot to a connoisseur, but its value is far less to someone who is untrained in appreciating wine, and doesn't taste much difference between one bottle and another; its value is even lower for a teetotaler. As simple as the subjectivity of value sounds, it's a concept Adam Smith lacked, and the absence of this insight is at the heart of Karl Marx's disastrous turn into totalitarianism—for if the economic value of things really could be objectively calculated, the idea of a planned economy becomes all but irresistible.

Marginal decision-making builds on the insight of subjective value. When you are deciding whether to buy oranges, for example, you start by considering the oranges' subjective value to you. You consider such factors as the nutritional benefits of vitamin C, the anticipated taste, and how many oranges you have already eaten today. But the oranges also come with opportunity costs: the money you spend, the other foods you won't eat if you eat these oranges, etc. "Marginal" decision-making comes in when we further assume that you make your decision based on the smallest increments available. If you decide to buy six oranges, you didn't make just one decision. You actually made seven distinct decisions: whether or not to purchase the first orange, the second, the third, the fourth, the fifth and the sixth, and then a seventh decision: not to buy a seventh orange. Once we understand that economic decisions are made on the margins, we are equipped to understand such decisions in much more sophisticated ways.

Austrian Resistance: Slow and Ineffective

The Austrians opposed the Keynesian school of economics, but their response had little practical effect on either public policy or public discourse outside the discipline of economics. Mark Skousen pulls no punches: "Except for Friedman, the free-market response to Keynesian theory was almost completely ineffectual" (Skousen 2001, 380). Skousen's "Friedman," of course, is Milton Friedman of the Chicago school. The Austrians have produced much important economic thought since the rise of Keynes, but it has not had the same public impact as the debate between Keynes and Chicago.

One reason for this is simply that the Austrians were slow to respond. The prominent Austrian figure Ludwig von Mises wrote very little that might be considered a response to Keynesianism. The index to his 1966 *Human Action* lists mentions of Keynes on only 15 of its nearly 900 pages, and four of those mentions are in footnotes (von Mises 2007). As Keynes was appearing on the cover of *Time*, Mises had little to say about him.

The rivalry between Keynes and Friedrich Hayek is celebrated today, including in a famous internet video depicting a rap battle between the two (EconStories 2010). The video is an excellent tool for introducing people to the debate over Keynesian macroeconomics, but it may create a false impression of the extent to which the two economists directly battled (via rap or otherwise) within their own lifetimes, as opposed to the later conflict between their followers.

In fact, Hayek did not respond to Keynes following the publication of the *General Theory* (Skousen 2001, 380; Wapshott 2011, 171–187). Keynes would have liked nothing better than a full-on public battle with Hayek and/or other prominent economists, not only because publicity sells books, but because Keynes dearly wanted to supplant entirely economists like Arthur Pigou (a major foil in the *General Theory*) and Hayek (Wapshott 2011, 172–174). But Hayek never countered Keynes when it would have been timely to do so.

Hayek himself reflected upon this later in his life. He said he hadn't reviewed Keynes' *General Theory* because he thought that doing so might prove pointless if "before I had completed my analysis he would have changed his mind." Later on, he admits that he never really considered the approach of the *General Theory* as something he might connect with, even at a critical level: "My disagreement with that book did not refer so much to any detail of the analysis as to the general approach followed in the whole work. The real issue was the validity of what we now call macroeconomics" (Skidelsky 1992, 459). Robert Skidelsky concludes "Hayek remained a bystander as the Keynesian revolution unfolded; and only started to reorganize a resistance after Keynes's death" (Skidelsky 1992, 459).

Nicholas Wapshott offers a different emphasis, saying Hayek did not offer immediate responses to the *General Theory* because he was focused on producing his own *magnum opus*, *The Pure Theory of Capital* (Wapshott 2011, 175–183). This book, being a work of equal ambition to the *General Theory*, would presumably stand as a comprehensive response to Keynes as well as to other alternatives. In a letter to Gottfried von Haberler, Hayek says: "I try to concentrate exclusively on the work on my book and must leave everything else"; of the *General Theory*, he says: "I should like to temporarily say nothing about it, since I am hopelessly stuck in Chapter 6" (Haberler Papers [various dates], box 67, Hayek to Haberler, February 15, 1936).

At long last, in the summer of 1940, Hayek finished his *Pure Theory of Capital*—the book that was supposed to render Keynes irrelevant. Alas, the world didn't notice. And one will find harsh critics of it among both Keynesians and anti-Keynesians. Paul Samuelson's assessment was that "Hayek's *The Pure Theory of Capital* was not stillborn. But it was a pebble thrown into the pool of economic science that seemingly left nary a ripple" (Wapshott 2011, 183). Even Friedman would later say: "I am an enormous admirer of Hayek, but not for his economics. I think *Prices and Production* was a very flawed book. I think his capital theory book is unreadable" (Wapshott 2011, 183). Following the publication of the *Pure Theory of Capital*, Hayek largely devoted himself to work that would be more accurately described as political philosophy, though he would also make other significant contributions to economic thought such as his 1945 "The Use of Knowledge in Society" (Hayek 1945). Wapshott quotes Hayek biographer Alan Ebenstein: "After Keynes published *The General Theory*...Hayek was virtually forgotten as a technical economist.... By the end of the decade, there was little interest in him" (Wapshott 2011, 181). Wapshott claims that Hayek's seminars at the London School of Economics became a place for young Keynesians to make fun of Hayek, who was seen as antiquated (Wapshott 2011, 181–182). John Kenneth Galbraith relates anecdotes of Keynesian students in Hayek's classroom that indicate the same thing (Galbraith 1981, 78).

Other Austrians didn't do much better. W.H. Hutt's *Keynesianism*, an effort he'd begun in the 1930s, didn't appear in print until 1963—at about the same time Mises published *Human Action* and Keynes was depicted on the cover of *Time*. Skousen refers to the book as "unclear and rambling" (Skousen 2001, 381).

Journalist Henry Hazlitt, most famous in economics circles for his legendary 1948 *Economics in One Lesson*, wrote what is perhaps the best-received and best-written Austrian response to the *General Theory*. In his 1959 *The Failure of the "New Economics,"* Hazlitt offers wide-ranging attacks on the analysis of the *General Theory*. However, Hazlitt assumes his readers are already deeply familiar with the *General Theory*. He engages with Keynes on Keynes' terms in the literal sense of adopting all his obscure jargon. So the book isn't of particular use to most readers, including most economists (since there has never been a time when the *General Theory* itself, in all its complex obscurity, was read carefully outside a small population of specialists). As a consequence, while it sold well for a book of its kind, it made little impact either among the public or in academia (Skousen 2001, 381).

One final gasp from the Austrians came in the form of two books by Murray Rothbard: *Man, Economy and State* in 1962 and *America's Great Depression* in 1963. Following the completion of his Ph.D. at Columbia, Rothbard set himself up as an academic outsider. He refused to accept a university post, instead agreeing to work at the William Volker Fund, a foundation that was interested in promoting and disseminating free-market ideas (McVicar 2011). Rothbard also refused to join the American Economic Association. Moreover, he preferred to put his ideas down in books rather than in peer-reviewed scholarly journals, and published his books with a non-academic publishing house (Skousen 2001, 382). Rothbard knew that the Austrian response to Keynes and the *General Theory*, as outlined above, remained far from adequate: "It is a mistake to dismiss [Keynesianism] brusquely, as many conservative economists have done…but failure to deal with the fallacies in detail and in depth has left the field of ideas open for Keynesianism to conquer" (Skousen 2001, 382). By deliberately setting himself outside of the discipline in every way, Rothbard guaranteed his ideas would lack influence. He is largely unknown outside a small circle of libertarian devotees.

Austrian Acquiescence in the Consumption Paradigm

Why was the Austrian response so slow and ineffective? Biographical factors may account for one or another figure being tardy or unsuccessful. But the whole school of thought—and a school with as much history and intellectual pedigree as the Austrians—simply failing to show up on the court calls for some larger explanation.

In his essay "Ethics on *The Road to Serfdom* and Beyond," Paul Heyne offers a promising starting point in seeking such an explanation. He suggests that the Austrians' response was inadequate because Keynes had cut past the secondary issues and raised the ultimate questions about the purpose and meaning of economic life, and the Austrians lacked a firm set of ultimate beliefs of their own from which to counter this challenge. Heyne uses Hayek's 1944 *Road to Serfdom* as a case study, showing that Hayek's approach to the big questions about economic organization demands a coherent set of underlying commitments about ultimate questions, but Hayek never supplies them. In the opening paragraph of the preface to the original edition, Hayek asserts: "All I shall have to say is derived from certain ultimate values. I hope…to make it clear beyond doubt what these ultimate values are on which the whole argument depends" (Hayek 2007, 37). Yet, as Heynes shows, Hayek never delivers the goods. He makes a compelling negative case against economic management, showing how it tends to lead to the destruction of the very ends its proponents seek to secure. But, as Hayek's own comment in the preface suggests, this is incomplete if the "ultimate values" upon which the argument is based are not specified. Yet they are not specified. Why? According to Heyne, Hayek "*was always troubled by the suspicion that he had no adequate grounds for his own most important convictions*" (Heyne 2008, 342; italics in original). It's challenging to argue against a worldview that makes ultimate claims about meaning and purpose if you are unsure about what your own proposed alternative might be.

Hayek's *Law, Legislation and Liberty* provides further evidence of the missing foundations in his thought. Hayek asserts that moral codes are nothing but social conventions with no rational basis. Moral law is no more than "a process of evolution and natural selection, an unintended product whose present significance may be wholly different from the intention of its creators" (Hayek 1976, vol. 2, p. 59). And Hayek puts his money where his mouth is:

> It would seem to me, for instance, to be clearly morally wrong to revive an already unconscious Eskimo who, at the beginning of their winter migration, in accordance with the morals of his people and with his approval, had been left behind by his group to die – and to be right only if I regarded it as right, and in my power, to transfer him into a wholly different society in which I was able and willing to provide for his survival. (Hayek 1976, vol. 2, p. 27)

Nothing is absolutely right or wrong; all morality is culturally relative.

With this in mind, let us return to the basic insights of the Marginal Revolution, to which the Austrians contributed so much: opportunity cost, the subjectivity of economic value, and marginal decision-making. We do not question the enormous value of these insights. These are true as far as they go, and modern economics has made many advances building upon them. But we should consider what would be necessary for someone to hold these insights and simultaneously resist the anthropology of the Consumption paradigm.

The Marginal Revolution model can accommodate the Consumption paradigm with impressive ease. The Consumption paradigm, as we have seen, relies on an instrumental view of rationality (in which reason does not dictate ends, but only calculates how to achieve those ends) and reverses the traditional relationship between gaining wealth and enjoying wealth (denying that production can have any end other than consumption). These are the core elements that produce the outcome of economic systems aimed solely at maximizing shallow satisfaction of consumer appetites. The Marginal Revolution, meanwhile, analyzes economic action in terms of actors who have preferences, and calculations undertaken by those actors to accomplish those preferences.

It is easy to see how the Marginal Revolution model does not, by itself, challenge the Consumption paradigm model. To the contrary, if you already believe in Keynes' version of *homo economicus*, you can adopt the Marginal Revolution model of decision-making without missing a beat.

Therefore, in any cultural environment where the Consumption paradigm anthropology has become the default assumption of how economic decisions are made, the Marginal Revolution model will tend to harmonize with that anthropology through a process so easy as to be unconscious. "Actors with preferences calculate how to satisfy them" can become, without anyone recognizing what has happened, "actors with [essentially irrational] preferences calculate how to satisfy them [through consumption]." The stronger a cultural grip the Consumption paradigm has, the easier and the more unconscious this process of assimilation will be.

To resist the Consumption paradigm effectively, then, an adherent of the Marginal Revolution model would have to consciously and firmly assert a substantive rationality (that some ends are rational and others are not) and a restoration of the old relationship between gaining wealth and enjoying wealth (affirming that consumption is not the only end of production). It is possible that this could be done simply by itself—that no other, larger scheme of philosophical commitments would be invoked. In most human thought, however, such commitments rarely stand by themselves. The development of a larger scheme of philosophical commitments about ultimate reality, speaking to the meaning purpose of economic life, would likely have to be involved.

Be that as it may, Austrian economists did not, and still do not, typically include a belief in these propositions as part of their economic analysis. They do not offer a model of economic action in which some ends are held to be rational, or draw any other kind of distinction between intrinsically good ends and bad ones. They do not affirm that production can serve other ends besides consumption.

Hayek, at least, in *Law, Legislation and Liberty*, affirmatively denies the only premises upon which the Consumption paradigm can be resisted. If morality is merely an unintended evolutionary process whose meaning may change to absolutely any extent from generation to generation or across cultures, then of course there can be no substantive rationality and nothing is intrinsically good. It follows that nothing has value except as fodder for consumption.

In the absence of a robust challenge to Keynes' version of *homo economicus* on these points, the ineffectiveness of the Austrian challenge to Keynes is easier to understand. Without rational ends, we are still (by default) operating within the economic psychology of "animal spirits" that respond to stimuli in easily manipulable ways. Without production that serves ends other than consumption, we are still (by default) operating in the economic psychology of the "paradox of thrift," in which a penny saved is a penny wasted. Absent a challenge on these points, not only is their failure easy to account for, it is difficult to see how their response could possibly have been effective.

The Chicago Response: We Can Do the Same Thing Better, Cheaper, and Faster!

Friedman, who was the public face of the Chicago school and exemplified all its central commitments, will be our focus for understanding the Chicago response to Keynes. For many who witnessed the very public battle between Samuelson and Friedman in the pages of *Newsweek*, or who have read Friedman's classics *Capitalism and Freedom* or *Free to Choose*, it may be difficult to accept that Friedman inadvertently played a part in the enduring influence of the Keynesian Revolution upon contemporary society. After all, Friedman was a free-market champion who deeply believed that less government intervention was better than more—in nearly every aspect of life. However, the means through which Friedman fought Keynesian economics surrendered entirely to Keynes' larger premises, fighting him on secondary questions.

We see this first in the choice of topics to fight about. It was Keynes who focused on broad monetary aggregates and their management through monetary policy. It was Keynes who focused on full employment. It was Keynes who focused on national income—GDP per person as the sole measurement of economic flourishing. And it was Keynes who recommended the use of both fiscal and monetary policy to get a recessionary economy back on track.

As we have mentioned above, the Chicago school did resist methodological aggregation. Their methods for analyzing economic phenomena focus on the "micro" decisions made by millions of economic actors. However, while the methods are micro, the goals are macro. The metric of success is the same as Keynes': to maximize annual GDP growth.

Friedman fought back with a "monetarist" model of the economy. This view holds that government tinkering with the money supply is the main driver of the business cycle. Hence it advises against discretionary changes in monetary policy, instead recommending a steady annual expansion of the money supply so people won't constantly need to guess what the Fed might do next.

Friedman's argument was that his model of the macroeconomy was better (i.e., more accurate) than the Keynesian one. As Skousen remarks, in a passage that celebrates Keynes:

> The…most surprising way in which Friedman attacked the Keynesian model was by using the same Keynesian language and theoretical apparatus to undermine Keynesianism and offer a countermodel known as monetarism. Many free-market economists have misunderstood this…brilliant and effective move.… In essence, Friedman, a scholar who was intimately familiar with the Keynesian system, used the language and apparatus of Keynes to prove him wrong. (Skousen 2001, 398–399)

The argument between Keynes and Friedman was like two people arguing over whether someone should have pizza or a hamburger for lunch, without asking whether the person is allergic to gluten or trying to lose weight.

Friedman was beholden to Keynes on an even deeper level, however. His economic models presuppose Keynes' anthropology—his version of *homo economicus*. For Friedman as for Keynes, economic actors are homogenous and controllable, pursuing essentially irrational preferences through predictable—and therefore manipulable—responses to stimuli.

For example, one of Friedman's first great modeling successes was his permanent income hypothesis, most completely fleshed out in his

A Theory of the Consumption Function (Friedman 1957). Recall that one of the fundamental propositions of Keynes' economics is that government spending can be used to stimulate overall spending in the economy through an expenditure multiplier. New government spending creates a ripple effect, because of the worker who receives an extra dollar of income as a result of government buying more goods and services. That worker will turn around and spend at least a portion of that dollar elsewhere, and the person who thereby gets it will turn around and spend it, and so forth. But according to the permanent income hypothesis, Friedman showed—using a massive historic set of U.S. income and consumption data—that people don't actually change their expenditure patterns much in response to short-term changes in their incomes. More specifically, Friedman's analysis suggested that we engage in consumption-smoothing behavior; we make plans for current spending based upon not just our current income, but the income levels we expect to have over our entire lifetimes. As a consequence of Friedman's analysis, there seemed to be little point to "priming the spending pump" through fiscal stimulus.

This singular example of Friedman's work powerfully illustrates Friedman's shrewdness in framing anti-Keynesian policy arguments within the context of Keynesian-style macroeconomic analysis. It also shows how he treats American households as homogenous, and conducts analysis on the assumption that we have no goals other than to maximize the satisfaction of consumption preferences. That is, Friedman contended that his models of "the economy" in Keynes' sense (GDP per person) were superior in "managing the economy" (maximizing annual growth in GDP per person). The only thing Keynes got wrong was to underestimate the quality of our instrumental rationality. We don't reason about ends, but we do reason about means better than Keynes thought we would.

An even clearer example may be found in his 1953 essay, "The Methodology of Positive Economics" (Friedman 1953). The first entry in a collection of his essays, it argued that the ultimate test of the merit of any economic model lay in its usefulness in explaining the past and, more importantly, predicting the future. Friedman believed that if an economist is struggling between two models—one with a great track record but some dubious assumptions, and one that seems more sensible but appears to have less predictive power—the economist should always choose the model with the dubious assumptions. In fact, Friedman calls a model's predictive power "the only relevant test." That is, it's totally acceptable to choose a model whose underlying assumptions are inconsistent with our general observations about human life and the world, as long as its mathematical formulae predict quantitative outcomes better than other, more theoretically justifiable models. A clearer example of the reduction of human beings to no more than loci of consumption data could not be imagined.

Friedman, and the Chicago school he exemplified, bought the Consumption paradigm wholesale. They accepted its aggregation of economic metrics and its reduction of the goal of economics to the maximization of consumer satisfaction. In doing so, they absorbed its anthropology of instrumental rationality and its view that production serves no end but consumption. Their opposition to the Keynesians on public policy questions was of course real and serious. But it amounted to offering a better way to achieve the same goals—we can do the same thing better, faster, and cheaper.

References

EconStories. 2010. Fear the Boom and Bust. https://www.youtube.com/watch?v=d0nERTFo-Sk. Accessed 31 Jan 2019.

Franklin, Benjamin. 1748. Advice to a Young Tradesman. July 21. https://founders.archives.gov/documents/Franklin/01-03-02-0130. Accessed 28 Jan 2019.

Friedman, Milton. 1953. The Methodology of Positive Economics. In *Essays in Positive Economics*, 3–43. Chicago: University of Chicago Press.

Friedman, Milton. 1957. *A Theory of the Consumption Function*. New Delhi: Oxford & IBH.

Friedman, Milton. 1968. Why Economists Disagree. In *Dollars and Deficits*. Englewood Cliffs, NJ: Prentice-Hall.

Galbraith, John Kenneth. 1981. *A Life in Our Times*. New York: Ballantine Books.

Haberler Papers. Various Dates. Stanford University.

Hayek, Friedrich. 1945. The Use of Knowledge in Society. *American Economic Review* 35: 519–530.

Hayek, Friedrich. 1976. *Law, Legislation and Liberty*. Chicago: University of Chicago Press.

Hayek, Friedrich. 2007 [1944]. *The Road to Serfdom*, 37. Chicago: University of Chicago Press.

Hazlitt, Henry. 2007 [1959]. *The Failure of the "New Economics"*. Auburn: Ludwig von Mises Institute.

Heyne, Paul. 2008. Ethics on *The Road to Serfdom* and Beyond. In *Are Economists Basically Immoral? And Other Essays on Economics, Ethics, and Religion*, 339–347. Indianapolis: Liberty Fund.

Hutt, W.H. 1963. *Keynesianism*. Chicago: Henry Regnery.

Kirzner, Israel M. (undated). Another Look at the Subjectivism of Costs. Working Paper. https://history.fee.org/media/2632/1290-another-look-at-the-subjectivism-of-costs.pdf. Accessed 28 Jan 2019.

McVicar, Michael J. 2011. Aggressive Philanthropy. *Missouri Historical Review* 105: 191–212.

Skidelsky, Robert. 1992. *John Maynard Keynes*. London: Penguin.

Skousen, Mark. 2001. *The Making of Modern Economics*. Armonk: M.E. Sharpe.

Stigler, George J. 1950. The Development of Utility Theory: I. *Journal of Political Economy* 58: 307–327.

von Mises, Ludwig. 2007 [1966]. *Human Action*. Indianapolis: Liberty Fund.

Wapshott, Nicholas. 2011. *Keynes Hayek*. New York: W. W. Norton.

PART III

Hollow Prosperity in the Empty Economy

CHAPTER 8

Pull Your Own Weight: Moral and Cultural Conditions for Productivity

The Keynesian Revolution was really a revolution, in every sense of that term. It involved the intellectual overturning of existing categories of thought, and the real-world overthrow of political, economic and social elites. As we have seen, economics was studied as a moral and cultural system for over 2000 years in the paradigms of the classical, Christian, and Enlightenment eras. The moral worldview of each approach was embedded in the cultural systems of civilizations, shaping how money and power were used. The aspiration to detach economics from these moral and cultural foundations had been growing among economists for more than a century before Keynes, culminating in the *methodenstreit* and its resolution in the work of John Neville Keynes. At the same time, the "palace gates" that had protected the old moral and cultural order against such revolutionary uprisings were being thrown open by a striking combination of exogenous historical factors. This paved the way for the arrival of the revolutionary leader, John Maynard Keynes, and the Consumption paradigm built by his successors.

In the next four chapters of this book, we will compare economic paradigms before and after Keynes in light of a question that surfaces the moral worldviews implicit in each paradigm. These four questions reveal the stark difference between the paradigms before and after Keynes, and help reveal the connection between the Keynesian Revolution and the hollow prosperity that contributes so much to our political, economic, and social crises:

V. V. Claar and G. Forster, *The Keynesian Revolution and Our Empty Economy*, https://doi.org/10.1007/978-3-030-15808-8_8

- In Chapter 8: How do economic systems allow us to make use of our world?
- In Chapter 9: How do economic systems connect us to our ancestors and descendants?
- In Chapter 10: How do economic systems shape the way we treat one another?
- In Chapter 11: How do economic systems embody moral realities that transcend human choice?

These are anthropological questions—questions about what it means to be human. That is why they surface the moral and cultural implications of economic paradigms. Human beings are economic creatures, and they are also moral and cultural creatures. The nexus that connects economics to moral and cultural realities is anthropology. The four questions examined in the following four chapters describe our relationship, as human beings, with (respectively) the non-human world, history, one another, and the transcendent.

As we will show, economics can neither avoid morality nor individualize it. Because each of these four questions raises moral concerns that will ubiquitously structure economic behavior, they show that the study of economics cannot avoid recognizing the importance of moral categories. And because each of these four questions involves moral commitments that are in large part culturally structured, the study of economics cannot radically individualize these moral concerns—that is, it cannot acknowledge that morality matters, then reduce morality to a matter of purely individual choice. As we have observed, you are free to announce that you are a chicken, but you are not free to live as a chicken unless everyone around you agrees to treat you as one. In the long run, sustaining your life as a chicken would involve changes to cultural structures that are outside anyone's individual control. Economic actors are, similarly, free to make moral choices given the constraints of cultural structures, but they are not free to live the kind of moral life they would be able to live if their cultural structures were different.

The book's conclusion will consider how economics might begin working toward what we are calling a Moral Consensus paradigm. This would be a paradigm that recognizes the need to study economic behavior as moral and cultural behavior. But it would also recognize the pluralistic nature of the social environment in advanced modernity—the impossibility of restoring, in the social conditions of the modern world, the cultural uniformity of the ancient world.

Production and Consumption

How do economic systems allow us to make use of our world? How do sand and petroleum become a smart phone? This is perhaps the most powerful question for revealing the moral and cultural dimensions of different approaches to economics. As with every other academic discipline, the definition of economics has been a matter of dispute; nonetheless, when economists consider what their discipline exists to study, answers usually center on how people make choices about the use of resources. (More precisely, they center on choices about the use of resources whose use is to some extent costly or limited.) This primarily means the use of the non-human world. True, social reputation is one type of resource, and the intersection of economics with social relationships will occupy our attention in Chapter 10. However, the primary resources occupying the attention of economists are material objects and time. Most economics is therefore the study of what we do (time) to make use of our world (material objects).

Economically, "making use of" the world is understood in terms of production and consumption. How economic systems allow us to make use of the world is a matter of how they understand what it means to "produce" and what it means to "consume," and especially how they connect the two. From one point of view, connecting production to consumption can be understood as the primary function of an economic system. This is why the most widely familiar image from academic economics is a graph of supply (production technologies and costs) and demand (consumption preferences and possibilities).

The Keynesian Revolution reversed how we understand the relationship between production and consumption. The major pre-Keynes paradigms treated production as primary and consumption as secondary, because making good use of the world meant, for them, pursuing a moral purpose (nature, God, reason) that could not be reduced to the satisfaction of consumer appetites. Productive human activity did, of course, serve consumption appetites; that was one of its functions. But it did not exist solely for that purpose. For the Consumption paradigm, production exists solely to serve consumption; consumption has become primary and production secondary, reversing the previous order. This is because after Keynes economics thinks "making good use of the world" can be reduced, at least for purposes of economic analysis, to satisfying consumer appetites.

There is a fatal ambiguity in the word "good" that allows the Consumption paradigm to eat its cake and also have it. Borrowing the nineteenth century economists' rhetoric of moral neutrality, economists say they do not incorporate any view of their own about what it means to make "good" use of the world. Consumers decide what is good, and economists tell them the most efficient way to satisfy the resulting consumption preferences. However, they do treat the maximizing of consumer satisfaction as morally and socially good—indeed, as the particular good to which economics as a discipline is dedicated, and a good so important that it calls for a moral crusade against those stuck in old ways.

As we will see, this makes an enormous difference to economic organization, and by implication other forms of social organization such as politics and the family, insofar as these intersect with economics. Older paradigms subordinated our consumption preferences to our duties. They permitted a role for our desires in shaping our economic lives, but insisting that the performance of duties should have a more profound influence over the way we live. The Consumption paradigm puts our consumption preferences in the driver's seat. Duties play a secondary role. They are boundaries, limits placed upon what has become the primary economic activity: satisfying our appetites. Where duties used to be primary and the need to satisfy consumer preferences was a constraint within which duties were to be satisfied, the order is now reversed. The economic systems and social organization implied in each view are radically different.

The key to this change is the reduction of teleology to no more than the satisfaction of consumer appetites. Teleology, recall, involves the question of what is intrinsically good. We treat the satisfaction of consumer appetites as intrinsically good, regardless of other factors. This means we have no categories for morally differentiating different kinds of consumer preferences and their satisfaction. And through the social influence of academic economics, that lack of moral categories—that moral indifference—has in turn shaped the structure of our economies.

Consumption is not bad in itself. As we saw in Chapter 2, Socrates' interlocutors objected to his description of an economy limited to survival needs, and Socrates himself accepted the objection. Human beings use their environment to accomplish the things they desire, and this not wrong as far as it goes.

But consumption is wrong when the desires it satisfies are wrong, or when it involves a wrong way of satisfying those desires. The Consumption paradigm valorizes consumption, elevating it to an intrinsic good. Thus it robs us of the ability to evaluate consumption morally. Through the social influence of economics, the assumption that all consumption is good in itself has gradually replaced teleological cultural commitments that structured the economy in light of moral standards against which consumption was evaluated.

The Nature Paradigm: Classical Views of Production and Consumption

The classical thinkers of the Nature paradigm believed the highest purpose in human life was wisdom or virtue. They treat economic topics for the purpose of outlining how to live a good (wise or virtuous) life. Recall from Chapter 2 that "economics" did not exist as a discipline or a distinct category of social thought before the modern era; Plato and Aristotle treat what we think of as economics in books on ethics and politics. While both devote significant attention to the role of consumer appetites, in both the goal of production is to facilitate the good life, understood as wisdom or virtue—the highest ends of nature—neither of which can be reduced merely to a set of consumption preferences, since they are concerned with more than consumption.

Plato

Plato's *Republic* is devoted to the question "what is justice?" and its portraits of cities and their social systems are introduced on grounds that describing what a just city looks like will help illustrate what justice is (Plato 1991, 45–46; 368c–369c). The dialogue reveals no independent interest in social systems for their own sake. The goal is to know justice; social systems are described in hopes of discovering what is just. Plato's sketches of the conventional and the utopian city are sketches of the *just* conventional or utopian city. In each case, the city's justice consists primarily in the right ordering of its economic arrangements—people specializing in the specific forms of work for which they are suited, and each specialist doing his own work well while not interfering with the others (Plato 1991, 123; 443b). The economic arrangements exist to serve justice, not justice to serve the arrangements.

Socrates' progress from the conventional to the utopian city illustrates the relationship between production and consumption. As we saw in Chapter 2, when Socrates introduces the conventional city, at first he puts in only the workers needed to provide for bare survival needs. Justice is achieved in a fairly straightforward way in this small and simple community. But Socrates' interlocutors point out that providing only for survival needs fails to satisfy people's desires for more comfortable and enjoyable lifestyles. Socrates had accounted only for those consumer appetites necessary for survival, but consumer appetites are never limited to mere survival. The increase of wealth needed to serve people's larger economic demands introduces much more complex questions of governance. In the simple version of the city, there are few quarrels because there is little to quarrel over, and few invasions because there is little for marauders to take. Comforts and luxuries, even in the smallest quantities, require increased wealth, and thus complex political and military systems to settle disputes and keep invaders at bay. Consideration of how these systems should be arranged ultimately leads into the depiction of the utopian city, where power is in the hands of the wise.

At each stage, as the analysis develops, production is arranged in such a manner as to both conform to justice and satisfy consumer appetites. However, the goal is justice. Satisfying consumer appetites is always a problem that has to be managed rather than a goal to be striven for.

The relationship between production and consumption emerges with particular clarity when we consider the reason the utopian city is utopian. The few who are wise should rule, Socrates says, because they are the only people who will consistently choose justice (and other wise ends) over the satisfaction of their material desires (Plato 1991, 153–161; 472c–480a). However, for precisely the same reason, it seems impossible that the wise ever really will rule. The wise, being good, do not desire power. And even if they did, the unwise would not allow the wise to rule, precisely because they know the wise will choose justice rather than material desires (Plato 1991, 274–275; 592a–592b).

One of Socrates' interlocutors offers the wry comment that the utopian city seems to be a utopia full of unhappy people. Socrates' response reveals the relationship between production and consumption with particular clarity. Socrates does not deny that the utopian city will contain unhappy people (Plato 1991, 97–98; 419a–421c). He holds that the wise few will always be incomparably happier than the unwise many, in any regime, just or unjust. The wise always get what they want (wisdom) while the unwise spend their lives futilely chasing after the satisfaction of desires that are fickle, contradictory and dependent upon uncontrollable circumstances. The point of the utopian regime is not to make individuals happy—a regime cannot make individuals more or less happy than their own level of virtue determines—but to conform to justice (Plato 1991, 198–200; 519d–521b).

To translate that into economic terms: We will be happy to the extent that we organize production in accordance with wisdom and justice, and unhappy to the extent that we organize it to satisfy consumer appetites. Economists today might ask: What does it mean to organize production in accordance with wisdom, if not to organize it in a way that satisfies consumer preferences? What other standard is there? A Platonic answer could begin with distinguishing wise from unwise consumer preferences, organizing the economy to satisfy wise preferences and not unwise ones. However, Plato's metaphysics suggests the possibility of a deeper answer. Wisdom, for Plato, meant knowledge of eternal truths, of which the things in the material world are a sort of shadow or inferior copy. A fully Platonic answer would probably involve organizing the economy so that its use of material things conformed more closely to the eternal truths of which those things are shadows or copies. This is suggested by his statement that while the utopian city might be impossible on earth, "in heaven…perhaps a pattern is laid up for the man who wants to see and found a city within himself on the basis of what he sees" (Plato 1991, 275; 592b). What that might mean depends on how one interprets Plato's notoriously difficult passages on metaphysics—as well as whether one reads the utopian city as a serious reform proposal, a satire or a metaphor—so we will not pursue it further here.

Aristotle

The first book of Aristotle's *Nicomachean Ethics* argues that the goal of human life is virtue, understood as both moral excellence and intellectual excellence (Aristotle 1980, 1–27; I). The *Ethics* and the *Politics* (which originally formed a single continuous work with the *Ethics*) proceed from this starting point. Economic activity is to be organized so that it facilitates the life of virtue. Aristotle's term for economic goods is "equipment," a term that suggests how totally he subordinates economics to virtue. Economic matters are simply the equipment needed for virtue. Indeed, the topic of economic goods does not come up until the *Ethics* has concluded and he has embarked upon the *Politics*, and it only comes up at all because the activity of acquiring and managing equipment is a necessary condition to develop and exercise the virtue for which the household is being organized. A man (for Aristotle, it must be a man) cannot practice diligence without the tools to do his work, generosity without money, or hospitality without a home (Aristotle 1992, 75–91; I.8–11).

The elite leisure class who have the capacity for the kind of life Aristotle considers truly virtuous—devotion to philosophy, art, politics, religion, etc.—cannot pursue that life unless others do the menial work of providing for their physical needs. Workers, including both slaves and free craftsmen, are thus a form of equipment—Aristotle even calls them "tools"—that the leisure class needs to exercise virtue (Aristotle 1992, 63–75; I.4–7). The workers exercise an imperfect or inferior form of virtue by doing what they are suited for and not aspiring to rise above their subordinate stations (Aristotle 1992, 96; I.13). This is the only kind of virtue the majority can aspire to. Their work, in turn, empowers the leisure class to pursue true virtue rather than work. Aristotle does not consider philosophy, art, politics, religion, etc. to be "work" because they involve the mind rather than the body (Aristotle 1992, 455–457; VIII.3).

The primary economic goal for Aristotle is to facilitate the increase of virtue. The desire to increase equipment rather than virtue is a sign of a base soul. To desire more equipment rather than more virtue is perverse, because equipment is supposed to serve virtue, and we are only supposed to care about it insofar as we need it for virtue (Aristotle 1992, 80–87; I.9–10).

The life of virtue also presupposes a stable and just public order that protects each household's use of its equipment for the virtuous life. Households join together in villages and cities to provide things that are necessary for the virtuous life and cannot be provided in isolated households (Aristotle 1992, 58–59; I.2). However, in economic affairs the sole goal of larger social organization is to protect each household's control of its own equipment and work. This is in contrast with "leisure" activities like philosophy, art or religion, which benefit from widely collective activity because they are, Aristotle thinks, mind-based and not body-based. In economics, therefore, private ownership of property by households is to be protected to the maximum extent possible, whereas education in leisure pursuits is to be maximally uniform (Aristotle 1992, 112–119; II.5 and 451–452; VIII.1).

A just economic order can be secured by either aristocracy or democracy. Note that "democracy" for Aristotle means democracy only among the landowning, nonworking leisure class, because anyone who works for a living cannot practice the true virtue of the leisured life, and therefore should not be allowed to participate in ruling (Aristotle 1992, 183–185; III.5). But there are poorer as well as richer people among the leisure class, so there can be "democracy" in which "the poor" (i.e. the poorer among the leisure class) rule through their greater numbers, or "aristocracy" in which "the rich" (i.e. the few among the leisure class who are *especially* rich) rule through a claim to excellence. The important point is not which form of government the city adopts, but whether the government seeks the proper good of the city—to empower its leisured citizens for lives of virtue—rather than the good of one group among the leisured citizens against the others. Aristotle presents the struggle between pure government and corrupt government primarily as a question of whether politics is dominated by a conflict between economic classes (the selfish interests of the poorer many v. the selfish interests of the richer few) or by rulers who do what is right regardless of which class it helps (Aristotle 1992, 189–190; III.7).

Moral education is therefore essential to a just political and economic order. Each form of government tends to produce citizens who admire and seek to emulate the dominant class—the many in a democracy, the rich in an aristocracy. Likewise, principles of justice that favor the dominant class are politically favored; democracies like equality and aristocracies like respect for superior station. The natural tendency of every city is therefore toward a public corruption that favors its dominant class. The only hope for a good public order is for democracies to teach their young people to respect the property of the rich and honor those who achieve excellence in high fields of endeavor, and for aristocracies to teach their young people to respect the property of the poor and treat them with justice and mercy (Aristotle 1992, 310–318; V.5–6).

To put this in production and consumption terms, for Aristotle production is to be arranged to serve those consumption preferences that facilitate virtue, and not those that do not facilitate virtue. The ultimate goal of production is not to satisfy consumption preferences but to facilitate the increase of virtue. To pursue consumption preferences for their own sake is perverse. And, when organized socially in the form of class conflict, the pursuit of consumption preferences for their own sake is *the* omnipresent threat to justice and social order.

The Nature paradigm's concept of production and consumption declined when social developments rendered it implausible. Wisdom and virtue were the ultimate objects of production because they were the highest ends of nature. The rise of Christianity rendered that understanding of nature problematic. Nature was still teleological, because God made it for a purpose. But now, nature pointed to something outside itself—to God. Wisdom and virtue were still good and important, but they no longer exhausted the ends of human life. For those who believed in a transcendent God, classical virtue wasn't enough.

The God Paradigm: Christian Views of Production and Consumption

Christians hold that the purpose of human life is to glorify, obey and enjoy God in Christ. In the God paradigm shaped by Christianity, the purpose of work, property, exchange and specialization of labor was to cultivate and maintain the created world in a way that glorifies, obeys and enjoys God. This applies both to individual economic activity (through work and property) and to community (through exchange and specialization).

The exact way Christian thinkers have related economic activity to glorifying, obeying and enjoying God has changed significantly over time and across Christian traditions. How Christian faith relates to the public order and economic systems of society has been a question to which the God paradigm produced an especially diverse array of answers. However, Christians have almost never attempted to disconnect the Christian faith entirely from public, including economic, questions. Even those schools of Christian thought that most strongly emphasize the need to keep the church distinct from the world, and avoid entanglement with the world's social systems, generally agree that the church should at least strive within its own domain to set an example of economic justice and flourishing for the world outside to see, and speak out as a prophetic witness against the world's economic injustices (Yoder 1994; Hauerwas and Willimon 1989).

Early Christianity

The ethics of most early Christian thinkers were strongly influenced by classical thought. To glorify, obey and enjoy God in Christ, at least as far as economic behavior was concerned, meant primarily to develop wisdom and virtue. There was biblical support for this approach; the book of Proverbs, for example, repeatedly stresses the intimate connection of wisdom and virtue with economics. Thus, on most specific economic topics, early Christian views of economics do not usually differ much from the classical views outlined above. The clearest exception was that Christians taught much stronger imperatives of generosity to the poor and resistance to injustice by the powerful than any classical thinker had done.

In spite of this general continuity on specific issues, there was a very palpable, overarching qualitative difference between Christian and classical approaches to economics. The stronger imperatives to generosity and prophetic resistance to injustice just mentioned arose from different motives than those of the classical thinkers. Those new and different motives were the result of a starkly different cosmological worldview, and that in turn produced a general difference in practical economic life.

Unlike classical thinkers, early Christianity affirmed equal human dignity across economic classes—even for slaves. The church did not so much challenge particular economic practices as the underlying ethos or mindset that shaped the whole system. The classical economy was designed on Aristotle's principle that the leisured class rules the working class—that workers exist to serve their superiors. The early church insisted that everyone at all points in the system existed to serve, glorify and enjoy God in Christ. Living within the still-dominant classical system, early Christians built an alternative way of life defined by their commitment to this principle. Christianity called for economic life characterized by excellent job performance, generosity, hospitality to strangers, and mutual recognition and contribution. The rich in classical culture gave gifts to the poor with the expectation of being repaid with loyalty and obedience; Christians were called to give without expectation of return, and were to view all people at all social levels as fellow workers (Rhee 2012, 103–138). The poor in classical culture did only as much as they had to, since they worked to serve lords and masters who cared little for their well-being; Christians, who worked to serve God, did such an excellent job in their work that even during periods when Christianity was illegal, a striking number of Christians were elevated to positions of important responsibility (Rhee 2012, 43–46). Christians stood out for their willingness to care for the poor and sick, whether Christian or not, even at risk to their own health and well-being (Ferngren 2011; Miller 2011).

Medieval and Early Modern Developments

In the early church, which had little social power, this new kind of economic life was not applied very much toward reform of economic systems. However, Christian affirmation of the equal dignity of all people, and its stronger calls to generosity and justice, would come to have far-reaching economic implications later on. The tight connection between economics and virtue was never repudiated. But Christian thought began to take on new concerns the classical authors had not prompted, and even repudiate some central commitments of classical thinking.

The equal dignity of all people became a direct challenge to the paternalistic systems that classical thought had legitimized. The most important of these was slavery, which was abolished in Western Europe after the fall of the western half of the Roman Empire (Stark 2005, 26–32). Protections for ordinary people's rights once again began to grow after the High Middle Ages (Stark 2005, 71–99). There was a slow but clear trend toward economic structures that recognized greater (though not yet equal) dignity in the role of the ordinary worker. Protections for property and contract rights facilitated the emergence of banks, trading companies and other autonomous economic firms in the later part of the Middle Ages (Stark 2005, 105–159).

This trend became more strongly connected, especially during the Reformation period, to a longstanding Christian theological commitment. Christian teaching had always held that human beings are made in the image of God, and one aspect of this image is human stewardship over the material environment. Medieval thinkers, largely due to the influence of classical ethics and metaphysics, conceived of this in static terms—to prevent the decay and corruption that were endemic to the world after humanity's fall into sin. In the Reformation period, a much more dynamic view of human stewardship emerged. Reviving a long-neglected theme from early figures like Irenaeus, the Reformers spoke of the world not as something to be merely preserved, but to be developed and cultivated over time into greater and greater manifestations of God's glory. The goal was not simply to clean up the world and preserve it, but to help it grow. God made humanity to make something of the world (Gunton 1998, 97–174).

This had a transformative impact on Christian understanding of economics. Human beings do not just move things around with their work and exchange. We create greater value. When our economic activity is good, it increases the degree to which the world glorifies God.

Within this framework, economic growth—the increase of the total amount of good, useful products and services in the world over time—became both plausible and legitimate. While the dramatic growth of the Industrial Revolution came later, the aggregate economy of Western Europe began to grow in the twelfth century (Maddison 2007, 382). Growth became plausible because God designed the world to grow. It became legitimate because growth, if pursued ethically, would fulfill God's intention for the world and glorify him more fully. The Reformers' revival of Irenaeus' view of history, in which the world was originally given to humanity as raw material for a project to be worked on rather than in a final state that was merely to be maintained, contributed especially to the legitimization of growth.

From the High Middle Ages on, there was an increased concern to systematize rules of justice. This was part of the general "scholastic" movement to systematize Christian thought during this period (de Roover 1958; Wittmer 2017). These more rigorous efforts to think through the requirements of Christian justice and form general rules for its application, which was carried on in modified form in the early modern period, contributed to a gradual strengthening of property and contract rights, which in turn provided essential conditions for the Industrial Revolution (Tierney 1997; Gregg 2007; North et al. 2009; McCloskey 2010; Allen 2011; Mokyr 2017). There was, of course, much more to the story, and the exact nature and extent of the contribution of Christianity to the Industrial Revolution is a hotly debated subject. But the role of the medieval scholastics and early modern Reformers and Counter-Reformers in building up greater support for property and contract rights is one important element.

In all this we see the gradual movement of the God paradigm away from the hierarchical dualism of classical thinkers, which divided humanity into workers who labored with their bodies and a class of philosophers (for Plato) or leisured citizens (for Aristotle) who pursued virtue and beauty with their minds. The view that human beings were made to make something of the world, not just with their minds but through their economic work, put all economic classes on more equal spiritual footing. The field hand was no less spiritual than the philosopher, because he was helping take care of the world and make it glorify God more; the philosopher was as much a "worker" as the field hand, because he was responsible to glorify God and contribute to God's world with his activities.

Christian Education for a Christian Economy

For Christian thinkers in all periods, moral education is essential to a well-ordered economy. All major Christian thinkers give a central place to the formation of virtue in their views of economics. This is one area where Christians never repudiated their classical influences. We have noted that the classical thinkers did not think in terms of "economics" as a category, but dealt with these issues as a subset of politics and ethics. Although specialized study of property and exchange did emerge in the late Middle Ages, there continued to be no distinct concept of "economics" until the modern era. Christians studied these issues as a subset of moral philosophy, which was itself subordinate to theology. If anything, the need for moral formation was strengthened with the rise of Christianity, given the Christian doctrine that all human beings are sinful by nature. The economy will only align with God's intention and flourish if people behave virtuously and public systems are just, but such behavior is even less natural in the Christian view than in the classical.

To the extent that Christian views differ from classical views on this topic, it is only in the introduction of two new issues that were not present for classical authors. One is the educational role of the church as a source of spiritual and moral formation. In the classical world, religious institutions were not a major source of moral training. Christianity claims that in addition to its other functions, its faith community must serve as a central source of such training. The second issue, which is related, is the relationship between Christian faith and the public order. Where classical thinkers presupposed a high level of cultural homogeneity within each city, from its earliest period Christianity had to wrestle with the fact that not all people in a given society are Christian. Must Christians work to establish a distinctly Christian public order? Participate in a shared (i.e. not distinctively Christian) public order, but in ways that reflect their Christian commitments? Form separate Christian communities, isolated as much as possible from the public order, and seek to build holy and pure lives in opposition to mainstream society? A breathtaking variety of views on how to deal with these issues emerged among Christians in the first few centuries of the faith, and the debate continues.

To put this in terms of production and consumption, for Christians the ideal economic arrangement orients production toward the achievement of things that glorify, obey and enjoy God. This includes satisfying many kinds of consumption preferences, from meeting the needs of our own households to taking care of the poor. But it is not limited to that—God appreciates goodness, truth and beauty, and wants us to produce a world in which these qualities are more and more fully manifested. And consumption preferences must never be an end in themselves; one of the most consistent warnings of the Bible and Christian ethics is the danger that consumption preferences will become ends in themselves rather than means of glorifying, obeying and enjoying God. Of course this ideal arrangement is not fully achievable, and (depending on whom you ask) may not even be much achievable, in a world where so many people do not want to glorify, obey and enjoy God. What concessions and compromises are appropriate to live as good citizens in the present life was always a topic of much debate for the God paradigm, and among Christians this debate continues today.

The God paradigm as a way of structuring economics, however, does not continue today. Even among Christians, there is not (to speak of) serious interest in reconstructing the old economic order. This is not because Christians have abandoned any of the beliefs described above. The Christian view of how production and consumption relate remains plausible to Christians. But the rise of social pluralism in the modern world—the ongoing coexistence of multiple cosmologies or worldviews within societies—makes it implausible that a whole economy can be organized on Christian principles (or the principles of any other particular religion or comprehensive worldview, for that matter). The God paradigm has been privatized, reduced to a system of life that can be appropriated by those who choose it, and ignored by those who do not. And as we have been emphasizing throughout this book, to privatize a moral view is to remove it from the cultural role of structuring the economy.

The Reason Paradigm: Enlightenment Views of Production and Consumption

In the Reason paradigm of the Enlightenment, the moral imperative to improve the world that emerged in later Christian thought is detached from specifically Christian commitments, and to a large extent from all specifically religious commitments. Reason operates without the benefit of revelation. Even those figures who identify as Christians begin to study economics in a way that is not much informed by theology. The goodness of justice, economic growth and progress remains at the center of economics, giving purpose and structure to all economic laws and practices. But now, improving the world is a moral end in itself rather than (or, at most, in addition to) a way of glorifying God.

This leads to a particular focus on the human condition rather than improving the world in more general terms. Work, property, exchange and specialization of labor are the engines of a historical process that is steadfastly improving the rationality, morality and material well-being of humanity. We are to use them to continue advancing this process. Without the mission to glorify God, human beings have become the exclusive focus of moral concern.

We see this clearly in the founder and paradigmatic representative of the Reason paradigm, Adam Smith. He wrote separate books on moral philosophy and economics, and this differentiation tells us something about how human thought was changing in the Enlightenment period. Nonetheless, he understood the two books as related, and he was right; the content of each cannot be understood without the other. Both books take the improvement of the human condition (intellectual, moral and material) as the central good to be achieved in all human action. The *Theory of Moral Sentiments* explains why we desire to improve the conditions of all people rather than only ourselves; the *Wealth of Nations* explains how this goal can best be achieved.

The goal was not to get rich as such, but to increase well-being. Smith and his peers especially opposed the idea that our goal should be simply to increase the amount of money and resources people had. He argued that we should seek to increase the production of good, useful products and services rather than the possession of money and things.

In fact, maximizing money income and the possession of precious resources was precisely the goal of Smith's greatest opponents, the mercantilists. Against their views, Smith held that it was the productive capacity of human labor to do good things that improve the human condition that ought to be maximized in a well-ordered economy.

Appetites and Duties

The relationship between consumer appetites and moral duties underwent a dramatic change in the Enlightenment period. Duty was still superior, but a much greater expectation of natural harmony between appetite and duty—between pursuing our self-interest and pursuing the interests of others—was introduced. It must be understood that this was a moral harmony. It was not that we were to do good to others solely or even primarily in order to gain advantages for ourselves, such that the motive to do good to others was ultimately selfish. Rather, through education and the use of reason, we were to overcome selfish passions and recognize that doing good to others is our own greatest good. Enlightened self-interest does not mean selfishness that has learned to calculate better. It means self-interest that has become *morally* enlightened. Enlightenment thought does not strive to repudiate altruism and embrace selfishness, but to harmonize morality with self-interest by teaching us to seek our own good through altruism. In this, the Enlightenment represented a return to the classical emphasis on virtue—recall Plato's happy philosophers, who always get what they want. But now, partly as a result of Christian influence, there is an emphasis on serving others and improving the world. To miss this point is to miss the essence of Enlightenment thought.

Once we have a rational and self-disciplined understanding of what our own interests are, a moral harmony between appetite and duty emerges. The same policies that advance knowledge and virtue also make us wealthier and better able to satisfy our consumption preferences. The economic policies of *The Wealth of Nations* are, on one level, recommended to national leaders as the best way to enrich their own nations. However, throughout the book these policies are also depicted as centrally important to an unfolding dynamic of progress in human history. "There is scarcely a page of the *Wealth of Nations* where history and theory are sundered from each other," wrote George Unwin (Unwin 1927, 18). This is especially obvious in Book III, on "the Progress of Opulence," whose first chapter is entitled "Of the Natural Progress of Opulence"; subsequent chapters describe how good policy permits, while bad policy hinders, this "natural progress." The interdependent development of greater reason, justice and wealth over time has revealed the wisdom of these policies and their beneficial effect on humanity at large. Smith is both a realist who appeals to national self-interest and an idealist who appeals to the good of the whole human race.

But how do we get to the point where people achieve a rational and self-disciplined understanding of their own interests? Honesty may well be the best policy, but only rational and self-disciplined people will know this. Smith and his peers were well aware of this problem.

Smith was particularly concerned that increased specialization of labor in the modern economy would lead ordinary workers to live in very small mental worlds. "The understandings of the greater part of men are necessarily formed by their ordinary employments," he wrote. The worker whose employments are very narrow and repetitive "has no occasion to exert his understanding" and is in danger of becoming "as stupid and ignorant as it is possible for a human creature to become" (Smith 1994, 840; V.1.3.ii). Concern for the ordinary worker's mental and moral development would be critical to both the worker's and society's economic and humane success.

Moral education was essential to achieve the envisioned harmony between appetite and duty. Smith devoted a long and carefully reasoned section of *The Wealth of Nations* to educational institutions. This included not only schools to educate the young, but churches as educational institutions to improve the people at large. Smith was as dissatisfied with the decrepit state of education in his society as he was with the Corn Laws, and he saw the same evil in both: government monopoly. He advocated broadening access to tuition subsidies in order to give parents a choice of schools, and greater religious freedom that would give congregants a choice of churches. This would reward the diligent and faithful teachers, while squeezing out the schoolmasters and pastors who hid behind the shield of state power while failing to meet people's needs—just as abolishing the Corn Laws would reward those who delivered corn to the hungry while squeezing out selfish rent-seekers (Smith 1994, 819–875; V.1.3.ii–iii).

In all this, we see a reconciliation of appetite and duty, which in earlier thought were perpetually opposed to each other, or at best in strong tension. But we do not see a reversal of underlying priorities. For Enlightenment thinkers, it is natural for our appetites to lead us to right behavior. A well-educated mind will see how obeying the moral rules will make us happier than breaking them, and this will lead to good behavior. This stands against the classical view that very few people have souls capable of the higher reaches of virtue, and reach it only by arduous training; it stands equally against the Christian view that sinful human nature darkens the mind and disorders the will in ways that only divine power can remedy. However, duty remains firmly in the driver's seat. Our appetites may align with what improves the human condition generally, but we have a duty to promote the good of humanity whether we happen to want to or not. The Enlightenment view that bad desires call for correction through education entails the view that some desires are good and others are bad, and that the public order must take care to correct the bad ones and encourage the good ones.

Crucially, Enlightenment thinkers treat improving the human condition—what it means to be rational, to be morally good, and to be materially well off—as objective rather than merely subjective. Which actions and desires are good or bad is not dependent on anyone's choices. The good for human beings is what it is, whether people want it to be that or not.

Recall Smith's attacks on Mandeville, which we saw in Chapter 2. Mandeville sough to explain all behavior with supposedly higher, transcendent motives as really a mask for the private selfishness of the individual. The wealthy patron doesn't fund art to further beauty, but to feed his vanity. Smith's reply, echoing the argument in Socrates' reply to Thrasymachus as well as key passages in Aristotle's *Ethics*, is that the actual human behavior we see around us cannot be explained without reference to external moral standards. Any given wealthy patron may well be a merely selfish person who wants to feed his vanity, but if everyone viewed art that way, beautiful art would not in fact feed anyone's vanity. Someone, somewhere, has to value beauty for its own sake to establish patronage of the arts as a prestigious activity. A particular selfish patron can feed his vanity by funding beautiful art only if it is already established as a general and fixed proposition that beauty is good (Smith 2006, 308–312; VII.4).

Smith's argument against Mandeville implies moral standards that are fixed (not dependent upon choice) and general (not the mere subjective desire of an individual). Similarly, the economics of the Enlightenment presupposes standards of what is good and bad in economics that are fixed and general. The idea that we could have a well-ordered and flourishing economy without taking great pains to structure it so it favored enlightenment over superstition, knowledge over ignorance, generosity over selfishness, frugality over prodigality and self-control over degeneracy struck most Enlightenment thinkers as unambiguously monstrous and detestable.

Human Progress

In production and consumption terms, the central goal of the Enlightenment for economics was to produce human progress. "Human progress" did not mean simply giving humans more and more of whatever they wanted. On the contrary, consumption appetites had to be ruthlessly and relentlessly reformed in order to change them from what they were to what they ought to be—to align consumption preferences with genuinely enlightened production preferences, not the other way around. Both the natural laziness and short-sightedness of human nature and the corrupt influence of selfish political and religious oppressors had established in humanity a morass of erroneous consumption preferences that the enlighteners set out to remove.

The Reason paradigm declined, as we have seen, because it lacked the deeper moral resources to maintain these robust moral standards. Everyone can see that wisdom and virtue must be normative if we believe that a teleological nature such as Plato and Aristotle believed in is the ultimate source of meaning in human life, or that glorifying, obeying and enjoying God must be normative if we believe that the even more teleological Christian God is the ultimate source of meaning in human life. It is not equally obvious that rationality demands these normative commitments, once "reason" is separated from higher sources of meaning in God or nature and set up as an ultimate standard. As the schools of thought launched by the Enlightenment separated themselves from the influences they had inherited from classical and Christian thought, their teleological commitments became more and more anemic. This led to a tendency to make fewer normative claims, and also a tendency to justify normative claims without higher teleological ends. The role of the former tendency in economics was the normative/positive split we saw in Chapter 3; the role of the latter was the moral crusade for maximal consumer satisfaction we saw in Chapter 4.

The Consumption Paradigm: Views of Production and Consumption After Keynes

The characterization of how production relates to consumption in the *General Theory* is one of the most important moves it makes for purposes of the emergence of the Consumption paradigm. Keynes reversed the prior paradigms' understanding of the relationship of production and consumption. He turned it on its head, making consumption primary and production secondary.

Reversing the Relationship

Keynes makes this move this bluntly, and prominently, but in a way calculated to minimize readers' awareness that a critical move is being made (and hence minimize reader consideration of whether the move is justifiable):

> All production is for the purpose of ultimately satisfying a consumer. (Keynes 2013, 46)
>
> Consumption—to repeat the obvious—is the sole end and object of all economic activity. (Keynes 2013, 104)

Almost as important as these statements themselves is the way Keynes presents them in the text of the *General Theory*. Appearing here, in stark isolation, these bold sentences convey the audacity of their author in making them. However, in the original context, they are presented as if they were merely obvious comments to which no sensible person would object—much as a physicist might stop before embarking on the description of a difficult problem to state, "of course we are assuming that this event is taking place on the earth's surface, with the standard gravity and air pressure and other conditions that prevail there. If we did this on Mars or in the stratosphere, we would get different results." The thing hardly needs to be said, and is said merely for the sake of completeness.

In fact, far from stating the obvious, Keynes is doing the economics equivalent of transferring a physics experiment to Jupiter. For it was precisely the central commitment of classical, Christian and Enlightenment approaches to economics that not all production is ultimately intended to satisfy a consumer, and consumption is thus not the sole end—it is not even the main end—of economic activity.

It is not accurate to cite Adam Smith as a precedent for these statements about all production serving consumption. In *The Wealth of Nations*, when Smith says that "consumption is the sole end and purpose of all production; and the interest of the producer ought to be attended to only so far as it may be necessary for promoting that of the consumer," the context of that statement is strictly limited to a discussion of trades that serve consumers, and were the object of mercantilist policy (Smith 1994, 715; IV.8). "All production" here means all production within the scope of the discussion at hand. Examples he cites include the production of wool, yarn, cloth, hides and furs. If Smith meant this statement to be absolutized across all economic behavior, as Keynes does, what are we to make of his section on expenses for the dignity of the state? (Smith 1994, 876; V.1.4). Smith is addressing the mercantilist argument that national economic policy should seek to enrich economic producers, i.e. companies. This is not an argument about the purpose of all economic activity or the general relationship between production and consumption. It is an argument about the purpose of one specific kind of economic activity (running a business) and the relationship between production and consumption in one specific form (commerce). Smith is holding up customer accountability against a crony capitalism that enriches businesses based on their political connections rather than whether they serve their customers well. His only point is that enriching producers does not enrich consumers. It was not his intention to detach economic production from a moral commitment to the goals of human progress, such as education, virtue and reform, to which he constantly appeals in his writings as fixed, objective teleological commitments.

Public Works with Purpose

Keynes himself invokes two telling examples that illustrate how he was reversing the relationship between production and consumption in a way Smith was not. Before this passage, Keynes has been complaining that government public works projects, which would keep people employed, face stiff political opposition. He then remarks:

> Ancient Egypt was doubly fortunate, and doubtless owed to this its fabled wealth, in that it possessed two activities, namely, pyramid-building as well as the search for the precious metals, the fruits of which, since they could not serve the needs of man by being consumed, did not stale with

> abundance. The Middle Ages built cathedrals and sang dirges. Two pyramids, two masses for the dead, are twice as good as one; but not so two railways from London to York. Thus we are so sensible, have schooled ourselves to so close a semblance of prudent financiers, taking careful thought before we add to the "financial" burdens of posterity by building them houses to live in, that we have no such easy escape from the sufferings of unemployment. We have to accept them as an inevitable result of applying to the conduct of the State the maxims which are best calculated to "enrich" an individual by enabling him to pile up claims to enjoyment which he does not intend to exercise at any definite time. (Keynes 2013, 131)

Pointing out this passage about how ancient and medieval civilizations in fact devoted huge effort and resources to things that "could not serve the needs of man by being consumed" is more than just a cheap "gotcha." In addition to exposing the falsehood of Keynes' insistence that it is simply obvious and unproblematic to say the end of all economic activity is consumption, it illustrates the depth and revolutionary character of the change Keynes is making.

Egypt and medieval Europe had this inexhaustible supply of politically palatable public works projects, which Keynes so envies, *precisely because they believed economic activity ought to be dedicated to something higher than consumption*. The pyramids and the cathedrals were built with the intention that they would last for eternity, standing forever as monuments to the gods, or God, and also as monuments to their own dedication to the divine. Of course, once the pyramids and the cathedrals are there, modes of consumption (such as tourism) can arise around them, but this is secondary. The question of whether "showing our dedication to the gods" can be understood as a consumption preference will be examined at greater length below; for now, it suffices to say that the Egyptians at least did not think of the pyramids this way, nor the medievals their cathedrals, and so on any possible view a radically different perspective from the one that prevailed before has been introduced.

This example shows that Keynes is doing something with the relationship between production and consumption that Smith was not doing. Smith was part of that bygone world in which people built things for higher purposes. That is the whole point of his critique of Mandeville. Where Mandeville looked at great art or beautiful churches and saw only the cheap vanity of their sponsors, Smith saw real higher purpose at work.

Teleology is the key to the change. Where consumer appetite is the only intrinsic good, no work is intrinsically good. All work is reduced to merely an instrumental good, valuable only as a way to earn a paycheck for consumption. A society that structures its economy on a view that some things are intrinsically good will never have trouble finding good work worth doing. It may encounter other kinds of difficulties, such as matching workers to jobs efficiently, but it will not lack for work that is publicly recognized as good. However, a society that structures its economy without a teleology beyond consumer appetite will not view any work as good work worth doing. It only sees good paychecks worth earning.

It is also worth noting that public projects seeking to produce intrinsic goods are perfectly possible in the advanced modern world; they are rare only because we have been taught not to want them. John F. Kennedy sold the moon landing to the American people as a grand project inherently worthy of undertaking regardless of tangible benefits (although he was careful to mention those, too). It would catapult humanity into a new age of history, crossing a threshold that could never be uncrossed. And he also stressed that the moral character of future life would be shaped by the moral character of those who led the way into new frontiers—if we love freedom and want the future to love freedom, we must get to space before the enemies of freedom do. This was not simply a matter of protecting the United States from Soviet space weapons in the short term (although it was that, too); it was an appeal to the inherent rightness of freedom and a claim that the United States owed it to the distant future to make sacrifices to ensure the future would be free (Kennedy 1962). And in all this he was right. That such projects of transcendent value have been getting more and more rare over the last century is partly a byproduct of the fact that in that period so many of them were poorly managed by large, unaccountable government bureaucracies. But it is also a byproduct of the success of the Keynesian Revolution, which has transformed the political and cultural landscape in ways that make such projects seem inherently implausible. Indeed, things now run so strongly in the other direction that presidents respond to major, traumatic national emergencies by urging people to go shopping for their country.

How This Reversal Shapes the General Theory of the General Theory

The reversal of the relationship between production and consumption is no minor thing in the *General Theory*. It shapes Keynes' theory at its core. To see this, we need only look at his summary of the general theory, which comes at the start of Chapter 18 of the book.

In the theory's calculations of what affects unemployment, some elements are considered "given." These are treated as fixed information. Such elements are not a subject of the analysis, but an environmental factor (so to speak) affecting the analysis. By contrast, the "independent variables" are the subject of the analysis. The general theory of the *General Theory* is a statement of how a given set of independent variables will affect the unemployment rate (the "dependent variable") under a given set of fixed circumstances.

It is therefore of utmost importance to note which elements Keynes uses as independent variables affecting unemployment, and which he treats as fixed circumstances. The only independent variables are the propensity to consume (i.e. the extent to which consumers will buy the things they want, as opposed to saving their money), interest rates and the marginal value of capital. Among the long list of fixed factors, Keynes includes the amount and skill level of available labor, and the tastes of the consumer (i.e. what people want to consume, rather than the extent to which they will in fact consume it).

Obviously any analysis must hold most of the factors in the world as fixed, and select only a relatively small number of factors to treat as variables. Otherwise, no analysis would be possible. But this is just another way of saying that the choice of what to consider fixed and what to consider variable is of paramount importance. It does not just affect the analysis, it constitutes the analysis.

Keynes treats propensity to consume as a variable, but not propensity to work. This embeds the primacy of consumption over production in the core of Keynes' theory. Why wouldn't the state of "animal spirits" among workers, whether anemic or excited, affect their productivity at work? And, on the margin, the employment rate? The underlying assumption is that people only work for a paycheck, i.e. that people have no economic motives other than consumption. Obviously the paycheck doesn't vary with animal spirits. All awareness of the role of workers' personal and social capital in employment (and, for that matter, the personal and social capital of the employers) is excluded by definition.

Treating consumer tastes as fixed also embeds the primacy consumption over production in the core of Keynes' theory. None of the previous major paradigms treated consumer preferences as fixed. On the contrary, changing the content of consumer preferences was a core concern for the

Nature, God and Reason paradigms alike. But if consumption is primary, consumer preferences must be considered fixed, for there is nothing above them to determine how they should change. There is no reference point in terms of which to evaluate how they ought to be different from what they are. On the contrary, they themselves are the reference point in terms of which everything else is to be evaluated and changed. You can measure whether the shoe fits your foot, and change it if it does not; you cannot measure whether your foot fits your foot, and change it if it does not.

A New View of Humanity

This is, in one way, the deepest level of the Keynesian Revolution. The revolution Keynes brought to economics can be summed up in the statement that where before, production of what was objectively good (virtue, glorifying God, human progress) was the purpose of economic life and consumption was organized to serve it, now consumption (satisfaction of people's appetites) is the purpose of economic life and production shall henceforth be organized to serve it.

This gives us a profoundly different picture of how human beings relate to their natural environment, which implies it gives us a profoundly different picture of what human beings are. In the classical Greco-Roman world, human beings were a part of nature—the rational and responsible part. Therefore the right use of nature was to cultivate intellectual and moral virtue, not seeking to change the world and concerned to preserve the achievements of reason and morality against inevitable decay. For Christians, human beings are drawn up by God's creative power *from* nature (hence their biological continuity with it) but are also set by God *over* nature with authority to manage it. Therefore the right use of nature was to glorify, obey and enjoy God. During the Enlightenment, human continuity with nature was even more attenuated. Human beings were seen as rational, responsible and perfectible users of nature, echoing the classical period in one sense (the emphasis on reason and moral agency) but now with the much more active and ambitious goal of seeking progress and improvement cumulatively over generations, in contrast to classical contentment and conservation. For Keynes, and for essentially all economics since Keynes, human beings are consumers of nature—bundles of appetites, attached to more-or-less clever brains that are capable of figuring out how to manipulate their environment to maximize the satisfaction of those appetites.

If consumption is primary, consumption appetites are sovereign. On all three of the older paradigms, one of the most essential economic responsibilities is to evaluate and regulate your consumption appetites. Hypothetically, consumers remain free to continue evaluating and regulating their own appetites in economics since Keynes, and to some extent they do. But there is a catch. Where before we were obligated to evaluate and regulate our appetites, now we are merely free to do so if we wish. But do we wish? That is a question about desires, not a question about obligations. Before, obligation was primary and desire was secondary. Now, desire is primary—even over obligation. We will regulate our appetites only to the extent that we *desire* to regulate our appetites. And, to repeat, we do in fact desire to regulate our appetites to some extent—partly because we can often get more gratification of our appetites by doing so, and partly because human beings do have a natural conscience. But an economy organized on the assumption we need only evaluate and regulate our appetites to the extent that we desire to do so will be very different from an economy organized on the assumption that the evaluation and regulation of consumer appetites is a primary human obligation, overriding other concerns.

Note that the long, slow extraction of humanity from nature across the earlier paradigms has been abruptly reversed. Over the course of the Nature, God and Reason paradigms, human beings became progressively less a *part of* nature and progressively more *set over* nature as its managers or stewards. In the Consumption paradigm, appetite is sovereign, and appetite is something that comes to us from nature. It is our nature that assigns to us desires to eat and sleep, desires to enjoy indulgences and avoid labor, desires for identity and recognition. It includes the spontaneous desire for moral self-approbation that we have referred to in the above paragraph as "natural conscience." Where appetite is sovereign, nature is sovereign.

The phrase "animal spirits" now begins to take on a sinister significance. In that passage, and indeed throughout the *General Theory*, consumers are treated not as rational and responsible agents but as creatures of instinct. The goal of the economist is to control the creatures by controlling the stimuli (hence the policy of "stimulus") that activate the consumer's instincts. In the Consumption paradigm, we are now so much a part of nature that we are not even the rational and responsible part of nature. We have fallen so far that we have fallen below even that level. We are merely an apparatus of nature. We respond to external input from nature (stimuli) in obedience to internal input from nature (desires). We are now below nature, subordinate to it. Nature gives us desires (our marching orders) and our job is to satisfy (obey) them.

Consequences of the New View

This new picture of how we use the world has far-reaching and revolutionary implications for every area of economic life. Keynes distils the center of his social vision in a single imperative: "I should support all sorts of policies for increasing the propensity to consume" (Keynes 2013, 325).

One striking passage shows unmistakably Keynes' flat reversal of the older relationship between production and consumption. The context, as with the passage about pyramids and cathedrals, is Keynes lamenting a lack of political support for public works projects such as housing:

> If the Treasury were to fill old bottles with banknotes, bury them at suitable depths in disused coalmines which are then filled up to the surface with town rubbish, and leave it to private enterprise on well-tried principles of *laissez-faire* to dig the notes up again (the right to do so being obtained, of course, by tendering for leases of the note-bearing territory), there need be no more unemployment and, with the help of the repercussions, the real income of the community, and its capital wealth also, would probably become a good deal greater than it actually is. It would, indeed, be more sensible to build houses and the like; but if there are political and practical difficulties in the way of this, the above would be better than nothing. (Keynes 2013, 129)

Try to imagine Smith, that great champion of productivity, writing anything remotely like this.

With this visionary scheme to hire workers to dig through caverns of garbage in search of cash—about the preferability of which to doing nothing Keynes appears to have been perfectly serious—Keynes discards any concern for productivity in our work. The only thing this work produces is paychecks. But for Keynes, that's the point. Doing anything—even work that is literally useless and meaningless—is good if it just gets money into people's hands in a socially acceptable way so they can get back to consuming. The consumption of the paycheck is literally all we care about.

Here we see, distilled in a sort of chemical purity, the effects of removing teleology from economics. Work, the activity that takes up the large majority of most people's waking hours, is purely an instrumental good. It is a means to the end of the paycheck, and for purposes of economics it has no other end for the worker. It builds nothing, accomplishes nothing, the worker cares about.

This is not, in fact, how people actually make decisions about their work. Keynes' theory has no place for that Uber driver in Omaha who took pride in seeing the fruits of his earlier labor as a glassworker while he drove around the city. As Keynes uses his formula to measure economic reality, he can only recognize the existence of consumption preferences. Production preferences don't exist in his universe.

This approach excludes traditional approaches to increasing employment that center on helping people become better (and therefore more productive and economically attractive) workers: schools and job training, moral education and reform. They are excluded not because they have failed; they have often been quite successful. They are excluded because the Consumption paradigm has arbitrarily ruled out the non-paycheck elements of employment, by definition. If paychecks are available, work will happen automatically, without much need to pay attention to things like building personal and social capital, such as a work ethic. The underlying anthropology of this view is animalistic—people are basically animals responding to stimuli, serving their consumption appetites and no higher end. We get them working by stimulating their appetites, not by helping them grow in their capacity to accomplish things that are worth accomplishing.

Or consider the paradox of thrift. Keynes scoffs at the idea that saving is morally virtuous. For Keynes, the only use of money is consuming it, so refusing to consume it is perverse. We are not building up a better world over time. Just as we do not create things to last forever, we do not save up to leave something to our grandchildren.

The paradox of thrift reverses the relationship between gaining wealth and enjoying wealth, productivity and consumption, in the *homo economicus* model. For Mill, the main goal of *homo economicus* was to gain wealth, and the desire to spend more than necessary in the present was an obstacle to be overcome. The clear implication is that Mill's *homo economicus* is striving to accumulate wealth over time, to save and build up something that will outlast one's own life. For Keynes, who puts consumption at the center, the obstacle is not the desire to spend but the desire to save. Where Mill's model is working to overcome the desire to spend, Keynes' is working to overcome the desire to save.

"Economic Possibilities for Our Grandchildren"

The new Keynesian view of production and consumption is also visible in Keynes' 1930 essay "Economic Possibilities for Our Grandchildren," an important precursor of the *General Theory*. In the early days of the Great Depression, when some began to speculate that economic growth might never return, Keynes had the foresight to see that the reverse was true, although he had a limited vision of the reasons. He predicted a future of ongoing economic growth, fueled by technological improvements and the money making magic of compound interest. In this world where automatic growth is the gift of inhuman things, machines and bank accounts, human work would matter less and less. People would spend less and less of their time working, until work would take up only a trivial portion of the day.

For Keynes, modern economic growth does not come from human beings and their capacity for production, as it did in the Reason paradigm. Things, not people, are the source of productivity growth. People consume what things produce. This view is sustained by a naïve reading of history, in which Keynes attributes the Industrial Revolution entirely to the accidental discovery of new machines and banking systems. With a shocking lack of basic historical knowledge, Keynes declares that before the Industrial Revolution, there was not only no technological development to speak of, but no economically important progress in "banking, statecraft, mathematics, astronomy and religion" (Keynes 1963, 2). Keynes has no categories of thought for understanding the human basis of productivity.

Keynes understood that his view of production and consumption implied a social revolution. He predicted that the decline of work would create a massive moral disruption in society, because it would upend the moral norms, woven deeply into the fabric of western culture, that people ought to find meaning and purpose through the good things they produce in their daily work. He observes a basic "purposiveness" in human psychology that would, at first, become badly dysfunctional when disconnected from its traditional objects, all of which are connected to daily work (Keynes 1963, 6). But he did not shy away from this dangerous social revolution; he welcomed it. He did not want a return to meaningful work. He wanted people to overcome the expectation that work would be meaningful. "We shall inquire more curiously than is safe to-day into the true character of this 'purposiveness' with which in varying degrees Nature has endowed almost all of us" (Keynes 1963, 6).

In the post-work future, there is almost nothing to do but relax and enjoy life. Economics as we now understand it—economics devoted to the goal of growth—would disappear, as its concerns would be provided for automatically by machines and bank accounts. Our survival needs securely provided for, Keynes expresses the hope that more people will be able to embrace a life similar to that of the Bloomsbury group elite, freeing themselves of attachment to materialistic greed, envy and vanity, simply enjoying life as it comes.

> We shall once more value ends above means and prefer the good to the useful. We shall honor those who can teach us how to pluck the hour and the day virtuously and well, the delightful people who are capable of taking direct enjoyment in things, the lilies of the field who toil not, neither do they spin. (Keynes 1963, 7)

Recall from Chapter 4 that what prevented the many from enjoying this kind of life, in the eyes of the Bloomsbury elite, was the way of life devoted to productive work in the modern economy. With the relentless need for productivity gone, human vanity would still divert many into materialistic goals, but it might become possible for more people to overcome that temptation. Human history reaches its final point of development: Bloomsbury bohemia for the masses.

The masses today, however, must be kept busy—and hence kept greedy:

> But beware! The time for all this [virtue] is not yet. For at least another hundred years we must pretend to ourselves and to every one that fair is foul and foul is fair; for foul is useful and fair is not. Avarice and usury and precaution must be our gods for a little longer still. For only they can lead us out of the tunnel of economic necessity into daylight. (Keynes 1963, 7)

The Bloomsbury life is not for the common worker, not yet; today, it is only for the elite. Until the glorious future arrives, the fires of mass consumption must be kept burning. The greed and vanity of the masses must be stoked and increased, not resisted. Only by constantly stirring up more and more greed, more and more materialistic consumer appetites, can we reach the glorious future where the need for work, and hence for the fires of consumption, can begin to fade away.

Keynes justifies this view of things, in a very Bloomsbury-esque move, by writing that we have only two kinds of consumption desires—survival needs and the envy-driven desires of vanity (Keynes 1963, 4). This is an empty vision of what work is for; human work produces only survival and vice. For anything else, we must look beyond economics to things like art and literature. Survival provided for, everyone will either collapse into vice or join the Bloomsbury bohemians and escape economics.

The emptiness of Keynes' vision of what work is for creates an emptiness—one that appears to trouble him—in his vision of what human beings will do in the future he foresees. He acknowledges that human "purposiveness" seems to be ineradicable, and that this suggests we will not be fully satisfied even by the life of pure enjoyment, accomplishing nothing beyond our own enjoyment, that awaits us:

> For purposiveness means that we are more concerned with the remote future results of our actions than with their own quality or their immediate effects on our own environment. The "purposive" man is always trying to secure a spurious and delusive immortality for his acts by pushing his interest in them forward into time. He does not love his cat, but his cat's kittens; nor, in truth, the kittens, but only the kittens' kittens, and so on forward forever to the end of cat-dom. (Keynes 1963, 6)

This is the source of the social dysfunction he predicts. But this does not lead him to go back and question his theory. He is surprisingly incurious about its consequences. Keynes simply does not seem to feel responsible to ask the question: What is the purpose of our purposiveness, if we are striving toward a utopia without purpose?

All three of the older paradigms avoid the problem Keynes encounters here because they are teleological. In these paradigms, producing things that are intrinsically good (virtue, wisdom, piety, progress, etc.) is a human need. This need cannot be reduced to a consumption preference, precisely because it is a need to produce things that are intrinsically good, as opposed to instrumentally good. The whole point is that we desire these things because we judge them to be good independent of our desire for them. Thus, there is always good work worth doing for each of these paradigms. Indeed, while there will always be difficulties in connecting workers with jobs, the closer we get to utopia the more good work worth doing we will have available.

The Moral Compass: Production Over Consumption

All major economic paradigms before the Keynesian Revolution began from a view that the purpose of human life was to do something intrinsically good, and economic systems were to be organized to serve that good. An economy that helped facilitate the pursuit of the good was viewed as rightly ordered. An economy that hindered it was disordered.

Production Comes First

This teleology—moral directedness—had the effect of placing production in a logically primary position, taking precedence over consumption. The reason is simple: in each case, economic life is to *produce* something over and above the satisfaction of consumer preferences. For classical thinkers, it was wisdom, justice and virtue. For Christian thinkers, it has been to glorify God and put God's love and holiness into action in the world. For the Enlightenment economists, it was the continuing progress of humanity in knowledge, virtue and material well-being. In each case, wherever consumer preferences conflict with the higher good, the economy is to prioritize producing the good over satisfying consumer preferences.

These teleologies can also be stated in more anthropological terms. In the Nature paradigm, a person is an animal (part of nature) with fixed capacities for reason and virtue, and a good person is a person maximizing their use of those capacities. In the God paradigm, a person is a being made in the image of God, and a good person is a person living in accordance with that identity. In the Reason paradigm, a person is an embodied mind with expandable capacities for reason and virtue, and a good person is a person seeking to expand their own and others' capacities, managing and reforming the world with and for ever-greater reason and virtue.

The higher goods elevated above consumption preferences by these pre-Keynes paradigms—virtue, wisdom, piety, progress—cannot themselves be understood as merely consumption preferences. The higher goods are higher precisely because they are not chosen. They are objectively good, not good because we desire them. This is the very reason the older paradigms placed them above and outside economic systems and behavior, guiding those systems and behavior. Economic flourishing required a relatively fixed and stable moral compass; "fixed and stable" is of course inconsistent with "dedicated to satisfying consumer appetites," even good ones.

Economic theory that does not recognize duty as a category distinct from appetites (or preference, desire, pleasure, utility, etc.) cannot account for our sense of duty by calling it an appetite. That fails to recognize what a duty is. Morality is not really morality if it is nothing more than a fuller awareness of one's own totally autonomous choices. This is because if the choices are really autonomous, they are idiosyncratic and arbitrary, and therefore morally meaningless. Conversely, if the choices are not arbitrary but have real moral content, they are not really autonomous, but are made within the context of some objective framework of meaning that is what it is regardless of our choices. If I choose to dedicate my life to charitable works and my neighbor dedicates his life to collecting pornography, how can either choice be morally evaluated if not with reference to some standard that is not dependent upon anyone's choices? And once we have such a standard, we cannot then reduce obedience to this standard to a mere consumer choice without robbing it of its objective status, which was the only reason we sought it out in the first place. Of course, for the virtuous person, doing your duty becomes itself a pleasure. But this can happen only when desire is subordinate to duty. The distinction between having a sense of duty to do something and the pleasure of knowing you did your duty remains, and remains important.

Productivity was the rock-bottom economic phenomenon for the major pre-Keynes economic paradigms. As we observed in Chapter 2, four common elements that have always run through the center of economics are work, property, exchange and specialization. These four things occur in a specific order of logical priority. Specialization is possible only because exchange happens; exchange is possible only because property happens; property is possible only because work happens. But work was not understood as something that existed solely to serve consumption or any other exclusively economic factor; rather, work existed to serve the good generally. If you tried to go "behind" work, logically speaking, you didn't find anything that was specifically economic; the only thing you found was the moral good as such. Work—productivity—was therefore the defining factor that divided what was economic from what was religious, political, etc.

Of course, the need to satisfy consumer preferences is an important factor in every serious approach to economics. Socrates' interlocutors in the *Republic* speak for the human race at large when they object to an economic theory so caught up in otherworldly moralizing that it is unwilling to make concessions to consumer preferences beyond survival needs. And Socrates conceded this point. One of the central challenges of economic theory since the *Republic* has been how we can have a morally good economy and also provide adequately for the satisfaction of consumer preferences.

That this challenge is a challenge—a problem—is the whole point. Aligning economic production to satisfy consumer preferences is easy, if production exists for no other purpose. For pre-Keynes paradigms, the whole challenge of economics was to dedicate economic production to some higher good, and still put hearty dinners rather than bean soup on people's tables (to say nothing of cars and smart phones and cures for deadly diseases).

Economics, Education and Social Order

The priority of production over consumption in the service of a moral good involved a social order committed to moral education of its members. People had to be trained to work, exchange and use resources rightly rather than simply doing whatever they wanted; there could be no sound economics without this concern at the center. This is why moral education was one of the core concerns of all major economic thinkers, and all public understanding of economic issues, from the dawn of history right up until the movement to detach economics from morality at the turn of the nineteenth century.

Confronted with people who made irrational, immoral or irresponsible use of time and resources, the classical thinker said: "To have a good economy, we must place people like this under the control of better people." The Christian said: "To have a good economy, we must push people like this to repent from their sin." The Enlightenment thinker said: "To have a good economy, we must educate people like this." All would predict that a failure to take such corrective action would lead to economic disorder and stagnation.

Even where people's actual behavior did not live up to the moral standard, the status of the standard itself was a given. It could not be dislodged without the overturning of the whole social order. In the classical world, highly virtuous governing elites would set the universal expectation of a certain baseline moral education in all households, and in this and other ways would see to it that everyone knew virtue was the proper purpose of economic activity. In Christian cultures, the teaching, ministry and authority of the church would set expectations for moral education in households, as well as conducting moral education, and in this and other ways would see to it that everyone knew glorifying, obeying and enjoying God in Christ was the proper purpose of economic activity. Where the Enlightenment held sway, educational institutions (primarily schools, churches and families) would see to it that everyone knew the improvement of the human condition in knowledge, virtue and material well-being was the purpose of economic activity.

Each approach affirms two levels of sociological responsibility for the moral compass. At one level, each affirms that it is every individual's responsibility to practice virtue, and to educate others (especially children) to do so. This is why the integrity of families and households is of particular importance in every major school of economic thought before the Keynesian Revolution, for it is in the household that people receive most of their moral formation. At another level, however, all three views affirm that there is a specific class of individuals and/or organizations (the leisure class, the church, the schools and churches) that plays a special role in clarifying and enforcing the boundaries of morality. This ensures at least a certain baseline level of shared public understanding of such things as the meanings of contested or ambiguous moral terms, or the application of moral rules to hard cases. In a cultural environment without such a baseline, morality begins to seem arbitrary and meaningless.

The Productive Virtues

The subordination of economic activity to teleology—higher purpose—also provided the necessary context for the formation of virtues such as diligence, honesty, self-control and frugality. These virtues can be inculcated with a high degree of success only where they are understood as transcending the human will and integral to the pursuit of the supreme good in human life (Hunter 2000). To the person who says, "why should I work hard if I hate my job?" or "what if my definition of honesty is different from other people's?" or "who's to say what's a good use of my money and what's a frivolous waste?" each of the major pre-Keynes paradigms had ready answers that would generally be accepted within their cultures. Their answers varied, and sometimes multiple schools of thought competed for influence. But all agreed that it was of utmost importance to have persuasive responses to such questions.

Virtue is essential to economic growth and flourishing. The baseline requirement for a community's economic success is that people produce at least as much economic value as they consume. It is work and exchange that create value; dilatory people will not do enough work, and dishonest people will not trade enough with one another. Meanwhile, spendthrift people will consume more than they produce regardless of their production rates. Without these virtues, the wealth accumulated by previous generations is gradually spent down, and when it runs out, panic will set in and people will start seizing their neighbors' resources. Many social pathologies are connected to the growing number of able-bodied people of working age who are not working (Murray 2013; Putnam 2016).

These two aspects of moral purpose in economic life—the stable, public moral compass and the formation of personal virtues—are interdependent. Where public systems radically individualize morality, treating it as no more than an arbitrary preference or autonomous lifestyle choice, it will be extremely difficult for people to maintain a sense of morality that transcends the will, and hence form virtues. Conversely, where people are in general selfish and dissolute in their behavior, any claim that there is a public moral compass will lack credibility.

Fracturing the Compass: Money as an End in Itself

Our very ideas of what "production" and "consumption" are have been emptied of meaning by the Keynesian revolution. Where production is primary and consumption serves production, we know what both are because we can define both relative to the higher good served by production. Where consumption is primary and production serves consumption, consumption and production become abstractions with virtually no content. Consumption means simply "whatever people want to do with their resources and opportunities," and anything is production if it helps people do what they want. This is the detritus left behind by the substantive and constructive goods that once defined the purpose of economic systems.

Consider the stark contrast between how economics treats gambling before and after the Keynesian Revolution. It would be a mistake to think that the earlier economic views called gambling economically unproductive because gambling was already ethically forbidden for other, unrelated reasons. The truth is precisely the opposite. Gambling was ethically forbidden because, and only because, it was economically unproductive. Money and time were to be consumed in ways that produced certain moral goods; gambling was a waste, and was therefore evil, because it consumed resources without producing those goods. After the Keynesian Revolution, however, casinos are considered highly productive. People have an appetite to gamble, and casinos satisfy that appetite by allowing them to consume gambling services.

Casinos are a prime example of producers manipulating, and even producing, the consumption appetites they serve. The casino treats the gambler as something less than equally human. The casino does not serve the gambler, it uses him.

The whole economy has become a casino in that respect since the rise of the Consumption paradigm. Without a publicly recognized teleology for economic activity, as production and consumption become empty categories, the relationship between producer and consumer becomes adversarial rather than cooperative. Big box stores, for example, are now laid out deliberately to manipulate customers' unconscious psychology in ways that keep them in the store longer, and more likely to buy things, in exactly the same way casinos use floor layout to keep people on the floor and gambling (Matarese 2018). Technology services harvest data from their users, data that the users don't want harvested, while using techniques borrowed from (you guessed it) casinos to keep people punching buttons—Big Tech uses its users the way casinos use gamblers (Thompson 2019). Customers know all this, but feel helpless to do anything about it.

Because production and consumption are now empty categories, money becomes an end in itself. If economic activity exists for consumption, our goal should always be more consumption. But "consumption" has little definite content. If anything that satisfies a preference is consumption, economists and other economic actors have something of a quandary when it comes to defining their purpose. If everything is consumption, what counts as more consumption? How do you measure growth? "Everything" is the one thing that can't be measured.

Money emerges as a convenient substitute. It is easily measurable, it is useful for satisfying a very great variety of desires, and there is relatively little cost to having more of it. Therefore having more of it is always desirable for all people. With no objective definition of what counts as good or desirable consumption, we usually cannot say very much about whether it is good that there should be more or less of any given product or activity. But we can safely generalize that everyone is better off with more money.

The key difference here is not the affirmation that having more money is good; the earlier views generally agreed, with some exceptions, that all things being equal it was better to have more money than less, even if only for the purpose of giving it away to those who need it more, or other good causes. The key difference is our inability to make almost any other generalizations about what is desirable or undesirable. For the older views, more money was generally better, but it was vastly less important than the questions they really cared about: Are we becoming good and wise people? Glorifying God? Spreading enlightenment and justice? Since the Keynesian Revolution, there are no such questions in economics. Whether we are getting richer is the only question that counts.

Thus economics becomes a sort of video game, with gross domestic product as the "score." In all the earlier paradigms, the economist is like a physician. Gross domestic product is for him a vital sign, like a heart rate—something that indicates the health of the patient. If your heart rate is slow, the physician diagnoses the cause and administers a treatment aimed at curing that cause. The physician does not start pounding on your chest to get your heart to go faster. Still less does the physician go around seeking out healthy people and pounding on their chests, on the theory that they will become even *healthier* if their hearts go faster! Yet this is something like what the Keynesian Revolution has reduced the economist to doing.

We must insist that the elevation of consumption over production is *not* a basic or necessary element of the modern economy itself. It has become commonplace for intellectual critics of modern economics to claim that the triumph of consumer appetites over higher goals is somehow unavoidable in any developed economy (Bell 1996). This determinism, which has deep roots in the materialistic historicism of Karl Marx and the social naturalism of Max Weber, does not square with the historical record. The triumph of consumption did not somehow percolate up from the vast world of economic activity, and then at long last achieve expression in the world of thought. As we have seen in Chapters 4 through 7, it was an idea first, and it was an idea that began not with economic development but with a vision of moral revolution. The idea originated with a single author. We know his name. We know the dates of his invention of the idea. And we can trace the spread of its influence through academic circles—accomplished by means that were not somehow intrinsically necessary, as if by natural law, to the real-world progress of economic development.

If we believe human beings have free will and are not enslaved to a Marxian materialistic determinism or Weberian social naturalism, there is no reason people could not have continued to hold the older views instead of adopting the new one. In fact, there are plenty of people around today who do hold economic views in clear continuity with those of Aristotle, Aquinas or Adam Smith (although of course the older views have been changed by their encounter with modern history). These views have no more than a marginal effect on the structure of our economy, not because some law of history has exiled them, but because the people who run the institutions that shape our culture have chosen other views.

Nonetheless, this architectonic change in the dominant understanding of economic systems has a ripple effect that cascades outward throughout the economy. The Consumption paradigm may not be a basic or necessary feature of modern economies, but by now it has become deeply embedded in virtually all economic structures. No matter how dirty the house gets, dirt is not a basic or necessary feature of a house—and yet, a house can get so dirty that its dirtiness becomes its most obvious and salient quality.

Hollow Prosperity: A Directionless World

The fracturing of the moral compass by the Keynesian Revolution inevitably leaves us with an empty economy whose prosperity feels hollow. It does not simply remove restraints on moral corruption, although that by itself would be bad enough. The absence of a teleological compass does not just permit moral deformation, it actively produces moral deformation.

An Economy Without Purpose

Where the human will operates with no purpose higher than itself, disconnected from teleology, its choices must become morally arbitrary and meaningless. This is a matter of logical necessity. We have many competing desires—desires for love, for justice, for comfort, for power, for pleasure, for dignity, for freedom, for safety, for candy bars. Without a sense of responsibility to a higher purpose, we lack any grounds for organizing or prioritizing these desires other than their momentary strength. The desires cannot organize and prioritize themselves, for each desire will place itself first if we listen to it, and without a higher standard we have no way to know which desires to listen to. Which should get the right of way in my decision-making, my desire to treat my neighbor fairly or my desire to have more stuff? If the answer is not determined by a responsibility that transcends the will, it will be determined by whichever desire happens to create a stronger appetite at any given moment. I am nothing but a puppet of my appetites, which in turn are nothing but products of my genetics and environment. My behavior is no more significant than that of a billiard ball. Human life is either transcendently moral or utterly meaningless.

When the Keynesian Revolution removes the teleological compass from economic structures, it removes conditions that are necessary in the long run for a sense of moral meaning and purpose in economic activity. All the normative commitments that are supposed to direct our economic action lose their definition. We may wag our normative fingers at big banks and corporations, telling them that they ought to prioritize serving their customers well instead of enriching themselves at the expense of their customers. However, without a publicly agreed upon teleology, what counts as "serving the customer well"? Doing what the customer wants? But they do that now. No one forces people to take out mortgages and credit card loans they can't pay back. No one forces people to buy complex securities instruments that have been dubiously declared safe by a government-organized cartel of politically connected accounting firms. Of course there are some practices that really are fraudulent or coercive, but the moral rot of our economic life (described in the introduction of this book) goes far deeper than that. We cannot restore general moral accountability to our overall economy by prosecuting particular cases of fraud or coercion any more than politicians could balance the federal budget by cutting only "waste, fraud and abuse."

There are serious limits on how much we can accomplish merely by stigmatizing or punishing bad behavior. To really direct economic activity to a moral end, we need positive, constructive motivations. Without a publicly agreed upon moral teleology, we can't provide a clear definition of what we're for, morally, any more than we can define what we're against.

At a deeper level, in a cultural environment defined by the Keynesian Revolution, our very attempts to promote moral behavior incorporate a presumption of selfish materialism that prevents our attempts from succeeding. Suppose we say to the bank, "you shouldn't make loans to people who won't be able to pay them back, because the customer will end up with less money than he started with." This implies that the customer's only interest is to gain more money and avoid losses. The bank might well reply: "If borrowers are only out to enrich themselves, why can't lenders do the same? The borrower will end up with less money, but we will end up with more money. Why is their gain good, but ours bad? We aren't stealing this money. Borrowers are coming to us and asking for loans, precisely because they want to maximize their income. Why is seeking to maximize income only evil when banks do it?" This is, in fact, more or less what defenders of the banks often say when confronted about ethical lending issues.

Nor can we reduce this to merely a question of behavior by individual banks. One might respond to these concerns by saying that even if the economic system is not moral, individual economic actors can seek a higher purpose in their behavior. This would be true in the short term, for some individual actors. However, economics is a cultural activity. Its moral element depends not only on individual decisions, but also on shared assumptions that are embedded in the structures of public relationships. Once again, you are free to call yourself a chicken, but you are not free to live as a chicken unless others agree that you are one. Similarly, you can do your best to live by a moral code as you understand it, and there is virtue in that. But if the economic structures you participate in do not publicly embody your moral assumptions, the influence of your virtue will be limited to yourself.

To continue the above example, one bank may refrain from making unethical loans, and that is praiseworthy. But if those ethical commitments do not inform the banking system at large (as embodied in such structures as law and government policy, media descriptions of banking practices, willingness of other economic actors to withdraw business from banks with unethical practices, etc.), the virtue of that bank will not create much positive moral influence on other banks. We can point to the good bank and say to the bad bank: "Why can't you be more like them?" But the bad bank will only reply: "Why should we?" Whatever answer we give to that question, the bad bank will be free to ignore it, and probably will not even understand it. There will be no common moral language within which our answer will be intelligible, plausible and legitimate. And that leaves us living in a social environment of unending anxiety about the moral core of our economic institutions—hollow prosperity.

The loss of higher purpose as an organizing principle of economic activity also leads people into the shallow, materialistic kind of life that calls into question the desirability and even the moral legitimacy of the modern economy. This is the problem of what is often called "consumerism," the question of whether economic growth is a good thing if (an important "if") it produces people whose lives have no purpose above the satisfaction of their own appetites. The dynamic world of economic growth and technological accomplishment that we enjoy was handed down to us as a result of the great personal sacrifices of our ancestors, who fought and died to give us just laws and secure freedom. Did they suffer and sacrifice so we could now relax and waste our lives by devoting ourselves to narcissistic entertainment? Was Nietzsche right that the bourgeois society of wealth and health must terminate in a squalid Last Man whose shallow selfishness proves that the whole enterprise was a disastrous mistake?

If not, the Consumption paradigm must go. Economic growth need not terminate in the Last Man, but the Consumption paradigm obviously must do so. And while Nietzsche was wrong to think that any system characterized by property rights and productive virtues must end in the Last Man, he was correct that if any system does in fact end in the Last Man, that system itself ought to end.

An Economy Without Virtue

The Keynesian Revolution also undermines the formation of virtues that are necessary to economic success. It becomes harder and harder to produce people who have the desire and ability to control their own behavior. The ability to say "no" (or "not yet") to one's own appetites for moral reasons is one of the most important foundations of economic flourishing. It lies behind diligent work, frugal saving, social solidarity and many other critical economic factors. These virtues become radically harder to form in the empty economy of hollow prosperity.

The absence of a belief that our appetites are answerable to a higher standard changes our appetites. We do have natural desires that include seeking the good of others, but where we do not think our appetites are subject to regulation by a standard that transcends them, the selfish appetites get much stronger. Our desires to seek the good of others do not create strong appetites that move us to action apart from a sincerely and deeply held belief that these desires are morally right and obligatory. Once we realize that all our appetites are on the same footing, the ones that reliably produce immediate pleasures for ourselves become much stronger.

Without an objective standard to which we know our behavior will be compared, we can even invent reasons why our selfish behavior is really beneficial for others as well. Such rationalizations may be fanciful. But who's going to call us out on it?

This dynamic is concealed from many people because they take as natural what is really the effect of moral education. Normally, we undergo moral training (in families, schools, churches, etc.) that greatly strengthens some of our natural appetites while teaching us to restrain others. However, in the empty economy of hollow prosperity created by the Keynesian Revolution, the motive for such education is much weaker and the difficulty of carrying it out is much greater.

Public policy on economic issues institutionalizes this anti-virtuous approach, and thus helps support and reproduce it. Whenever there is a downturn in GDP growth, Keynesians demand a fiscal stimulus that will summon forth economic growth without anyone having to work harder or tighten their belts. The magic of the multiplier effect will give us all something for nothing. Critics will advocate other policies—monetary stimulus, tax cuts—that similarly promise (or are presented in public rhetoric as promising) a return to economic growth without a demand for more work and less waste on the part of the ordinary consumer.

The implicit message of all voices in every such debate is: You can get something for nothing. You ought to get something for nothing. You ought to demand something for nothing. If you're not getting something for nothing, you've been betrayed by those evil scoundrels in the other party.

Our greatly reduced ability to form moral virtues in an empty economy of hollow prosperity lies behind many of the serious economic problems facing us. The rate of able-bodied adult males of working age who are not employed is rising to historically unprecedented levels. Our social bonds are undermined by long-term economic dependency—not just on government welfare programs at the bottom of the socioeconomic spectrum, but on people at all levels living off families and partners without making a contribution. Whenever people are disconnected from work, social dysfunction follows—drugs, family breakup, mental illness, suicide (Murray 2013; Putnam 2016).

New business formation is likewise declining (U.S. Census Bureau 2018). Entrepreneurship requires the productive virtues of diligence and self-control alongside a high risk tolerance and a personality that takes satisfaction in finding new ways to accomplish good purposes. It requires, in short, an especially productivity-centered approach to life.

When Lyndon Johnson unveiled his plans for a Great Society, our culture still had such strong moral concerns about these issues that he had to promise us, over and over, that he abhorred long-term dependency and was trying to help people up to where they would no longer need help. He denounced the idea of an economic "dole" in harsh terms, swearing mighty oaths that his programs would not become a dole:

> We are not content to accept the endless growth of relief rolls or welfare rolls….Our American answer to poverty is not to make the poor more secure in their poverty but to reach down and to help them lift themselves out of the ruts of poverty and move with the large majority along the high road of hope and prosperity. The days of the dole in our country are numbered. (Eberstadt 2014)

This language of the evils of the dole hearkened back to a historical memory of the late Roman Empire, when the cruel and powerful wealthy would dole out money to the peons to keep them quiet.

Today, such moral qualms about the dangers of dependency seem to have vanished. Even as concern about an "opioid epidemic" and "deaths of despair" increases, we are now debating the idea of a universal basic income. This breaks the connection between work and wages much more fundamentally than any welfare program. A culture that puts production first can still easily justify safety-net programs for people who are unable to work, or unable to do work that is economically valuable enough to support themselves. But a universal basic income establishes consumption as the fundamental economic fact. It is the clear triumph of the Consumption paradigm, and can only incentivize greater disconnection from work, with the resulting increase in social dysfunction. The abject failure of the Great Society to accomplish its aims—Sergeant Shriver once declared that the war on poverty would be won in ten years—seems to have taught us few lessons (Will 2015).

We can use gimmicks to goose the GDP in the short term. In the long term, only virtuous workers given direction by a moral culture can produce economic flourishing that lasts.

We already know that death is not the end of life—that the purpose of life is not simply to stay alive. To find our way back from hollow prosperity, we do not need to invent a new morality, or have some demagogue impose it on us. To be human is to act with moral assumptions, as we have seen. We already possess the teleological awareness we need. We know that some things are intrinsically good, and that it is the pursuit of these things that makes life meaningful.

We just need to reconnect our economic lives to those higher purposes. And because we are cultural creatures as well as moral, doing this in our own decision-making is not enough. The economic systems and larger cultural structures that define and arrange our individual economic decisions must themselves be designed in such a way that the pursuit of these purposes will be treated as something normal rather than as something abnormal, as it is treated now. We must rediscover purpose as individuals, but also to some extent together.

References

Allen, Douglas W. 2011. *The Institutional Revolution*. Chicago: University of Chicago Press.

Aristotle. 1980. *Ethics*. Oxford and New York: Oxford University Press.

Aristotle. 1992. *Politics*. London and New York: Penguin Books.

Bell, Daniel. 1996. *The Cultural Contradictions of Capitalism*. New York: Basic Books.

Eberstadt, Nicholas. 2014. The Great Society at 50. *The Weekly Standard*, May 9.

Ferngren, Gary. 2011. A New Era in Roman Health Care. *Christian History* 101: 6–12.

Gregg, Samuel. 2007. *The Commercial Society*. Lanham: Lexington.

Gunton, Colin. 1998. *The Triune Creator*. Grand Rapids: Eerdmans.

Hauerwas, Stanley, and William H. Willimon. 1989. *Resident Aliens*. Nashville: Abingdon Press.

Hunter, James Davison. 2000. *The Death of Character*. New York: Basic Books.

Kennedy, John F. 1962. Speech at Rice Stadium, Sept 12. https://er.jsc.nasa.gov/seh/ricetalk.htm. Accessed 23 Jan 2019.

Keynes, John Maynard. 1963 [1930]. Economic Possibilities for Our Grandchildren; Scanned by Yale University Economics Department from John Maynard Keynes, *Essays in Persuasion*, Norton, 358–373. http://www.econ.yale.edu/smith/econ116a/keynes1.pdf. Accessed 23 Jan 2019.

Keynes, John Maynard. 2013 [1936]. *The General Theory of Employment, Interest and Money*. Cambridge: Cambridge University Press.

Maddison, Angus. 2007. *Countours of the World Economy*. Oxford and New York: Oxford University Press.

Matarese, John. 2018. How Grocery Stores Are Just Like Casinos. KGUN-9, Feb 14. https://www.kgun9.com/money/consumer/dont-waste-your-money/how-grocery-stores-are-just-like-casinos. Accessed 23 Jan 2019.

McCloskey, Deirdre N. 2010. *Bourgeois Dignity*. Chicago: University of Chicago Press.

Miller, Timothy S. 2011. Basil's House of Healing. *Christian History* 101: 13–16.

Mokyr, Joel. 2017. *A Culture of Growth*. Princeton: Princeton University Press.

Murray, Charles. 2013. *Coming Apart*. New York: Crown Forum.

North, Douglass C., John Joseph Wallis, and Barry R. Weingast. 2009. *Violence and Social Orders*. Cambridge and New York: Cambridge University Press.

Plato. 1991. *Republic*. New York: Basic Books.

Putnam, Robert D. 2016. *Our Kids*. New York: Simon & Schuster.

Rhee, Helen. 2012. *Loving the Poor Saving the Rich*. Baker: Grand Rapids.

de Roover, Raymond. 1958. The Concept of the Just Price. *Journal of Economic History* 18 (4): 418–434.

Smith, Adam. 1994. *The Wealth of Nations*. New York: Modern Library.

Smith, Adam. 2006. *Theory of Moral Sentiments*. Mineola: Dover Publications.

Stark, Rodney. 2005. *The Victory of Reason*. New York: Random House.

Thompson, Andrew. 2019. Engineers of Addiction. The Verge. https://www.theverge.com/2015/5/6/8544303/casino-slot-machine-gambling-addiction-psychology-mobile-games. Accessed 23 Jan 2019.

Tierney, Brian. 1997. *The Idea of Natural Rights*. Grand Rapids: Eerdmans.

Unwin, George. 1927. *Studies in Economic History*. New York: Macmillan.

U.S. Census Bureau. 2018. Business Formation Statistics, Feb 8. https://www.census.gov/newsroom/blogs/research-matters/2018/02/bfs.html. Accessed 23 Jan 2019.

Wittmer, Michael. 2017. Is a Just Price Enough? *Journal of Markets and Morality* 20 (2): 263–278.

Will, George F. 2015. What Patrick Moynihan Knew About the Importance of Two Parents. *Washington Post*, Mar 13.

Yoder, John Howard. 1994 [1972]. *The Politics of Jesus*. Grand Rapids: Eerdmans.

CHAPTER 9

Leave It Better Than You Found It: Moral and Cultural Conditions for Stewardship

The discipline of economics is uncomfortable with both the future and the past. Economists are trained to be careful when building models of the future—not to say, "if we do X, Y will happen," but rather, "in our model of this scenario, which we have refined over time using empirical data, if we specify X, the model indicates Y. On the other hand, if we specify…" Hence the old joke about wanting to consult a one-handed economist! Of course, outsiders are only interested in the model because they want predictions of the future as a basis for plans and decision-making. Economists, who know that they are speaking about a model and not about the concrete reality of human beings with free will, prefer to speak in the present tense rather than the future tense ("the model suggests Y" as opposed to "Y will happen with certainty"). As for the past, the study of the history of economics has been eliminated from the training of economists. The discipline carries on its nineteenth century aspiration to model itself on the physical sciences, and nobody thinks chemists need to know the history of chemistry. The history of economic thought is studied now primarily by historians and sociologists, who often have little or no training in economics. Only a handful of historians of economics are left in economics departments, a sort of saving remnant of the earlier days when the discipline thought it needed to understand human action from the inside as well as from the outside.

Economists may not be interested in history, but history is interested in economists. Human beings are historical creatures, living within a sequence of events. We are dependent upon seeing and understanding

V. V. Claar and G. Forster, *The Keynesian Revolution and Our Empty Economy*, https://doi.org/10.1007/978-3-030-15808-8_9

the sequences—the connections between what happens in the past, present and future—to understand the meaning of our lives. The past forms our identity, and our actions are aimed at forming the future. All this applies in economics as much as anywhere else.

Recognizing this, earlier paradigms for the study of economics gave a central place to understanding how our economic lives connected us to the past and the future. They defined the horizon of time that was of proper concern for economic decision-making—a year, a life, a span of generations. They defined what the past had provided that was of concern in economic life, and what duties we had toward those who would come after us.

The Consumption paradigm also has something to say about time horizons, and this is another key factor in our moral anxieties. It radically shrunk the horizon of time we were responsible to think about, which helps explain why our prosperity feels so hollow and our economy so empty. We live within economic structures and discourses that strongly discourage us from building anything to last, and whatever is not lasting cannot have lasting purpose.

As for duties to future generations, Keynes himself said it best: "In the long run we are all dead" (Keynes 2013b, 65).

The Present and Its History

How do economic systems connect us to our ancestors and descendants? The past shapes our economic decisions, and our economic decisions shape the future. History—the legacy left us by our ancestors and the legacy we are leaving to those whose ancestors we will be—plays a dominant, if underappreciated, role in economic analysis. As we have seen, economists focus on the decisions people make about the use of resources. Each economic decision represents an isolated moment in time. But each is made within a vast and complex array of conditions, created in the present by the events of the past, and each is motivated by preferences that concern how the decision will affect the future.

To see how economic decisions are shaped by conditions (from the past) and preferences (about the future), consider my decision whether to make myself a ham sandwich for lunch or go out for pizza. The conditions range from my tastes and my income to my health and my proximity to the pizza place to the kind of work I have to do that afternoon and whom I might meet if I went out. These are all the legacy of the past to me, including not only the immediate past of this morning but the whole course of my life and even the longer history that built up the community around me. They are created by my own past decisions and the past decisions of countless others. The preferences include my desires to have a tasty meal, to be full rather than hungry this afternoon, to have more money available for future needs, to get my work done today and to meet (or not meet) others during lunch. These shape what kind of future I want to have, including the immediate future implicated in my desire to be full and the longer future implicated in my desire to get my work done. My choice will create different states of affairs—including the conditions of future choices. The number and intricacy of these conditions and preferences is so enormous as to be bewildering if I try to think about them all, which is why—like everyone else—I rarely think about more than a few of them and never attempt to tally them in total.

Cost-benefit calculations, which are at the heart of all our economic decisions, change dramatically based upon the time horizon we are concerned about. People who think only about the immediate future will work less and relax more, save less and spend more. People with a more intense concern about what their lives, and the world around them, will look like in ten years (or a hundred years) will behave very differently.

Above all, time horizons are closely connected to ethics. What it means to "act responsibly" depends upon what span of time we consider ourselves "responsible" for. This is why it is commonplace to refer to a person who only thinks about the very short term when making decisions as "irresponsible." If I knew for certain that I would be annihilated in one hour, and would never exist again in this or any other world, there would be no sound moral objection to my spending that hour doing just about anything I want (as long as I don't harm others). Acting responsibly becomes an empty concept if there is no future for which I am responsible. That is why systems of moral formation, such as religions and ethical philosophies, expend so much effort convincing people to make their daily choices thinking about the long term and not just the short term. And it is why every major world religion draws important connections between ethics in the present world and what happens to us after we die.

In one sense, economists are constantly thinking about history because they are always being asked questions about the future. As we have noted, they are trained to be careful when modeling the future; however, as we have noted, history is interested in economists even if economists are not interested in history. Economists are asked to predict the movements of growth rates, employment rates and stock market indexes; to predict the length of business cycles and bubbles; to predict the outcome of adopting this or that change in policy. They are even, in contradiction of the most basic tenets of their discipline, asked to predict the behavior of individual people and organizations when confronted with specific economic choices. (The problem is not that such predictions are impossible, although they are; the problem is that if such predictions were possible, we should be asking their spouses rather than economists.) There is little they are not asked to predict. And the discipline is willing to provide its models as the functional equivalent of predictions; corporations and governments employ countless thousands of economists, because it believes their models predict the future. That the economist is treated as the modern equivalent of the tribal priest, reading entrails and omens, is already a joke so old as to have become trite.

In another sense, however, history does not get the attention it deserves from modern economists—and that is one of the primary results of the Keynesian Revolution. We have seen that earlier economic paradigms began with the view that there is an overarching purpose to human life, and economic systems were well-designed and well-functioning only to the extent that they facilitated this purpose. We now add the observation that these overarching views of life's purpose involved specific perspectives on history as well as specific perspectives on production and consumption. The understanding of what was truly productive in the Nature, God and Reason paradigms was inextricably connected to those paradigms' understandings of how the present is related to the past and the future across a long horizon—where we all came from and where we are all going. No such views systematically inform economic analysis since the Keynesian Revolution. In our economic thought, the present exists largely in a vacuum.

In particular, older paradigms demanded that we recognize responsibilities to our ancestors and descendants—responsibilities specific in nature and powerful in their influence over our daily lives and ongoing social organization. After the Keynesian Revolution, only the individual making each particular economic choice is of essential consideration. No responsibilities to ancestors or descendants necessarily inform an economist's analysis; such attachments will appear important to the economist only to the extent that individuals making economic choices are consciously and measurably motivated by them. When people buy memberships in ancestry-tracking websites or invest in college savings accounts for their children, economists will naturally recognize that such decisions are motivated by preferences that involve ancestors and descendants. But such cases make up only a small portion of all economic phenomena, and outside this sphere the modern economist will not look for such generational connections.

The Keynesian Revolution's overturning of the relationship between production and consumption is interdependent with a revolutionary overturning of the relationship between the present and history. We have seen that the Consumption paradigm assumes we do not exist to produce or accomplish anything outside our own appetites. This is an assumption about our relationship with history as much as it is an assumption about our relationship with the non-human world—as was the older assumption that we *did* exist for a purpose higher than our own appetites.

The difference this makes to economic organization is much more significant than at first it may seem. Savings and investment, risk-taking in startups and new enterprises, debt, entitlement policy and much else is shaped by how (or whether) we think about what the present owes the future. The role we assign to government, and to mediating institutions like families and churches, in forming our economic systems is shaped by how (or whether) we think about what the present owes the past. However, as we are socially conditioned by the Consumption paradigm to think about economics only in terms of the present generation, we require a mental effort to see how that conditioning impacts economic behavior. That effort is the burden of this chapter.

The Nature Paradigm: Classical Views of History

The classical philosophers of the Nature paradigm operated in a culture whose view of history was cyclical and traditionalist. It was cyclical in that it expected civilizations to rise and fall endlessly, each civilization repeating the same sequence of growth and degeneration, with no essential change from cycle to cycle. (Here we see how they viewed human beings as part of nature—human communities have an endlessly repeating and unchanging life cycle, just like all other animals.) It was traditionalist in the sense that it emphasized responsibilities to ancestors—to respect the wisdom of past generations and maintain the social forms they passed down.

This is not to say it was more concerned about the past than the future. On the contrary, traditionalism is even more concerned about the future than the past. Traditionalism is a desire to *pass on* the traditions.

That said, in another sense the past did dominate. While responsibilities to descendants were at the center, those responsibilities were largely understood in terms of deference to ancestors. What we owed our descendants primarily consisted of passing on to them what our ancestors passed on to us, with as little deviation or decay as possible.

The cyclical nature of this view was the cause of its traditionalism. At all periods in the history of a civilization after its initial founding, the central problem is the deterioration of that civilization toward its inevitable ruin at some point in the future. A civilization's past is always better than its future. The central goal is therefore to slow down the process of decay as much as possible. Thus the view that all civilizations are inevitably declining subordinates the future almost totally to the past, since the only way to improve the future is to maintain as much of the past as possible. (Even in the founding moment, when a civilization began, its power and energy were understood to be the last remaining legacy of whatever had been worth preserving from some prior, now-ruined civilization—such as Rome rising from the ashes of Troy.)

Plato and Aristotle

The great philosophers challenged some aspects of the prevailing view of history. In particular, from Socrates forward they challenged the demand that we defer to the wisdom of ancestors. The practice of philosophy consists in testing the truth value of received claims. Whether the claims are subsequently accepted or rejected, the mere act of testing their truth by our own lights removes them from their accustomed position of authority. (This is why Athens responded to Socrates' inquiries by executing him rather than by answering his questions—his sacrilege lay not in his answers to the questions, but in the act of asking of such questions at all.) Socrates occasionally invokes the epics of Homer to draw strategically on their authority, such as when he answered the charge that he was foolish to philosophize if philosophizing led to his death by asking whether Achilles was foolish to fight when fighting led to his death. However, he spends much more time attacking Homer and the other prevailing myths, for example discussing at length why any story that depicts the gods in conflict with one another must be false and corrupting (Plato 1991, 55–58; 377b–380c). This assertion of our right to think for ourselves even against the authority of our ancestors represented a key break from the dominant understanding of history, and was essential to the distinct character of classical culture shaped by philosophy's presence.

However, the philosophers affirmed their culture's cyclical view of history. They posited that the universe had existed forever and would exist forever, in more or less its present form.[1] This provided cosmological support for the cyclical view—an eternal theater, upon whose stage the drama of history would be eternally reenacted. Plato even proposed the possibility of reincarnation, with souls returning to earth from the afterlife through a process that resembles the drafting of players onto teams in modern sports. The future lives of all people being born at a certain time would be laid out on display; the soul who had been most virtuous in the prior life got first choice of what life to be born into next, followed by the second most virtuous soul, and so on in order until the least virtuous soul had to take whatever life was left unchosen by all the others (Plato 1991, 297–303; 614b–621d).

When it came to political and economic affairs, the philosophers mostly affirmed their cultures' traditionalism. In the case of Plato, this was simply because he did not think there were many who could philosophize. Only those who were able to think for themselves had a right to think for themselves; all others would inevitably defer to received opinion, and any attempt to push them in another direction would only be futile and destructive. This is the point of the notorious "noble lie," the purely fictional cosmology invented by the philosopher-kings to justify the ways of the utopian city to the masses, whose belief in its justice is essential to the public good but who lack the philosophical wherewithal to grasp its justice rationally (Plato 1991, 93–94; 414b–415d). The philosopher-kings are pseudo-traditionalists; having rejected the inherited traditions as irrational, they deceive people into believing in a new, phony tradition that supports the city's rationally designed institutions. Plato then goes on to sketch how the processes of moral decay would inevitably cause the utopian city of the philosopher-kings to degenerate into a more ordinary aristocracy (the rule of gentlemen and heroes),

[1] See Aristotle's *Physics*, 251b14–26; Plato's *Timaeus* may be an exception, depending on how it is interpreted, but (as we will see below) in the *Republic* history is unambiguously cyclical.

the aristocracy into an oligarchy, the oligarchy into a democracy and the democracy into a tyranny (Plato 1991, 222–249; 544e–569c). The striking level of detail in which Plato draws these hypothetical historical sketches reveals how important the cyclical and traditionalist view of history was to him. In the life of a philosopher, it was possible to question ancestors and break out of the tyranny of history; in the life of a city, moral decay and a resulting need for traditionalism (even to the extent of inventing noble lies!) was the rule.

Aristotle comes to similar conclusions by different routes, and the differences produce a social ethic of a subtly different character. He is much less invested than is Plato in drawing a sharp distinction between philosophers and other classes of educated people, allowing more room for real rational reflection in political action. But he is no less convinced that moral degeneration is a ubiquitous social phenomenon, and therefore is no less cyclical and conservationist than Plato in his political and economic thought.

As we saw in Chapter 8, Aristotle was not very concerned with comparative evaluations of aristocracy and democracy aimed at determining which was best. He does offer comments on that question, but his real interest is in the level of moral purity or degeneracy in any given polity (Aristotle 1992, 189–190; III.7). Each city inherits a certain type of constitution, and its concern should be to preserve purity in that constitution by fighting moral decay (Aristotle 1992, 310–318; V.5–6). The possibility of switching between systems, from democracy to aristocracy or vice versa, is not an important consideration. Instead, throughout the *Politics*, his primary concern is to slow the breakdown of political institutions. The underlying cause of this decay, he writes, is the ubiquitous moral corruption of human nature (Aristotle 1992, 369; VI.4).

However, because Aristotle allows for some level of wisdom among educated citizens, rather than limiting it to a tiny and socially isolated class of philosophers, his political thought is more conservationist than traditionalist. The goal is still to conserve and pass on to our descendants the political institutions that have been bequeathed to us by our ancestors, working to slow the inevitable cycle of decay. But, in a sharp contrast with Plato, Aristotle displays almost no interest in preserving inherited belief systems that justify political institutions. Hence there is no noble lie in Aristotle; arguments justifying political institutions stand or fall on their merits. This explains Aristotle's intense interest in the moral purity of a city's political systems—the city can only be conserved if it can be shown to deserve conservation. Where a city's rulers prioritize the public good, sound rational arguments to preserve the city's institutions will never be lacking. Where a city's rulers seek only their own good, arguments defending the city's institutions will ring hollow. All this adds up to a concern for conservation that does not involve much interest in tradition as such. Some passages in the *Politics* on the moral purity of the system can even sound to modern ears like calls for reform, as they demand just and merciful treatment of the weak. Aristotle understood this not as reform in the modern sense of progress, but as moral virtue—consistent with, and necessary for the conservation of, the established order handed down to us by our ancestors.

The Nature Paradigm and History

This is not to say that the philosophers' challenge to ancestral authority had no effect on social life. One distinct contribution that can plausibly be traced to their influence is an increased emphasis on education in wisdom and virtue. If we can think for ourselves, we had better learn to do so in a way that is not socially destructive. Even if we would prefer not to think for ourselves, we have no choice but to do so once there are philosophers loose in the culture, running around challenging social authorities to defend their beliefs and ways. And, of course, not all social authorities viewed philosophy with hostility; to the extent that some valued it, the importance of education in wisdom and virtue only rose even further.

In economic terms, this view of history set the Nature paradigm against the main behaviors associated with economic growth in the modern world. People lived in a rigid class structure, in which social mobility was rare, and even doing a different job from your father's job was abnormal. This social rigidity was seen as necessary as a preservative against decay; its effect was to prevent all but the most low-level sorting of workers to match productive talents with jobs. If a field worker had a son born with a bad leg, that son might get a job as a servant inside the house rather than in the field. He would be extremely unlikely to have even an opportunity to try to become, say, a skilled worker like a carpenter. Those jobs went to the carpenters' sons, who were raised to them from birth.

Innovation and entrepreneurship would have been deeply opposed to the dominant norms of conservative traditionalism. Risk tolerances were extremely low by our standards. Moreover, the expectation of continual decay disposed people not to believe in the possibility of long-term economic growth. This was a major factor in taboos against lending money at interest, among other things, because in a no-growth environment it doesn't make sense to think of money as a productive asset.

The God Paradigm: Christian Views of History

How the rise of Christianity affected our understanding of history is a notoriously difficult subject. A typical approach to summarizing it is to say that Christianity moved us from a cyclical view of history to a linear view, with a clear beginning and end, and that this opened the door to the possibility of innovation and progress over time. The Christian gospel of salvation can even be stated straightforwardly as a repudiation of the cyclical view: Because of Christ, human history no longer has to be just the same damned thing over and over again.

Christianity and Progress

Christianity involves the claim that by Christ's power, Christians can overcome (at least to a large degree) the ubiquitous sinfulness of human nature. This eventually allowed Christians to remove the expectation of inevitable decay that underlay classical traditionalism. As we have seen, early Christians drew a great deal from the classical emphasis on wisdom and virtue as the proper ends of life, but Christianity gradually developed more distinct understandings of what is wise and virtuous, and began to be more concerned about how we care for the physical world. The Christian view of history played a key role in these developments. The belief that God made the world and then it fell away from him into sin, but it is now being redeemed in Christ, suggests that those who are following Christ should be active in repairing the world, resisting the effects of the fall into sin and restoring things as much as possible to the way they would have been without the fall. And the belief that Jesus is coming back at the end of history to redeem the world fully—not just individual people or the church but the whole cosmos, including the material creation—suggests that those who are following Christ should try to live today in a way that anticipates the perfection he will enact at his return. These imperatives make it plausible that with Christ's help,

Christians might lead the way in breaking the cycles of history and introduce real improvements.

All of this is, as we have said, a typical way of summarizing the difference that the Christian view of history made. There is much truth to it historically, and it has substantial biblical support (Gunton 1998). But it also requires some important correction.

Christianity does undeniably demand a linear history in the sense that it demands a clear beginning and end. The Christian community decisively repudiated early Christian theories (such as those of Origen) that tried to reconcile Christian theology with the classical view of an eternal universe, and it has continued to do so. And it is true that this implies at least some possibility of breaking out of the old, classical cycle of inevitable decay in some ways.

However, it does not necessarily follow from this that we must expect innovation and progress to be welcomed at the social level, outside the true church, where worldly powers will continue to rage against God until Jesus returns and destroys them. The extent to which Christians have expected progress has always depended on the complex theological challenge of interpreting not the beginning and the end, but the middle part of the biblical story. A bewildering variety of views about the form and extent of possible social progress in the period in between the first and second comings of Jesus have been present in every period of Christian history (Niebuhr 1975; Carson 2012). Christian progressives and their critics both can point to substantial biblical and philosophical warrant for their views.

The great danger of an overly simple narrative of inevitable Christian progressivism, at least for our purposes here, is that it often reduces the role of Christianity merely to removing classical pessimism and paving the way for Enlightenment optimism. This seriously distorts the real content of Christian thinking—and also of classical thinking, and Enlightenment thinking to boot. In fact, there are important ways in which the rationalism of classical and Enlightenment views harmonize with each other, in opposition to the irreducible mysticism that characterizes Christianity in even its most philosophical forms. Jean-Jacques Rousseau and Voltaire did not believe that Adam plunged all humanity into sin, or that Jesus was coming back to redeem the whole world at the end of history, any more than Plato or Aristotle did.

Early Christianity

Diverse views of history, with diverse implications for social ethics and progress, emerge early in the Christian period. Irenaeus and Eusebius represented two very different ways of justifying an expectation of progress in light of Christian history. Irenaeus, living in a period when Christianity was still illegal and persecuted, nonetheless expected great things because God had not originally made a static world but a great, dynamic project, with human beings in charge of seeking progress. With Christ's coming, God was putting that project of change and progress back on track. Spiritual transformation in the hearts of believers would express itself in everyday lives characterized by virtue, justice, reconciliation and peace, rejecting greed and materialism for service to God and others (Gunton 1998, 52–56). Eusebius, who lived through the legalization of Christianity, sought progress not through spiritual transformation but national and ecclesial institutions. The nations of the world had fallen away from God, but with the founding of the church they were now being reclaimed. Priests and bishops would join hands with emperors and lords to Christianize the world, imposing justice and virtue on the recalcitrant people of the nations (O'Donovan 1996, 197–199).

However, as Christianity completed the transition from a persecuted church to an official church, the view that ultimately gained the most influence was strongly skeptical of power and of social progress. Augustine, drawing on earlier stands of Christian thought as well as important classical influences, provided a lengthy and masterful analysis of the culture and civilization of Rome in light of the larger cosmic narrative of Christianity in *The City of God*. His conclusion was that the coming of Christ had indeed inaugurated a new period in history, but the dominant reality of this new era was not progress but conflict. Until Jesus returns to complete his work, those who accept Christ and those who reject him are stuck with each other. They're all Romans, so they have to find some way to live together—but their different views and values on every subject of public concern leave them constantly squabbling with each other and struggling to maintain even a minimal level of civil harmony. The future is not worse than the past, as the classical view had held, but it's not better, either; Augustine offers no expectation of constructive innovation or social progress, and no expectation of inevitable degeneration (Augustine 1984, 843–894; XIX).

Augustine accepts an official role for Christianity if the emperor seeks it, but distrusts political authority and emphasizes the enormous distance between the kind of lives we live in the present age and the lives we will have after Jesus returns (Deane 1963, 116–153, 172–220). The cold realities of political and economic systems are harsh and deeply tragic; while we have no choice but to participate (dropping out would be irresponsible) we ought to do so in a spirit of lament, longing to be released from the harsh necessities of political and economic life (Augustine 1984, 859–861; XIX.6). This shares some affinity with Plato's view of the political life as something separate from and decisively inferior to philosophizing, but on the whole it has a character starkly different from either classical virtue politics or Enlightenment progress politics.

Augustine's influence over Christian thought in the western world is hard to overstate, but eventually Christians in the west did become more comfortable asserting the interdependence of political and religious institutions. This led to a greatly increased political role for the church—the "Christendom" social model, in which everyone in a given nation was expected to be Christian (with rare exceptions) and required to live accordingly. Christendom represented a more positive assessment of what the church could accomplish in the present age. Rather than accept a permanent stalemate between those who do and don't follow Jesus, medieval Christendom believed it was possible to govern society in an unambiguously Christian way. Christ's first coming had ushered in a new age.

Medieval and Early Modern Developments

Because of this view that much could be accomplished for God in the present, the Middle Ages were characterized by the steady growth of what Charles Taylor has called a "spirit of Reform," with a capital R (Taylor 2007, 25–218). Moral and social reform was pursued more and more extensively and systematically. Medieval Christians were not, of course, naïve about the corruption and failures that occurred in both political and ecclesial leadership. And the border between political and ecclesial institutions was always a hotly contested frontier, with kings and popes constantly pushing to expand the scope of their power at one another's expense. Nonetheless, as we have mentioned above, protections for property and contract rights facilitated the emergence of banks, companies and firms in the later centuries of the Middle Ages.

This same spirit of Reform fueled early colonialism and conquest in the later parts of the Middle Ages and the early modern period. As economies began to grow and technological progress began to accelerate, as a result of the spirit of Reform, European nations began to have more power to exploit and enslave other populations. Inhabitants of the world beyond Europe were seen as benighted pagans, in need of not just the Christian message but the social Reform that would come with it. Christians (i.e. Europeans) knew how to run a society properly, thanks to the benefit of Christian revelation and experience; they would only be doing the non-Christians (i.e. non-Europeans) a favor if they ran their societies for them. Later, as Europe began secularizing and as Christian religious leadership became unwilling to continue turning a blind eye to the evils of colonialism, the justification for colonialism and conquest shifted from religious grounds to racial grounds. It began, however, with religious justification, associated with the spirit of Reform (Frederickson 2002, 15–47).

The Christendom spirit of Reform culminated in a dramatic reform of Christendom itself—the Reformation, which in addition to being an unprecedented theological upheaval was also an unprecedented social upheaval. Protestants moved to overthrow unjust social structures seen as rooted in Roman Catholic traditions, while Roman Catholics moved to overthrow unjust social structures whose injustice was seen as having lent plausibility to the Reformers. The sale of indulgences is only the most famous among countless examples of traditional institutions eliminated or radically reinvented in the Reformation era. More ominously, because church and state were interdependent in the Christendom model, a conflict over who had authority in the church inevitably became a conflict over who had authority in the state. This led to extensive wars of religion.

After the cataclysm of the Reformation, Christian social ethics diverged into many competing schools of thought. Leading reformers like Luther and Calvin, heavily influenced by Augustine and associating Christendom with the corruption of the church in the Middle Ages, sought to reduce and impose controls upon (although not eliminate) the political role of the church. The Roman Catholic Church, chastened by the Reformation, undertook dramatic reforms to force priests and bishops to focus on speaking to moral and religious questions rather than directly brokering political and economic power, and to crack down on those who used ecclesial offices for their own political and economic gain. This Counter-Reformation did not amount to a repudiation of Christendom, but it did greatly retrench the church's political and economic role. Meanwhile, more radical reformers on the Protestant side embraced strategies ranging from Christian political utopianism to withdrawal into isolated communities that largely rejected the civil political community (such as the Mennonites; Forster 2008, 107–141).

Christianity and Traditions

An underappreciated side of this story is the complex Christian attitude toward traditions and the inherited wisdom of the past. Classical philosophers, while claiming the right to question their ancestors, nonetheless devoted their politics largely to preserving and passing on whatever the past had left us. But when the Christian message went out into the world, it called on people to turn from the beliefs and practices in which they had been raised. "You were ransomed from the futile ways inherited from your forefathers," said Peter to first-century believers (I Peter 1:18). Jews had standing to claim there was wisdom in their traditions, since those were from God (Romans 3:1–4); other nations had to heed the words of Paul, who warned that "in past generations [God] allowed all the nations to walk in their own ways," but now "we bring you good news, that you should turn from these vain things to a living God" (Acts 14:15–16). This theme resounds in the works of early Christians, and especially in Augustine.

Later, however, things became much more complicated. On the one hand, as the nations of Europe were transformed by Christianity, their traditions came to be seen as Christian traditions that held much wisdom and ought to be preserved. On the other hand, as we have seen, growing political power sparked a spirit of Reform that sought to use political power for godly ends, to reform society and destroy injustices. This complexity persists to the present day, as Christian views run the gamut from traditionalistic to revolutionary.

The God Paradigm and History

In economic terms, this view of history positioned the God paradigm to make important contributions to economic development. Risk tolerances were expanded by the belief that God comforts the afflicted in the present age, and cares more about their relationship with him than about their financial security while they await the restoration of all things in Christ's return. The medieval spirit of Reform introduced social support for innovation and entrepreneurship; breaking with "the futile ways inherited from your forefathers" could be redemptive. The potential for long-term economic growth was recognized, especially after the revival of Irenaeus' view of history in the Reformation period. If God gave us the world as a dynamic project, in which human action would cultivate the world more and more fully, we could expect economic growth. Likewise, Augustine's skepticism about the prospects for using political and economic power to remake the world in the present age, muted during the era of Christendom, experienced a great revival after the Reformation and the end of the Christendom model. This provided invaluable intellectual tools for restraining the power of the state and affirming protections for property and contract rights, and for extending religious freedom. On the other hand, the wrong turn of colonialism created barriers to the extension of those rights to non-European populations, and established social conditions that invited the rise of economic mercantilism, with its focus on seizing resources.

The fragmentation of Christian social ethics after the Reformation crisis was also the beginning of the end for the God paradigm. We have already noted that the God paradigm declined because of persistent social pluralism, and that this pluralism began as a pluralism within Christianity as a result of the Reformation crisis. In large part, this was a pluralism about interpreting the middle part of the biblical account of history—the part we live in. Unable to agree on how much and what kind of Reform we could expect in the present age, between the first and second comings of Christ, Christianity could no longer sustain a single paradigm for social action.

The Reason Paradigm: Enlightenment Views of History

Historical narrative dominates the Enlightenment thought that formed the Reason paradigm. The very term "Enlightenment" represents a historical claim—that the explosion of new thinking in modernity has inaugurated a new era, a transition from darkness to light. Before, fear and superstition prevented the general spread of knowledge, along with the political and economic revolutions implicit in that spread of knowledge. While the more honest Enlightenment figures recognize precursors to their movement in earlier periods, they held that the decisive change came not with the Reformation and Counter-Reformation but with the rise of modern science, liberal democracy and religious freedom. With the unleashing of knowledge ("Enlightenment") it now becomes possible to exponentially accelerate the process of improving the state of the human race in its rationality, morality and material well-being.

This process of Enlightenment unfolds naturally and, in a sense, inevitably. People do have free will, of course, but they also have certain consistent preferences. They like truth better than superstition (once they have come to see the superstition for what it is), they like freedom better than slavery and they like material well-being better than poverty. Once a new technology is invented, it is never un-invented; similarly, once the thrones and altars are disenchanted they will not be reenchanted. The spread of knowledge can be slowed down, and sometimes temporarily suppressed, by the kings and priests whose power that knowledge will undermine. But you can't kill an idea, and the opposition of the powerful can only delay rather than stop the spread of Enlightenment.

The proper goal of life is to join in this unfolding enterprise of Enlightenment. To build a better world for our grandchildren is a high honor and privilege. Participating in this enterprise is the best and happiest life available to us. In a sense, there is almost nothing to the Enlightenment other than this call to move history forward.

This exciting project to build the future produced much good and also much evil. The economic growth and general spread of well-being associated with the Industrial Revolution speaks for itself (Appleby 2010). The transition to constitutional democracy and religious freedom, while they partly grow from roots in the Christian movements of early modernity, are also to a large extent products of the Enlightenment (Bloom 1987). At the same time, the march of progress also became associated with destructive movements. European colonialism took on the Enlightenment mantle of progress as it exploited and enslaved "unenlightened" populations for their own good; politicians whipped up fervor for wars and other military adventures on the belief, or pretense, that they would make the world safe for democracy and progress (Frederickson 2002, 49–95).

Past Wisdom and Future Possibilities

The past is no longer looked to as a source of wisdom in Enlightenment thought. It appears mostly as a source of ignorance and superstition, and the vices that result from them. Even those willing to acknowledge the availability of wisdom in the past do not think we need to go back and get it there; the wisdom of the present is superior. And, of course, the dominant tone of Enlightenment discourse did not even go so far as to acknowledge the existence of much wisdom in the past. More common is the striking attitude one finds, for example, in the passage of John Locke's *Essay Concerning Human Understanding* in which Plato and Aristotle are briefly—and dismissively—mentioned as "the old heathen philosophers" (Locke 1975, 68; I.3.5). No need to stop and explain why these views are inadequate for our purposes; that they are old and heathen is explanation enough.

The future is as attractive in the Reason paradigm as the past is unattractive. As we drain our swamp of its fetid waters of prejudice and fear, we may look back now and then to contemplate the deep and wide seas of ignorance that preceded the swamp. But we will more often look forward to the dry land of reason and virtue that will follow it, upon which our descendants will stand, thanks to our sacrifices.

For the Reason paradigm, the future is much more knowable than it is unknowable. That the swamp of ignorance will be drained and the land will be dry is beyond doubt. Not only that, we can characterize what life on the dry land will be like when it comes, for reason is teleological. It teaches us the natural law. We can have rational knowledge not only of what means will serve given ends, but of what the ends are. We know that the enlightened future will be a place of honesty, diligence, self-control, cooperation and generosity, and that its social structure will emphasize democracy, education, productive enterprise and monogamous domestic affection. The tendency to depict the enlightened future as an unknowable brave new world, that while we are still draining the swamp we cannot say what the dry land will look like, came in much later as the teleological reason of the early Enlightenment gave way to such anti-teleological developments as utilitarianism and the positive/normative split.

The Reason Paradigm and History

These are hardly original observations. They are even trite. However, they are not always applied to the economic aspect of the Enlightenment. The works of Adam Smith are as dominated by historical narrative as those of Rousseau, Voltaire or Thomas Paine—if not more so.

Large portions of the *Wealth of Nations* are devoted to history. It doesn't just explain, for example, how the division of labor works. It tells the story of how the division of labor has progressed historically, and what that progress has produced. Technological development in communications and transportation gradually increased the scope of markets. Thus, through trade, a much greater diversity of options for distributing tasks among workers became possible; markets were able to realize enormous new efficiencies. This in turn produced a commercial middle class that derived its wealth from trade. This commercial class undermined the medieval social order, which was built to accommodate lords and serfs, and struggled to manage the presence of those who had wealth but did not owe it to the feudal system's ancestral titles and land holdings. Smith attributes even the Reformation to technology's tendency to increase the power of local authorities at the expense of the emperor and the pope (Smith 1994, 862–863; V.1.3.iii).

The Reason paradigm's view of history obviously sets up much stronger expectations of economic growth; to make progress in well-being is the whole point of the enterprise. Contempt for the past and hope for the future strongly incentivizes high risk tolerance. And the Reason paradigm unambiguously supports innovation and entrepreneurship. The God paradigm had introduced a break between "the futile ways inherited from your forefathers" and the possibility of progress after the first coming of Christ. But it had persistent doubts about how much of that progress would be possible before Christ's second coming, and it also felt responsible to preserve the wisdom of Christian traditions. The Reason paradigm welcomed innovation unambiguously and felt no substantial ties to old ways of any type.

At the same time, the unwillingness of the Reason paradigm to learn from the wisdom of the past has not aged well. It would be unfair to blame the Reason paradigm for all the unprecedented evils of the twentieth century, since they came after the paradigm had dissolved. But there were evils enough during the Enlightenment period itself. Moreover, the dissolution of the moral foundations of the paradigm, as we have observed, was remarkably rapid when compared to the endurance of the Nature and God paradigms over so many centuries. The moral instability of the paradigm comes down to its unwarranted faith that "reason" could support the teleological weight previously carried by nature and God. This is, from one angle, about history. The question of what is intrinsically good in human life cannot be detached from human nature, and human nature is in turn largely a question of where humans come from. If we come from nature, that implies a standard of what is good; if we come from God, that implies another standard of what is good; if we come from nowhere—if we have no past that matters—that implies no stable standards for what is good. And so it proved in practice. ("I cannot deny my past, to which my self is wed/the woven figure cannot undo its thread." Louis MacNeice, "Valediction.")

The Consumption Paradigm: Views of History After Keynes

In the Consumption paradigm, where consumption is primary and productivity has no value except to provide for consumption, there is nothing to build up over time. Satisfaction of consumer appetites is all that matters. And that always takes place in the present. Economics comes to live in an Eternal Now, an everlasting present disconnected from the future and the past.

As we saw in Chapter 8, when Keynes lamented the lack of reliable political support for public works projects, he pointed to the pyramids and cathedrals of earlier civilizations. Egypt built pyramids and Europe built cathedrals to stand for eternity, or as close to it as the uncertainties of life would permit. That was the reason they never ran out of such works. Keynes saw in this only something that would keep people earning paychecks to spend on ephemeral enjoyment.

And as we have seen in Chapter 4, where we looked at the "paradox of thrift," for Keynes a penny saved is a penny wasted. Where Mill and the other classical economists made building up wealth over time the goal of economics, for Keynes the only goal is to spend and enjoy. Mill's *homo economicus* seeks to gain wealth as the primary goal of economics, and encounters the desire to spend or relax as distractions or obstacles toward the goal. Keynes' *homo economicus* seeks only to spend and relax, and goes after wealth only for that purpose.

The Keynesian version still seeks to gain wealth, but only because he wants to enjoy that wealth. The change here involves the time frame. Mill's version is building up for the distant future. This would naturally support the expectation that he is not building only for himself; he may not be building primarily for himself. Keynes' version is not building anything. He is enjoying. He looks forward to no future.

Keynes works hard to detach us from our traditional tendency to encourage a future orientation. He recognizes that the tradition he is fighting is a moral one, arguing that it is misguided, and a new morality is needed that will not encourage the thrift that leads to liquidity traps. Consider this passage:

> That the world after several millennia of steady individual saving, is so poor as it is in accumulated capital-assets, is to be explained, in my opinion, neither by the improvident propensities of mankind, nor even by the destruction of war, but by the high liquidity-premiums formerly attaching to the ownership of land and now attaching to money. I differ in this from the older view as expressed by Marshall with an unusual dogmatic force in his *Principles of Economics*, p. 581:
>
> Everyone is aware that the accumulation of wealth is held in check, and the rate of interest so far sustained, by the preference which the great mass of humanity have for present over deferred gratifications, or, in other words, by their unwillingness to "wait". (Keynes 2013a [1936], 242)

Note not only Keynes' pointed references to the older view's decidedly moral terminology ("improvident") in promoting savings, but his sardonic description of the "dogmatic force" of the old view. A dogma is a doctrine about transcendent moral or metaphysical truth that has been formulated and promulgated by teachers with recognized authority to interpret and deliver such doctrine. That is not a bad description of how the old, robustly teleological economists admonished us to save our money.

Keynes' attack on the old moral virtue of saving is not always wry and indirect. It is sometimes much more forthright:

> Thus, after all, the actual rates of aggregate saving and spending do not depend on Precaution, Foresight, Calculation, Improvement, Independence, Enterprise, Pride or Avarice. Virtue and vice play no part. It all depends on how far the rate of interest is favorable to investment, after taking account of the marginal efficiency of capital. No, this is an overstatement. If the rate of interest were so governed as to maintain continuous full employment, Virtue would resume her sway; the rate of capital accumulation would depend on the weakness of the propensity to consume. (Keynes 2013a, 111–112).

"Virtue," far from being found in encouragement to save, is found in cheap money that facilitates full employment. That cheap money (i.e. low interest) also punishes savings is a bonus—for, as we have seen, a penny saved is a penny wasted.

Or consider his view of the stock market. Investors must ignore the long run, according to Keynes. A given stock buyer, to be smart, must be a speculator—trying to guess what the market will guess, then invest in that guess a little before the market does. You must be a speculator because all the other stock buyers are speculators; when most people are investing for the short term, the incentives are aligned to punish you if you buy and hold companies that are actually good long-term bets because of their underlying business. "There is no clear evidence from experience that the investment policy which is socially advantageous coincides with that which is most profitable," Keynes declares (Keynes 2013a, 157).

And why is it that all the other investors are speculators, necessitating that you must also be a speculator if you seek to do well? Because "life is not long enough," declares Keynes (Keynes 2013a, 157). If our time horizon is only our own lifetime, investing in productivity doesn't make sense.

There is, thankfully, one agency that has a longer time horizon. "I expect to see the state, which is in a position to calculate the marginal efficiency of capital goods on long views and on the basis of the general social advantage, taking an even greater responsibility for directly organizing investment" (Keynes 2013a, 164). Visionary policy elites—the Bloomsbury know-it-more-than-anybody-else set—may not care about what kind of world our grandchildren live in, but they can at least rise above the even pettier short-sightedness in which the ordinary person is sunk. They can be trusted to see accurately and enact selflessly that "investment policy which is socially advantageous" but not profitable for investors. The goal of those elites, as we have seen, is to manage consumers into ever greater self-indulgence in the Eternal Now within which they live; here we add investors to the list of the managed.

Keynes' radical narrowing of the time horizon for economics, like his reversal of the relationship between production and consumption, shapes the core of his economic theory. In his summary of the theory at the beginning of Chapter 18 of the *General Theory*, Keynes holds available labor and the tastes of the consumer as fixed. As we have observed, what gets held as fixed and what is a variable is not just important to the analysis, it constitutes the analysis.

Treating available labor and consumer tastes as fixed traps us in an Eternal Now. It rules out most the primary means employed by all three of the previous paradigms, and especially by the Reason paradigm, for building up a flourishing economy *over time*. Education and training can expand people's productive capacities, increasing the personal and social capital they need to make more and better employment options available to them. Moral reform can reduce forms of consumption that undermine the productive virtues—including not only the obviously vicious forms of consumption, but more broadly the squandering of money on frivolous luxuries that trains us to value ephemeral pleasures rather than delaying gratification. When available labor and consumer tastes are held fixed, we do not even see the possibility of improving the economy and reducing unemployment by these means.

While "Economic Possibilities for Our Grandchildren" might seem to represent a concern for future generations, the reverse is the case—surprising as that may sound. That essay actually attacks those who were emphasizing that we should save up and consume less for the sake of our grandchildren, because the Great Depression had shown that the prosperity of the future was in doubt. Against these calls for discipline and frugality, Keynes sneeringly wrote: "The 'purposive' man is always trying to secure a spurious and delusive immortality for his acts by pushing his interest in them forward into time. He does not love his cat, but his cat's kittens; nor, in truth, the kittens, but only the kittens' kittens, and so on forward forever to the end of cat-dom" (Keynes 1963, 6).

Keynes claims the well-being of our grandchildren is something we need not concern ourselves about, because their prosperity is assured by the automatic workings of technological progress and compound interest (Keynes 1963, 2). The only thing he tells us to do for the good of our grandchildren is to continue telling people consume selfishly and enjoy themselves, to keep the consumption-driven engine of growth running:

> But beware! The time for all this [transcending work and greed] is not yet. For at least another hundred years we must pretend to ourselves and to every one that fair is foul and foul is fair; for foul is useful and fair is not. Avarice and usury and precaution must be our gods for a little longer still. For only they can lead us out of the tunnel of economic necessity into daylight. (Keynes 1963, 7)

How convenient! The ordinary person is, of course, not able to see this far into the future; thankfully, Keynes of the Bloomsbury know-it-more-than-anyone-else set can see it, and he admonishes his fellow elites to suppress the calls for thrift and keep the pigs' heads in the trough where they belong.

The Moral Compass: Future Orientation

The major pre-Keynes paradigms began from a view that we are powerfully shaped by our ancestors, and our highest purposes in life all lead us to a concern for our descendants. Concern for what kind of world and way of life we would leave for our grandchildren was thus to be a central factor in structuring the economy, from public policy to business strategy to household management. We did not structure the economy this way as a matter of consumer preferences; rather, consumer preferences were to be determined within this structure.

This historical consciousness is a direct result of teleological consciousness. We saw in the last chapter that for all three of the major pre-Keynes paradigms, the purpose of human life was to do something intrinsically good, and the economy was to be ordered by this higher purpose. Such a view, if seriously pursued, quickly leads us to put concern for our descendants at the center of life. This is partly for philosophical and theological reasons, as the metaphysical worldview of each of these paradigms connects moral goodness with intergenerational development.

However, this connection between teleology and the future is also based on much less highfalutin considerations. To begin with, if we want to maximize the accomplishment of good goals, investing in the future rather than the present produces a multiplier effect. We can't do much good for the dead, so the primary objects of moral concern are the living and future generations. And no matter how great the world population grows, there will always be more potential future people than there are people walking around alive at any given time. The future has a permanent moral advantage just from sheer numbers. Moreover, all three paradigms recognized that the universe is (for practical purposes) capricious in the short term, striking down even the most promising individuals with accidents, disasters and injustices. An investment in my own well-being is unreliable. An investment in the good of posterity is more certain to produce benefits for somebody somewhere, even if the universe's short-term caprice hinders me from predicting exactly what good will be done for whom how.

Thus, concern for the future—a future orientation—is always a high priority for those who put teleological considerations first in life. Even those who preach reverence for the past most strongly, and have the most negative views of future prospects, still have a future orientation. For the classical Greco-Roman mind, and for those among modern conservatives whose thought resembles theirs, reverence for the past is motivated by concern for the future. The reason we must learn to honor our elders and carry on our traditions is because our descendants will suffer if we do not. A social ethic focused on slowing the inevitable future decline represents an increased, not a decreased, level of concern about the well-being of the future. Whether classicists or conservatives or doomsday prophets, those who warn fervently that the future will never be as good as the past show by that act how concerned they are about the future.

Of course, the past also mattered for all these pre-Keynes paradigms. In the Nature paradigm, the past was a model to be preserved and emulated, inestimably valuable because it was our only source of virtue in an ever-decaying world. In the God paradigm, the past was the record of what God had done for humanity in history, and thus our only available source of information of what he has to say to us (for revelation comes to us from the past) as well as the only guide for anticipating what he might be doing in our midst in the present and future. In the Reason paradigm, the past is used negatively—but it is nonetheless used. The Enlightenment defines itself and its mission in opposition to the benighted past. It did not value the wisdom of the past, but it did value an understanding of what was wrong with the past; only that could tell us what it meant to be enlightened and to build an enlightened future.

The role of the past in these views was not accidental, it was necessary. The only way to orient ourselves toward the future rather than the present is in light of the past. If we only know where we are now, we have no way to guess where we are going next. If we know not only where we are now but the path by which we got there, we have much more information by which to understand where we might be going. The future is unpredictable in detail, but it is not absolutely undetermined and chaotic. For the future will grow, in broadly intelligible ways, out of the present—just as the present grew, in broadly intelligible ways, from the past.

In this chapter we have traced how important this future orientation, with its corresponding concern for knowledge of the past, has been in the economic thought of each approach. Their understanding of their responsibilities to the future was part of the moral compass that guided their economic lives. And their future orientation was inextricably linked with their teleological commitment to prioritize production over consumption.

The views of history shaped by teleology in these paradigms can be stated in more anthropological terms. In the Nature paradigm, a person is a product of the past, and a good person is a guardian of the past for the sake of the future. In the God paradigm, a person is a descendent of Adam, who fell from God's plan, and a good person is a person who strives through Christ to live by the plan God made Adam for, anticipating Christ's restoration of that plan when he returns. In the Reason paradigm, a person is builder of the future, and a good person is a person who seeks to build a better future.

Fracturing the Compass: We're All Dead

"In the long run we are all dead" said Keynes to his critics, when the critics said that economists should care about the long run. That statement embodies the Consumption paradigm's approach to history. We will, apparently, have no descendants—or at least none whose future we care enough about to manage our economic affairs with the long run in mind.

If production is primary and consumption is secondary, the purpose of productivity is to build something up over time. It might be to preserve civilization for future generations against the slow decay of generational corruption. It might be to participate in the unfolding plan of Christ as his return approaches. It might be to drain the swamp of ignorance to clear a dry land of enlightenment we will never live to see. In each case, we have powerful reasons to care about the long run. What is one year if the purpose of my work is to build a world for my grandchildren? It is not nothing, of course. I still need to put food on the table every day. Moreover, I can't build a world for my grandchildren unless I make progress toward that goal year by year. The point is that, in older paradigms, we had to balance attention to immediate concerns with long-term goals. And in that balance, the long-term goals mattered more.

The Consumption paradigm does not even try to balance immediate and long-term goals. Immediate goals are all that count. In the long run, we're all dead.

Since Keynes, economics has been all about the present. The main goal of policymakers in the Consumption paradigm is to raise annual GDP growth. In a sense, the burden of this chapter is to convey how short a term one year is by the standards of all major economic approaches before the time of Keynes. In contemporary economic thinking, a year feels like a long time. Large businesses, under the discipline of capital markets, focus on quarterly earnings. A year feels like a long time in comparison. Periods of time longer than a year come into our economic view rarely, usually when policymakers offer us transparently unrealistic projections of future growth, or spending cuts, to justify a policy they want to enact in the present.

But one year looks like a very short time in the perspective of any of the earlier economic paradigms. This was partly because they had agricultural economies in mind, where production was tied to the crop cycle, and one year was thus the smallest unit of time that made sense for most purposes. But it was at least as much because those paradigms placed the goal of economic action so much further into the future.

Individual actors within the economy can and do make decisions with the long run in mind. They may care about what kind of lives their grandchildren live. But the economic paradigm that dominates policy and management structures, and defines the conceptual framework for our discourse about economics, is made on the assumption that the immediate goals are the ones that really count. I as an individual may care what kind of lives my grandchildren live, but we as a nation do not care what kind of world our grandchildren live in. And those economic structures, in turn, form the kind of people we are as we live and think within them. Public structures that don't care about the long run make it harder for individuals to care about the long run.

The Consumption paradigm has no language of sustainability. As we have seen, by holding available labor and consumer tastes fixed in his economic theory, Keynes removes from our view the traditional concerns for building up a sustainable economy over time: education, training, moral reform. These concerns are not important to Keynes because for him, the purpose of economics is not to build sustainable economies. It is to rack up the highest GDP growth we can get this year. We can worry about next year, next year.

We are back to economics as video game, with GDP as the score. Each year is one "play" of the game. The player begins from scratch each time, and when the game is over, it is forgotten and we move on to the next game. Nothing builds up or carries over from game to game.

Hollow Prosperity: An Eternal Now

When economists and the policymakers and economic leaders they influence have no goals that last longer than a year, the rest of us are affected by the empty economy they create. Their moral crusade to hike short-term GDP shapes both public policy and the public discourse. When those who control systems of power and institutions of disproportionate cultural influence live in an Eternal Now and build nothing up, it becomes much harder for all of us to orient our own behavior toward future generations.

The well-being of the economy is framed in our culture entirely in terms of short-term metrics, such as GDP, stock market levels and "consumer confidence." This last emphasizes the strong norms in our culture that we ought to spend, spend, spend for the sake of the public good. Keynes' view that a penny saved is a penny wasted has percolated into our wider culture, where it shapes our assumptions in ways we typically aren't even aware of. Tempted to buy one of those costly indulgences—the ones Mill gently regretted and Keynes put at the center of economics—we say with knowing irony, "it'll stimulate the economy," and then go ahead and squander our money. And why would we not do this, when going to the mall and squandering our money is what the president begged us to do to save the country after 9/11?

Savings rates are far below historic levels, because the huge web of cultural norms associated with saving money has been shredded. Within living memory, banks advertised their savings accounts with ads that summoned us to live up to these moral norms. Now, banks advertise loans for consumption, not accounts for saving. Recently, one of the authors of this book saw an advertisement in a bank encouraging customers to go on vacation and finance it by taking out a loan—an outrageously irresponsible course of action even for a financially stable household.

Credit card debt is, as is widely known, well beyond any kind of rational level. People no longer possess the personal virtue to spend within their means. And why should they, when their government has not done so in generations, and shows no sign of doing so? Levels of debt—both personal and government—are outrageously out of control, and this is not only familiar but feels like a permanent background fact of life. Yet there seems to be nothing anyone can do about it. We are all simply resigned to ever-increasing indebtedness. Here is as clear an example as one could find of the hollow prosperity of an empty economy.

Debt is only the beginning of the mess caused at the national level by short-term thinking. Unsustainable entitlement programs and debasement of the currency are obvious train wrecks in the making, with obvious (if far from painless) solutions. Yet, again, nothing is done and nothing can be done.

Entrepreneurial risk-taking, as measured (for example) by rates of formation of new businesses, is in decline, as we have seen. We want gratification now, not to build new things that will change the future. And, of course, launching new businesses requires capital, which in turn requires a reservoir of savings.

The family, and other mediating institutions essential to the formation of personal and social capital that people need for economic success—churches, voluntary associations—are in ongoing jeopardy (Murray 2013; Putnam 2016). These institutions are future-oriented. Their survival depends on our willingness to make sacrifices now in order to sustain institutions that we know we need in the long run.

We can, of course, exercise heroic virtue and live for future generations even as our whole economic and cultural system tells us not to and punishes us for doing so. But things that take heroic virtue are not going to be done by many. Anyone who has been involved in educational activities designed to help people acquire sound financial practices can testify to how difficult it has become to lead people into even rudimentary levels of self-control and future orientation.

At a deeper level, our short-term mentality causes feelings of anomie and hopelessness. "Deaths of despair"—from drug abuse, suicide and health problems related to obesity and poor self-care—and mental illnesses are rising, as we have seen.

We build and do almost nothing for eternity. What do we produce that will still be here in a hundred years? Egypt built pyramids and medieval Europe built cathedrals; for a civilization on our scale to build nothing that would make a similarly permanent contribution to humanity would have struck our ancestors as decadent and contemptible. The lack of permanent physical objects might be forgivable if we were doing great deeds that would have a permanent effect on human history and last forever in memory. It is now fifty years since we went to the moon. What have we done since that our grandchildren will remember?

In the 1880s, we went out to a little Spanish colony town in the middle of nowhere, isolated in the wasteland of the southern California desert. It was so tiny it could barely be said to exist. And we said to ourselves: "You know what would go really well right here? One of the biggest and most influential cities in the history of the world." And we built it. We built a trans-continental railroad to connect it to Chicago. We built irrigation systems across hundreds of miles to supply fresh water in the desert. We threw open the golden door to enterprising people from Mexico and Asia. We invented the motion picture camera, one of the most consequential inventions in history, and in that town in the desert we built a new global industry that has permanently changed the way the whole human race does one of the most important things it does: tell stories. Because we used to be the kind of people who did that kind of thing.

Where is the next Los Angeles? We have the resources and the human and social capital to build three such cities from scratch over the course of a single generation, if we wanted to. With a little more time we could build one on the moon, if we wanted to. But we have been taught not to want to, by an economic paradigm that stunts our horizon of time.

Here and there it is still possible to find something we build with the intention that it would be permanent, giving us a small-scale glimpse of the kind of things we could be building and doing on a bigger scale. The recently built National Museum of African American History and Culture stands out brazenly on Washington, DC's famous National Mall, with an architectural distinctiveness that seems designed to declare: "This building is now a permanent presence on the Mall. From now on, you will not be able to take your children to the Mall to absorb the American story without taking account of what this building stands for."

We cannot, of course, build dozens of museums on the National Mall. But every city could find a project like that one—and then another, and another. Think of the public spirit and solidarity that could be mustered in New York to rebuild the original Penn Station, atoning for one of the most criminal acts in that city's history. Indeed, the comparison between the splendor of the old Penn Station and the squalor of the new one illustrates the vertiginous fall from the grandeur of the Reason paradigm, with all its faults, to the sub-utilitarian materialism of the Consumption paradigm. Why not climb back up—or build something even better than the original?

Consider that remarkable glass dome in Omaha, which prompted the conversation with an Uber driver who took such pride in having helped build it. How often do we build things like that, things our grandchildren will admire? Our nation has a lot of cities with a lot of civic space that is currently occupied by hideous buildings and even more hideous public art. We have a Superfund for cleaning up the toxic sites left behind by generations of polluters, from before we became more conscientious about the environment. Why not a Superfund to clean up toxic sites left behind by generations of equally offensive artistic despoilage?

How long until we go back to the moon? To Mars? Beyond? When do we colonize the ocean floors? Or the skies?

Living in an Eternal Now, unaffected by what came before and only vaguely concerned by what will come after, we cannot build economic lives that are morally satisfying. And if we cannot do that, we cannot pass on to our grandchildren the long-term economic growth bequeathed to us by our ancestors. Only virtuous workers given direction by a moral culture can sustain the productive virtues—diligence, honesty, self-control, risk-taking—upon which long-term growth depends.

We already know that we cannot pursue ends worth pursuing if we live in an Eternal Now. We do not need a new morality or a demagogue to find our way back. We only need to take seriously our own teleological awareness, and follow that thread where it leads. But we must be prepared to sacrifice comfort and leisure to the extent that building for our grandchildren demands it. We cannot eat our cake and have it; if we do not want to be stuck on earth, we must stretch ourselves painfully to reach for the skies.

References

Appleby, Joyce. 2010. *The Relentless Revolution*. New York: W. W. Norton.

Aristotle. 1992. *Politics*. London and New York: Penguin Books.

Augustine. 1984. *City of God*. London and New York: Penguin Books.

Bloom, Allan. 1987, *The Closing of the American Mind*. New York: Simon & Schuster.

Carson, D.A. 2012. *Christ and Culture Revisited*. Grand Rapids: Eerdmans.

Deane, Herbert A. 1963, *The Political and Social Ideas of St. Augustine*. New York: Columbia University Press.

Forster, Greg. 2008. *The Contested Public Square*. Downers Grove: InterVarsity Press.

Frederickson, George M. 2002. *Racism*. Princeton: Princeton University Press.

Gunton, Colin. 1998. *The Triune Creator*. Grand Rapids: Eerdmans.

Keynes, John Maynard. 1963, "Economic Possibilities for Our Grandchildren," Scanned by Yale University Economics Department from John Maynard Keynes, *Essays in Persuasion*, Norton, 358–373. http://www.econ.yale.edu/smith/econ116a/keynes1.pdf. Accessed 23 Jan 2019.

Keynes, John Maynard. 2013 [1936]. *The General Theory of Employment, Interest and Money*. Cambridge: Cambridge University Press.

Keynes, John Maynard. 2013. *A Tract on Monetary Reform*. Cambridge: Cambridge University Press.

Locke, John. 1975. *An Essay Concerning Human Understanding*. Oxford and New York: Oxford University Press.

Murray, Charles. 2013. *Coming Apart*. New York: Crown Forum.

Niebuhr, H. Richard. 1975. *Christ and Culture*. New York: HarperCollins.

O'Donovan, Oliver. 1996. *The Desire of the Nations*. Cambridge and New York: Cambridge University Press.

Plato. 1991. *Republic*. New York: Basic Books.

Putnam, Robert D. 2016. *Our Kids*. New York: Simon & Schuster.

Smith, Adam. 1994. *The Wealth of Nations*. New York: Random House.

Taylor, Charles. 2007. *A Secular Age*. Cambridge: Harvard University Press.

CHAPTER 10

Respect Other People: Moral and Cultural Conditions of Human Dignity

The conflict between the rhetoric of moral neutrality among economists and the strongly normative rhetoric that dominates popular discussions of economic issues is one of the biggest areas of dissonance in our national discourse. We do not experience the same level of dissonance with most other social sciences. Political scientists and sociologists study poverty (for example) as well as economists. They may not always be fully aware of, or fully willing to confess to, the moral presuppositions upon which they rely, so their analyses are sometimes biased or distorted. But they are much less likely to make aggressive claims about their own moral neutrality, asserting that their analysis of poverty is purely positive and untouched by the warping influence of normative beliefs. Political scientists and sociologists who study poverty will usually admit that their studies are directed to those subjects by a desire to help society alleviate poverty. Dialogue about moral realities can therefore occur, and to some extent does occur, between popular movements and academic researchers in these disciplines. It does not occur with economists. (Recall from the Introduction Peter Berger's "one group of social scientists with whom it was generally impossible to work.")

This dissonance and lack of dialogue helps to conceal one of the worst aspects of hollow prosperity and the empty economy: the tendency to slowly dissolve ethical constraints in both business and government. This ultimately leads to ever-greater political control over the economy.

V. V. Claar and G. Forster, *The Keynesian Revolution and Our Empty Economy*, https://doi.org/10.1007/978-3-030-15808-8_10

Legal and political restraint must substitute for the absence of moral self-restraint on the part of businesses, and political leaders themselves become less morally self-constrained in demanding more power over others.

It may not seem obvious that statements like "all production is for the purpose of ultimately satisfying a consumer" or "in the long run we are all dead" are connected to Keynes' desire to have government control the economy at levels comparable to those in socialist states, or to his statement that politicians should "manage" our "human nature" to keep us "strongly addicted to the money-making passion." But they are connected.

The connection is anthropological. The same view of human nature that leads the Consumption paradigm to elevate consumption over production and radically narrow our time horizon is also a view of human nature that cannot sustain ethical limits on what it is permissible to do to people. Businesses that act upon the view of human nature formed by the policy structure and cultural influence of the Consumption paradigm will find it harder and harder to justify ethical limits. Governments will find it even harder to limit their own power—and will see in the collapse of business ethics an urgent need to expand their power.

"Management of the economy" is another way of saying "government management of our daily lives." Thinking of the economy as a thing that can be managed by highly educated technocratic elites is not merely a step in the direction of unlimited political control over all aspects of human life; it constitutes unlimited political control over all aspects of human life. Since our economic lives include our most intimate and important personal decisions, political control over the economy implies political control over almost every decision people make. This creeping totalitarianism of economic management is the gravest threat we see in hollow prosperity.

Human Dignity

How do economic systems shape the way we treat one another? Ethics involves at least three dimensions: purposes (the teleological), virtues (moral character), and rules (the normative). Purposes and virtues are internal to moral action. They constitute what we ought to do and how. Rules are external to it. They limit what we may do. The last two chapters have been concerned primarily with purposes and virtues; they concern the content of proper economic action. In this chapter, we turn to the rules.

This is, as we have seen, the one area where economics has not abandoned morality, although it claims to have done so. Purposes and virtues—teleology and moral character—really were minimized in economics after the nineteenth century. However, Keynes was vigorously and openly normative, proudly prescribing what we ought to do. His followers, in building the Consumption paradigm, merged Keynes' moral crusade with the nineteenth-century economists' rhetoric of moral neutrality. Economics since Keynes has truly excluded purposes and virtues, but it has all kinds of rules, even though it claims not to. It is crypto-normative.

That a society's ethical rules have a profound effect on its economic systems is too obvious a point to be worth belaboring. The easing, in the late Middle Ages, of norms against charging interest for money loans—sternly discountenanced in both classical and earlier Christian thought—had an impact sufficiently enormous to establish the important role ethical boundaries play in economic systems. Even Milton Friedman, when making his famous statement that corporations have no social responsibility other than to make a profit, was careful to qualify it by adding that corporations were also obliged to obey the laws (including laws enacted to achieve moral ends) and the prevailing ethical norms of honest business practice in their societies.[1]

While the last two chapters dealt with topics that are closely connected to our moral duties to others, this chapter turns to a direct

[1] The full quote is: "There is one and only one social responsibility of business – to use its resources and engage in activities designed to increase its profits so long as it stays within the rules of the game, which is to say, engages in open and free competition without deception or fraud" (Friedman 1970). Friedman added that the people running the business should obey the moral duties they discern themselves to be under to their consciences, their families and their nations; and that it is government's responsibility to pass laws to accomplish social ends, and businesses must comply with these laws. His argument is that the business itself is distinct from the people running it and from the government regulating it, and it ought to leave moral discernment and social regulation to these two agencies respectively. We may ask whether it is desirable, or even possible, for a business to operate without institutionalizing in its practices ethical judgments that reach beyond the bounds Friedman permits; even Friedman acknowledges that because businesses are "artificial persons" they may have "artificial responsibilities." But there is no question that Friedman acknowledges the pervasive presence of social and governmental moral influence upon business activity.

consideration of those duties. What are we allowed and not allowed to do to our neighbors? As a result, this chapter turns much more explicitly to the question of anthropology.

What is a person? The way we treat something corresponds to what we think it is. If I find a piece of wood and conclude that it broke off from a priceless antique, I will save it carefully and see if I can restore it to its rightful place. But if I conclude that it is just scrap left over from yesterday's carpentry, I will think that its rightful place is the trash can, and act accordingly. So when we ask how we ought to treat people, our answer will depend on what we think a person is.

"What is a person?" is therefore a question with far-reaching consequences for economics (as well as all the other social sciences). Whenever we order our economic arrangements, whether in public policy or the household budget, we are taking a stand about the right way to treat people; this involves taking a stand about what a person is. Even if we merely seek to understand economics, we require these kinds of moral assumptions to form the categories of thought we use to construct that understanding. That is why we measure GDP per person but not per yak.

Scholars increasingly use the concept of "human dignity" to process questions about the moral significance of human beings (Lewis 2007; Nussbaum 2008; Rosen 2012; Düwell et al. 2014; Barak 2015; Waldron 2017). This concept originated in classical antiquity and has a robust history in Christian and Enlightenment thought. The concept of human dignity has taken on a different meaning in each of the three corresponding economic paradigms. Today, the way we understand human dignity is changing significantly once again. That is a complex story and mostly beyond the scope of this book. But in the field of economics, the Keynesian Revolution is at the center of the story of how our concepts of dignity are changing.

The Nature Paradigm: Classical Views of Human Dignity

The classical philosophy of the Nature paradigm grounded the concept of human dignity in reason and virtue. The earliest known appearance of the phrase "the dignity of humanity" is in the philosophy of the Roman Stoics. The Latin *dignitas* refers to rank or standing; Adam Schulman writes that it "means something like 'worthiness for honor and esteem'" (Schulman 2009, 6). The "dignity" of humanity in this sense meant the superiority of human beings over the other parts of nature. This superiority entitled them to a position of authority over the rest of the natural world, and also obligated them to practice reason and virtue. Our right to harness the ox and plow the field was connected to our responsibility to tell the truth and exercise self-control. The rights and responsibilities both came from our elevated rank or status ("dignity") in the diverse spectrum of nature.

The concept is even older than the phrase. From the beginning, classical philosophy was built on the idea that there was something unique in human beings that made them morally significant. And this special status for human beings was always connected with reason and virtue.

Plato argued that people must have immortal souls because (among other arguments) they are capable of reason. We cannot learn any knowledge unless we already possess certain kinds of knowledge, the kinds of knowledge needed to assimilate and make sense of new knowledge. (Later philosophers would call this a priori knowledge.) Therefore the reasoning element in us cannot come into being and grow the way the body does. It must have an ongoing existence.[2] Our ability to know truth, which is eternal and transcendent, is our participation in the higher world of ideas that exists above the world of physical bodies. This places us above the other parts of nature, which are trapped in the physical world and have no eternal element.[3]

Plato also connected the soul to moral responsibility. The line between reason and virtue is less clear in Plato than it is in Aristotle. For Plato, behaving virtuously sometimes seems to be identical with behaving rationally (Plato 1991, 198–200; 519d–521b). But while these categories are not carefully distinguished, there is a clear moral element in Plato's understanding of rationality. As we observed in the previous chapter, he proposed the possibility of reincarnation, with souls allowed to choose their future lives in priority order based on the virtue of their past lives. He did not imagine such a process for the lower animals. The details of this celestial "draft" were admittedly speculative; its significance for Plato was that human beings, using their reason, cannot make sense of the universe and their place in it without a moral accountability to which all people are subject (Plato 1991, 297–303; 614b–621d).

[2] See Plato's *Meno*.

[3] See Plato's *Phaedo*.

For Aristotle, the special status of human beings is even more clearly linked to reason and virtue. For Aristotle, each thing in nature has one or more forms of excellence that it exists to achieve. Aristotle identifies the two highest forms of human excellence as intellectual excellence and moral excellence—reason and virtue (Aristotle 1980, 1–27; I). It is these forms of excellence that make human beings stand out above the other parts of nature, which achieve lower forms of excellence. What distinguishes humans is that they speak together (reason) about the good (virtue). This is why they are able to accomplish so much that the lower animals cannot, and why they are the pinnacle of nature's pyramid (Aristotle 1992, 59–61; I.2).

For purposes of economics, perhaps the most important thing to grasp about the classical view of human dignity is that it was dependent upon social roles and hierarchy. In the classical view, a human being does not have any dignity simply as a human being. Dignity is not intrinsic. A person has dignity to the extent that, exercising reason and virtue, they fulfill the roles determined by their nature and their relations with others—by being a good husband, father, household manager, citizen, etc.

This means dignity is unevenly distributed. Roles deemed to require higher levels of reason and virtue convey more human dignity. The ancients held that a man has higher dignity than a woman, a free man has more than a slave, a citizen more than a foreigner, etc. This hierarchal thinking was of course the very reason why the Latin word for rank or standing—*dignitas*—came to be used for what we now call "dignity."

The Nature Paradigm and Dignity

The connection between hierarchy and dignity is important to economics for at least two reasons. First, it implied that people could not choose their social role, including the type of work they were to do. In the classical world, people were assigned to roles and jobs based primarily on their birth and on decisions made for them early in their lives by their parents. If it is your role that gives you your significance as a person, clearly you cannot be permitted to choose your role. Your choice cannot change your role, because it is your role that dictates what kinds of choices you ought to make. If you are supposed to make all your choices on the basis of your role, on what basis could you possibly choose a role?

Second, economic roles were a central factor in the distribution of dignity. Those who had to work to support themselves were deemed to have much lower dignity, because they did not have the leisure time to pursue those activities—politics, religion, philosophy, etc.—that were held to be essential for the higher development of reason and virtue. Aristotle says explicitly that no one who works for a living should be allowed to vote, and that such people are not fully human but are "tools" (his word) used by their masters and employers in the leisure class to accomplish the ends of reason and virtue (Aristotle 1992, 63–75; I.4–7). Management of economic affairs is necessary for the virtuous life. The leisure class must have something to eat, so some attention to economic matters is therefore legitimate. But the economic sphere of life was decidedly lower in dignity and value than the higher realms of politics, religion, and philosophy—and so were people whose lives were chiefly occupied with economic affairs.

This meant the economy of the classical world was rigidly controlled and highly stratified. This ensured a high level of conformity to ethical standards, but at great cost both to economic development and moral recognition of human beings. People were not free to pursue the kinds of work they were best suited to. Men had to do the jobs their fathers did, mostly farming. Women, having married the men their fathers selected for them, had to do the work assigned to women in the household. And the overwhelming majority of the population had no secure property or contract rights. As members of the less rational and virtuous working class, they could not be trusted with such rights. Their place was to obey their social superiors, ensuring the rule of reason over ignorance and of virtue over vice.

Owner/slave and master/servant relations were as central to classical culture as male/female and parent/child relations. Alongside these formal, personal relations was a paternalistic conception of the more general relationship between the wealthier and the lower classes. If the rich chose to provide for the needs of the poor, they did so on the expectation that the poor would reciprocate this gift with loyalty, obedience, and submission to the stratified social order (Rhee 2012, 14–19).

In such a society, sustained economic growth was not possible. The rigidity of social roles prevented all but a very few members of society from discovering and exercising the full use of their productive capacities, or inventing new ways of doing things. The strict hierarchy within which all social activity was subject to the control of a very small ruling class prevented the development of markets with a wide scope of exchange, limiting the extent to which new efficiencies could be discovered and realized through the division of labor. And, of course, where the ruling class has that much power over people, people are not incentivized to be highly productive—whatever they build can simply be taken from them.

The God Paradigm: Christian Views of Human Dignity

Christian understandings of human dignity are rooted in the scriptural doctrine that human beings are the only creatures in the natural world who are made in the image of God. This idea is one of the most important foundations of the God paradigm in economics.

Because this idea occurs frequently in scripture, with different contexts and associations, there have been multiple approaches to explaining it. These approaches do not necessarily conflict, but they can differ widely in emphasis. While all three approaches have existed at all stages of Christian history, different approaches have dominated at different times.

Medieval Christianity emphasized the image of God as a reflection of divine characteristics. In a lesser and creaturely way, we possess some of God's attributes (reason, will, emotion, agency, responsibility). This emphasis harmonizes in some respects with the classical view, as reason and virtue were emphasized almost as much in medieval Christianity as they were in classical philosophy. But, as we will see, there were also sharp differences (Horton 2011, 391–392).

Reformation theology emphasized the image of God as conferring a status of authority over nature. As God's official representatives, human beings have the right and responsibility to be stewards of—to rule and develop and protect—the animals, plants, and minerals (Horton 2011, 396–400). More recent biblical scholarship has reinforced this aspect of the doctrine by showing that it aligns with the use of the phrase "image of god" in ancient Near East literature to describe kings; the Old Testament seems to be appropriating the phrase to suggest that humanity is a royal race, every member of which participates in a monarchical authority over the nonhuman world (Motyer 1996, 71).

Finally, a third approach—one receiving more attention today—emphasizes the relational nature of human personality and community. Human beings have a paradoxical nature that is both individual and social simultaneously. Our individual identities and purposes are structured by our relations with others, yet our social relations are also structured by the capacity of individuals to assert their own identities and purposes. For some, this paradox is an image of the triune Christian God. God is, in Christian theology, one being who is three persons united forever in love and mutual self-giving. The paradoxical individual-and-social nature of human beings is seen by some as an image of God's unity-in-diversity and diversity-in-unity; we were made to live together in loving and fruitful relationship with God and with one another (Horton 2011, 392–393).

This Christian idea of the image of God introduces two changes from the classical view that have enormous consequences for economics. In the classical view, dignity was conferred upon each individual by their social role, but in the Christian view dignity is intrinsic to human nature. A person's dignity does not vary by or depend upon their social role; on the contrary, social roles must conform to the dignity of the human person rather than vice versa. And where the classical view distributed dignity unequally, Christianity declares all human beings to be of equal dignity. The king may have more power and authority than the subject, but not more human dignity.

As Christianity spread, the first major economic impact was the assertion of a moral duty to care for the poor out of pure generosity rather than out of expectation that the poor would repay this help through loyalty and service. This conflict of ethical principles rose to the surface early in the history of Christianity's growth. Christians became known not only for personal generosity in caring for the poor, but for organizing institutions in the public square for that purpose (they invented the first hospitals) and calling upon social elites to do the same. Over time, this moral witness played a critical role in the increasing public legitimacy and authority of Christianity (Rhee 2012, 159–190).

During the Middle Ages, after Christianity had been established as the norm in principle, attention turned to reforming traditional economic and political structures so they conformed more fully to that norm in practice. Through the use of reason, we could discern the natural law—a moral lawfulness that God had ordained to govern human affairs. On the basis of this moral law discernable in nature, we could figure out more just and fruitful ways to arrange even our most fundamental economic and other social structures. This is the "spirit of Reform" (capital R) we have noted above. Greater legal protection for economic rights—to work, own property and enter into enforceable contracts—was extended to those outside royal families. Some traditional inhibitions on economic practices were relaxed; of particular importance, where charging interest on money loans had previously been seen as oppressive, increasingly the prohibition on interest itself came to be seen as oppressive (Grabill 2007, xiii–xxxv). The first economic firms, such as banks, were founded (Stark 2005, 105–159).

The Reformation brought with it a major revival in an old and neglected idea called the doctrine of vocation—that every Christian is "called" by God to exercise love for God and neighbor through their daily work. This greatly increased levels of social respect for ordinary workers (Wingren 2004). The classical idea that people who worked with their hands were inferior in reason was only somewhat challenged, since the education necessary to develop the mind was still available only to a few (although it was during this era that the first attempts to extend education to all people were made, on grounds that even the ordinary worker was made in God's image and ought to be developed; Glenn 2002). By contrast, the idea that the ordinary worker was *morally* inferior suffered a catastrophic collapse. The doctrine of vocation struck directly at the classical belief that there was a tradeoff between time spent on work and time spent on moral development. Work, even supposedly "menial" work, was held to be morally edifying because it was carrying out the call to love God and neighbor. Martin Luther's sermon on marriage provides an instructive window into this change in attitudes. Against the view that those who marry and raise children are less suitable for the priesthood because they have to spend time changing dirty diapers instead of reading books about God, Luther asserts that changing dirty diapers makes a man more suitable for the priesthood, as it trains him to love God by loving and serving his neighbor (Luther 1522).

Of course, the rise of Christianity did not by itself overthrow hierarchical social institutions. Continued exercise of authority by kings, popes, etc. was justified as necessary to social order. It did, however, strip these hierarchical institutions of much of their mystique of moral superiority. With the Reformation, this effect was extended even to the church itself. All Christians, not just clergy, were servants of God doing work that was equally valuable and pleasing in God's sight. This change in moral attitudes was an essential contributing factor in the egalitarian revolutions that later emerged.

The aggregate economy of Western Europe began to show sustained growth, at a slow but steady pace, starting in the twelfth century (Maddison 2007, 382). The changes that had been gradually introduced by the God paradigm played a key role in this growth. As we have noted above, new policy structures protecting property and contract rights for a wider scope of people were implemented to bring the economy into closer conformity to the natural law. At least as important was a social ethos that increasingly affirmed the equal moral and religious dignity of all work—and hence of all workers. These were the original formal and informal building blocks of sustained growth.

The Reason Paradigm: Enlightenment Views of Human Dignity

Enlightenment views of human dignity vary even more than Christian views, so the story for the Reason paradigm is complex. Some key Enlightenment figures were Christians who incorporated a Christian view of human dignity into Enlightenment thought, or non-Christians who were heavily influenced by Christian patterns of thinking; Renee Descartes and John Locke fall into this category. Another line of thought is represented by Thomas Hobbes and David Hume, for whom the ability to use reason when calculating how to satisfy appetites and passions—instrumental reason—is more or less the only difference between human beings and other animals, reducing human dignity to a minimal level; this line of thought includes the Physiocrats. A third line of thought, one that was particularly influential on Adam Smith, attempted to build a substantive reason that would set moral ends, but grounded in moral sentiments rather than direct appeals to God—although God was usually identified as the author of the sentiments. Jean-Jacques Rousseau, the founder of this school, wrote that God had implanted all human beings with sympathy for one another and compassion for others' suffering, and these moral sentiments were the basis of ethics (Rousseau 1979, 266–294). This is substantive reason, in that reason is obligated to recognize the authority of the moral sentiments, and failure to follow them is labeled irrational. But it grounds the moral element of substantive reason subjectively, entirely within the human psyche, rather than in objective relations with God. The role of God is to justify treating our subjective moral sentimentality as authoritative.

Nonetheless, we can observe a number of consistent patterns in Enlightenment views of human dignity. One is an elevation of reason to the point where it became the paradigmatic sign of our humanity. The very term "Enlightenment" reflects the central focus on reason in this period. This continued a trend toward the elevation of reason that began with natural law thought in the Middle Ages (Gunton 1998, 125–130). One of the key challenges of the Enlightenment was to articulate how reason related to morality, and it is in how they wrestled with this issue that the differences between the Christian/quasi-Christian, Hobbesian/Humean, and Rousseauian/Romantic schools are most clearly visible.

A second consistent trend was a reduced emphasis on the relational nature of human beings. For classical thought, relationships with others and the social roles they convey were at the center. Human dignity depended upon them. In Christian thought, dignity in the image of God became independent of social roles, but human nature was still held to be deeply relational, embedding us in identities, moral duties, and social roles not of our own choosing. During the Enlightenment, the individual became more morally autonomous. Moral duties to others that were not of our own choosing became suspect (Taylor 2007; Berger 2014, 1–16).

This narrative of the Enlightenment's individualism is often carried too far. The extreme individualism common in advanced modernity (so-called "postmodern" thought) is sometimes read backward into Enlightenment thinkers. In fact, Enlightenment thinkers consistently held that some social institutions—especially the family and government—were necessary and had a permanent, objective grounding in human nature. They did emphasize the role of social conventions in structuring these institutions, and that is the basis of the common but misleading oversimplification that they thought these institutions were "artificial rather than natural." In fact, they did not believe we were free to simply get rid of these institutions or change them in any arbitrary way we wanted. They were quite clear that human nature absolutely demanded these institutions, and that it would continue to do so as long as human beings were human. We see this, for example, in their stern admonitions to marital fidelity and the nurturing of children, demanded by the natural and permanent institution of the family. The conviction that some institutions were natural and permanent placed firm limits on how we could legitimately restructure them.

What did change was the role that individual choice—alongside reason—was held to play in legitimizing these institutions. Politics and the family were legitimate, and obedience to their commands obligatory, because if they did not exist any rational person (note that important phrase) would freely consent (another important phrase) to create them and be subject to them. If people refuse to submit to legitimate political authority or the most basic imperatives of family life, that person is being irrational. Such people could legitimately be compelled to obey in these cases, because the individual choice they would make if they were rational is more important than the individual choices they actually do make as irrational people. But compelling them is only legitimate because in these particular cases we know with certainty what the rational choice would be, and we know that because we can say with confidence that any rational person would freely make that choice. Individual choice stands alongside reason as a basic legitimizing principle of Enlightenment thought.

During this period, the public respect accorded to ordinary work, and the respect for moral equality that goes with that social recognition, reached its peak. The connection between recognizing all people's equal moral dignity and recognizing the moral value of their work is important to grasp. The Enlightenment inaugurated an age, through which we are still living, of democratic political revolutions and of extending recognition of the human rights of those who were previously oppressed. This is the *political* corollary of the Enlightenment's *economic* emphasis on the dignity of doing an honest day's work for an honest day's wage. It is primarily because ordinary workers have a right to keep the fruits of their labor that oppressive economic and political orders are unjust and must be overthrown. And it is because the ordinary worker's work is morally edifying that the common people can be trusted to exercise this right (Forster 2005).

The Consumption Paradigm: Views of Human Dignity After Keynes

As we have seen, Keynes reinvented *homo economicus*, the representative economic agent who is wealth-maximizing, costly-indulgence-enjoying and labor-averse. John Stuart Mill's original model of *homo economicus*, avaricious though he was, carried forward at least some of the moral assumptions of the Reason paradigm, and was intended to be used only for purposes of empirical modeling. Keynes changed the "rationality" of the model from Mill's still somewhat-substantive rationality, which prescribed ends, to a purely instrumental rationality, leaving ends to be determined by animal instinct. And Keynes did not just build models, he went on a moral crusade to *produce* this person through normative political and social influence. His followers, who built the Consumption paradigm, adopted the nineteenth-century rhetoric of moral neutrality, but carried on Keynes' moral crusade to remake us as *homo economicus.*

Bundles of Appetites

Economics in the Consumption paradigm requires us to treat people as if human beings were, most fundamentally, nothing but bundles of appetites. It is not simply that people do their best to satisfy their appetites as a matter of fact. The Consumption paradigm establishes a normative obligation to do our best to satisfy our appetites.

That we are nothing but a bundle of appetites, at least for purposes of economic thought, is established by the norm demanding that we satisfy our appetites. If there were anything else in us—a mind capable of evaluating appetites, a will responsible to regulate appetites—there could be no *carte-blanche* endorsement of the goodness of satisfying appetites simply as such. The satisfaction of our appetites (which is "the good" for our appetites) would have to be integrated with other goals ("the good" for the other parts of us).

If human nature is complex, made up of multiple types of components, any serious view of what is good for human beings would also have to be complex, incorporating what is good for each aspect of our nature into a comprehensive whole. A discipline that operates with a view of the good that is simple rather than complex (satisfy consumer appetites!) necessarily assumes an anthropology that is simple rather than complex (a person is nothing but a bundle of appetites). And by assuming this anthropology, it reproduces it by forming our actual behavior.

This assumption that we are nothing but bundles of appetites shapes the core of Keynes' theory in the *General Theory.* At the beginning of Chapter 18 of the book, where he summarizes the theory, consumer tastes are fixed. They are not to be evaluated or regulated, but merely satisfied. Only the propensity to consume—how far we are willing to go to satisfy our appetites—is variable. A theory of economics that allowed for moral evaluation of appetites could not hold those appetites constant. They would have to be variable. And since what is fixed and what is variable constitutes the analysis, the theory would be fundamentally different theory.

The *homo economicus* whose behavior constitutes Keynes' analysis is closer to an animal than a person. It does whatever its consumption preferences—its immediate appetites—tell it to do. The only question is how much of that activity it will engage in, a variable determined by its "animal spirits."

We can treat people as bundles of appetites to be satisfied or as persons with intrinsic worth, but not both. If people are what the Consumption paradigm says they are, we cannot attribute moral significance to the human person, either intrinsically (with the God paradigm) or in the fulfillment of roles (with the Nature paradigm) or some amalgam (with the Reason paradigm). If we are under an obligation to satisfy our appetites, we cannot be thinking, decision-making beings obligated to evaluate our appetites and regulate which are to be satisfied when.

Economists in the Consumption paradigm may, of course, hold moral or religious beliefs that attribute intrinsic value to the person. But their theories of economics are not able to assimilate these beliefs.

From "Economy" to "The Economy"

This view of the person is interdependent with a shift in the focus of economics, also brought about by the Keynesian Revolution. Economics before Keynes was primarily concerned with understanding the economic decisions of households, businesses, and other discrete economic actors. After Keynes, economics primarily studies the management of "the economy" as an aggregate whole.

Even the term "the economy" is a relatively recent development. The word "economy" used to refer to a personal virtue: frugality and good stewardship of resources. There was no "the economy," because the aggregate state of economic arrangements at any given moment was not what mattered.

Timothy Mitchell asserts that as late as the 1930s, the definite article "the" was not used in front of the word "economy"; the locution "the economy" became commonplace during the 1940s and 1950s (Mitchell 2002, 80–82). The text of the *General Theory*, where we would expect to find this term throughout the book if it were in common use, seems to confirm Mitchell. Keynes uses "the economy" only once in the *General Theory* (Keynes 2013, 13).

The new focus on the aggregate is facilitated by the reduction of human beings to mere bundles of appetites. *Homo economicus* has uniform goals that can be satisfied in the aggregate. And this is even truer of Keynes' model of *homo economicus* than of Mill's.

Rational and responsible moral agents have some goals that can be aggregated (e.g. national defense). However, for the most part the decisions they face are unique to themselves. The moral goodness or badness of an action is extensively dependent upon who does it, in what situation, and how.

If the human person has a teleology, we definitely will not be able to aggregate much of our economic analysis. If the human person—not the human race as a whole, or the nations and other groups it forms, but the human person as such—exists to accomplish things that are intrinsically good, every person must accomplish those good things in their own life. They flourish as thinkers and actors.

Such people will, of course, band together in groups to accomplish good things. But they will have to do so organically, under no artificial compulsion (so the teleology of the individual, who flourishes as a thinker and actor, is respected) and in a wide variety of particular forms and modes (corresponding to the goal in view for each group). Human beings have a social nature, but that sociability is expressed in a bewildering variety of types of social units. Some are organic (families), some synthetic (nations), and some contractual (businesses). In none do people simply melt down into a big pot of undifferentiated soup.

The Decline of Business Ethics and the Rise of Unlimited Politics

This anthropology is a major factor in the continuing decline of business ethics. In Chapter 8, we examined this decline with an emphasis on the impossibility of setting clear ethical standards if we have no substantive definition of economic productivity. Here, we add the anthropological dimension of the ethical breakdown. Anyone who views the human person as nothing but a bundle of appetites will have difficulty justifying ethical limits on what can be done to people. While business schools are not economics departments, the discipline of economics exercises enormous influence over what future business leaders are taught about human behavior. The discipline of economics provides the language and thought categories in which economic behavior is described. Economists also influence policymakers whose decisions shape the business environment. And, of course, business leaders hire their own economists and take their advice.

As virtually every political philosopher since Plato has observed, a serious decline in public morals will be followed almost inevitably by the rise of tyrannical political control. Ominously, the new focus on aggregate methods in economics emerged in tandem with Keynes' desire to manipulate and control whole populations. He wants economists to decide such things as how much buying consumers should be doing, and how much money should be invested in the stock market, at each given moment. And he wants the state to use policy to push real economic actors to conform to these aggregate targets. If people are saving too much and buying too little, the state needs to stimulate their shopping spirits, as we saw in Chapter 4. The state should also take direct control of how much money is in the stock market, as we saw in Chapter 9.

Keynes thinks economists can use mathematical methods to analyze data with sufficient complexity to reach conclusions about the best way to manipulate aggregate economic factors for better results. He acknowledges that "too large a proportion of recent 'mathematical' economics are merely concoctions, as imprecise as the initial assumptions they rest on, which allow the author to lose sight of the complexities and interdependencies of the real world in a maze of pretentious and unhelpful symbols" (Keynes 2013, 298). However, he still asserts that "if we have all the facts before us, we shall have enough simultaneous equations to give us a determinate result" (Keynes 2013, 299).

In light of the extensive state control of markets Keynes advocates, his explanation for why he thinks socialism is unnecessary is downright sinister:

> It is not the ownership of the instruments of production which it is important for the State to assume. If the State is able to determine the aggregate amount of resources devoted to augmenting the instruments and the basic rate of reward to those who own them, it will have accomplished all that is necessary. (Keynes 2013, 378)

Keynes shares Marx's goal of giving the state control over our economic lives, which is to say, over all the most intimate and important decisions we make. He just thinks the state can accomplish this control without seizing ownership of assets.

That is not even the most sinister passage in the *General Theory*. Consider:

> The task of transmuting human nature must not be confused with the task of managing it. Though in the ideal commonwealth men may have been taught or bred to take no interest in the stakes, it may still be wise and prudent statesmanship to allow the game to be played, subject to rules and limitations so long as the average man, or even a significant section of the community, is in fact strongly addicted to the money-making passion. (Keynes 2013, 374)

To unpack the disturbing implications of this passage requires some careful attention:

- In an ideal state, we would "transmute" human nature, raising people not to care how much money they end up with after playing the "game" of money-making.
- However, for now we need to keep the game going. If we stop, we'll have nothing to eat; the economy runs not on productive work but on satisfying consumer appetites.
- Thus it is the responsibility of government to keep the game going.
- Keeping the game going involves all the players being highly motivated and playing to win—"strongly addicted to the money-making passion."
- The wise and prudent statesman will therefore "manage" human nature, keeping it in a state of socially beneficial greed, rather than attempt to "transmute" it toward real selflessness, at least so long as we live in the current state and not the ideal state.

This passage about manipulating the masses to take advantage of their greed for social purposes must be read in light of Keynes' even more candid comments just a few years earlier in "Economic Possibilities for Our Grandchildren":

> But beware! The time for all this [virtue] is not yet. For at least another hundred years we must pretend to ourselves and to every one that fair is foul and foul is fair; for foul is useful and fair is not. Avarice and usury and precaution must be our gods for a little longer still. For only they can lead us out of the tunnel of economic necessity into daylight. (Keynes 1963, 7)

The task of "managing" human nature in its present state of wickedness does not merely mean coping with that wickedness while working to overcome it. The wickedness must be actively encouraged, so the benighted masses will keep "playing the game" to win. If greed slackens, the economy crashes.

Keynes' desire for government to exercise control over our desires and ideas, in order to manipulate the kind of people we are and what motivates us, was not merely theoretical. He was actively involved in the design and launch of new government initiatives to fund the arts—with the goal of establishing government influence over the content of the arts. "Keynes hoped for a moral and ethical transition in society, and his economic and cultural policies sought to create the conditions for that transition," writes Anna Rosser Upchurch in her history of Keynes' involvement in government arts programs (Upchurch 2011, 70).

Living under political leaders who manipulate us to keep us as greedy as possible is a lamentable disadvantage of not living in Keynes' "ideal state." However, it does not follow that a transition to the ideal state would be preferable from our point of view. The ideal state to which Keynes refers in the *General Theory* may have been the future he described in "Economic Possibilities for Our Grandchildren"; if so, it is not necessarily an ideal we would share.

It appears, from external evidence, that Keynes looked forward to a rosy future in "Economic Possibilities for Our Grandchildren" because he anticipated a heavy-handed eugenic campaign to purge the human race of its less desirable members. Phillip Magness and James Harrigan have uncovered an extensive correspondence on this topic between Keynes and H.G. Wells from 1926 to 1934. Moreover, it is clear that Keynes himself saw "Grandchildren" as part of this discussion; as Magness and Harrigan point out, when he published "Grandchildren" in a collection of essays, Keynes paired it with a review he had written of Wells' eugenicist novel *The World of William Clissold*, publishing the two essays under the shared heading "The Future." In a joint appearance before the strongly eugenicist Malthusian League in 1927, Keynes and Wells both connected their work to the hope for a eugenically cleansed, scientifically managed society. Keynes had been an enthusiastic eugenicist from early in his career, including a whole chapter devoted to it in his 1919 *Economic Consequences of the Peace*; but the correspondence uncovered by Magness and Harrigan, and Keynes' direct linking of "Grandchildren" with Wells' eugenic novel, greatly increases the importance of eugenics as a context for "Grandchildren" (Magness and Harrigan, undated; Magness and Hernandez 2017).

So when Keynes talks about "transmuting human nature" in the *General Theory*, we should take that literally. He served as director of the British Eugenics Society from 1937 to 1944. At a 1946 dinner of the society, just two months before his death, he declared eugenics to be "the most important, significant and, I would add, genuine branch of sociology which exists" (Magness and Hernandez 2017, 79).

Keynes' direct interactions with communist and fascist dictators are sobering to consider. In 1925, as Stalin was consolidating his power,

Keynes—already an internationally respected figure—traveled to the Soviet Union to speak. He warned that the Soviet Union had an overpopulation problem, and should find a way to reduce its surplus population. "There is no greater danger than [population growth] to the economic future of Russia," he declared. "There is no more important object of deliberate state policy than to secure a balanced budget of population" (Keynes 1925). Estimates of the death toll from the government-induced Soviet famine of 1932–1933 vary from 5 million to 10 million people.[4]

No doubt the famines would have happened without Keynes' advice, nor is it plausible that Keynes would have approved of mass murder. On the other hand, it is chilling to consider Keynes' profound insensitivity to the nature of the Soviet regime and what it was capable of, which should have been clear to informed observers like himself. It is even more chilling to read Keynes' writings after 1933 asking whether this close encounter with mass murder chastened him at all in his enthusiasm for eugenics and social planning.

Judging from the introduction Keynes wrote for the German edition of the *General Theory*, published in 1936 as Hitler was ascendant, Keynes seems not to have been chastened:

> The theory of aggregate production, which is the point of the following book, nevertheless can be much easier adapted to the conditions of a totalitarian state than the theory of production and distribution of a given production put forth under conditions of free competition and a large degree of *laissez-faire*. This is one of the reasons that justifies the fact that I call my theory a *general* theory. (Hazlitt 1959, 277; see also Singh 1994, Lipka and Šťastný 2008)

Despite this casual observation that his policies would work more smoothly in a "totalitarian state" than in a liberal one, Keynes was not a totalitarian. The worst we ought to say of him in this connection is that he was unaware of his own limitations, and the limitations of his fellow

[4]Estimated deaths in Ukraine range from 3.3 million (Snyder 2010, 53) to 7.5 million (Marples 2007, 50) and about 2 million died in Kazakhstan (Pianciola 2001).

know-it-more-than-anyone-else elites. He was insensitive to the danger of overreaching power.

But that is just another way of saying that he possessed no serious moral inhibitions that would steer him out of the path of totalitarianism. As he said, he was laying the groundwork for political control of the economy comparable to that in a socialist state, and more easily accomplished in a totalitarian state, so political leaders could manage human nature to ensure that we remained addicted to the money-making passion.

There is nothing wrong with thinking about "the economy" as a social reality, and measuring aggregate data. There really is a social level of human life, so having a term for referring to it is an advance. Measuring GDP growth is, as we have noted in Chapter 8, an important indicator that can help us diagnose whether there are problems in our economies that need attention.

The point is that it is supremely dangerous to think of the economy as something that can be manipulated and controlled. When we manipulate the economy, we manipulate human beings in their most intimate and important life decisions. If human beings have a teleology, managing the economy takes that teleology away from them.

The Moral Compass: Persons with Purpose

All three major economic paradigms before the Keynesian Revolution began from a view that the meaning of our lives and our duties to other people were mostly "given." That is, we did not invent them for ourselves. They were grounded in the fixed facts of human nature and reason. Even the Enlightenment, when it elevated the importance of individual choice, required that choices must be rational to be legitimate and deserve protection—and reason might permit a wide scope of possibilities in some ways, but in other ways it was given in human nature.

As a result, lives of service to other people and respect for key social institutions like the family, church and government were closely associated with the special dignity of human beings. People could make moral claims against being mistreated by these institutions, because they possessed human dignity. However, this same human dignity placed moral claims on them as well. In the Nature paradigm, human dignity entitled people to the rights of their social role, and required the duties of that role. In the God paradigm, human dignity entitled people to be treated in accordance with Christian love and holiness, but also required them to live up to that same standard. In the Reason paradigm, human dignity entitled people to respect for their rights, within the boundaries of reason, but also required people to work productively within the structures of family and civil society.

Economic systems and behaviors were to be structured in accordance with these requirements. Businesses were expected to treat people with the dignity appropriate to them under the understanding of the dominant paradigm. Laws governing work, property, and exchange had to prioritize protection of the moral claims made by human dignity. This included both the claims people could make against mistreatment on grounds that they possessed human dignity, and the claims made on those same people requiring them to live up to the standards of behavior required by human dignity.

Two important consequences followed from this structure. One is that economic systems were based upon, and therefore socially reinforced, moral principles that placed absolute limits on what you were allowed to do to people. Individuals and businesses were all under these restrictions. In the classical world, the agrarian economy normally gave autonomy to the household against interference from outsiders. This protection did not do much for the workers, who were viewed as possessing lower dignity; however, the protection typically enjoyed by the leisure-class landowners against arbitrary abuse was considerable. Under Christianity, concern for the poor gradually led to better treatment for them, including the abolition of slavery in late antiquity. Under natural law doctrine, legal protection for property and contract rights began to be extended beyond the leisure class, facilitating the creation of economic firms. During the Enlightenment, arguments for the equal rights of all people continued this trend, and led to large-scale political and economic reform as well as revolution.

The other consequence is that economic systems were based upon, and therefore socially reinforced, a strong affirmation of the rights and responsibilities of non-economic institutions such as family, church, and government. Society was a complex structure with interlocking institutions playing a variety of roles. Laws governing work, property, and exchange were required to protect the roles of these institutions. Economic preferences of employers, workers, or consumers that would have the effect of crippling these institutions were not to be given the same level of legal and regulatory protection as economic preferences consistent with these institutions' health and flourishing. If consumers wanted to buy, say, pornography, then those consumers were just out of luck. Economic systems had no responsibility to protect and facilitate transactions inimical to the social health of the structures necessary to social organization.

The views of human dignity shaped by teleology in these paradigms can be stated in more anthropological terms. In the Nature paradigm, a person is to be treated as a bearer of rights over their inferiors and of responsibilities to their superiors. In the God paradigm, a person is to be treated as a fellow bearer of the image of God, called to love God and neighbor and be loved in return. In the Reason paradigm, a person is to be treated as an embodied mind capable of knowing and building, with corresponding rights and responsibilities.

If we wish to maintain ethical standards and political freedom, we must not only hold that the human person has a teleology, but build social systems on the assumption of that teleology. That means social systems cannot be morally neutral, but must know at least enough about the purpose of human life to know where the limits are. This does not mean we must impose social uniformity on the meaning of life, for doing so would violate the very purpose of maintaining ethical standards and political freedom. But it does mean we need to build at least enough moral consensus to establish shared foundations for ethics and freedom.

Fracturing the Compass: Persons as Things to Be Managed

The human being considered as a mere bundle of appetites is not something that can make a plausible claim to dignity that must be respected. We can continue making louder and louder normative claims that businesses and government ought to respect our human dignity. But without a teleology for the human person, we cannot ground that claim in anything that compels the respect we demand.

Substantive reason, which can reason about ends, can offer rational arguments for the dignity of the human person. As we have seen, Keynes swapped the last remaining vestiges of substantive reason left over from the Reason paradigm for a purely instrumental rationality that does not reason about ends. Ends are irrational, grounded in the appetites. Having no rational argument for an end of human life, we have no rational argument for the dignity of the person.

We therefore have no argument against the limitless expansion of government power. If a person is merely a bundle of appetites, why not take control of it? Appetites come to us from outside our immediate control anyway. If, as we have seen, the human being as bundle of appetites has abandoned its position above nature, and even within nature, and become a mere slave to nature, why not make it a slave to rational controllers instead?

And instrumental reason is ridiculously easy to control. It merely calculates how to achieve the goals supplied to it, based on the situation—the environment—supplied to it. So if you control the environment to which the person with instrumental reason is exposed, you control the person. All you have to do is supply the appropriate *stimulus* for the response you wish to produce.

Take control of the options for accumulating wealth, enjoying indulgences and avoiding labor, and you take control of *homo economicus.* If consumers can be limited to a narrower range of options, they can be herded in whatever direction that makes "the economy" look good—assuming "the economy" is defined in terms of large aggregate measures like GDP and the unemployment rate, rather than a substantive understanding of human well-being as it is experienced at the individual and micro-social (i.e. local institutional) level.

By examining only the quantitative and aggregate aspects of economic behavior, the Consumption paradigm methodologically privileges the treatment of human beings as interchangeable cogs. By identifying the goal of economics as maximizing the gratification of appetites, it creates a built-in impetus to use political power to use people as instruments of public policy. Each individual human person is ruthlessly subordinated to the appetites of the mass.

This approach does not merely invite, but actually establishes, unlimited political control over all aspects of human life. Not all of life is economic, but there is no human activity that is not at least deeply intertwined with the economic side of life. The economic manipulators cannot effectively take control of the economy unless they take control of everything that has a major impact on the economy—which is to say, everything. In other words, when we have said that we want economic experts to use public policy to produce a higher GDP, we have already surrendered (in principle) all of human life to (in principle) unlimited political control.

This is "economics as video game" in the most chilling sense. There are no real people in a video game, just objects to be manipulated by the players. Economists and politicians, and the social elites who have the most power to lobby the politicians, are the players in this game. We are the objects on the screen that they control—control for the purpose of racking up a high score for them, not us.

Moreover, the economic technocrats who thus gain unlimited power over us can never successfully fulfill the purported purpose of this political consolidation of power. It is, in fact, intrinsically impossible to gather the information that would be needed for successful economic planning—impossible not because we lack the computing power, but because the information simply cannot be collected (Hayek 1991). Agency problems also undermine economic planning. A large number of people must exercise a large amount of power to carry it out, which creates enormous incentives for the people running the system to cheat or sell out in various ways, and there is no effective way to control them all.

The persistent failure of economic management to accomplish its goals ensures that those in power will constantly need to blame economic shortfalls on enemies and malefactors, real and imagined. Power over economic policy will tend to shift over time away from economists and into the hands of political elites whose loyalty is not to economic flourishing (in any sense) but to their own dominance (Hayek 2007, 157–170).

Hollow Prosperity: A Pointless Life

When we view ourselves as bundles of appetites, even if "only for economic purposes," our lives lose a sense of meaning and purpose. "Economic purposes" are one of the most important factors in the structure of our daily lives. If we are not meaningful creatures "for economic purposes," if we live in a morally empty economy, then our daily lives will lack meaning.

This is part and parcel of the moral disorders we have looked at in previous chapters. It's easy to treat the poor as dehumanized wards of the state if we view people as bundles of appetites. The comfortable can satisfy their own appetites, but the poor need our provision—our help—to do so. And that help implies control, because those who make you happy and provide for your needs (and in the Consumption paradigm, with no teleological scheme to set firm priorities, all our consumer preferences tend to be elevated to "needs") cannot avoid controlling you. The breakdown or vulnerability of mediating institutions needed for economic flourishing, like families and churches, is inevitable if we think of ourselves as bundles of appetites. These mediating institutions only make sense if we think that we are much more than bundles of appetites—they exist to help us learn to regulate our appetites in light of what is higher in us.

That seeing ourselves as bundles of appetites "for purposes of economics" means seeing ourselves that way in daily life is the very reason political control over the economy means political control over daily life. We have ever-increasing difficulty restraining political powers from taking over our lives because public discourse in its current state does not permit public recognition of any meaning or purpose in our daily lives that demands respect.

It may sound alarmist to describe our situation as one of "creeping totalitarianism." People associate the idea of tyranny arising from economic management with Marxism. They think this problem is in the past since Marxist economic theory is discredited. Of course, more than one billion people are still enslaved by communist regimes, discredited theory or no. But the more immediate point here is that the threat to our humanity was never exclusively "out there" in illiberal states. It was always "in here" as well, in liberal states, where wise people have been sounding the alarm for a century about the slow disintegration of moral standards enforceable against the state.

Consider that where consumers are managed by politicians, there can be no common goals between the politician manipulating and the consumer manipulated. They do not and cannot interact on the level of ends, but only of means. The whole justification for economic management is that consumers do not have the knowledge or inclination to make choices for the common good. They are neither economic experts with mathematics capable of analyzing aggregate outcomes, nor are they rational and responsible agents making choices based on a teleology.

The point of economic management is that the politicians *use* the consumers to accomplish the politicians', not the consumers', ends. That is what management is. It is in this disconnect between the ends of the politician and the ends of the consumer that the danger of creeping totalitarianism lies.

In theory, the economic manager is acting for the common good. But in the relationship between manager and managed, there can be no common good—no shared ends. Consumers are assumed not to have the knowledge or inclination to participate in the deliberation about ends that guides the politicians. No economic management would be going on in the first place if that assumption were not made. Deliberation about ends occurs not among everyone, but only among the political and economic elite.

Like Keynes, those on the Right (nationalists) and Left (socialists) now calling for more government control of the economy are not themselves totalitarians. That is why we call our problem "creeping" totalitarianism. If it were open totalitarianism, it would be easier to mobilize a moral response. Nationalism and socialism never begin as open and explicit totalitarianism. But once the moral guardrails are down, all bets are off on how quickly they can get to their logical conclusions.

In observing that seemingly harmless economic management produces creeping totalitarianism, Friedrich Hayek—for all the other problems in his thought—was dead right and demands a fresh audience. His 1944 *The Road to Serfdom* is an invaluable guide to seeing how the first, apparently innocent steps in the direction of economic management contain within them both the impulses that lead to totalitarianism and the dismantling of the only moral barriers that can prevent it. We particularly recommend Chapter 10: "Why the Worst Get on Top."

Another author from that era worthy of fresh attention is Whittaker Chambers, a Soviet spy who broke with communism and became one of the century's most insightful opponents of totalitarianism. He refused to join William F. Buckley's conservative movement because he objected to its idolatry of free markets as the solution to every problem, so he is no wild-eyed libertarian ideologue (Chambers 1987, 260–275). In his 1952 masterpiece *Witness*, he puts his finger on the root cause of totalitarianism: the decline of teleology, the attempt to live as if we were not subordinate to a purpose higher than humanity. When we believe that the human mind has no standard of truth higher than its own thought, and no standard of right higher than its own will, no effective limits remain on the permissible exercise of power over human beings. There is nothing upon which to ground such limits that we are unconditionally bound to respect (Chambers 2014, xxxiii–l).

A third author in need of rediscovery is Wilhelm Röpke, to whom this book is dedicated. The title and subtitle of his 1958 *A Humane*

Economy: The Social Framework of the Free Market, express in miniature the aspiration to an integrated empirical, moral, and cultural understanding of free and virtuous economic life for which our own book is a plea. Frustrated with the morally bankrupt ideology that had come to dominate the free-market movement, he asked at the beginning of *A Humane Economy*: "Where does a man of my kind take his stand if he is to attack socialism because he believes it to be wrong?" (Röpke 1999, 3) He would defenestrate himself from the Mont Pelerin society a mere three years later.

Once again, we do not need a new morality or a demagogue to lead us out of this danger. We only need to remember what we already know: that our lives are morally meaningful, that the daily life of each and every one of us has a higher purpose that can't be pursued by anyone else on our behalf. A society that forgets these facts in the organization of its economic systems cannot remain free or virtuous, or sustain the moral foundations of a flourishing economy. We have not forgotten these facts, and can recover them when we wish. As Hayek emphasized in *The Road to Serfdom*, while economic management by a technocratic elite must always lead us toward totalitarian control so long as we pursue it, we are always free to stop pursuing it. "It is because everybody wants it that we are moving in this direction. There are no objective facts which make it inevitable" (Hayek 2007, 59).

References

Aristotle. 1980. *Ethics*. Oxford and New York: Oxford University Press.

Aristotle. 1992. *Politics*. London and New York: Penguin Books.

Barak, Aharon. 2015. *Human Dignity*. Cambridge: Cambridge University Press.

Berger, Peter L. 2014. *The Many Altars of Modernity*. Boston: De Gruyter.

Chambers, Whittaker. 1987. *Odyssey of a Friend*. Washington, DC: Regnery.

Chambers, Whittaker. 2014 [1952]. *Witness*. Washington, DC: Regnery.

Düwell, Marcus, Jens Braarvig, Roger Brownsword, and Dietmar Mieth (eds.). 2014. *The Cambridge Handbook of Human Dignity*. Cambridge: Cambridge University Press.

Forster, Greg. 2005. *John Locke's Politics of Moral Consensus*. Cambridge and New York: Cambridge University Press.

Friedman, Milton. 1970. A Friedman Doctrine. *New York Times*, Sept 13.

Glenn, Charles Leslie, Jr. 2002. *The Myth of the Common School*. Oakland: Institute for Contemporary Studies.

Grabill, Stephen J. 2007. Editor's Introduction. In *Sourcebook in Late-Scholastic Monetary Theory*, ed. Stephen J. Grabill. Lanham: Lexington.
Gunton, Colin. 1998. *The Triune Creator*. Grand Rapids: Eerdmans.
Hayek, Friedrich. 1991. *The Fatal Conceit*. Chicago: University of Chicago Press.
Hayek, Friedrich. 2007 [1944]. *The Road to Serfdom*. Chicago: University of Chicago Press.
Hazlitt, Henry. 1959. *The Failure of the "New Economics"*. Auburn: Ludwig von Mises Institute.
Horton, Michael. 2011. *The Christian Faith*. Grand Rapids: Zondervan.
Keynes, John Maynard. 1925. The Economic Position of England. http://www.hetwebsite.net/het/texts/keynes/keynes1925moscow.htm. Accessed 30 Jan 2019.
Keynes, John Maynard. 1963 [1930]. Economic Possibilities for Our Grandchildren; Scanned by Yale University Economics Department from John Maynard Keynes, *Essays in Persuasion*, Norton, 358–373. http://www.econ.yale.edu/smith/econ116a/keynes1.pdf. Accessed 23 Jan 2019.
Keynes, John Maynard. 2013 [1936]. *The General Theory of Employment, Interest and Money*. Cambridge: Cambridge University Press.
Lewis, M. 2007. A Brief History of Human Dignity. In *Perspectives on Human Dignity*, ed. J. Malpas and N. Lickiss. Dordrecht: Springer.
Lipka, David, and Dan Šťastný. 2008. John Maynard Keynes, Socialism and Economic Policy of Nazi Germany. *Acta Oeconomica Pragensia* 1: 108–116.
Luther, Martin. 1522. The Estate of Marriage. https://pages.uoregon.edu/dluebke/Reformations441/LutherMarriage.htm. Accessed 29 Jan 2019.
Maddison, Angus. 2007. *Countours of the World Economy*. Oxford and New York: Oxford University Press.
Magness, Phillip W., and James R. Harrigan. Undated. John Maynard Keynes, H.G. Wells, and a Problematic Utopia. Working Paper (Cited with Permission).
Magness, Phillip W., and Sean J. Hernandez. 2017. The Economic Eugenicism of John Maynard Keynes. *Journal of Markets and Morality* 20 (1): 79–100.
Marples, David R. 2007. *Heroes and Villains*. Budapest: Central European University Press.
Mitchell, Timothy. 2002. *The Rule of Experts*. Berkeley: University of California Press.
Motyer, Alec. 1996. *Look to the Rock*. Grand Rapids: Kregel.
Nussbaum, Martha. 2008. Human Dignity and Political Entitlements. In *Human Dignity* and *Bioethics*. Washington, DC: President's Council on Bioethics.
Pianciola, Niccolo. 2001. The Collectivization Famine in Kazakhstan, 1931–1933. *Harvard Ukrainian Studies* 25: 237–251.
Plato. 1991. *Republic*. New York: Basic Books.
Rhee, Helen. 2012. *Loving the Poor, Saving the Rich*. Grand Rapids: Baker.

Röpke, Wilhelm. 1999 [1958]. *A Humane Economy*. Wilmington: ISI Books.
Rosen, Michael. 2012. *Dignity*. Cambridge: Harvard University Press.
Rousseau, Jean-Jacques. 1979. *Emile*. New York: Basic Books.
Schulman, Adam. 2009. *Human Dignity and Bioethics*. Notre Dame: University of Notre Dame Press.
Singh, Narindar. 1994. Keynes and Hitler. *Economic and Political Weekly* 29 (42): 2755–2766.
Snyder, Timothy. 2010. *Bloodlands*. London: Bodley Head.
Stark, Rodney. 2005. *The Victory of Reason*. New York: Random House.
Taylor, Charles. 2007. *A Secular Age*. Cambridge: Harvard University Press.
Upchurch, Anna Rosser. 2011. Keynes' Legacy. *International Journal of Cultural Policy* 17 (1): 69–80.
Waldron, Jeremy. 2017. *One Another's Equals*. Cambridge: Harvard University Press.
Wingren, Gustaf. 2004. *Luther on Vocation*. Eugene: Wipf & Stock.

CHAPTER 11

Putting First Things First: Moral Consensus for a Flourishing Economic Culture

In this chapter we reveal our hidden agenda: moral consensus. We do not think the discipline of economics as a whole can or should restore the approach of earlier paradigms, each of which grew out of a single ultimate worldview: classical reverence for nature, Christian reverence for God or Enlightenment reverence for Reason. Social worlds built on a single worldview, such as these, were always held together by unjust violence and oppression of those who thought differently. We now live in a pluralistic social world because we have rightly decided to stop using force to create coherent social worlds, and without such force, social worlds do not cohere in the same tight and uniform way. We need a new approach for a new social world in which people do not all revere the same things.

We propose consensus rather than uniformity. If we want to escape the Consumption paradigm, it is necessary for people who have different beliefs about ultimate reality to agree with one another about some transcendent moral claims. When it comes to higher realities, we will never agree about everything; we will not even agree about the things that matter most to us. But we can agree about enough to provide the basis for an economic paradigm that overcomes the deadly combination of instrumental reason, short-term perspective and an undignified view of the human person that define the Consumption paradigm.

This chapter will show why a Moral Consensus paradigm for the study of economics is necessary if we seek an effective alternative to the Consumption paradigm. The conclusion will propose first steps toward building it.

V. V. Claar and G. Forster, *The Keynesian Revolution and Our Empty Economy*, https://doi.org/10.1007/978-3-030-15808-8_11

What Does It Take to Challenge the Consumption Paradigm?

While the public policy positions of Keynesian economists are always contested by the anti-Keynesian schools in political debate, that same conflict actually solidifies the dominance of the Keynesian Revolution and its Consumption paradigm at the deeper level of moral and cultural norms. Both sides of the public policy conflict implicitly reinforce the core tenets of the revolution. Chicago and Austria, for the most part if not always to the same extent as the Keynesians, tend to treat human beings as if they were most fundamentally consumers rather than producers, responsible for the short term rather than the long term—a bundle of desires lacking any characteristics that would justify attributing to it an inviolable dignity.

These core anthropological tenets are rarely even explicitly discussed; all sides take them for granted as premises rather than debate them as positions. Thus these premises achieve the status of unquestionable, uncontestable commitments in our culture. They are woven into the fabric of public policy and public discourse alike, shaping our economic actions and our very conceptions of what economics is, without our realizing it. The more heated the dispute between Keynesians and anti-Keynesians becomes, the more the unconscious and unquestionable cultural dominance of these core anthropological commitments is reinforced.

Because the two counter-revolutionary movements reinforce the core commitments of the Consumption paradigm, they can have no lasting victory over their Keynesian rivals even on the level of public policy. Austrian and Chicago economists resist Keynesian arguments for economic management by government, as well as the Keynesians' methodological aggregation and (for the Austrians) methodological focus on quantitative methods. However, they either acquiesce in or explicitly affirm the anthropological commitments that lead logically and naturally to the Keynesian conclusions. Government management of the economy and methodological aggregation make perfect sense if we adopt Keynes' model of *homo economicus* and the consequent view that the purpose of economics is to maximize satisfaction of consumer appetites. The harder the Austrian and Chicago schools fight the Keynesians on these secondary questions, the more strongly they reinforce the primary anthropological commitments that shift the battleground to Keynes.

In Chapter 10 we have strongly endorsed Hayek's warnings against the implicitly totalitarian logic of economic management in *The Road to Serfdom*. However, while Hayek saw the danger clearly, he did not find an adequate remedy. So long as the Consumption paradigm defines what we think economics is and what we want from it—which to say, what we think a human being is and what they need from an economic system—the Keynesian school will usually be the most plausible approach in public policy debates. Until the Consumption paradigm is challenged, the anti-Keynesian schools are unlikely to do much more than temporarily hinder the dominance of the Keynesian one.

Nor would it be enough merely to tear off the mask of "moral neutrality" and recover the frank normativity of Keynes himself. Granted, Keynes' completely unselfconscious tone of high-handed prescriptiveness can be a refreshing alternative to the oppressive hypocrisy of economists who are constantly telling us what we ought to do, while also constantly telling us their observations are merely positive and involve no moral evaluation. The unashamed moral judgment exercised in the *General Theory* does make John Stuart Mill's reductive, robotic *homo economicus* look as ridiculous and monstrous as it really is. However, as we have seen, the same Keynes who so openly embraced normativity was the originator of what became the even more reductive, even more monstrous Consumption paradigm. Clearly, normative prescription simply as such is not what was lacking.

To escape the Consumption paradigm, economists must return to teleology—to a robust conviction that economic activity serves a higher purpose beyond satisfying our own appetites, accomplishing ends that are intrinsically good. Without teleology, we cannot escape the instrumental reason that reduces our humanity by anchoring our decisions in the irrational urges of "animal spirits." A substantive rationality requires a substantive good that has a status above our reasoning rather than below it—a good that is good whether we choose it or not. With teleology we can have substantive goods, and therefore substantive reason, and therefore we can be producers first and consumers second rather than the other way around. Otherwise, we cannot.

Moreover, without teleology we cannot sustainably escape the confinement of cost-benefit calculations to a short time frame, trapped in a shallow and irresponsible Eternal Now that sees saving as a "paradox of thrift" and proclaims that "in the long run we are all dead." It is literally impossible for us to care whether we are leaving a good world for our grandchildren if the word "good" means "whatever people choose." We do not know what our grandchildren will choose. "Leaving a good world for our grandchildren" becomes a phrase without meaning.

Normativity without teleology is unmoored. We can and do admonish people to be productive, serve the future, and respect others. Our admonitions are ineffective because, in practice and increasingly even in theory, we are unwilling to supply any meaning to those moral terms (productive, serve, respect) beyond "whatever people choose for these terms to mean."

Acknowledging Transcendence

How do economic systems embody moral realities that transcend human choice? Any return to teleology implies a return to some form of transcendence. That is a scary word, we know. But there is no getting away from it.

Teleology involves placing us back underneath our moral responsibilities, obligated to pursue them whether we want to or not, rather than thinking we are above our responsibilities and able to choose them. It is impossible to invent the meaning of your own life; if you invented it, and could just as easily have invented anything else, your invention is merely arbitrary and therefore not meaningful.

If we are under our responsibilities rather than over them, we are acknowledging that there is some kind of moral reality that exists beyond or above human choice. That fixed moral reality is what makes each of our particular moral choices meaningful. That is what we mean by the transcendent.

Transcendence need not be religious, and often is not. Aristotle's appeal to a teleology grounded in a transcendent Nature (capital N) was not religious. Neither was Adam Smith's appeal to Reason (capital R). The fiercely atheistic system of communism, which is famously organized around a theory of History (capital H) by whose unbreakable historical laws all events must proceed, appeals to the transcendent as a basis for public action perhaps more aggressively than any other political ideology.

The extremely rapid collapse of the Reason paradigm by itself shows how urgently we need not only transcendence, but a full and robust account of the transcendent. The Reason paradigm attempted to have a substantive rationality rather than an instrumental rationality, but it typically held (in practice if not always in theory) that nothing was transcendent but Reason. The problem was that Reason did not, by itself, provide a sufficient justification to sustain substantive rationality after the influence of Christian metaphysics (and thus natural law) declined, or defend substantive rationality against the attacks arising from Rousseau and the diverse movements inspired by his thought. The Nature and God paradigms could maintain a stable environment for the integration of empirical, moral, and cultural observation because they had transcendent objects of such a kind as to demand this integration. Substantive rationality requires something to be substantive about; it does not invent, but perceives, transcendent goods.

The high moral hope of the Enlightenment, that advanced knowledge and reasoning powers would by themselves bring us advanced virtue and wisdom, has disintegrated into a history of world wars, genocide and cultural fragmentation. With the benefit of this hindsight, the inadequacy of Reason as an ultimate standard for arranging human life is now widely recognized by philosophers across a variety of beliefs and schools of thought (Nietzsche 2009; Weber 2004; Lewis 1943; Berger 1967; MacIntyre 1981; Haidt 2013).

The Challenge of Pluralism

For all of human history, every society—with no known exceptions—has organized its public structures, including its economic structures, with reference to the transcendent. Classical societies were organized around a combination of their gods and an understanding of Nature. Medieval societies were organized around the Christian God.

Things in the modern era are more complex, but modernity is no exception to the rule that all societies build their public structures around the transcendent. A greater number of transcendent claims are admitted within each society. Over the course of the last few centuries, efforts were made first to accommodate multiple religions within the same society, and then to accommodate both religious and non-religious accounts of ultimate reality. However, the old narrative of "secularization," which held that claims about the transcendent were declining, has been pretty thoroughly debunked by historians and social scientists. A better concept for what is happening is "pluralization." Many accounts of transcendence, including religious and non-religious accounts, are being accommodated simultaneously in the same society (Berger 2014, 1–16). The rise of pluralism can be plausibly attributed to the rise of moral norms against the use of force in matters of belief, increases in internal divisions within religious systems, increased daily exposure to multiple views becoming inevitable with economic and technological progress, changes in our conception of how human beings relate to nature arising from modern science, increased differentiation as highly developed societies become more complex, and other causes (Taylor 2007; Luhmann 2013; Berger 2014).

The thing to notice about modern societies is that their strategies for managing pluralism are always themselves grounded in transcendent claims. Permission for pluralism in early modern Europe was often justified with appeal to Christian norms against the use of unjust violence (Forster 2005; Loconte 2016). Later, appeals to Reason emerged as a justification for permitting pluralism; these appeals were sometimes based on religious theories of natural law, sometimes on a non-religious secular Reason that was nonetheless beyond human choice and therefore transcendent, and sometimes on a calculated ambiguity that appealed to both (Berger 2014, 1–16). In modern India, Hindus have invented special new castes for Christians and Muslims, allowing a social system predominantly shaped by Hindu belief in a transcendent caste structure to accommodate Christians and Muslims who refuse to accept their traditionally assigned caste identities (Berger 2014, 83).

This should not be surprising. Social systems, including economic systems, can only continue their own existence by justifying themselves in moral terms. People will not support the continuation of the system if they don't think it's morally justified. And such justifications must find some basis on which to make their appeal. Ultimately, there is no avoiding transcendence.

So the challenge facing economics is not whether the transcendent can be admitted. It already is. The question is how to admit it in a pluralistic context where people have different views about the transcendent, and we refuse to impose uniformity.

Treating Autonomous Choice as Transcendent

The Consumption paradigm looks different when understood in the context of pluralism. Coping with the challenge of pluralism—the difficulty of accommodating multiple views about the transcendent within a single society—is one of the most important factors shaping social life in the advanced modern world. The Consumption paradigm, which creates so much moral dissatisfaction and anxiety, makes much more sense if we see how it harmonizes extensively with a natural, but ultimately unsuccessful, response to the pluralism problem.

A very common strategy for coping with the challenge of pluralism, in economics and other settings, is to set up respect for people's individual choices about the transcendent as our only shared transcendent commitment (Berger 2014, 11–12; Hunter 2000, 31–80). We are not, according to this approach, imposing a single view about the transcendent. We are allowing maximum individual freedom for all such views. This requires us to set up one shared transcendent commitment—respect for people's choices about their values, conceptions of the good, and transcendent beliefs. Other than that, let a thousand flowers bloom.

There are several problems with this approach. One is that the single shared transcendent commitment cannot be justified. As we have just noted, moral justification must make reference to some kind of transcendent moral reality. But a society or a group (such as the discipline of economics) that has only one transcendent commitment obviously has no other transcendent grounds upon which that one commitment can be justified. This is why social settings relying on such a strategy for coping with pluralism tend to be highly unstable (Bloom 1975; Hunter 2000, 151–176).

A deeper problem, and one with greater consequences for the topic of this book, is that setting up respect for everyone's choices about the transcendent as the only socially shared transcendent principle—the only thing about the transcendent that everyone is required to affirm—fundamentally changes the nature of our choices about the transcendent. The principle of respect for choices is the only principle that has been placed, in practice, above our power of choice. If I am an individual living within this social system, everything else is a matter of unconstrained choice for me; this one principle is imposed on me without my choice. In other words, this principle is for me the only really transcendent principle. All my other choices about transcendent are not in fact about the transcendent, for I have the power to make my own choices about them. And whatever I can choose is not transcendent; it is the essence of the transcendent that it is above or beyond our choices.

This approach reveres Autonomous Choice the same way the classical philosophers revered Nature, Christians revere God or the Enlightenment philosophers revered Reason. As a result, although it begins as a strategy for coping with pluralism, it ends up stamping out pluralism. All real, substantive views of the higher good come under a regime of constant inspection by suspicious regulators, who are ever on the lookout for anything that seems like it might not respect Autonomous Choice. Under this regime, only one view of the transcendent is consistently safe from the inspection regime: the view that reveres only Autonomous Choice and has no other transcendent values. This relativistic viewpoint becomes socially privileged, while real and substantive views of the good are marginalized (Hunter 2000, 81–150). As Peter Berger puts it, taking up a standpoint of cultural relativism (all views of the good must be treated as equally valid) necessarily involves developing an attitude of cognitive privilege (most people reject cultural relativism; I am one of the wise few who have achieved enlightenment) that explains all other views of the good as false consciousness (Berger 2014, 11–12). Far from succeeding as a strategy for avoiding the imposition of a single, uniform worldview, this approach ends up in practice as just another single, uniform worldview built around reverence for a single object.

The connection between this strategy and the Consumption paradigm should be obvious. Obviously the Consumption paradigm did not begin or develop as a response to the problem of pluralism; it began and developed as a response to the problem of unemployment. But equally obviously, the Consumption paradigm has an enormous built-in appeal for people who are looking for an escape from the challenge of pluralism. It elevates consumer choice to a level of absolute autonomy. It is probably the only economic system that could possibly be constructed in a society committed to the elevation of Autonomous Choice as a response to the challenge of pluralism. The rise of the Consumption paradigm has been a social change on a truly vast scale, and no social change can occur on that scale without multiple factors contributing to its success. Its harmony with a very common and natural, if futile, strategy for coping with pluralism must be a major reason the Consumption paradigm has had the success it has had.

And it is a major reason the Consumption paradigm is morally and culturally unsustainable. We have described the study and practice of economics within the Consumption paradigm using the metaphor of economics as a video game. Here, we come to the most profound application of that metaphor.

A video game is not a real struggle to accomplish really good ends—saving imperiled princesses, killing Nazi soldiers, recovering sacred artifacts, destroying villainous superweapons. It is merely the simulation of such struggles. Simulations are enjoyable because they are simpler and easier than the real thing (ask anyone who has actually had to fight Nazi soldiers) and there are no real stakes if you lose. Video games can be simpler and easier, and have no stakes, precisely because they are not real. But for the same reason, because they are not real, they are not meaningful. A life devoted to video games cannot produce the kind of deep satisfaction and moral confidence that real accomplishment provides. In the same way, economic life under the Consumption paradigm is morally unreal—hollow, empty.

Let's adjust the metaphor of a game, to illustrate the need for real transcendence more directly. If you are inventing the rules of a game, you can simulate gameplay in order to test the rules and see how they work. If your game is too hard, you can make the rules easier; if your game is too complex, you can make the rules simpler. But as long as you retain the power to change the rules, you are merely simulating the game and not really playing it. No one would stake anything really important on the outcome of the game if they knew you had the power to change the rules mid-stream. Only when the rules are fixed and beyond your control can you really play.

Similarly, our lives can only have meaning within some higher framework of what counts as meaningful—a framework we cannot control. Without that, we are only simulating a meaningful life rather than living it.

This helps explain why more and more of life in the empty economy is devoted to controlling perceptions—constructing identities and performative gestures, especially on social media—than about reality. For example, recent research concludes that taking pictures—which has become a ubiquitous of almost every activity in the age of Instagram—actually reduces our ability to remember the experiences we take pictures of (Henkel 2014, 396–402; Soares and Storm 2018, 154–160). Rather than authentically experience life, we increasingly act as our own photographers and biographers, becoming spectators rather than participants in our own lives.

Is an economic system that structures life as an endless simulation sustainable? The rising tide of nationalism and socialism, fueled by moral anxieties about the emptiness of our economy, suggests it may not be.

Evil Is Good: The Dead Beehive

In economics, this strategy to treat Autonomous Choice as if it were transcendent is at the heart of the Consumption paradigm. That is why the Consumption paradigm ends up imposing, through public policy and social discourse, a single hegemonic reverence for consumer choice that slowly pushes all other transcendent beliefs and commitments to the social margins. We can see this whole process clearly in Keynes' own writings.

Every economic paradigm produces an economic culture, and every economic culture in turn reproduces its economic paradigm. The Nature paradigm both produced and was produced by the economic culture of the ancient *polis*, with its seemingly eternal and unchanging social structures. The God paradigm both produced and was produced by the economic culture of Europe from late antiquity through early modernity, with its public piety. The Reason paradigm both produced and was produced by the economic culture of the eighteenth and nineteenth centuries, notably including the Industrial Revolution.

We do not need to guess what kind of economic culture Keynes hoped his moral crusade to reform society would produce. In the penultimate chapter of the *General Theory*, he tells us himself. Keynes strives to produce the culture of Bernard Mandeville's beehive.

Mandeville, as we saw in Chapter 2, was a cynical anti-moralist who sought to tear down all pretensions of virtue and higher purpose in the economy, elevating instead frankly selfish lives devoted to consumer satisfaction as the path to a wealthy society. Mandeville was excoriated in aggressive language by Adam Smith, and by virtually every other significant voice in any part of Europe who became familiar with his work. As Keynes himself asserts, with a sort of perverse pride, no one in all history other than the always-idiosyncratic Samuel Johnson had ever had a good word to say about Mandeville (Keynes 2013, 359).

No one, that is, until Keynes. The *General Theory* concludes with a chapter titled, "Concluding Notes on the Social Philosophy Towards Which the General Theory Might Lead." This chapter contains many of the reflections quoted earlier in this book on the kind of reform Keynes hoped to achieve in society. In the immediately preceding chapter, Keynes reviews the history of modern economic thought outside the dominant Reason paradigm. He finds many good things to say about the mercantilists, and sundry other marginal figures. But his real hero is Mandeville.

Mandeville's 1714 *Fable of the Bees* is an allegorical poem, followed by a commentary on what the poem illustrates about social and economic life. The poem is about a beehive that symbolically represents human society.

One day, all the bees decide to practice self-control and frugality. They dutifully save up their money instead of spending on luxuries. Their leaders likewise curb wasteful spending on acquisitive wars, reducing the army to no more than is needed for self-defense.

The result is disaster. First, most of the people employed producing luxuries and armaments lose their jobs. Then, as those unemployed people have no paychecks to buy goods and services, people in other industries lose their jobs. The catastrophic ripple effect brings the beehive to its knees:

> The building trade is quite destroy'd,
> Artificers are not employ'd;
> No limner for his art is fam'd,
> Stone-cutters, carvers are not nam'd. (Keynes 2013, 361)

Mandeville's notorious conclusion is that evil is good: "Private vices, by the dexterous management of a skillful politician, may be turned into public benefits" (Mandeville 1806, 237).

Keynes unabashedly tells us that his *General Theory* is grounded in Mandeville's evil-is-good philosophy. And, as he shows, it is. Keynes credits Mandeville as the first writer to bring a "theory of underconsumption" (as Keynes' chapter title puts it) into wide public view, but this is only the first of the similarities Keynes observes between his theory and Mandeville's. Like Keynes, Mandeville excoriates savings as a waste of good money that could be spent on consumer appetites instead, producing jobs for the hive. And Mandeville calls on government to take control of the economy to keep people practicing those "private vices" in ways that produce "public benefits." Note that the popular, latter-day Mandevillian epigram "private vice is public virtue" leaves out, for the sake of brevity, Mandeville's important qualifier about putting people's lives under "the dexterous management of a skillful politician" who can manipulate private vice into public benefits.

The deepest common basis of the two theories, however, is in their definition of what constitutes a flourishing society and economy. Keynes approvingly quotes Mandeville: "The great art to make a nation happy, and what we call flourishing, consists in giving everybody an opportunity of being employed" (Keynes 2013, 361). Note that the general happiness and flourishing of the nation is here collapsed into merely economic success and no more, and economic success is likewise collapsed into employment. And the value of employment is not to make sure everyone has meaningful work that makes a really good contribution to the world, like that Uber driver in Omaha reflecting on his glasswork. To the contrary, Mandeville's aspiration is to produce wasteful and pointless luxuries—and even conduct acquisitive wars—to ensure everyone has a paycheck. And the paycheck is to be devoted solely to consuming, as Mandeville's (and Keynes') attitude toward savings demonstrates. "No wonder that such wicked sentiments," says Keynes of Mandeville, tongue firmly planted in cheek, "called down the opprobrium of two centuries of moralists and economists who felt much more virtuous in possession of their austere doctrine that no sound remedy was discoverable except in the utmost of thrift and economy both by the individual and by the state" (Keynes 2013, 362).

For Keynes, as for Mandeville, national happiness is no more than economics; economics is no more than jobs; jobs are no more than paychecks; and paychecks are no more than consumption. Private vice, managed by skillful politicians, is public virtue. Evil is good.

This is the rock-bottom cause of the empty economy and its hollow prosperity. The policy structures and cultural discourse that define our economic lives begin from the assumption that evil is good—that private vice is public virtue, when managed by skillful politicians. This is why we have such difficulty forming the productive virtues, finding a sense of meaning and purpose in our daily activity, building for the long term and sustaining ethics in business and government that treat people with human dignity.

At the end of the fable, the hive dies. Most of the bees perish from starvation. Those that remain abandon the hive and settle down in new and more humble surroundings, content with their honest and virtuous poverty. The glory of the hive is gone forever—and the surviving bees are so content with their goodness, they don't even miss it.

Is it the virtuous hive that is dead in the long run? Mandeville and Keynes think so. And if we think that the mere distribution of money is sufficient to call a nation flourishing ("the great art to make a nation happy, and what we call flourishing, consists in giving everybody an opportunity of being employed") they may seem at first to be right. But if evil is good and private vice is public virtue, where will we get the productive virtues necessary to keep people working and new businesses starting up? How will the consciences of the bees—their need to feel that their lives are good—be placated? How does a thriving hive get passed on from generation to generation if we aren't virtuous enough to care what kind of world we are leaving to our grandchildren?

And if private vice produces public benefits when managed by skillful politicians, where in our culture of celebrating vice will we find politicians who are virtuous enough to manage our vices for public benefit, rather than their own?

Inadequate Responses: More Than One Way to Kill a Beehive

After Mandeville, Keynes has another and very different figure to celebrate. The variance between these two figures demonstrates how easy it is to end up in Mandeville's beehive. Well-meaning and highly virtuous people can end up promoting the Consumption paradigm if they are unaware of, or unwilling to challenge, its basic anthropological tenets.

Keynes identifies the highly moralistic pastor and reformer Thomas Malthus as another precursor of the *General Theory*. Here it is important to recall the distinction between Malthus and Malthusianism. As we have discussed in Chapter 2, Malthus himself did not articulate the theory, now known as Malthusianism, holding that economic growth ends in catastrophic crashes. As a Christian and an advocate of the poor, Malthus certainly would have disapproved of the Malthusian Society in Keynes' day, which advocated eugenics as a path to a scientifically improved society (an enthusiasm embraced by Keynes throughout his career).

However, Keynes is correct in identifying Malthus as someone who advocated a "theory of underconsumption," and an opponent of high savings rates as a result. As Keynes shows with quotations, "in the later phase of Malthus the notion of the insufficiency of effective demand takes a definite place as a scientific explanation of unemployment" (Keynes 2013, 362). Malthus wrote to David Ricardo:

> We see in almost every part of the world vast powers of production which are not put into action, and I explain this phenomenon by saying that from the want of a proper distribution of the actual produce adequate motives are not furnished to continued production....I distinctly maintain that an attempt to accumulate [i.e. save] very rapidly, which necessarily implies a considerable diminution of unproductive consumption, by greatly impairing the usual motives to production must prematurely check the progress of wealth. (Keynes 2013, 362)

This passage shows that the traditional moral emphasis on productivity still has a hold on Malthus. However, he has embraced the view that if we want to increase production, we should increase consumption. He has become an embryonic Keynesian.

What led the virtue loving Malthus into the beehive of the vice loving Mandeville and Keynes? It appears to have been precisely his virtue—his concern for the poor. Malthus' goal is to get more money into the hands of the poor, so they can buy necessities. In other words, so they can consume. Laudable as that goal is, other goals take no place alongside it. We want to improve the material well-being of the poor, but do we want to put people to work in jobs without moral meaning in order to accomplish that goal? If we did decide to do that, we should at least be aware of the moral price we are paying, so we can keep our eyes out for a better approach as soon as one can be found. But Malthus elevates the immediate, material solution to the status of policy ideal. The wider scope of moral concerns, and the whole teleological view of economic life, that Malthus' Christian faith might have suggested to him ("man does not live by bread alone"), has dropped from sight in his analysis. He has become functionally non-teleological, and his policy conclusion (society must increase "unproductive consumption") reflects this.

Like the well-intentioned Malthus, the Austrian and Chicago schools continually find themselves in Mandeville's beehive. The Chicago school does not even try to avoid it. On the contrary, they rush into the beehive, confident that they know better than Mandeville how to produce public virtue from private vice. While their commitment to morally neutral language does not permit them to assert explicitly that "private vice is public virtue," that is what their view ultimately resolves to. Consumers seek to maximize the satisfaction of their appetites, and the purpose of economic systems is to facilitate that maximization. Mandeville, who stands in for Keynes in this metaphor, wants to manipulate the selfish consumption preferences of the bees to serve the prosperity of the hive. The Chicago beekeepers say, in effect, "we know how to do that job better."

Austrian economists do not intentionally rush into the beehive, but nor are they willing to take a clear stand on the only ground that can keep them out of it: substantive rationality, production with purpose, and (ultimately) transcendent commitment to teleological goods. The key insights of the Marginal Revolution—opportunity cost, the subjectivity of economic value, and marginal decision-making—need not commit us to the anthropology of the Consumption paradigm. But they will commit us to it by default if we do not affirmatively supply an alternative anthropology. The subjectivity of economic value does not exclude, and must not be allowed to exclude, true generalizations (which may be true only as generalizations) about what people do, in fact, hold to be intrinsically good. We need not only models of how people make decisions, but models of what transcendent ends people typically or characteristically make decisions in light of. The difference between "I think X is good" and "X is good because I think so" may be subtle, but it is a subtlety without which we cannot be human.

The Moral Consensus We Require Is Possible

We must return to transcendence, but we must not impose a single, ultimate worldview. We must reject both the hegemonic homogeneity of the older paradigms and also the equally hegemonic homogeneity of the Consumption paradigm. This implies we need moral consensus—not full agreement on all moral questions, but enough agreement on enough moral questions for us to conduct the study and practice of economics on the basis of teleological rather than reductionist assumptions.

The basic points of agreement that would be required for such a consensus have been laid out in the preceding chapters. We would need to study economics on the assumption that human beings are substantively rational and not just instrumentally rational. The ultimate basis of their economic decision-making is not irrational "animal spirits" but a desire for the things that human reason says are really, objectively good—such as health, shelter, material necessities, mobility, satisfying work, time for relationships with others, and leisure to enjoy things that are good, true, and beautiful. We would need to study economics on the assumption that human beings are part of a vast, intergenerational chain through history, in which the present generation does not just strive to enjoy certain objective economic goods, but also cares whether those goods are passed down to their grandchildren. And we would need to study economics on the assumption that the end of economic activity is not some aggregate metric, but for human beings in their non-aggregate, concrete reality to enjoy these objective goods through their own moral, intellectual, and physical efforts. This implies there are limits on what we can do to people in the name of economic efficiency.

That Uber driver in Omaha, whose pride in his glasswork demonstrates the bankruptcy of the Consumption paradigm, could have belonged to any faith or to none. What he said would be affirmed by almost everyone, of every faith or none. That consensus is the beginning of the end of the Consumption paradigm. There is, we think, not that much difficulty in reaching agreement about the moral commitments we have outlined above.

There will, of course, be very important differences at a secondary level. If doing economics this way were going to be easy, we would already be doing it and the Consumption paradigm would have been relegated to the dustbin of history long ago. Defining the meanings of terms will be an acute challenge.

But there is no need to paint the picture as worse than it really is. Differences and difficulties of this kind exist within every paradigm. Read Aristotle's critique of Plato, or the debates over political philosophy between Thomas Aquinas and William of Ockham. There was never a golden age of intellectual harmony where moral terms had fixed and stable meanings. On the contrary, each paradigm could be defined not by its agreement over moral terms, but by which debates over the meaning of moral terms are important. We know that we have passed from the God paradigm to the Reason paradigm when we no longer care about (or understand) the heated arguments about morally permissible interest rates among the doctors of the School of Salamanca in Spain, having crossed the Pyrenees to hear the equally fierce debates of the Physiocrats in the salons of Paris.

The great challenge is not to create agreement that economic life is shaped by real, teleological transcendence. It is to admit that we already agree about that to a great extent, and permit the study of economics to be shaped by this consensus rather than by a Consumption paradigm that denies what we all, in fact, believe.

We do not know much about what such a paradigm would look like after it was built. The main thing we know about it is the moral commitments it would have to start from. In our pluralistic social world, it would be wrong to try to ground these commitments in one ultimate worldview. We propose that people of different ultimate worldviews can reach enough of a consensus on these propositions to study economics together. For this reason, we refer to the alternative we hope to see emerge as a Moral Consensus paradigm.

We have shown in the last three chapters how the foundations of economic success are moral and cultural. If our society can pull together around a moral consensus, we can recover a flourishing economic culture. Given that the study of economics exerts so much influence over our economic policy structure and our public discourse about economics, one indispensable element of such a renewal must be a reform of the discipline of economics around a similar moral consensus.

Of course, it would be wrong to adopt such reforms in an intellectual discipline on grounds that they are socially necessary. However, as we have shown in this book, there are strong internal, theoretical grounds for such a reform. The pretense that the empirical observations of economics involve no moral or cultural premises, if taken seriously, would leave us unable to explain why we measure GDP per person but not GDP per yak.

Economics, like all social science, is already a moral and cultural discipline. Economists incessantly tell us what we ought to do. We all know this. We might as well admit it.

In the conclusion of this book, we will suggest a few practical examples of what "admitting it" might look like.

References

Berger, Peter L. 1967. *The Sacred Canopy*. Garden City: Anchor Books.

Berger, Peter L. 2014. *The Many Altars of Modernity*. Berlin and Boston: De Gruyter.

Bloom, Allan. 1975. Justice. *American Political Science Review* 69 (2): 648–662.

Forster, Greg. 2005. *John Locke's Politics of Moral Consensus*. Cambridge and New York: Cambridge University Press.

Haidt, Jonathan. 2013. *The Righteous Mind*. New York: Vintage.

Henkel, Linda A. 2014. Point-and-Shoot Memories. *Psychological Science* 25: 396–402.

Hunter, James Davison. 2000. *The Death of Character*. New York: Basic Books.

Keynes, John Maynard. 2013 [1936]. *The General Theory of Employment, Interest and Money*. Cambridge: Cambridge University Press.

Lewis, C.S. 1943. *The Abolition of Man*. Oxford: Oxford University Press.

Loconte, Joseph. 2016. *God, Locke and Liberty*. Lanham: Lexington.

Luhmann, Niklas. 2013. *Theory of Society, Vol. II*. Stanford: Stanford University Press.

MacIntyre, Alasdair. 1981. *After Virtue*. Notre Dame: University of Notre Dame Press.

Mandeville, Bernard. 1806. *Fable of the Bees*. London: T. Ostell.
Nietzsche, Friedrich. 2009 [1887]. *The Genealogy of Morals*. Oxford and New York: Oxford University Press.
Soares, Julia S., and Benjamin C. Storm 2018. Forget in a Flash. *Journal of Applied Research in Memory and Cognition* 7: 154–160.
Taylor, Charles. 2007. *A Secular Age*. Cambridge: Harvard University Press.
Weber, Max. 2004 [1919]. *The Vocation Lectures*. Indianapolis: Hackett.

CHAPTER 12

Conclusion: Toward a Moral Consensus Paradigm

This is a highly polarized moment. The empty economy produces polarization, because our daily economic activities no longer convey meaning and purpose (leaving us to seek those things in extreme movements) and because our daily economic activities no longer establish shared, public moral commitments (leaving us convinced we have no common ground with our neighbors). In economics as in every other area of our shared life, Left and Right seem to be competing to outdo each other in how much of their moral self-restraint they can trade away for short-term access to money and power. Between the ascendance of immoral nationalism on the Right and immoral socialism on the Left, this would seem to be the worst possible moment to call for a moral consensus.

However, the shoe may be on the other foot. The very desperation produced by our national lack of moral consensus—the ongoing social dysfunction and policy disasters created by our leaders' refusal to find common ground on what is right—serves to demonstrate that moral consensus is necessary. The worst polarization may be followed by the best reconciliation, if only because the combatants have learned what the alternative to consensus really is. There are historical precedents for such a hope; the history of the European wars of religion is instructive in this regard. The roar of the waterfall gets louder as the boat approaches it, and the noise may awaken the captain in time to start the engine and turn around.

V. V. Claar and G. Forster, *The Keynesian Revolution and Our Empty Economy*, https://doi.org/10.1007/978-3-030-15808-8_12

That might sound like a version of "it's so crazy, it just might work!" If so, consider the alternatives. How else are we to escape the deadlock of endless polarization, which not only wrecks public policy, but ruins more and more of our everyday lives with political conflict? Do people want an economy governed by an ever-rotating parade of nationalist recriminations against socialists and socialist recriminations against nationalists, in which you can't even buy a chicken sandwich, a cup of coffee, a shoe, a moisturizer, or a razor without becoming a combatant in the culture war? Is the future really, as Orwell feared, a boot stamping on a human face forever? If not, where else will we turn for an alternative but to some kind of moral consensus?

Among those who have thought most deeply about the causes of our polarization, there is increasing realization that a return to higher things—carried out in a way that maintains social pluralism—is the starting point for a serious solution. Before he became justly famous for *The Righteous Mind* (Haidt 2013), Jonathan Haidt published *The Happiness Hypothesis*, whose subtitle is *Finding Modern Truth in Ancient Wisdom* (Haidt 2006). Peter Berger summarized his lifetime of work on this problem in *The Many Altars of Modernity*, which concludes with an endorsement of a pluralism that welcomes transcendent commitments within a shared structure of public life (Berger 2014). Two of the most important conservative books of the past decade were Yuval Levin's *The Fractured Republic* and Jonah Goldberg's *Suicide of the West*, both of which center on reconciling pluralism with higher moral principles (Levin 2017; Goldberg 2018). Senator Ben Sasse has published *Them*, a call to overcome polarization, and *The Vanishing American Adult*, which highlights the points of moral consensus around which people can come together (Sasse 2017, 2018). Haidt is a progressive secularist who explains social phenomena with reference to evolutionary psychology; Berger was a progressive and very theologically liberal Lutheran; Levin is a politically conservative Jew who also writes a good deal on Jewish religion, while Goldberg is also politically conservative and ethnically Jewish, but thoroughly secular; Sasse attends a church in an evangelical, theologically traditionalist denomination and has served on the board of a seminary associated with that tradition. The common ground among them is deeply impressive.

We have shown in this book why we think economics cannot accomplish the goals for which it exists as a discipline without working its way out of the Consumption paradigm. We have suggested a Moral

Consensus paradigm as an alternative because we do not see any other way out of the Consumption paradigm's anthropological dead end. But we also think that if the discipline of economics undertakes such a difficult regeneration, it will have something vitally important to contribute to the emerging search for moral consensus in society as a whole.

Economics matters a lot. That's why we love it so much. For a variety of reasons, the influence of academic disciplines (like economics) upon our cultures and societies is not as great now as it was in the early and middle parts of the twentieth century. But it is still very great. Economics departments train the people who make public policy for economic life, who run the national and international organizations that carry out a wide variety of economic missions, and who steer decisions in all our banks and large companies. Economics teaches these women and men what economic action is and how it works. In doing so, it trains them to think in certain ways about what it means to be a human being, and how we relate to one another in society. The sooner economics fixes its own anthropological problems, the sooner it will help everyone else fix theirs.

What would it look like to study economics on the assumption that people really do have higher purposes in life, but that we need not agree about everything concerning those purposes? Below, we suggest four starting points, drawing upon the four big anthropological questions that structured Chapters 8 through 11 of this book. These suggestions are tentative, as any must be at so early a stage. We expect that if a Moral Consensus paradigm does develop, it will eventually look different from these proposed starting points in ways we cannot now predict. That is, after all, how science progresses.

First Things First: Commitments that Transcend Choice

How do economic systems embody moral realities that transcend human choice? Putting first things first, we consider this question as a starting point to provide the basis for returning to productivity, stewardship, and respect with a new approach.

People hold some things to be intrinsically good. They hold these things to be good whether or not anyone recognizes them as good or makes choices to pursue them. That is, they hold some things to be good with a goodness that is above or beyond human choice.

How should the discipline of economics reckon with these preferences in analyzing economic behavior? Two further facts will help us develop an answer to this question.

First, the existence of this type of preference, and its exertion of an important influence over economic behavior, is the human norm. It is consistent across cultures and historical periods, so it is not the mere accident of some local or historical factor. While it may not be universal in the sense of covering absolutely every individual, it is certainly universal in the sense that it would be a necessary element in any realistic model of normal or typical human behavior. It is the hard-core existentialists and amoralists, who say with Hamlet that "nothing is good or bad, but thinking makes it so," who are the rare exceptions that can be left out of account in a general model.[1]

Second, a partial but not complete agreement exists—again, across cultures and times—on the question of what is intrinsically good. That all human societies impose upon their members a consistent set of moral basics—don't kill, don't steal, tell the truth, keep your promises, help your neighbor in need—is one of the oldest observations of human thought.[2] The classic philosophical triumvirate of the good, the true and the beautiful expresses the aspirations of human life from ancient China to modern Chile. At the same time, interpreting what these higher things mean (What is beautiful? What is truth? Which killings are murders? What counts as theft?) consistently produces profound disagreement.

It appears that there has never been a society that did not subscribe to the basic human morality, and also that there has never been a society that did not disagree to some extent about what that morality meant. These disagreements are not arbitrary and unlimited; they take place within the narrow boundaries of the common human morality. People have disagreed about whether, and under what conditions, you are obligated to keep a promise made under duress. But they do not (except in cases so bizarre as to be ignorable) disagree about whether you are ever obligated to keep any promises ever. On the contrary, it is precisely

[1] Act II, Scene ii.

[2] Aristotle's *Ethics*, in spite of the clear opinion of its author that Greek culture is superior, really represents an attempt to generalize about what human societies hold to be morally good. For a classic argument in favor of this position in modern times, see Lewis (1943).

because we all agree—and agree so strongly—that we must *normally* keep all our promises that the disagreement about promises made under duress is so intense and socially important.

Here is the really important point for economics: Because our disagreements are not limitless, but take place within the narrow bounds of a universal human morality, it is possible to rely on the universal morality as a basis of understanding human behavior without having to resolve all our differences about its meaning. Below, we will suggest three areas of moral agreement upon which economics can build. In brief, they are:

- People have production preferences as well as consumption preferences, including a desire to participate personally in the production of the intrinsically good. A sustainable economic life must account for both types of preferences (production and consumption) at the individual and cultural level.
- Production preferences can also be understood as stewardship preferences, meaning a desire to leave the world with more intrinsic good than it had when we arrived. A sustainable economic life must account in complex ways with the long-term time frames within which people make cost-benefit calculations, at the individual and cultural level.
- People are substantive reasoners who have the right and responsibility to discern the intrinsic good for themselves and participate personally in its production. A sustainable economic life must make this personal process of discernment and participation, not impersonal aggregate metrics, the goal of economic policy and discourse.

Pull Your Own Weight: Productivity

How do economic systems allow us to make use of our world? The Consumption paradigm reversed the previous relationship between production and consumption, accumulating wealth and enjoying wealth. It asserted that consumption is the only end of production. This change goes hand-in-hand with the rise of a purely instrumental rationality, in which reason does not dictate ends, but only discerns the means by which we can accomplish ends dictated by non-rational psychological factors ("animal spirits").

Against this, a Moral Consensus paradigm could assert that because people hold some things to be intrinsically good, people have production preferences that are independent of their own or anyone else's consumption preferences. People want certain good things produced—brought into being and maintained—not in response to some consumer appetite, but for their own sake.

Of course, as anyone with a basic understanding of economics already knows, satisfaction of these production preferences will not be economically sustainable if consumption preferences are simply ignored. But in this case, what's sauce for the goose is sauce for the gander: the satisfaction of consumption preferences is equally unsustainable if production preferences are simply ignored. The growing dysfunction in our economic public policy and public discourse reveals this. If people feel that their prosperity is hollow and their economy is empty, they become easier and easier prey for nationalists and socialists who know how to exploit popular moral anxieties for their own ends.

The model economics needs is neither all consumption preferences nor all production preferences. It is a realistic acknowledgment that both kinds of preferences matter and the great challenge of economic life is to find the best feasible use of our time and resources that takes them all into account. Economic analysis need not assume economic activity serves only the end of satisfying consumer appetites. If people have production preferences, economics can identify multiple ends of economic activity. The satisfaction of consumer appetites would certainly be one of these ends, but not the only one.

We can take this model even further. People don't just prefer that certain good things be produced; they want to be busy producing good things themselves. People want to have work, not just for a paycheck but to be genuinely productive. They are dissatisfied if they do not spend a substantial portion of their time doing work that accomplishes good ends. That is, production preferences are to some extent preferences about our own activity; people want to satisfy their production preferences in large part through their own direct action.

A culture of work matters for the formation of the productive virtues. In economic terms, the production preferences of individuals are (like all preferences) influenced by the formal and informal institutional structures within which people live.

An interesting research agenda could be built on such assertions (in this section we are particularly indebted to McMullen and Steen 2017):

- If Sam Sloth has a trust-fund income of \$40,000 per year and plays video games all day, while Polly Productive has an income of \$40,000 from her job as a plumbing saleswoman, the Consumption paradigm says Sam is better off while the Moral Consensus paradigm says Polly is better off. How can we test that proposition?
- What are the elements of Polly's work that make her better off—can we identify what it is about having a job rather than not having one that makes it preferable to have one? Are there jobs that are not preferable to nonwork, and if so, what factors make them so? The enormous literature in the field of business management on employee behavior and preferences would by itself provide extensive fodder for new economic research interests in this area.
- What social conditions cause what changes in production preferences? In other words, what forms the productive virtues?
- How can we refine, and bring to the forefront of the profession, more complex measures of unemployment that take account of workers' preferences about their work (such as quantitative and qualitative underemployment), as opposed to the crude "unemployment rate" that tells us only what percentage of those in the workforce are receiving a paycheck?
- Can we connect the new research on production preferences to these more complex metrics of unemployment? In other words, how do changes in production preferences affect the quality and quantity of work performed, and its compensation?
- In the Consumption paradigm model, people value all leisure time equally, because its only value consists in avoiding work. However, if having good work to do can be a positive value, how does this affect our conception of how people value leisure time?
- In what other ways can we measure non-pecuniary economic preferences and outcomes? Steps have already been taken in this direction in development economics through the use of indexes of social factors associated with development. How might we expand our diagnostic toolkit so we have a wide variety of ways to measure how the economy is doing?
- Do changes in consumer tastes have visible effects on macroeconomic outcomes? If so, is this because some consumer tastes undermine the productive virtues while others reinforce them?

Leave It Better Than You Found It: Stewardship

How do economic systems connect us to our ancestors and descendants? The Consumption paradigm holds that there is no value in building things up over time. A penny saved is a penny wasted, according to the paradox of thrift. If the only end of economic activity is to satisfy consumer appetites, we cannot make economic decisions today based on what will provide a better economy for our grandchildren; we do not know what our grandchildren will want.

Against this, a Moral Consensus paradigm could assert that because people hold some things to be intrinsically good, their economic activity is partly motivated by a desire to build up a world over time that has more rather than less of those good things. That is, people want to be good stewards of the world, leaving it better than they found it. Production preferences could also be understood as stewardship preferences.

Economic analysis would therefore have to consider in more complex ways the time frames within which people make their cost-benefit calculations. People care, sometimes intensely, about what kind of world they are leaving for their grandchildren. They care about this on the personal level, in their own household decisions, and on the social level, where public policy and public discourse are shaped by appeals to this powerful motive. Nationalist and socialist policies gain ground by appealing to fears about the long-term cultural sustainability of the economy—fears that are not addressed by advocates of market liberalism who can only talk about short-term GDP growth rates.

A culture of stewardship matters for the formation of stewardship virtues. Although people care about what kind of world they leave, self-discipline and prudent planning are needed to put those preferences into action. These moral virtues require formation, alongside the productive virtues. Formal and informal social institutions affect the extent to which people form such virtues.

Once again, an interesting research agenda suggests itself:

- Mainstream economics today often assumes that cost-benefit calculations are made within a time frame of one year or shorter. To what extent is this true?
- How are the time frames within which people calculate related to outcomes? Initial research into this question, such as the famous

marshmallow experiment, is inconclusive so far. That is to be expected in a new line of inquiry. Given that the time frame has such a dramatic effect on the content of a cost-benefit calculation, the amount of research done on this question to date would seem to be far less than the question deserves.

- What experiences and social conditions impact the time frame within which people make cost-benefit calculations? Can we identify conditions that lead people to adopt longer time frames?
- Do people save money only to facilitate future consumption? Or do they have other motives? To the extent that future consumption is in view, how much of it is their own future consumption and how much is it a desire to pass on wealth to future generations for their use?
- What do people do in their economic lives—work, saving, consumption—that they hope will have an effect lasting beyond their own lifetimes, or even a permanent effect?

Respect Other People: Human Dignity

How do economic systems shape the way we treat one another? The Consumption paradigm uses a model of human beings in which a person is just a bundle of appetites. It holds that the only goal of economic activity is to satisfy those appetites. There is nothing in this conception of a human being that would justify attributing dignity to the human person. Moreover, the purely instrumental view of reason in the Consumption paradigm removes the role of the human being as reasoner with the right and responsibility of discerning what is good. If we build economic systems based solely on what will maximize an aggregate measurement of appetite satisfaction (for which GDP per person is a proxy), we will build a system without concern for whether individuals are treated with dignity or whether their rights are respected.

Against this, a Moral Consensus paradigm could assert that because people hold some things to be intrinsically good, the purpose of economic life is for people to pursue those goods for themselves. Economic activity begins with the human being as a substantively rational decision-maker. Rather than an appetitive consumer, the human being at the center of this economic model is a reasoner who has a right and a responsibility to make decisions that conform to good ends. We may not fully agree on what ends are good, but some ends will be widely agreed upon, and conceptual frameworks for accommodating disputed ends can also be developed. The point is not to specify fully and precisely what the good ends are (that is the job of philosophy and theology, not social science) but to conceptualize human action as something that is oriented toward ends, and ought to be oriented toward good ends.

Recent research in behavioral economics has already begun to challenge the Consumption paradigm on precisely these lines, showing that human dignity matters to economic behavior. Now-familiar experiments such as the "dictator game" reveal that people do not, in fact, strive to maximize their own economic advantage without regard to concerns such as fair play and respect for others. Test subjects behave this way even when the others affected by their decisions are strangers who will never meet them or even know their name, so there are no social or reputational consequences at stake (Guala and Mittone 2010).

A culture of respect matters for the formation of respectful virtues. The experiments of behavior economics point to this cultural dimension of respect for human dignity; test subjects in different cultural environments play the dictator game differently, as the rules of fair play depend upon cultural institutions (Buchan et al. 2006, 373–398). Even small variations of the conditions of the game within the same culture produce unpredictable results (Guala and Mittone 2010, 581). Economics must study institutions and not just individual decisions to understand how imperatives of fair play and respect form economic behavior.

This research agenda investigating human dignity as an economic phenomenon could be multiplied:

- Are large organizations less likely to treat people—customers, business partners, their own employees—according to norms of fair play and respect than small organizations?
- Do more aggressive public policies in economics, such as tightening of regulation, incentivize small economic organizations to merge and become large, or to seek acquisition by large organizations, so they can more effectively survive and seek advantages under tighter government control? Does this undermine the ethics of these organizations and their respectful treatment of customers and partners? In other words, whereas the Consumption paradigm under Galbraith's influence has told us that we need big government to protect us from the evils of big business, does big government actually create big business (and its evils)?

- How do social controversies about what is fair and right, ranging from highly specific public controversies to much broader and deeper questions about the origin and legitimacy of the liberal market order, shape economic activity?
- How has the personal and social capital of demographic groups today been impacted by historic injustices? How does that shape the structure of economic life and institutions?
- To what extent do people trust one another to engage in honest and fair exchange? To what extent do they trust the producers and services providers they buy from? How do these trust levels affect economic life?
- When people are coerced into participating in economic activity, how does that activity change relative to parallel voluntary behaviors? Are the factors that make jobs beneficial to those who have them (part of the research agenda on production preferences, above) attenuated or removed by the exercise of coercion? How are the people themselves affected—do they make other economic decisions differently after the experience of coercion?

What Comes Next

In the long run, we are all dead—but life will go on when we are gone. We all know this, and in our economic lives we do not always behave as shallow, short-term consumers who don't care what we leave behind. If the discipline of economics wants to understand economic behavior as it really is, it must come to terms with the moral reality of human life. To ignore normative and teleological realities is to ignore the human, and to ignore the human is strange way to conduct a scientific study of how humans behave.

If we do not care what kind of world we are leaving, our economic systems will continue to be wracked by moral anxiety and the outrage it produces. Nationalists and socialists have their own reasons for wanting to block any movement toward a moral renewal that would restore confidence in our systems, but the rest of us should be seeking such a renewal with all the energy that the urgency of our situation demands. A return to economic vitality must begin with a restoration of confidence in our economic systems and practices, on the basis of a sustainable moral consensus for a pluralistic society.

We love economics. We love it because it matters—a lot. Tough new questions that overturn old certainties are already being asked in the discipline. We look forward to finding out what comes next.

References

Berger, Peter L. 2014. *The Many Altars of Modernity*. Berlin and Boston: De Gruyter.

Buchan, Nancy R., Eric J. Johnson, and Rachel T.A. Croson. 2006. Let's Get Personal. *Journal of Economic Behavior and Organization* 60 (3): 373–398.

Goldberg, Jonah. 2018. *Suicide of the West*. New York: Crown Forum.

Guala, Francesco, and Luigi Mittone. 2010. "Paradigmatic Experiments: The Dictator Game. *The Journal of Socio-Economics* 39: 578–584.

Haidt, Jonathan. 2006. *The Happiness Hypothesis*. New York: Basic Books.

Haidt, Jonathan. 2013. *The Righteous Mind*. New York: Vintage.

Levin, Yuval. 2017. *The Fractured Republic*. New York: Basic Books.

Lewis, C.S. 1943. *The Abolition of Man*. Oxford: Oxford University Press.

McMullen, Steven, and Todd P. Steen, 2017. Does Current Economic Theory Impose a Materialistic View of Work? *Journal of Markets and Morality* 20 (1): 165–178.

Sasse, Ben. 2017. *The Vanishing American Adult*. New York: St. Martin's Press.

Sasse, Ben. 2018. *Them*. New York: St. Martin's Press.

Author Index

V. V. Claar and G. Forster, *The Keynesian Revolution and Our Empty Economy*, https://doi.org/10.1007/978-3-030-15808-8

Subject Index

V. V. Claar and G. Forster, *The Keynesian Revolution and Our Empty Economy*, https://doi.org/10.1007/978-3-030-15808-8

CPSIA information can be obtained
at www.ICGtesting.com
Printed in the USA
LVHW031247261119
638462LV00014B/1721/P

9 783030 158071